In 1898 the United States went to war with Spain over the future of Cuba. The American navy had, in the preceding decade, been revived after years of neglect, and was much stronger than anything that the Spanish could bring against it. In the Philippines, Admiral George Dewey easily destroyed a weak Spanish squadron. A military invasion of Cuba was supported by the rest of the US Navy, under the command of Admiral William T Sampson. An important part of this force was the Flying Squadron, led by Commodore Winfield Scott Schley. Meanwhile a Spanish squadron under Admiral Pascual Cervera sailed from Europe to the Caribbean and, after disappearing for some days, reached the port of Santiago de Cuba. Schley was the first on the scene; his movements were later to be severely criticised. When Sampson arrived with the rest of the fleet, a blockade of the port was instituted. In the end, Cervera was obliged to make an attempt to break out, but his squadron of four cruisers was overwhelmed and destroyed. During the battle on Sunday July 3, Schley was in effective command, as Sampson had gone ashore to confer with the army commander. Although the Americans had won another easy victory, a bitter dispute arose between the respective supporters of Schley and Sampson as to who was entitled to the credit. Fanned by the popular press, the issue split the U S Navy to the point where its morale was seriously affected. Matters came to a head with the publication of a book violently attacking Schley's conduct. He demanded a Court of Inquiry; this sat for forty days at the Washington Navy Yard, presided over by Admiral Dewey. It was one of the great trials of American history, as the lawyers refought the campaign in minute detail. In the end, the verdict went against Schley, though this was offset by a minority opinion from Dewey that he had indeed been in command and deserved the credit for the victory. This book explores the rights and wrongs of the conduct of those principally involved in a battle that marked the dawn of the American empire, and closely examines the dramatic proceedings of the Court of Inquiry.

Quintin Barry is a solicitor and a retired Employment Judge. He has also held a variety of offices in both the public and private sector, including the NHS and local radio. He is presently Chief Executive of an international group of law firms. Following a lifelong interest in history & naval history, he is the author of a number of books on military and naval history. These include an acclaimed two-volume history of the Franco-Prussian War of 1870–1871, a history of the Austro-Prussian War of 1866, and the first modern history of the Russo-Turkish War of 1877–1878. He has made a particular study of the life and career of Helmuth von Moltke. He has also written a biography of the 17th Earl of Derby, which was published in 2012. His most recent books are: *The War in the North Sea 1914-1918* and *Far Distant Ships*, a study of the blockade of Brest during the Napoleonic Wars.

DISPUTED VICTORY

The series *Warfare in the Victorian Age* looks at conflict globally throughout the Victorian Era. Although as a British publisher the initial output will largely concentrate on the British experience during this era, it is in no way limited to this. We hope in the future to examine European warfare during this period as well as the United States and indeed the entire globe.

Although largely confined to the dates Queen Victoria's reign, 1837-1901, there will be some latitude either side. The late Georgian period is important as a lead in to the Victorian Era. The early years of the twentieth century also carry on the 'story' of the Victorian Era. The period was one of great technological change. Consequently there was also considerable tactical change, although as is often the case this rarely kept pace with the new and emerging technology. There are important lessons to be learnt from the study of military history in this age. The Victorian Era illustrates the consequence of the Napoleonic Wars. It is also essential in understanding the movements toward the First World War. The series allows the opportunity for writers and historians to present their work on an era that is sadly too often neglected. Whilst many of the books in the series will look at individual battles and campaigns it is not limited to this. The series will also explore wider issues of the age and consider warfare in a wider sense, along with technology, individuals, and weaponry.

1. *The Battle of Majuba Hill. The Transvaal Campaign 1880-1881* John Laband (ISBN 978-1-911512-38-7)*
2. *Forgotten Victorian Generals. Studies in the Exercise of Command and Control in the British Army 1837-1901* Edited by Christopher Brice (ISBN 978-1-910777-20-6)
3. *For Queen and Company. Vignettes of the Irish Soldier in the Indian Mutiny* David Truesdale (ISBN 978-1-911512-79-0)*
4. *The Siege of Lucknow 1857. Victorian Warfare in Defeat and Victory* Edward Gosling (ISBN 978-1-911512-90-5)*
5. *Disputed Victory. Schley, Sampson and the Spanish-American War of 1898* Quintin Barry (ISBN 978-1-912174-91-1)

* Denotes books are paperback 248mm × 180mm, other books are hardback.

Disputed Victory

Schley, Sampson and the Spanish-American War of 1898

Quintin Barry

Helion & Company Limited

Helion & Company Limited
26 Willow Road
Solihull
West Midlands
B91 1UE
England
Tel. 0121 705 3393
Fax 0121 711 4075
Email: info@helion.co.uk
Website: www.helion.co.uk
Twitter: @helionbooks
Visit our blog http://blog.helion.co.uk/

Published by Helion & Company 2018
Designed and typeset by Mach 3 Solutions Ltd (www.mach3solutions.co.uk)
Cover designed by Paul Hewitt, Battlefield Design (www.battlefield-design.co.uk)
Printed by Short Run Press, Exeter, Devon

Images author's collection unless otherwise noted.
Maps drawn by George Anderson © Helion & Company 2018
Front cover: Rear Admiral William T Sampson (left), Rear Admiral Winfield S Schley (right), USS *Brooklyn*. Rear cover: USS *Massachusetts*.

ISBN 978-1-912174-91-1

British Library Cataloguing-in-Publication Data.
A catalogue record for this book is available from the British Library.

For details of other military history titles published by Helion & Company Limited contact the above address, or visit our website: http://www.helion.co.uk.

We always welcome receiving book proposals from prospective authors.

Contents

List of Photographs

In Plate Section

List of Maps

Acknowledgements

It is always a particular pleasure to be able to express one's gratitude to those that have helped in the production of a book. I am grateful as always to Duncan Rogers of Helion and his colleagues for their assistance in preparing this book for publication, particularly in relation to the maps and illustrations. My thanks go also to Tim Readman, who read the book in draft; to Jean Hawkes, who typed it with her usual patience and understanding; to Jerome A Busch, of counsel to the law firm of Vogt Resnick Sherak of California, and formerly of the US Navy's Judge Advocate General's Department, who provided helpful comments about the course of the Spanish American War, and advice about the legal processes involved in the Court of Inquiry; to my grandson Laurence Townsend for his considerable assistance with the illustrations; to George Anderson who drew the maps; and to Kim McSweeney for the typesetting.

Prologue: The Washington Navy Yard

On Thursday September 12 1901, at 1:00 p.m., there began at the Washington Navy Yard a remarkable court hearing. Open to the general public, it took place in the spacious hall known as the 'Gunner's Workshop', which had been specially fitted out for the purpose. It was large enough to accommodate over three hundred people. No expense had been spared in preparing the hall for the hearing. A California newspaper published a report that a small fortune was being spent by the Navy Department, and described the preparations that had been made:

> The meetings of the court are to be held in the most richly appointed apartment of the Navy Department, the floors of which are covered with expensive carpets, the walls elaborately decorated and hung with valuable paintings of former secretaries, and which is furnished with mahogany tables, settees and big easy chairs upholstered in leather.[1]

The *Mariposa Gazette* went on to consider the huge cost in the salaries of the officers that would be required to attend, as well as the travel cost of bringing them from distant stations to Washington: 'In addition to the cost of bringing witnesses there are the running expenses of the court. Stenographers and a clerical force are required, while the item of stationery will not be inconsiderable.' There was a sense of barely suppressed excitement among the onlookers as they began to file in to take their seats. Over fifty journalists representing newspapers from all over the United States were also present to record the proceedings.

They had all come to witness what in naval terms was the most sensational legal spectacle since the court martial of the British Admiral Keppel in the eighteenth century. As had been the case with those proceedings, the issues and the personalities involved in the present case had bitterly divided both a navy and nation. During the course of the hearing, one of the lawyers concerned remarked, with perhaps understandable hyperbole: 'I doubt if the naval history of the world presents, or ever has presented, a case of the important character of that in which we have been so long engaged. I doubt if a tribunal more exalted in the character of the officers who composed it has ever sat in judgment upon a brother officer's acts'.[2]

The fashionable crowds which flocked to the Washington Navy Yard were there to watch Rear Admiral Winfield Scott Schley defend himself against a series of allegations arising out of his conduct during the Spanish-American War of 1898. At the heart of the dispute was the question of whether he, or Rear Admiral William T Sampson, deserved the credit for the victory of the American fleet in the battle fought off Santiago de Cuba on July 3 1898. One way or another practically all the senior officers of the US navy had taken a view in the matter. The flames of the dispute had been fanned by the popular press, a large section of which had come down firmly on the side of Admiral Schley, believing that he was being unfairly treated by the Navy Department.

Fiercely partisan views had been expressed on both sides of the argument over a period of more than three years. So violent had been the debate that the US Secretary of the Navy, John D Long, had been obliged to issue an instruction prohibiting American naval officers from discussing the issues in public, because the questions raised were damaging the morale of the US navy.

In ordering the inquiry, Secretary Long had insisted that, in deference to the importance and dignity of the occasion, the officers should wear full dress uniform. Since, however, the weather in August in Washington would be unbearably hot, the opening of the inquiry was deferred until mid-September. All the formal proprieties were to be observed, including the employment of a party of marines to act as ushers under the command of Captain Henry Carpenter. In the Gunners' Workshop the acoustics were perfect, and the audience could hear every word spoken in the course of the proceedings.

On September 12 well wishers crowded round Schley to shake his hand as he took his place with his legal team. He had appointed three distinguished lawyers to represent him during the inquiry, all old friends. These were Judge Jeremiah M Wilson, of Washington DC; Isidor Rayner, of Baltimore; and retired naval Captain James Parker, of Perth Amboy, New Jersey. The Judge Advocate General of the US Navy, Captain Samuel C Lemly, served as judge advocate to the inquiry; he was assisted by Edwin P Hanna, Solicitor General to the Navy Department.

Feelings among the spectators would run high throughout the hearing; in spite of the frequent use of his gavel, the President experienced difficulty at times in maintaining order. As the hearing continued, there would often be bitter disputes between the lawyers, arising from arguments about the scope and conduct of the proceedings and the relevant law.

The Court of Inquiry was presided over by Admiral George Dewey. At 63, he was as fit and wiry as a much younger man. Five foot seven inches tall, it was said of him that his personal ambition was in inverse proportion to his height. Extremely vain, he had become an American national hero with his victory over the Spanish at the battle of Manila Bay. Invariably well turned out, with a beaky nose and flowing white moustache, he was immaculate in his heavy full dress uniform. The other two members of the court were Rear Admiral EK Benham and Rear Admiral Henry L Howison.

The proceedings began with the reading by the Judge Advocate General of the precept convening the inquiry, the purpose of which was stated as being to inquire 'into the conduct of the said Schley, Commodore in the Navy, during the recent war with Spain and in connection with the events thereof.' The document went on to set out ten specifications into which the Court was to inquire The precept had been drafted by Captain Lemly in terms which, in the view of Schley's lawyers, were deliberately designed to make it as difficult as possible to rebut the allegations made against him. To them, this was a clear indication that the Navy Department, and Secretary Long in particular, was determined that Schley should not be able to clear his name. The ten points of the precept into which the Court was to inquire were as follows:

1 His conduct in connection with the events of the Santiago campaign.
2 The circumstances attending, the reasons controlling, and the propriety of the movements of the "Flying Squadron" off Cienfuegos in May, 1898.
3 The circumstances attending, the reasons controlling, and the propriety of the movements of the said squadron in proceeding from Cienfuegos to Santiago.

4 The circumstances attending and the arrival of the "Flying Squadron" off Santiago, the reasons for its retrograde turn westward and departure from off Santiago, and the propriety thereof.
5 The circumstances attending and the reasons for the disobedience by Commodore Schley of the orders of the Department contained in its dispatch dated May 27, 1898 and the propriety of his conduct in the premises.
6 The condition of the coal supply of the "Flying Squadron" on and about May 27, 1898; its coaling facilities; the necessity, if any, for, or advisability of, the return of the squadron to Key West to coal; and the accuracy and propriety of the official reports made by Commodore Schley with respect to this matter.
7 Whether or not every effort incumbent upon the commanding officer of a fleet under such circumstances was made to capture or destroy the Spanish cruiser *Colon* as she lay at anchor in the entrance to Santiago Harbour May 27 to 31, inclusive, and the necessity for, or advisability of, engaging the batteries at the entrance to Santiago Harbour, and the Spanish vessels at anchor within the entrance to said harbour, at the ranges used, and the propriety of Commodore Schley's conduct in the premises.
8 The necessity, if any, for, and advisability of, withdrawing at night the "Flying Squadron" from the entrance to Santiago Harbour to a distance at sea, if such shall be found to have been the case; the extent and character of such withdrawal; and whether or not a close or adequate blockade of said harbour, to prevent the escape of the enemy's vessels therefrom, was established, and the propriety of Commodore Schley's conduct in the premises.
9 The position of the *Brooklyn* on the morning of July 3, 1898, at the time of the exit of the Spanish vessels from the harbour of Santiago. The circumstances attending, the reasons for, and the incidents resulting from the turning of the *Brooklyn* in the direction in which she turned at or about the beginning of the action with said Spanish vessels, and the possibility of thereby colliding with or endangering any other of the vessels of the United States fleet, and the propriety of Commodore Schley's conduct in the promises.
10 The circumstances leading to, and the incidents and results of, a controversy with Lieutenant Albon C. Hodgson, U.S. Navy, who, on July 3, 1898, during the battle of Santiago, was navigator of the *Brooklyn,* in relation to the turning of the *Brooklyn;* also the colloquy at that time between Commodore Schley and Lieutenant Hodgson and the ensuing correspondence between them on the subject thereof, and the propriety of the conduct of Admiral Schley in the premises.

During the course of the hearing, which some newspapers had mistakenly supposed would be of short duration, the Court would hear evidence, in minute detail, from a large number of witnesses, and would sit sit for no less than forty days; the oral evidence before it was contained in transcripts which ran to over 1,800 pages, with a large number of documents submitted by both sides. One witness from whom the Court would not hear, however, was Admiral Sampson, who was too ill to testify. His absence meant, in the view of many observers, that the proceedings would amount to Hamlet without the Prince of Denmark. Attempts by Admiral Schley's lawyers to introduce evidence relating to Sampson's conduct would be invariably ruled out of order. It remained to be seen whether, when all had been said, the Court would be able to produce a final opinion that would command general respect and bring all controversy to an end. It would not be an easy task.

1

The American Navy

With the ending of the Civil War, the United States found itself in possession of a huge navy, the raison d'etre for which had disappeared, and not surprisingly, in view of the cost of maintaining such a force, steps were immediately taken to run it down. Within a very few years it had returned to a strength suitable to the resumption of its pre-war activities. The extent of the reduction was described by Harold and Margaret Sprout:

> In December 1864 the Navy List included nearly 700 vessels, aggregating half a million tons, and mounting almost 5,000 guns. By the end of 1870, this force had shrunk to less than 200 vessels, aggregating less than 200,000 tons, and capable of mounting only about 1,300 guns. In reality the shrinkage was even greater, for many of these vessels were worn out or otherwise unfit for service. The total number in commission, including store ships and hospital ships, was only 52, mounting altogether less than 500 guns, most of which were now obsolete.[1]

The peacetime activities of the US Navy required that overseas squadrons should be maintained for the purpose of showing the flag in tacit support of American trade. The advent of steam created a serious problem, because the United States did not possess a network of coaling stations. As a result, the policy was to insist that all naval vessels should have 'full sail power,' and steam was not to be used unless absolutely necessary. The cruising function of the navy meant that no fleet organisation was possible, while the reluctance to use steam power meant that the navy's steam cruisers were adapted to maximise their sailing qualities, with a consequent marked reduction in their speed. Furthermore, these cruisers were armed with obsolete muzzle-loading smooth bore guns, or makeshift rifled guns, which left them far behind their European counterparts in offensive power. Nor were these vessels adequately protected by armour; as late as 1872 the Navy Department was still seeking authority to build wooden cruisers in spite of the wartime experience which had shown their extreme vulnerability.[2]

This decline in the fighting power of the US navy was not merely the result of a desire to reduce cost. Leading naval officers argued that the country's needs were best met by the policy that was pursued. Admiral Case told a congressional committee in 1876 that professional opinion was opposed to the building of heavily armoured vessels, explaining: 'We have no near naval neighbours, nor is it probable that we will have for a century to come, or that there will be fleet-fights when we do.'[3]

Much of the impetus towards the adoption of a reactionary policy derived from the influence of Vice Admiral David D Porter, who was allowed, by the appointment by President US Grant of a figurehead, Adolph E Borie, as Secretary of the Navy, to assume total control. Porter, in spite of his experience in the use of steam power during the Civil War, was an extreme exponent of sail power, and ordered a return to its use, requiring all ships to undertake constant exercise with sails and spars. Although Borie was soon replaced, by George M Robeson, Porter's pernicious influence continued; Robeson boasted at the end of his eight year tenure of office of his achievement in sparing the country from the cost of building an armoured fleet.[4]

The decay of the US Navy continued. With no foreign complications requiring the use of naval force, the Secretary of the Navy in the Hayes administration, Richard W Thompson, who followed Robeson, is remembered for an astonishing ignorance about the uses of a navy and about the ships of which it was composed. He reported to Congress his belief that 'heavy armour-plated, gun-bearing vessels' were incapable of sea service, being suited for little but harbour defence. His term of office was the nadir of American naval administration; but in 1881 the pendulum of decline began at last to swing the other way, when President Garfield appointed William H Hunt as Secretary. Hunt brought to the post a long standing interest in the navy together with the energy and tact to do something about a situation which he recognised as disastrous. He appointed a board of naval officers to plan the reconstruction of the navy, and established a good working relationship with Congress. He had set in motion a process of reform which continued after his brief term of office when, soon after Garfield's assassination, he was sent by President Arthur as ambassador to St Petersburg, and was succeeded by William E Chandler.

Hunt's board had reported in November 1881, pronouncing the existing unarmoured vessels as altogether inadequate. In considering their replacements, the board concluded that steel ships should be designed, as 'notwithstanding the greater cost of steel as a shipbuilding material, the lack of experience in the manufacture of steel frames in this country, and the experimental stage that steel shipbuilding is passing through in Europe, it should be recommended as material of construction.'[5] The board went on to call for the expenditure of $29 million, on the construction of sixty eight vessels. The size of this programme was eminently justified; at that time the condition of the navy had become desperate:

> The year 1881, when Garfield succeeded to the Presidency, marks the lowest point to which the navy has ever sunk since the days when the United States had to pay a ransom to Algiers. Out of the 140 vessels on the navy list in 1881, twenty five were tugs, and only a few of the rest in condition to make a cruise. Not a single ship was fit for warfare.[6]

The Congress, however, was unimpressed, rejecting the report outright. International conditions were not, the politicians reckoned, such as to suggest that the huge expenditure recommended was justified. The most that the House Naval Committee was prepared to do was to approve a building programme of six cruisers and a ram, after the chairman of the committee, Benjamin Harris, had individually interrogated the members of the board. It was Harris's conclusion that the recommendations were extravagant and politically unworkable, and he responded unfavourably to what he regarded as a slur on Congress for not doing more in the past.[7] In the end, the number of vessels that Congress finally authorised was reduced to two steel cruisers, and in any case no funds were appropriated for their construction. The Act of

1882 which authorised the construction of the two cruisers also set up a new advisory board composed of a president, five officers and two civilian experts

Recognising the impossibility of achieving overnight the large scale programme that had been rejected by Congress, the new board, which was led by Commodore Robert W Shufeldt, carefully reduced its recommendations to what was considered viable in political terms It put forward a request for four steel cruisers and a despatch vessel. The Act of 1882 had also imposed a limit on the cost of repairs to the existing wooden vessels to a maximum of 30% of the cost of a similar new vessel, and next year reduced this to 20%. This accelerated the process of necessary replacement; and the proposal of Shufeldt's board was accepted, though limited to only three cruisers and the despatch vessel. These became known as the ABCD vessels; the cruisers were *Atlanta*, *Boston* and *Chicago*, and the despatch vessel was *Dolphin*. Chandler was severely criticised over his choice of shipbuilder; he selected John Roach, a substantial contributor to the Republican Party; when the ships came to be built, Roach's lack of experience in modern warship construction severely hampered progress. Nevertheless they were in due course completed, and formed into the so called 'White Squadron' to work out tactics and combined operations. They were, however, fitted with a full suit of masts, spars and sails, with the inevitable reduction in their speed. Even after their completion, so pervasive was the belief in sail power that their first evolutions as a squadron were conducted at the outset under sail alone. Only when it seemed that they would be late for the reception at the end of the first day was it found appropriate to use the engines.[8]

The three steel protected cruisers were not of great fighting power. They had an armoured deck three inches thick, and were equipped with modern breech loading rifled guns of up to 8-inch calibre. The largest of them, *Chicago*, was of 4,500 tons. All four vessels had a designed speed of 14 knots, although in their trials none of them attained this. But they marked a huge step forward in the rebirth of the US navy, and were perfectly suited to the navy's traditional role of protecting American trade. It was the first time since the Civil War that Congress had authorised the building of significant new warships, and these stimulated popular enthusiasm to the point at which further appropriations became politically acceptable.[9]

Apart from beginning the long climb back of the US navy towards respectability in terms of warships, Chandler's term of office was marked by an important step towards establishing what the United States actually needed a navy for. Commodore Stephen B Luce, who had headed the Department of Seamanship at the US Naval Academy during the Civil War, in the course of which he also commanded a number of warships, had for some time been strongly urging the establishment of a Naval War College. In October 1884 this was launched at Newport, Rhode Island, with Luce as its first president, in which capacity he served until taking command of the North Atlantic Squadron in June 1886. He was succeeded by Captain Alfred Thayer Mahan who had supported Luce in his campaign to set up the Naval War College. Together the two men revolutionised American naval thinking.

Luce was an old friend of Admiral David Porter, and his influence had had its effect on that profoundly conservative individual. As early as 1871 it became apparent to the latter that Navy Secretary Robeson was unable or unwilling to grasp the extent of the navy's deterioration, and he produced a report to show just how weak was the naval situation of the United States. At that point in time the navy possessed only twenty nine warships that could be counted as serviceable. Robeson, however, was unmoved; and in spite of Luce's continuing influence over Porter, the senior admiral of the navy, the situation did not improve.[10]

Luce's first successful step towards reform came with his foundation in 1873 of the Naval Institute. The Institute's *Proceedings* provided an opportunity for naval officers all too well aware of the state of the navy to argue for reform of the strategic policy to be applied, as well as the need to build warships capable of executing that policy. These officers were able to watch, enviously, the rapid advances in warship design in Europe. But the climate was changing, albeit very slowly; and when Hunt, followed by Chandler, began to do something about the problem, they found that the door was beginning to swing open.

Chandler was the subject of extravagant criticism for the scandal over the award of the construction contacts to John Roach; Allan Nevis described Roach as an 'illiterate, elderly, infirm ironmaster,' and accused Chandler of being immorally prepared to cheat the government in order to pay back a political debt.[11] Nevertheless, he was prepared to take on the Republican establishment, for instance over attempts to reinstate officers who had been dismissed for good reason. And in 1884 he made a huge contribution to the process of reform when he accepted Luce's arguments for the establishment of a Naval War College. To protect the independence of the fledgling institution, he placed it under the Bureau of Navigation.

In setting up the Naval War College, Luce had a clear idea of the men he wanted to work with him, appointing Captain Mahan to head the Naval Branch and Professor James R Soley, of the Naval Academy, as lecturer in international law. More controversially, he wished to appoint an army officer, Lieutenant Tasker H Bliss, to head the Military Branch., although it was only after enlisting Chandler's support that he was able to overcome professional naval objections to a soldier instructing sailors in land warfare.[12] One of the objections came from Captain Francis M Ramsay, the superintendent of the Naval Academy, who argued that the functions of the Naval War College should be treated as an extension of the work of the Academy.

In establishing the Naval War College Luce aimed at developing and teaching a modern concept of warfare as a scientific study. As a young officer taking part in the siege of Charleston he came to realise that the conduct of war must be on fundamental and unchanging principles, and that this must be taught professionally. Years later he recalled how, listening to Sherman explain how when he reached South Carolina and cut Charleston's communications, it would fall into the navy's hands 'like a ripe pear:'

> After hearing General Sherman's clear exposition of the situation, the scales seemed to fall from my eyes. It dawned upon me that there were certain fundamental principles underlying military operations – principles of general application whether the operations were conducted on land or at sea.[13]

It was his selection of the head of the Naval Branch of the College that Luce made his most important contribution to the development of professionalism in the US Navy. Alfred Thayer Mahan was born at West Point in 1840, where his father, Dennis Hart Mahan, was Professor of Mathematics. At the age of sixteen, over his father's objections, he became a cadet at the Naval Academy at Annapolis: a model student, with a strong religious belief, Mahan was not popular with the other cadets, whom he generally despised. On leaving the Academy in 1859 Mahan was assigned to the frigate *Congress*, on the Brazilian Station. *Congress* was one of the last of the sailing frigates of the American navy, and was to meet her end in the Civil War at the hands of the Confederate ironclad *Virginia* in Hampton Roads. With the outbreak of the Civil War, the *Congress* was ordered home. Midshipman Mahan was ordered to the converted merchantman *James Adger*, which was being fitted out as a blockader; and then, promoted to lieutenant, he became executive officer of the steamer *Pocahontas*. She arrived late, but just in time to take part in the battle of Port Royal on November 7 1861, which proved to be Mahan's only battle. Thereafter, he spent ten months on blockade duty, after which he was posted to Newport to lecture on seamanship. Here he made the acquaintance of Lieutenant Luce, his head of department, and the two men, in spite of an age difference of 13 years, became close friends.[14]

In the last year of the war, Mahan was sent back to blockade duty in the Western Gulf on the steam corvette *Seminole*, which he found 'desperately tedious.' After three months, however, he joined Admiral Dahlgren's squadron off Charleston, where he greatly enjoyed serving as a staff officer to the admiral. After the end of the war, now promoted to Lieutenant Commander, Mahan in 1869 returned to the United States, where he fell in love with the eleven years younger Ellen Lyle Evans, whom he married in 1872. Promoted to commander, he was assigned to the command of *Wasp* on the South American Station, a posting which lasted until 1875

In 1877, he was posted to the Naval Academy as head of the Department of Gunnery; he found, however, that the running of gunnery drills was taken over by the Superintendent. This provided him with time for writing, and from then on his course was set, although the results were not immediate. In 1882, however, he was asked by the publishers Scribners to write the third volume of their Civil War series, which was published as *The Gulf and Inland Waters*. Next year he was disappointed not to be appointed to the command of *Pensacola*, flagship of the European Squadron, a post which went to Commander George Dewey. Mahan did not enjoy the posting he received, to the *Wachusett*, on the Pacific Station where he did not have a very successful time, among other thing colliding with a sailing barque. He was ultimately relieved by the invitation from Luce to join the Naval War College, although it was 1885 before he escaped from the *Wachusett* and took up his duties; the College began to operate in September of that year.[15] Mahan may not have liked the navy any more than the navy liked him, and he was an indifferent seaman; but he was about to become one of the most influential naval officers in the world.

Meanwhile in March 1885, following the inauguration of Democrat President Grover Cleveland, a new Secretary of the Navy took office. William C Whitney was a successful corporation lawyer; he was appointed with a brief to clean up the Navy Department after the worst excesses of the Chandler era. Of a somewhat puritanical disposition, he was well fitted to tackle the financial abuses which he found, although he encountered real difficulty in eradicating the political misconduct of party bosses in obtaining employment for their supporters.

In 1886 Whitney organised an inventory of the stores held in naval depots, discovering over $1m worth of rotting clothes and canvas, which prompted him to introduce a new supply policy. Pursuant to this, he published a single advertisement calling for bids for steel hull plates from domestic steelmakers; the Bethlehem Steel Company was the successful bidder, giving a promise to build a special mill for rolling such plates.[16]

In that year a board examining the question of coast defence led by the Secretary of War, William Endicott, reported on the need for a vast network of fortifications and a fleet of monitors. This board had two naval members in Commanders William T Sampson and Caspar F Goodrich. The former had been one of the members of a board that recommended the establishment of the Naval War College, and was seen as a coming man in the navy. The Endicott board included an appendix by Sampson which outlined the various types of vessels that would be required, and the assumption was made by the board that these would include numerous heavy ironclads able 'to act offensively and not be confined to the defence of ports.'[17]

One of the issues which Whitney inherited was the quality of the construction in Roach's yards of the ABCD vessels, and he was fierce in his condemnation of the structural defects said to exist in them. There is evidently some controversy about Whitney's motivation for his attack on Roach; Walter R Herrick notes that in any case, all three cruisers exceeded expectations on their trials.[18] They were, however, of modest dimensions and offensive power compared to contemporary vessels in Europe, where battleships of up to 15,000 tons displacement were being built. The largest of the ABCD vessels, *Chicago*, carried four 8-inch steel rifled guns as her main armament.

During Whitney's time as Navy Secretary, some thirty new ships were added to the US navy. In 1886 the armoured cruisers *Maine* and *Texas* were authorised. These were to be of over 6,000 tons carrying four 10-inch rifled guns, and capable of speeds of 18.5 knots. They were subsequently rated as coast defence battleships. Another addition was the protected cruiser *Baltimore*, designed to attain 20 knots. In the following year Congress authorised seven warships, two of which were destined to play a significant part in the war with Spain. The largest was the armoured cruiser *New York*, of 8,000 tons, mounting six 8-inch guns, and capable of 20 knots, while the protected cruiser *Olympia* of 6,000 tons, carrying four 8-inch guns, was capable of 22 knots.

In June 1886 the Naval War College lost its president when Luce was appointed to the command of the North Atlantic Squadron. He was succeeded by Mahan. Unfortunately Whitney disliked Mahan. Perhaps this contributed to the Navy Secretary's decision to transfer responsibility for the college from the Bureau of Navigation, and ordering that it be relocated at Torpedo Station on Goat Island, on the other side of Narragansett Bay. Whitney's lack of sympathy for Mahan, and for the War College, led to a loss of appropriations for the College, hampering its work. In 1888 Whitney assigned Mahan to the role of president of the board established to select a site on Puget Sound, near Seattle, which interrupted his academic work for a year.

Whitney's term of office had certainly produced administrative reform, as well as the expansion of the fleet, although Herrick notes that 'he ignored strategy and left naval policy basically as it had been in the days of Thomas Jefferson.'[19] With the inauguration of President Benjamin Harrison in March 1889, a new Secretary of the Navy took office who was to have an even greater influence on the Navy's development. The new Republican president had the advantage of a clear majority for his party in both houses of Congress, enabling him to pursue his policy of developing a strong navy.

Benjamin Franklin Tracy was born in 1830. He practised as a successful lawyer until the outbreak of the Civil War, in which he served with distinction, rising to the rank of brigadier general. Thereafter, he moved to Brooklyn and resumed the practice of the law, serving as the US District Attorney for the eastern district of New York before returning to his successful private practice. Later, after an unsuccessful campaign to became mayor of Brooklyn, he became Chief Justice of the state Court of Appeal. He was active in politics and was closely associated with Thomas Collier Platt, the leader of the Republican state machine in New York. After Harrison's election Platt had hoped to be made Secretary of the Treasury; to console him for his bitter disappointment, Harrison offered to appoint to his cabinet any nominee that Platt put forward. It was in this way that Tracy became Secretary of the Navy, in which post he showed himself from the outset a staunch exponent of Harrison's big navy policy.

Tracy was heavily influenced by Mahan, who at that time was engaged in writing the book that was to make his name. International conditions ensured that naval policy was central to the early policy of the Harrison administration. Two of the leading historians of the US navy described how that policy was shaped by the politician's high regard for the naval officer:

> Mahan, whose book was approaching completion in the summer and autumn of 1889, provided an ideological basis which made Secretary Tracy's annual report for that year one of the most forceful documents in the entire history of American naval policy. Whether Tracy had access to Mahan's manuscript, or whether he merely consulted him, it is difficult to say, but the ideas were indubitably Mahan's.[20]

Tracy might, some thought, have been more appropriately appointed to head the Department of Justice as Attorney-General, but he was soon able to demonstrate that he was the right man in the right place, as one newspaper editorial observed in October 1889:

> No doubt General Tracy, as Attorney-General, would have been an unspeakable improvement on his predecessor, but there is no reason for moving him. Gen. Tracy is the strongest man in the cabinet... and is doing about the only work that reflects much credit on the administration. He is the first thoroughly honed and...capable Republican Secretary of the Navy since the end of the Civil War.[21]

Tracy's success in the post had not been taken for granted by everyone; Admiral David Porter had been mindful of the extent to which the bureau chiefs had dominated Secretary Whitney, and had hoodwinked him into believing that he was master of the situation. Writing to Luce, Porter thought that Tracy was very accessible, but listened quietly and did not commit himself:

> From certain questions which he asked me about the Bureau of Equipment, I imagine that Whitney left the chief ... to Mr Tracy to aid the latter in the task of tuning the Navy, hoping that his successor would fail as egregiously as Whitney himself. Whitney and Tracy having been friends, the latter may well fall into that trap.[22]

The chief of the Bureau of Equipment to whom Porter was referred was Captain Winfield S Schley; soon after taking office, Schley chose to resign and go to sea in command of the cruiser *Baltimore*. Tracy was in fact determined not to allow himself to became subservient to the bureau chiefs, who for their part, accustomed to controlling the civilian Secretary of the Navy, openly challenged his judgement on many issues. Tracy, however, was not to be deflected from his purposes by such disloyalty, and he was determined to stand up for himself against their efforts to impose their professional authority and expertise on him.

Tracy's report to the Congress was dramatic in the scope of its recommendations. Although emphasising that defence, not conquest, was the object of naval policy, he argued that this required 'a fighting force', which must contain armoured battleships capable not only of beating off an enemy's fleet on its approach to the American coast but also of threatening its own coast. He called for the construction of twenty battleships, with twelve assigned to the Atlantic and eight to the Pacific, such vessels to be of a quality and power to match the best in the world, and be of uniformly high speed. In addition sixty fast cruisers were required, both to serve with the fleet and to protect merchant shipping as well as to attach that of the enemy. Finally there should be at least twenty heavily armoured coast defence vessels.

Tracy was hopeful that his recommendations would be an acceptable basis for the development of the navy. In December 1889 Senator Hale introduced four bills incorporating the first stages of Tracy's programme. The first proposed the building of eight battleships (of from 7,500 – 10,000 tons), two armoured monitors, three cruisers and five torpedo boats. The second bill proposed that battleships be named after states and cruisers after cities, to promote public identification with the vessels. The third improved the terms and conditions of seamen, and the fourth bill provided for a survey of the American merchant fleet from which auxiliaries might be enlisted in wartime.[23]

However, the hoped for progress was effectually scuppered by the publication of the report of the Policy Board which Tracy had established to determine the country's naval requirements. The board consisted of six naval officers, under the chairmanship of Commodore WP Mc Cann; Captain Sampson was one of its members. Tracy had intended that the substance of the board's report should be kept confidential, rightly supposing that its contents provided a mixture that was far too rich for Congressional palates, and he was dismayed by its unauthorised publication.

The Board's recommendations fell on the ears of Congress like a clap of thunder. It advised the adoption of a construction programme of 192 ships at an approximate cost of $281,550,000, made up as to thirty five battleships, ten rams, forty four cruisers, three torpedo depot ships and one hundred torpedo boats. Ten of these ships were to be 'first class battleships of great endurance,' comparable to foreign contemporaries, with a range of 5400 miles at 10 knots. The other twenty five battleships would be designed for starter range operations.[24]

Even allowing for the comfortable surpluses accruing in the US Treasury, the scope of the recommendations prompted violent protest in Congress, and Tracy felt unable to support it. Even newspapers that had shown themselves to be pro-navy rejected the report. However, in June 1890 the House Naval Affairs Committee provided for the construction of three battleships, of about 8,500 tons. Even this modest proposal attracted strong opposition, but in the end the House voted 131 to 105 in favour and the senate 33 to 18. It has been pointed out that in supporting the proposal the legislators did not realise what they had done, accepting the suggestion that it was 'merely the continuance' of a policy settled by the War of 1812 which had thereafter been consistently followed:

> On the contrary, the battleship section of the Act of 1890 implied Congressional endorsement of a revolutionary departure in our system of naval defense. This legislation, as its sponsors openly admitted, was but the first step toward creating a fighting fleet to seize command of the open sea; but not all the open sea. The Act carried highly important qualifying words. The phrase 'sea-going, coast-line battleships', and the stipulated fuel endurance of only five thousand nautical miles obviously implied, and were unquestionably intended to imply, that our bid for naval supremacy was not to extend much, if at all, beyond a thousand miles or so from the continental seaboard of the United States.[25]

However, notwithstanding the limitations referred to in the Act, the decision meant that Pandora's Box had been opened; the Congress would have very considerable difficulty if it wished to close it again. The three ships were the *Indiana* class; apart from the name ship, there were *Massachusetts* and *Oregon*. They displaced between 10,163 and 10,540 tons; had a trial speed of between 15.5 and 16.8 knots; had an armoured belt of up to 18 inches; and were powerfully armed with four 13-inch guns in two centre line turrets, and eight 8-inch guns mounted in four wing turrets on the upper deck. Their low freeboard meant that they became awash in heavy seas.[26] They cost between $5,500,000 and $6,500,000.

Tracy, meanwhile, had also been working on a restructuring of the administration of the Navy Department. He created a board of five bureau chiefs which would oversee his building programme, hoping thereby to achieve a consensus and avoid interdepartmental disputes. He also took steps to restore the Naval War College to its independent status, although it took a year to be able to restore it to its original habitat. In the meantime, he saw to it that Mahan was recalled from his exile at Puget Sound and was reinstated as president. Mahan returned with considerable anxieties about the college's future, and, mindful of the strength of the opposition to the college's very existence, cast about for allies. He found the man he needed in Admiral Porter, whose Damascene conversion from reactionary to progressive, under the influence of Luce, allied to his unchallenged seniority in the naval profession, made him the ideal protector.

Tracy's admiration for Mahan had preceded the publication, on May 13 1890, of *The Influence of Sea Power upon History 1660-1783*, but its almost immediate success confirmed his opinion of its author. The book was reviewed by the 31 year old Theodore Roosevelt, then serving as a Civil Service Commissioner, and provoked widespread favourable comment. Mahan was evolving a strong and clear set of beliefs about the position of his country in the world; he 'did not regard the United States as permanently destined to remain an isolated Continental Power.'[27] On the contrary, he believed that its destiny was to become a world Power, which would require the possession of powerful naval resources to support its position:

> Already, in 1890, he beheld indications that the American people were at last awakening to the greater opportunities awaiting them overseas. And with a view to hastening this process, he plunged into the congenial task of indoctrinating his countrymen with his vision of national power and destiny. In a series of magazine articles, appearing at intervals between 1890 and 1897, and marvellously synchronised with the march of events and the 'broadening horizons' of the nineties, he set forth his view of America's imperial destiny.[28]

His views chimed with those of Secretary Tracy, who believed that America must reach out for its place in the sun. One historian has summarised Tracy's policy: 'He wanted battleships. He wanted overseas bases. He wanted colonial empire.'[29] If his policy was as crudely direct as that, he could certainly find intellectual support in Mahan's writings. In these, Mahan sought to illustrate the ways in which an enemy threat might develop. In the first of his articles, published under the title '*The United States looking Outward*, he gave as an example of a possible threat the fact that 'all over the world German commercial and colonial push is coming into collision with other nations.' He underlined this by going on to observe, as an added warning:

> It is note worthy that, while these various contentions are sustained with the aggressive military spirit characteristic of the German Empire, they are credibly said to arise from the national temper more than from the deliberate policy of the government, which in this matter does not lead, but follows, the feeling of the people, – a condition much more formidable.[30]

Mahan argued that a nation must either expand or decline. If America was now beginning to look outward, so were other nations, who were developing 'aspirations for commercial extension, for colonies, and for influence in distant regions, which may bring … them into collision with ourselves.'[31]

In mid February 1890 Tracy suffered an appalling personal tragedy, when a fire destroyed his house, killing his wife and younger daughter; his elder daughter saved herself and her child by jumping from a window, and Tracy himself narrowly escaped death. President Harrison at once ordered that Tracy be moved to the White House where he gradually recovered, forming as he did so a close personal friendship with Harrison. The two men shared a feeling that real progress was being made with the expansion of the navy; two cruisers and two gunboats had been commissioned, while *Texas* and *Maine*, with six protected cruisers, were nearing completion. As time went by, Tracy's influence on the president steadily increased, as Harrison relied on him for advice on a wide range of issues.

By now Porter's serious illness in the winter of 1889-1890 had left Mahan as Tracy's chief consultant. This did not, however, mean that Mahan was in an entirely secure position. The appointment of Rear Admiral Francis M Ramsay as chief of the Bureau of Navigation in succession to the more sympathetic Rear Admiral Walker was a grave setback. Ramsay's original hostility to the setting up of the War College had not abated. Although Tracy had brought before Congress a proposal to restore the War College to its original location on Coaster's Island, Mahan learned that Ramsay was planning to send him back to sea. It took the removal of the college from the supervision of the Bureau of Navigation to avert this disaster, enabling Mahan to plan the building of the new college, as well as embarking on a sequel to *The Influence of Sea Power upon History*. The new building was completed in the summer of 1892; and in December there was published *The Influence of Sea Power upon the French Revolution and Empire 1793-1812*, to enormous acclaim both in the United States and abroad, where especially in Britain and Germany Mahan's reputation was already high. In America, *The Army and Navy Journal* observed that his two books on the influence of sea power 'have done much to restore our naval prestige … if the college had done nothing more than to inspire these admirable studies in naval history it would have fully justified its existence.' *The Edinburgh Review* called Mahan's writing 'a splendid apotheosis of English courage, of English skill and of English power.' describing the latest book as important 'to the statesman, the administrator, the ship owner, the merchant and the tradesman, equally with the naval officer.'[32]

In Germany, Mahan's first book on sea power had struck an immediate chord with Kaiser William II. Having parted with Bismarck over the issue of Germany's future as a world power, William found in Mahan's writing exactly the kind of endorsement of his country's requirement for sea power that he needed. In June 1892 he quoted Mahan in a famous speech justifying his call for a strong navy. He later ordered that a copy of the *Influence of Sea Power* be supplied to all the warships of the Imperial German Navy; before the end of the decade copies of a translation had been supplied to all German public libraries, schools and government institutions.[33]

His book was greatly admired by professional writers on naval affairs. Perhaps the most striking description of its effect came from the pen of Sir Julian Corbett, looking back many years later at its publication:

> For the first time naval history was placed on a philosophical basis. From the mass of facts which had hitherto done duty for naval history, broad generalisations were possible. The

> ears of statesmen and publicists were opened, and a new note began to sound in world politics. Regarded as a political pamphlet in the higher sense – for that is how the famous book is best characterised – it has few equals in the sudden and far reaching effect it produced on political thought and action.[34]

Other British naval writers took a similar view. Rear Admiral Philip Colomb wrote: 'I was delighted to see by the publication of Captain Mahan's *Influence of Sea Power* that on the other side of the Atlantic, an abler pen and a deeper thinker had been at work on thoughts something like our own.'[35] This opinion was shared by such as Sir George Sydenham Clarke, John K Laughton, Thomas G Bowles and James R Thursfield. The latter, the naval correspondent of *The Times*, described Mahan as 'the originator and first exponent of what may be called the philosophy of naval history.' On the other side of the Channel, Captain Darrieus of the French navy wrote that Mahan's work should be read and re-read, and in his own books warmly endorsed the conclusions drawn by Mahan.

Before leaving the huge influence which Mahan was soon to exert on political opinion in the United States and abroad, it should be noted that, in the words of one of his biographers, 'in general, Mahan did not in 1890 consider the United States a likely candidate for imperialism, colonialism, or militarism.' In 1884 he had expressed his concerns:

> I dread outlying colonies, to maintain which large military establishments are necessary. I see in them the oncoming of a 'strong' central government … or perhaps a subversion of really free government.[36]

2

Battleships

In autumn 1891, at a press conference, Tracy bluntly set out his imperialist beliefs; 'the sea will be the future seat of empire. And we shall rule it as certainly as the sun doth rise! To a pre-eminent rank among nations, colonies are of greatest help.'[1] His position was not exactly the same as that of Mahan, who said he was an imperialist, because he was not an isolationist, and was not primarily interested in colonies:

> I am frankly an imperialist, in the sense that I believe that no nation, certainly no great nation, should henceforth maintain the policy of isolation which fitted our early history; above all should not on that outlived plea refuse to intervene in events obviously thrust upon its conscience.[2]

What Mahan did foresee, in the first of his articles, written in 1890, awakening the United States to the reality of its situation, was the dangers that would accompany the opening of a canal through the Central American isthmus. This, he argued, while inducing a great increase of trade though the Caribbean, would give every position there 'an enhanced commercial and military value, and the canal itself will become a strategic centre of the most vital importance.'[3]

President Harrison's foreign policy was such that it inevitably involved the US navy directly and indirectly in its implementation. Apart from the abortive attempt to annex Hawaii, the issues that most threatened to test the navy in actual hostilities arose in Chile. Here, in January 1891, a civil war broke out between the forces supporting President Balmaceda and those supporting the Congress. Tracy sent Rear Admiral William P McCann to Valparaiso in the old wooden cruiser *Pensacola*, where he was reinforced by the modern cruisers *Baltimore* and *San Francisco*; thereafter he became involved in trying, unsuccessfully, to negotiate a ceasefire. McCann was also concerned with the activities of a ship, the *Itata*, carrying a cargo of guns intended for the insurgents; Tracy sent another cruiser, *Charleston*, south to intercept the vessel which, in the end, she did. This led to strong anti American feeling on the part of the insurgents, which was increased when Tracy authorised United States warships to take on prominent Balmacedist refugees. Another incident arose when the cruiser *Baltimore* supervised the connection of a new telegraph cable to Valparaiso in the teeth of the insurgents' protests.

A much more serious crisis erupted later in the year. By mid October 1891 the Congressional insurgents had gained the upper hand in the civil war, and controlled both Santiago and Valparaiso. The captain of *Baltimore* was Commander Winfield S Schley, who reported to Tracy from Valparaiso that everything was peaceful there, and that there was no continuing reason to station a vessel there. Balmaceda had committed suicide, and the population was quiet. Tracy thought that *Baltimore* should remain, however, so Schley imprudently decided to allow two boat loads of liberty men to go ashore. At about 1:30 p.m. on October 16 the cruiser's boats landed, and a number of the men made their way to bars in the seedier part of Valparaiso. At about 6:30 p.m. a fight developed; who started it became a matter of extreme controversy, but it ended with two Americans dead and thirty six under arrest, many of them wounded. The prisoners were soon released, but the incident aroused violent anti-American feeling in Chile. Schley reported to Tracy, claiming that his men were sober when attacked, an improbable assertion based on the outcome of a three member Court of Inquiry which he appointed to investigate what had occurred. Tracy felt obliged to accept this version; he realised, however, that Schley was not the man to handle a serious diplomatic incident, and he ordered the gunboat *Yorktown*, commanded by Commander Robley D Evans, to Valparaiso to relieve *Baltimore*. Accordingly, at the end of November, Schley put to sea, leaving Evans to deal with a situation that was rapidly deteriorating.

Evans regarded the attack on the sailors as 'about the most cowardly and brutal thing I ever heard of'; but he disapproved of Schley's attempt to argue that his men were 'perfectly sober' at the time:

> I did not agree with him in this, for in the first place I doubted the fact, and in the second it was not an issue worth discussing. His men were probably drunk on shore, properly drunk; they went ashore, many of them, for the purpose of getting drunk, which they did on Chilean rum paid for with good United States money. When in this condition they were more entitled to protection than if they had been sober.[4]

In both Valparaiso and Washington feelings were running very high, to the point at which war seemed a serious possibility. Behind the scenes, according to one of Mahan's biographers, Tracy began to prepare for a possible war, creating an informal Naval Strategy Board consisting of Assistant Secretary Soley, Mahan, Captain William M Folger and officers from the office of Naval Intelligence.[5] Another of Mahan's biographers, Robert Seager, seems not to accept that this was the case, suggesting that Mahan had only a 'peripheral interest' in the Chilean crisis beginning as late as December 17, when he was called to Washington. He does, however, quote from a letter which Mahan wrote to Luce on January 10:

> I wait impatiently and somewhat anxiously the outcome of the Chilean trouble. That their rulers are aware of the impolicy of forcing us to war, I am sure; but I doubt that they may too much fear their mob. It is astounding that our government should allow matters to drag so, when there is a question of so formidable a vessel as the [Chilean battleship] *Prat* thus getting time to escape. We are so confident in our bigness and so little realise the great extra load entailed by the distance of Chile, in case of war. The ultimate result, I suppose can be little doubtful, but we may first get some eye openers.[6]

The better view, however, is surely that Mahan was indeed a member of the strategy board, although was disappointed in the informal nature of that body, hoping that a proper Naval Staff would be established; many years later, he wrote to Luce to describe what had been expected of him:

> I was….. directed to study the military side of the question, to be ready to prepare plans, or to express opinions, as a result of my reflections; but Mr Tracy kept matters in his own hands, consulted when he wished to consult, and acted without consultation as he chose… Occasionally, once or twice, I gave brief written expression to my views; but these were simply memoranda, and I do not think that they ever went on file.[7]

At all events, the efforts of the Navy Department were such that in very short order the navy had been put on what was effectively a war footing. This lent determination to Harrison and his Secretary of State James G Blaine, who delivered an ultimatum to Chile on January 21 1892, threatening to break off diplomatic relations. In the face of this, the Chileans gave way, agreeing to make an apology and to pay an indemnity of $75,000 to the wounded sailors and the families of the two who died.

Tracy himself had worked like a beaver in making preparations for the war. He later described the care that had been taken to conceal these from the public:

> These were carried out so quietly that it never has been known just how far we went. The reason that we were… able to keep what we were doing from the public was that all the preparations… were controlled by one person, who carried on all his transactions with principals, not agents.[8]

He went on to summarise the strategy which it was intended to pursue if war did break out, a strategy which would have been completely beyond the US navy less than a decade earlier:

> According to this plan, the first order was to concentrate the fleet. A point of concentration was agreed on, and this was to be telegraphed to the three fleet commanders with the orders… to begin operations. Admiral Gherardi was to be in command of the combined fleets. After the fleets had concentrated, they were to proceed to Chile, drive the Chilean men-of-war under the guns of the fort in Valparaiso, then attack the whole coast ot Chile. The coalmines in the southern part were to be seized, thus cutting off the coal supply for the warships of the enemy, and all other details were to be looked after.[9]

After the crisis had passed, Tracy was asked by a reporter if it was true that every member of Harrison's cabinet had been in favour of declaring war on Chile except the Secretary of State. Tracy indignantly repudiated the suggestion that he was a warmonger:

> I did not know I was a war man; I rather thought that I was peaceably inclined, but I am also inclined to maintaining the dignity of the United Sates government and its power to protect its civilians, soldiers and sailors when abroad. If that leads to war, then I am for war; if it leads as I believe it will, to peace, then I am for peace.[10]

Tracy's work to expand the US navy was severely hampered by the political situation in Congress, after the mid-term elections of November 1890, which left the Republicans with a majority of only six in the Senate, while the Democrats had a huge majority in the House of Representatives. Between April and December 1891 no significant warships were authorised. During this period Tracy embarked on a programme of navy yard reform, the effect of which would be to reduce very severely the patronage which the two parties had been used to exploiting. Not surprisingly, this prompted violent opposition from the leaders of the political machines, in private at any rate; but Tracy was unmoved, and he proceeded to introduce new regulations for the navy yards.

Another issue which occupied a good deal of Tracy's time was the determination of the Chief of the Bureau of Navigation, Francis M Ramsay, to send Mahan to sea, which would scupper any question of his returning to the presidency of the War College. Tracy told Ramsay that Mahan's presence was required during the duration of the Chilean crisis. While noting that the extent of Mahan's work on the Naval Strategy Board is still unknown, Herrick quotes from a letter which Mahan wrote to Tracy on January 2 1892 which suggests that the board 'had instructions to prepare for eventualities more hazardous than a naval war with Chile:'

> The progress of that duty is as follows: I drew up a paper containing my views in case of England and sent it over six weeks ago to Folger. I wrote yesterday for data needed to take up the cases of Spain and Germany, and West Indies generally.[11]

Ramsay, once the Chilean crisis had passed, tried again to order Mahan to sea, and brushed aside Mahan's protests that he would be more useful to the navy while continuing to write ashore, remarking: 'It is not the business of naval officers to write books.' Tracy however, again intervened, ordering that Mahan remain ashore.

Notwithstanding the unfavourable domestic political climate, Tracy pressed on with his plan to expand the navy; in this he was supported by President Harrison, whose third annual message to Congress called for funds to be appropriated for the construction of a fleet of the 'best modern type.' Debates began in April 1893 on the proposals put forward by Tracy, which included two more battleships of the *Oregon* class, a second *New York* class armoured cruiser, a torpedo cruiser and a flotilla of light torpedo boats. In the event, as Tracy had more or less expected, his shopping list was cut down; the Navy Act of 1892 authorised only one battleship and an armoured cruiser.

The battleship became the *Iowa*, the most powerful vessel so far built in the United States. Displacing 11,340 tons, she was twelve feet longer than the *Indiana* class. She was armed with four 12-inch guns, which resulted in a saving of weight of 18 tons per gun compared to the 13-inch guns of the preceding class. Her secondary armament consisted of eight 8-inch guns mounted in four wing turrets and six 4-inch guns. She had a designed speed of 16 knots and was capable of steaming 4,500 nautical miles at ten knots. Her armour layout was similar to that of the *Indiana* class, save that the main belt was some four inches thinner, but the citadel extended three quarters of her length compared to their two thirds. She was considered to be a much better sea boat, due in part to her higher freeboard, and a more stable gun platform. She was of striking appearance, with two remarkably tall funnels.[12]

The armoured cruiser that was authorised became the *Brooklyn*. She displaced 9,215 tons, and carried eight 8-inch and twelve 5-inch guns, and was designed to attain a speed of 21 knots. The Navy Department boasted that she could steam from New York to San Francisco without recoaling At 400 feet in length, she was 40 feet longer than *Iowa*. She, too, was designed with very tall funnels, three in number.

During 1892, Tracy's navy was kept busy. A dispute with Britain over sealing in the Bering Sea led to the despatch of a squadron under the command of Robley D Evans. Gherardi was put in command of a squadron of cruisers to show the flag along the east coast of Latin American. Other cruisers were kept on patrol in Venezuelan waters due to a boundary dispute between that country and British Guiana, while in the Far East a squadron of five ships of the Asiatic Squadron were sent to make their presence felt. There could be no doubt that, as a significant force, the US navy had arrived.

During the year Mahan was again becoming anxious about the future of the War College, and pressed Tracy to take steps to secure its status. Tracy responded positively, to Mahan's great relief; but bad news came in November, with the Democrat success in the presidential election which returned Grover Cleveland to the White House. It seemed that Cleveland would probably appoint Congressman Hilary A Herbert as his Secretary of the Navy, a man with whom Mahan had crossed swords in 1888, and from whom he could expect no favours. Tracy was unable to persuade Herbert, in advance of his taking office, to allow Mahan to remain at the War College and to continue his writing rather than be sent to sea.

Herbert, a Confederate veteran of the Civil War, came from South Carolina, and had taken an active interest in naval questions as chairman of the House Naval Affairs Committee, generally supporting expansionist measures. Cleveland appointed as Assistant Secretary William G McAdoo, another supporter of naval expansion, so Tracy has good reason to hope that his policies would be continued under the new administration. Mahan, however, could have no such hope for his own future; Herbert wrote of Ramsay: 'I have never known a man more upright and just minded than Admiral Ramsay.'[13] Mahan's fears were soon justified; Ramsay insisted that Mahan must return to sea, ordering him to take command of the cruiser *Chicago*, which he did on May 11 1893.

Herbert had not felt able to interfere with Ramsay's decision, but unbeknown to the latter, who continued to reject Mahan's theories about the primacy of the capital ship, the new Secretary had been convinced by the *Influence of Sea Power on the French Revolution and Empire*. In his first annual report he called for the construction of at least one battleship and six torpedo boats in the coming year, arguing that the navy must be kept in such a condition 'as to give weight to whatever policy it may be thought wise on the part of the government to assume.'[14] In endorsing Mahan's capital ship theories, Herbert firmly rejected the policy of building unarmoured cruisers, which he contended could destroy merchant ships and fight against similar vessels but would be helpless against armoured ships. It was the British fleets of capital ships that had won the naval war against Napoleon; what the US navy required was more battleships. Herbert's policy of naval expansion was a marked departure from Democrat tradition but was justified by his statement of the requirement to support public policy:

> The Navy was not merely an agency for the defence of the homeland in war, but also an instrument of power with which to promote national interests abroad and generally to put teeth into civilian diplomacy in time of peace. The Navy was to be the spearhead of commercial expansion, to advance and protect American interests in the Far East, the south seas, Central and South America, and other distant places.[15]

Herbert's plan to build more battleships was held up by the state of the US Treasury, which in 1893 was no longer so flush with money as it had previously been. Cleveland insisted that large scale naval construction must wait for the time being. Events elsewhere, however, ensured that the interruption in the expansion of the navy was brief. Overseas, the naval battles of the Sino-Japanese war of 1894-1895 appeared to point to the fighting value of capital ships, while foreign navies were accelerating their building programmes. A number of disputes with Britain emphasised the importance of a strong navy, while the US navy continued to play an important role in protecting American interests. An instance of this came in January 1894, when insurgent forces in Brazil sought to prevent American merchantmen from docking at Rio de Janeiro. The local US commander, Commodore Stanton, appeared to be adopting an even handed approach between the two sides, and he was recalled, being replaced by Rear Admiral Andrew EK Benham, who insisted that the American merchant vessels be allowed to dock. The insurgent leader on the spot threatened to fire on them; Benham at once cleared his small squadron for action, opening fire when an insurgent vessel fired a warning shot. Benham's decisive action did the trick, and the insurgents backed down.[16]

By late 1894, although the financial situation had not yet entirely recovered, Herbert felt able to resume his push for renewed naval construction, arguing that its cessation would jeopardise the armour plate and other industries on which the navy depended. He was helped in his campaign by the fact that Mahan's theories were by now widely known, and commanded a lot of sympathy in political circles. In December 1894 Cleveland endorsed Herbert's proposal to build three more battleships; the Senate reduced this to two, which the House accepted in order to save the bill, which was passed in March 1895.

These battleships were the *Kearsarge* class. The name ship was unique in not being named after a state; this came about because the famous *Kearsarge* dating from the Civil War had been wrecked in 1894, and Herbert asked Congress to make an exception to the law to allow the new battleship to bear the honoured name. The second ship of the class was *Kentucky*. These vessels displaced 11,549 tons, and were armed with four 13-inch guns and 4 8-inch guns, the latter in two twin turrets mounted directly on top of the 13-inch turrets. There was a secondary armament of fourteen 5-guns in main deck broadside casemates. Armour was a 16.5-inch belt. On their trials, the two ships attained a speed of just under 17 knots. They had a range at 10 knots of 5,316 nautical miles. Their construction time was much the same as the earlier battleships, from the laying of the keel on June 30 1896 to commissioning on February 20 1900.[17]

A further sign of the willingness of Congress to vote funds for battleship construction came in the following year. Herbert asked for two battleships; the House of Representatives, which was once more under the control of the Republican Party, voted for four; when the bill came to the Senate the number was reduced to two; and in the end a compromise was reached on three. These would be the *Illinois* class, consisting of *Illinois*, *Alabama* and *Wisconsin*. It had become customary for each new battleship authorisation to be described in the legislation as 'seagoing coastline battleships.' But like their predecessors the new ships were to have an extensive steaming range at 10 knots of about 4,500 miles, and were equipped with four 13-inch guns as their main armament. The super firing 8-inch guns were dispensed with; instead, these vessels carried fourteen 6-inch guns, five pairs of which were mounted in hull casemates at main deck level, with the remaining four guns in sponsons on the upper deck. Armour protection was the same as in the *Kearsarge* class. Although designed for a speed of 16 knots, all three ships attained 17 knots on their trials. These would be the last battleships authorised before the outbreak of the Spanish American War.[18]

In his annual report for 1896, in which he had asked for two battleships, Herbert published a table showing the relative strength of the world's navies in battleships. This put the US navy in sixth place, behind Britain, France, Russia, Italy and Germany; but for the first time Spain ranked after the United States, with three battleships, although possessing seven armoured cruisers compared to America's two. In a change of policy that would prove significant in the following decade, Japan had recently placed orders for six battleships, rather than confine the fleet to cruisers as had previously been the case.[19]

Meanwhile Alfred Mahan had reluctantly taken his cruiser *Chicago* to sea, sailing for Europe as the flagship of Rear Admiral Henry Erben, a man totally out of sympathy with Mahan and with the concept of a War College. It was a relationship that was unlikely to prosper in any case, but the popular adulation heaped on Mahan once they had reached Europe infuriated Erben to an even greater extent than his professional view of Mahan as captain of the vessel. Wherever they went, Mahan's reputation had preceded him, and he received a host of invitations from the great and the good. In October 1893 *The Times* declared in an editorial:

> By his pregnant conception of sea power and his masterly exposition of its influence upon the history of the British Isles, Captain Mahan may almost be said to have effected a revolution in the study of naval history similar in kind to that effected by Copernicus in the domain of astronomy.[20]

One item of news which cheered Mahan as he continued his round of social invitations was a letter from Commander French Ensor Chadwick. who wrote: 'The War College is safe. The Secretary read your last book and that convinced him. He told me some time since he was opposed to it. He now tells me he has informed Ramsay that he has changed his mind.'[21] Mahan had by now organised his not very demanding shipboard duties to enable him to work on his biography of Nelson, and Erben's awareness of this did nothing to improve the Admiral's temper. In November 1893 he wrote a fitness report which reflected his opinion of Mahan's literary endeavours:

> I state herewith that Capt. Mahan always appears to advantage to the service in all that does not appertain to ship life or matters, but in this particular he is lacking in interest, as he has frankly admitted to me. His interests are entirely outside the service, for which, I am satisfied, he cares but little, and is therefore not a good naval officer. He is not at all observant regarding officers tending to the ship's general welfare or appearance, nor does he inspire or suggest anything in this connection. In fact, the first few weeks of the cruise she was positively discreditable. In fact, Capt Mahan's interests lie wholly in the direction of literary work and in no other way connected with the service.[22]

Although he could not deny an element of truth in some of Erben's remarks, Mahan was outraged at the contents of a report which he did not see until January 1894. His allies back home concluded that it would be unwise to press for an inquiry; Henry Cabot Lodge saw Herbert privately, who agreed that the matter could in effect be quietly dropped, and Mahan wisely accepted the advice of his friends to leave the matter there. In the meantime, the cruise of the *Chicago* continued, with the relationship between admiral and captain remaining one of unconcealed hostility until Erben finally hauled down his flag in September 1894, and was replaced by Rear Admiral William A Kirkland. Meanwhile Mahan had continued his triumphant tour of Europe, where he was lionised on all sides, especially in England. In the course of an almost endless round of public engagements he met and talked with many of the great men of the time, and was left in no doubt of the high regard in which he was held. When Kirkland shifted his flag from *Chicago* to *San Francisco* he wrote to the Navy Department to comment on a memorandum he had received from Erben, when he took over the command, that was highly critical of Mahan. He therefore considered it an act of justice to report his own observations of the *Chicago*'s captain:

> Captain AT Mahan USN, is a careful yet bold Navigator – never afraid of his ship. He is a just and careful administrator of the Regulations and Laws of the Navy, to his officers and crew. He is indefatigable in his efforts to obtain the best results in efficiency so far as he is permitted by the regulations. He is subordinate and cheerful in carrying out the instructions of his superiors. Of his abilities and his gentlemanly and officer like conduct everyone is aware.[23]

By the time that Mahan returned to New York aboard the *Chicago* in March 1895 he had made up his mind to apply for a year's leave and then retire from a profession which he enjoyed no more than at any time since he had entered it. His last seagoing command may, in respect of the long running feud with Erben, not have been particularly pleasant, but it has been pointed out that if Ramsay had been his best friend anxious to do all he could for him, he could have done nothing better for Mahan than to send him to Europe. His time spent in European waters or, to be more accurate, ashore there, cemented his growing reputation. Mahan was a happy man; therefore, when on November 17 1896 he went on the retired list, having since his return from Europe been able to continue his literary career uninterrupted.[24]

3

Winfield Scott Schley

Winfield Scott Schley was born in Frederick County Maryland on October 9 1839, where his father was a farmer. He was descended from John Thomas Schley, one of two brothers who emigrated from Bavaria in the middle of the eighteenth century. He owed his name to the friendship between his father, also John T Schley, and General Winfield Scott, widely revered as a hero of the war of 1812; the latter became his godfather. In 1848 Schley's mother died, and John Schley moved with his family to the city of Frederick, where he prospered. He maintained his friendship with General Winfield Scott, who suggested that the young Schley might pursue a military career, promising to help secure an appointment to West Point. As it happened, however, Scott was without influence at the material time, having fallen out with Jefferson Davis, then the Secretary of War. Schley, however had by then become attracted by a naval career, and with the aid of Congressman William H Hoffmann, another influential contact of his father, secured a place at the Naval Academy at Annapolis, which he entered in September 1856, as an acting midshipman.

He was not a studious youth, writing in his autobiography that he 'held pleasure and holidays in higher esteem than plodding study, which was more interesting in some such ratio as the square of the distance separating us from books.'[1] Once at Annapolis he became the leader of a group of students known as the Pelicans, dedicated to enjoying themselves rather than devoting themselves to their work. There is a glimpse of him at Annapolis from Mahan who in a letter to a friend described a typical incident:

> A crowd of fellows had assembled in Paddock's room to hear music and some of them prevailed on Jim [O'Kane] to give them a tune on the violin He struck up a dance, not much time in it I must say, and 'Ye Pelicans', each with a cigar in mouth, gyrated around in the mazes of the dance. But alas! A change came o'er the spirit of the scene. One of Ye Pelicans, yclept Schley, unwarily trod on Jim's pedestal where a very sore corn had made its appearance. Away went violin in one corner of the room, bow in another, while Jim, exclaiming in shocking profanity… The room was convulsed with laughter, while Schley, taking possession of the discarded violin, commenced a series of performance that only Schley could give.[2]

Schley made no reference to Mahan in his autobiography, *Forty Five Years Under the Flag*, either at Annapolis or subsequently. One of Mahan's biographers has suggested that 'there is no certain evidence that Mahan particularly disliked Schley during their midshipman days together,'and that the violent hostility which he displayed only came later. The outlook and personalities of the two men were, however, so opposed that it is unlikely that they ever had much to do with each other. There was a marked contrast between the reserved and intellectual Mahan, and the popular, athletic and attractive Schley.[3]

The students at Annapolis made an annual cruise to learn seamanship in a sailing sloop, which Schley enjoyed much more than the classroom at the Academy. He recalled the experience, during his first cruise in 1857, of taking his turn at the wheel, going aloft to reef and furl the sails, of small boat drills, always in wet clothing, living in crowded unventilated quarters, with great pleasure. They lived, he wrote, on rations of 'hard tack, salt junk, pork and beans, weevily rice, wormy cheese, rancid butter,' and were allowed only one gallon of water per day for all purposes. These hardships, he wrote, produced a 'camaraderie of the older officers and men… which bound them together in loyal attachment to country and to each other.'[4] They also led Schley to develop a sympathetic understanding of the daily lives of the seamen who came under his command.

Schley graduated in June 1860, and was posted to the steam frigate *Niagara*, aboard which he undertook a cruise to the Far East, aware as he went of the darkening political shadows at home. Returning in May 1861, the crew of the *Niagara* were greeted with the news of secession, and almost at once the frigate was ordered to take up a blockading station off Charleston. Within the first two days a prize was taken, the *General Parkhill*, suspected of Confederate sympathies, and Schley, with a prize crew of twelve men, was sent to take her in to Philadelphia. Once there, Schley was granted leave to visit his family in Maryland before being assigned in August 1861 with the rank of master to the *Potomac*, part of the Western Gulf Squadron under Farragut. Before joining her, he became engaged to Annie Rebecca Franklin, whom he had known since he was at Annapolis.

Aboard the *Potomac*, Schley was one of nine masters and midshipmen; immediately below him on the list of her officers was Master William T Sampson, who had just graduated from the Naval Academy. In terms of personality they could hardly have been less alike, but they appear to have had a reasonably equable relationship.

For the next nine months the *Potomac* served on blockade duty. It was a dreary time. The *Potomac*, a sailing frigate, was too slow to overhaul and capture any blockade runner, so she was confined to the task of patrolling the waters off Mobile Bay. In May 1862 she was sent to Vera Cruz to monitor the French invasion of Mexico and the activities of British, Spanish and French ships that had been sent there for the purposes of debt collection. This proved to be the *Potomac*'s last assignment and she sailed to Pensacola, where she was laid up. Schley was now ordered to join the steam gunboat *Winona*, serving off Mobile, as her executive officer.

In this posting it was Schley's unpleasant duty to have Captain Thornton, the *Winona*'s commander confined to his cabin and examined by the surgeon, who concluded that he was suffering from delirium tremens due to excessive alcohol. Reporting this to Captain James Alden, the senior officer present, Schley was relieved to have his actions approved. Under a new commander the *Winona*, not a very seaworthy vessel, was assigned by Farragut to operate in the Mississippi River, where although she was frequently damaged by enemy fire, Schley himself survived unscathed.

During one of these actions Schley was on deck, casting the lead because of the severe danger of running aground, and about to hand it to the master's mate at his side when a shell hit the

Winona, killing the master's mate. Moments later, the ship went aground briefly on a bar off Profit's Island. Schley described what followed:

> Unfortunately in her position only one gun could bear upon the enemy's battery and for ten or fifteen minutes this disadvantage continued, while a storm of projectiles from artillery and musketry swept the ship. The chief engineer was directed to let steam run up to the highest safe pressure and then to open her engines wide astern. After a few moments the *Winona* glided off into deeper water. She then steamed ahead to straighten up with head to the current. She took her position abreast the battery and for an hour poured her heaviest fire into the enemy's position, driving his forces from the field with considerable loss, notwithstanding that they were behind the levee.[5]

He was next assigned to the large steam sloop *Richmond*, in which, due to the absence ashore of the executive officer, and the temporary absence of Captain Alden, he found himself as acting commanding officer during Farragut's operations against Port Hudson on May 24 1863. The *Richmond* led the line as the fleet moved up to bombard Port Hudson, her target being a battery on a height known as the Citadel. Schley understandably wanted to make a good impression on Admiral Farragut, and ignored the flagship's signal to break off the action and retire, telling himself that it did not apply to the *Richmond*. When it became obvious that this was not the case, Schley obeyed the instruction. Reporting aboard the flagship, he found Farragut extremely displeased. Had Schley not seen the signal to withdraw which had been flying for an hour? In reply, Schley's stammering explanation, that the conditions of visibility made it difficult to see the signal, and that he thought it did not apply to him, did not go down well. Farragut said that he 'wanted none of this Nelson business in his squadron about not seeing signals'.[6] Inviting the young officer into his cabin, however, Farragut relaxed, telling Schley that he had been obliged to censure him publicly for disregarding his orders, but adding: 'I desire to commend you and your officers and men for doing what you believed right under the circumstances. Do it again whenever in your judgment it is necessary to carry out your concept of duty.' So saying, he poured Schley a glass of wine. It was an incident which understandably, had a considerable effect on Schley, powerfully reinforcing his self confidence.

As was the case with so many of the officers who served under him, Farragut made a huge impression on the young Schley, who wrote of him in his autobiography:

> The admiral was a man of perhaps five feet seven inches in height. His gait and step were those of a very young man, and in conversation he was an animated and interesting talker. His information and experience were general, and upon almost all subjects – professional, scientific or political – he was interesting and attractive. Like all great men, he was affable and accessible. His manner was one of great mildness and self poise. His ideas were clear and his methods of doing things were always decided. When he had made up his mind to give battle in a certain way, it was realised that his way was the best. In any of the emergencies of battle his towering genius was readiest and his cool self-possession was an inspiration to everybody. The wide difference that was apparent between this sprightly, kind, mild and pleasing gentlemen, even when under a heavy load of responsibility, and his lion-like character and presence when battle was going on was the contrast between sunshine

and storm. His judgment of men was excellent, as the choice of officers with whom he surrounded himself indicated.[7]

Once Port Hudson had fallen in July 1863, Schley's combat experience during the Civil War came to an end. After a spell in the Bureau of Ordnance in Washington, in the course of which he married Annie Franklin on September 10, his next posting was as executive officer of the experimental double ended ship *Wateree*, which was sent to the Pacific in part to test her effectiveness as a warship, and in part to join the unsuccessful hunt for the Confederate raider *Shenandoah*.

As the war ended, the *Wateree* was engaged in operations along the west coast of Latin America, in particular being concerned with the protection of American lives and property during an election in Nicaragua. Schley returned home in April 1866; promoted to lieutenant commander, he was next sent to the Naval Academy to serve as a member of the Department of Discipline. His career during the Civil War had shown him to be a resourceful and courageous officer but, like Dewey but in contrast with Mahan and Sampson, not especially intellectual. He did, however make a contribution to the better education of the students when in his second and third years at Annapolis he served as assistant professor of Spanish. During this stint there he was working alongside both Dewey and Sampson. The former was concerned largely with administrative duties, becoming aide to the superintendent. Sampson in 1867 took up a post as head of the newly established Department of Physics and Chemistry.[8]

In November 1869 Schley's appointment at Annapolis came to an end with his assignment to the newly commissioned *Benicia* on the Asiatic Station, as executive officer. The vessel was part of a squadron commanded by Admiral John Rodgers, who was entrusted with a mission to the closed 'Hermit Kingdom' of Korea. He had two principal objectives. The first was to find out what had happened to the American merchantman *General Sherman* which had disappeared without trace off the coast of Korea. There was a strong suspicion that she had fallen a victim to the notorious pirates that infested the Korean coast; these were, one New York newspaper wrote, 'pirates of the worst sort. No one escapes them. They capture a ship, pillage it, burn it, and kill all the crew.'[9] It was an international problem that Prussian Minister President Otto von Bismarck had suggested to US Secretary of State Hamilton Fish should be dealt with by joint action of Britain, France, the North German Confederation and the United States. It was a proposal that did not survive the outbreak of the Franco Prussian War, but the US government was prepared to act alone if necessary. The second objective that Rodgers was given was to open up to Western trade and influence the secretive and isolationist kingdom of Korea, by negotiating a treaty similar to that obtained by Commodore Perry in Japan.

Rodgers, after taking the former US Secretary of State William Seward first to Japan and then to China, headed for the Korean coast, requesting permission to carry out a survey. No apparent objection was raised, and the survey ships started work. At Kangwha Island, however, there were five forts, manned by an estimated 2,000 men, which opened fire on the surveyors. Rodgers received a note from a counsellor of the Korean king to the effect that Korea would have nothing to do with foreign nations. This was not good enough; Rodgers demanded an apology and explanation for the forts having opened fire. None was forthcoming, and on June 10 he put ashore a 650 strong landing party under Captain LA Kimberly, to whom Schley served as adjutant. This soon captured the lesser batteries, and moved forward to assault the main fort on the following day. In the fighting that ensued, Schley was slightly wounded in the arm; 3 Americans and 243 Koreans were killed, and half a dozen Americans and an unknown number of Koreans were wounded, as the fort was taken. Before withdrawing, the landing party dismounted the fort guns and destroyed its magazines and storehouses. After this incident, there was no question of the Koreans agreeing to a treaty such as the United States had proposed.[10]

After three years in the Far East, Schley found himself at Annapolis again where, with the rank of commander, he became head of the Modern Languages Department. Characteristically he came to the conclusion that too much time was spent on grammar and vocabulary, and not enough on learning to speak a language. He decreed that more time should be devoted to conversation. Foreign languages were, however, low down on the priorities, given the enormous range of other subjects that the midshipmen had to study.

It was a time when the US navy was at perhaps its lowest ebb since the end of the Civil War, and Schley was one of those naval officers who agitated for a proper understanding of the need for the navy's restoration. He joined the newly formed US Naval Institute, established to promote the growth and efficiency of the service. He had returned to the Naval Academy in the autumn of 1872, and served four years there before his next assignment took him back to sea as captain of the screw steamer *Essex,* a command which he held from 1876 to 1879, and which took him far afield. Secretary of the Navy Thompson offered him the congratulations and thanks of the Navy Board for a successful commission:

> The *Essex,* after a cruise of unusual activity and often exposed to the severest weather both in the tropic and temperate zones, returns in an almost perfect condition save ordinary wear and tear, and could again be dispatched on distant service. All this is most gratifying evidence of the excellent qualities of the ship, the faithful manner in which she was fitted and her able and careful management.[11]

Having returned in October 1879, Schley's next appointment was as a member of the Lighthouse Board, headed by Commander George Dewey. He was responsible for the Second District, extending from Newburyport, Massachusetts to Newport, Rhode Island, and was based in Boston. It was a pleasant time, bringing him into contact with a wide range of people outside the inward looking world of the navy, in the course of which he gained valuable experience of the commercial world at large. When this four year term of duty came to an end in 1883, he returned to Washington to work in the Navy Department, quickly becoming a valuable support to Secretary William E Chandler, at that time at loggerheads with the US Senate. Schley became deeply involved in negotiating a settlement with shipbuilding companies over the terms of their government contracts.

It was while working in Washington that Schley received an assignment that made him a national hero. A polar expedition led by Lieutenant Adolphus Greely of the US army had been stranded in the Arctic when the steam whaler *Proteus* had been crushed in the ice and sunk. Two attempts to rescue Greely and his men had failed, and President Chester Arthur decided that the rescue expedition should be conducted by the navy. Chandler offered the command to Schley, who accepted at once, stipulating that he should be allowed to pick his own officers. Special ships were prepared and strengthened, and Schley sailed from New York on April 21 1884 in the *Thetis*, with the *Bear* and the *Alert*, seen off by huge crowds on shore.

It was a hazardous mission, involving threading through the ice which threatened to block the progress of his little squadron. Schley spent as much as twenty hours at a time in the crow's nest of the *Thetis*, studying the ice through which he must pass. He was accompanied by a number of whalers, whose captains were sceptical of Schley's ability to succeed, due to his lack of experience of the conditions, Schley, however, thought otherwise; his mission was to rescue Greely, and experience was of little value in this aim; he wrote later that 'they who know nothing fear nothing. This proved to be the dominant factor in the expedition's work.'[12]

News that Greely might be found at Cape Sabine gave hope of success, and on June 22 the *Bear* reached the survivors there. Eighteen of Greely's men had died; he and six others were at the last extremity, as they lay in sleeping bags in a violent gale. The rescue was, as Harold Langley wrote, 'the high point of Schley's professional career.' To the press and to the public of America he had demonstrated outstanding heroic qualities, and he was greeted with enormous national enthusiasm when he returned to New York, where President Arthur came to thank him personally. The *Army and Navy Journal* observed that 'not a whisper of hostile criticism had been heard on Commander Schley's management of the expedition, but he received credit for good judgment and energy from all quarters;' while the *United Service Magazine* wrote that it 'was a notable feat, this dash through howling tempest and ice straight to the goal, and the American heart was thrilled as it had not been since Richmond fell.'[13]

Schley was rewarded by President Arthur by appointment to the post of Chief of the Bureau of Recruiting and Equipment. It was an important post and the influence it gave him in Washington was enhanced by his enormous popular reputation. Always affable and outgoing, he was admired by pressmen and politicians alike, and at the relatively young age of forty two was at the centre of the American naval revolution that under Secretaries Chandler, then Whitney and finally Tracy was to reverse the long decades of decline.

He was also able to mingle with the leading figures of the American army and navy and those of the government, getting to know many of them very well. They included many of the outstanding individuals of the Civil War, both Union and Confederate. Schley enjoyed the experience of meeting such men, writing that: 'at close range all these men were accessible, pleasing in conversation, interesting in relating experiences, simple in their modes of life, and forceful in character'.[14]

Schley embarked on his administrative duties very conscious that they would call for skills different from those required at sea:

> The new field to which the President had assigned the commander embraced duties that were new and almost unknown to him. They were approached with some misgivings, lest this post of honour, with its multifarious ramifications, might transcend the business capacity of the new appointee … The duties, as well as the personnel, of the bureau had to be studied with some care before changes could be made, or its systems of business modified in any particular.[15]

Schley's bureau was particularly concerned with the questions arising from the fitting out of the new vessels being added to the navy and the naval supplies and stores for them. One such question arose from the use of steel where iron had formerly been used. It caused, as Schley recalled, 'some friction between the department and the manufacturers who, in some instances, expressed the belief that what the department demanded could not be produced in the United States.'[16] During Schley's term at the bureau, he took over also the duties of chief of the Bureau of Provisions and Clothing, and it was at this time that a standard uniform was introduced for

US Navy seamen. Another innovation, for which Schley particularly pressed, was the removal of the barriers which prevented a seaman to be promoted beyond the grade of warrant officer, thus permitting them to attain commissioned rank.

In addition to the specific duties of his office, Schley was also involved with many of the key policy issues with which the Navy Department was concerned. In the autumn of the year of his appointment, the presidential election had brought the Democrat Grover Cleveland to the White House, while the new Navy Secretary was William C Whitney. Schley enjoyed a good relationship with his new political master, whose reservations about the establishment of a War College soon became apparent. In authorising this, Chandler, his predecessor, had done so in the face of considerable opposition within the navy. Whitney, although at first not displaying any hostility to the War College, disliked Mahan, who had become its president in 1886. When, in1888, he decided to transfer responsibility for the oversight of the college to the Bureau of Equipment, he did so with Schley's encouragement. Mahan was furious at the Navy Secretary's decision, which led him to a violent outburst against Whitney's probity:

> Whitney is considered by men in the Navy able to judge as one of the strongest men in the Cabinet; but he is corrupt (politically) in the in the use of patronage and I gather that in that respect the Navy is worse than it had ever been in my time… in this respect he is as bad or worse than Chandler or Robeson.[17]

Mahan, who could never comprehend any point of view contrary to his own, was in no doubt that he had Schley to blame for Whitney's decision; if there had been no personal enmity between him and Schley previously, there certainly was now. He told Luce of this, and wrote to his old friend Sam Ashe:

> I will not ask you to believe, what I believe but do not know, but which is commonly believed in the Navy, that the Secretary is largely influenced by a man named Schley – who you may remember – who has never achieved more than a second-rate reputation, if that, among his brother officers.[18]

The issue led Mahan to mobilise all the resources available to him in a desperate bid to prevent the Naval War College being consolidated with the Torpedo Station and thus coming under the control of the hated Schley. In November 1888, the election brought back the Republicans, under Benjamin Harrison, who defeated the outgoing President Grover Cleveland; this gave Mahan some hope that that Whitney's successor would be more amenable to Mahan's wishes, and, in the event, when Benjamin Franklin Tracy took office, this turned out to be the case. Before this, however, Whitney had had his way, and a few weeks before he left office he finally ordered the move of the college to Goat Island, where it was consolidated with the Torpedo Station, while its buildings were assigned to Schley's Bureau of Equipment for use as a training facility for apprentice seamen. Mahan meanwhile was sent off to chair the commission considering the site for the new navy yard north of Seattle. It was only in July 1889, when Tracy paid his first visit to the Naval War College, that its supporters could feel that the tide had turned, and that the Navy Department had at its head a man profoundly sympathetic to the role and needs of the college.

Meanwhile Schley, after more than four years in his administrative posting, was keen to get back to sea, and he asked Tracy to agree to this. The Secretary was happy to oblige; Schley stayed on for a few months to ensure continuity before formally sending in his resignation on June 25 1889. He had no hesitation in responding to Tracy's request for a recommendation for his successor, putting forward the name of his good friend Captain George Dewey, who was duly appointed to the post at the end of July.

Schley, meantime had been delighted to receive his new orders as captain of the protected cruiser *Baltimore*, then nearing completion at the shipyard of William Cramp and Sons at Philadelphia. The *Baltimore*, of 4413 tons, mounted twelve 6-inch guns; her deck armour was four inches thick. She was capable or 20 knots. After completion, the cruiser sailed from Philadelphia on January 13 1890 to Norfolk, where she completed her sea trials before joining the North Atlantic Station, based at Key West. After a voyage to Europe to carry the body of the inventor John Ericsson to Sweden, where Schley enjoyed visiting with the King and members of his family, the cruiser spent some time on the Mediterranean station. Her next assignment was to the coast of Chile, where a revolution had broken out; she arrived in Valparaiso on April 7 1891 to join the American warships already operating in those waters. On August 28 the insurgent forces took Valparaiso, and after a period of unrest conditions in the city quietened down. The *Baltimore* had been lying at anchor in the harbour, and remained there as a protection to the American Consulate, for the rebels still suspected the United States of sympathising with the Balmacedist government and greatly resented this. Schley, in view of the popular feeling, did not give his crew liberty.

By October 16, since the other foreign warships present were allowing their crews ashore and it was a long time since his men had been granted liberty, Schley reckoned it safe to allow some 115 of them to go ashore.

It was a decision which led to the major diplomatic incident described in Chapter 2. Schley's immediate response was to appoint his own board of investigation, which established to his satisfaction that his men had not been drunk, a finding which Robley Evans found hard to believe. Schley and the *Baltimore* left the station in December and sailed for San Francisco, where the Judge Advocate General of the Navy conducted his own investigation, while Schley went off to Washington to report to the President and the Navy Department.

Schley's next appointment was as inspector of the Third Lighthouse District, based at Staten Island. There was no suggestion that any blame attached to him for the Chilean incident; instead, Schley's progress across the continent was somewhat of a triumphal progress, at least in his account:

> Everywhere when the train stopped large crowds of our people had assembled to give expression of their approval of the commander's action in protecting his crew and in standing for the rights and honor of the Nation in far-off countries.[19]

All this can have done no harm to Schley's not inconsiderable self confidence.

The new post was not particularly demanding. Schley was able to maintain all his government, service and social; contacts, and also to undertake some consultative work for the Navy Department. One question on which he successfully offered advice was that of the retention of woodwork in the ceilings and bulkheads of the latest ships. He wrote to Hilary A Herbert, Navy Secretary since the Republican defeat of 1892, on October 27 1894:

> 1st. Under the action of modern artillery and high explosives there is grave danger of fire from the lodgement and explosion of shells behind or near such ceilings or bulkheads.
>
> 2nd. When in action there is serious danger to officers and men from splinters driven inboard by the rapid machine and other gunfire, and no one who has ever had the experience of battle in wooden ships can ever forget the casualties from this cause, often at points remote from that struck by shot or shell.
>
> 3rd. The saving of weight by omitting ceilings and bulkheads could be better utilised if given over to the coal supply, so as to increase the steaming radius of the new vessels, as well as to increase the interior accommodation for stores and personnel.[20]

Leaving the Third Lighthouse District in March 1895, Schley served for six months in the Navy Department's Board of Inspection, before being appointed to command the armoured cruiser *New York*, the flagship of the North Atlantic Squadron. It was an uneventful posting; it continued for two years before he returned ashore, once again as a member of the Lighthouse Board, of which he was elected chairman. In February 1898, while serving in this capacity, he was promoted to the rank of commodore. Before this could become effective, he was obliged to appear before a medical board, which 'scrupulously overhauled the person and, as well, the medical history' of the candidate, whose service record was then minutely examined.

4

William Thomas Sampson

Born in 1840 at Palmyra, New York to poor Scottish-Irish immigrants, William Thomas Sampson showed great aptitude for study at the local schools, so much so that his teachers strongly recommended him as a candidate for one of the national service academies. With the support of Congressman Edwin B Morgan a place was obtained for him at the Naval Academy in 1857. His admission was in its way remarkable; according to Peter Karsten, the author of 'The Naval Aristocracy' less than 7 percent of cadets came from a working class background. Although slightly older than Mahan, Sampson arrived at Annapolis a year later; the younger boy was immediately impressed by the shy slightly awkward country boy. He remembered him as having an 'unusually fine complexion, delicate regular features, and brown eyes remarkable both in shape and color.' Sampson from the first took a special interest in gunnery; he demonstrated a keen interest in acquiring technical knowledge of all kinds, as Mahan recalled:

> At our first meeting, Sampson began as he afterwards continued, putting me through a searching series of questions concerning the matters around him. He clearly, if unconsciously, intended not to wait till knowledge came to him of itself, if he could compel it to hasten.[1]

Sampson did well at the Academy, ranking top of his class of twenty seven cadets in each of his last three years there, displaying a particular interest in scientific and technological questions. His reserved personality led him to stand aloof from his fellow midshipmen, unlike the more boisterous and less intellectual individuals such as Dewey and Schley. The outbreak of the Civil War found him still at Annapolis, where he was at once plunged into conflict when a crowd of Southern sympathisers rioted outside the Academy, threatening violence to the Yankee cadets within. Sampson was in command of a company of armed midshipmen ready to defend the gate and walls of the Academy. As a member of the senior class of cadets, he was at once ordered on active service. He served briefly at the Washington Navy Yard, where he caught the eye of the renowned gun designer Commander John Dahlgren, before being assigned to the frigate *Pocahontas*, patrolling the River Potomac, Her principal task was in convoying the troopships and ammunition vessels that were supporting the intended thrust southwards which ended in the first battle of Bull Run.

On June 1 Sampson was assigned next as acting master aboard the frigate *Potomac*, at that time undergoing repairs in Brooklyn Navy Yard, which gave him the chance of home leave. The

Potomac was ready for sea on August 20, and Sampson served in her alongside Schley for the best part of a year, before on July 16 1862 being promoted to lieutenant and sent as an instructor to the Naval Academy. The institution had been moved for the time being for security reasons to Newport, Rhode Island. Sampson served for two years there. In spite of the war, the standard arrangement for the cadets to go on a practice cruise was adhered to, and aboard the *Macedonian* Sampson found himself a shipmate of Alfred Mahan, as they taught a generation of cadets that would in due course play a prominent part in the Spanish American War. Sampson's interest in technology, and ordnance in particular, had not abated and his enthusiasm for these subjects got rather too much for Mahan: 'the ingenuity of the machinery, the variety and beauty of the blocks, the many excellencies, had the changes rung upon them meal after meal, till I could hear the whir of the wheels in my head and see the chips fly.'[2]

In 1863 Sampson married Margaret Sexton Aldrich, with whom he had five daughters, one of whom, Susan, died at the age of two. The marriage was a happy one, until ended by tragedy in 1878, when Margaret Sampson died of typhoid fever. Sampson, still reserved to the point of diffidence, enjoyed his time at the Academy, where he could continue his study of his profession. In August 1864 this period of his career ended when he was assigned as executive officer of the monitor *Patapsco*, serving in Rear Admiral John Dahlgren's South Atlantic Blockading Squadron. Built generally on the lines of the *Monitor*, the *Patapsco* had her pilot house placed on top of her gun turret, away from the risk of danger from her own guns, while her funnel was protected by heavy armour. She had, however, been in service for eighteen months and was sadly in need of a dockyard overhaul, bearing the scars from action against Fort Sumter and Fort Moultrie. Her turret could only be turned through ninety degrees, while only one of her guns was still serviceable. Her bottom was foul, and salt deposits had reduced the effectiveness of her boilers. The experience of serving aboard such a vessel, however, was invaluable to an officer of Sampson's concern with technological problems.[3]

On the night of January 15 1865, the *Patapsco* was ordered, as part of the squadron's operations against Charleston, to remove a number of Confederate mines laid between Fort Sumter and Fort Moultrie. Her task was to escort a number of picket launches, whose crews dragged for the mines: it was a moonless night and Sampson, piloting the *Patapsco* from on top of the turret, could see little as he steered the vessel back and forth outside the supposed location of the mines. On her third run she struck a mine; Sampson's official report described the event:

> The torpedo struck the vessel on the port side just abreast the bitts, and appeared to raise the deck, through which the smoke issued. My first impression on hearing the report was that a shot had struck the overhang just below the water; but the column of smoke and water which immediately shot upward convinced me of the real nature of the explosion.[4]

Almost at once, the ship's stern lifted clear of the water, and she sank in fifteen seconds. Sampson, extricating himself from some rope netting, was hauled on board one of the picket launches.

Next day he and the *Patapsco*'s captain reported in person to Dahlgren: the latter wrote in his report that 'the cool intrepidity displayed by Lieutenant Sampson deserves the highest praise.' Mahan, who heard from Sampson at first hand his description of what had occurred, observed that when he saw him, 'he was as unaffectedly and without effort unperturbed as though nothing remarkable had occurred'.[5]

When the Civil War came to an end, Sampson and his brother officers had all had practical combat experience. For more than three decades thereafter there was not much more of it for any of them. Sampson, though, had learnt much from Dahlgren's example; he was not to be deflected from his purposes, whatever might be the situation.

His next two years, having been during that time promoted to the rank of lieutenant commander, were served aboard the steam frigate *Colorado*, on the European station. It was an unremarkable posting, although in the course of it he caught the eye of Lieutenant Commander George Dewey, executive officer of the *Colorado*. He wrote of him:

> Nature had been kind to Sampson. Not only had he a most brilliant mind and the qualities of a practical and efficient officer on board ship, but he was, in those days of his youth, one of the handsomest of men I have ever seen, with a bearing at once modest and dignified. Already he was a marked man among his fellow officers, who, in a profession which is so strictly technical, are the best judges of a confrère's abilities. As a mess companion he was an inspiration, and many were the professional discussions we had, now agreeing and now disagreeing with equal earnestness. As young men we were looking ahead to the future developments of naval science which had been given such an impetus from '61 to '65, while we still enjoyed the traditions of the old sailing ship days, and frequently, in passage from port to port, had the *Colorado* under full sail, while our engines were silent.[6]

In 1867 Sampson was appointed once more to the Naval Academy, now restored to Annapolis, where in due course he became head of the newly established Department of Physics and Chemistry. He enjoyed life at the Academy, and in particular recognised the considerable significance for a cadet of the scientific training which he received there, writing:

> Every branch of a naval officer's profession furnishes many illustrations of the application of science… It may not be absolutely necessary that an officer should understand the chemical and physical difference between cast-iron, wrought iron, or steel gun; yet, I think there can be no question that such knowledge will be serviceable many times… The objects of the course in this department are to develop the cadet's powers of observation, and make him prompt and correct in interpreting the impression of his senses.[7]

In June 1871 Sampson again went to sea, as executive officer of the screw sloop *Congress*, on the European Station. He was thus again able to see at first hand the progress made by European navies, and what he saw was extremely depressing. The quality of the latest vessels in commission, even in the most modest of navies, was greatly superior to the United States vessels; it was obvious to Sampson that their 'modern breech loading cannon could outrange the *Congress*' cast iron smoothbores and in a matter of minutes reduce her white oak walls to rubble.'[8] Sampson cannot have regretted leaving this posting in mid 1874: at the end of the fleet manoeuvres that were ordered in February of that year as a response to the *Virginius* affair he was ordered to Washington to report on them. They had shown very clearly that the US Navy was entirely inadequate even to take on a navy such as that of Spain. The *Congress* was sent back to Europe, but Sampson gratefully returned to his former post as head of the Department of Physics and Chemistry, convinced of the rapidly increasing need for scientific training of a naval officer if he was to do his job properly, and the importance of ensuring his ability to respond to the rapid advance in naval technology and the changes that it would bring with it. He wrote:

> Great and rapid changes are liable at any moment to arise in his profession. If a naval engagement were to take place today between two modern fleets, the result might entirely revolutionise our ideas of naval warfare. He who would be most prompt to appreciate the new condition of things, and adapt himself thereto, will be the best officer. Now, I think this readiness for the future is only to be secured by arming the graduates of this institution at all points by such scientific training as will best prepare them for any contingency.[9]

Before going to sea again Sampson was able to engage in a number of scientific ventures. Most notable of these was his sponsorship of Albert A Michelson, whose experiments ultimately resulted in 1879 in his accurate measurement of the speed of light. Sampson also participated in a scientific expedition to Wyoming to observe a solar eclipse. During this posting at the Academy Sampson was able to arrange conducted tours for his cadets of important manufacturers along the east coast, including the major shipyards in Philadelphia and New York. They were also able to witness the development of explosives and fuses at the new Torpedo Station at Newport.

This exciting time for Sampson came to an end in December 1879 with his posting to command the screw gunboat *Swatara* on the Asiatic Station. It was a cruise that was generally uneventful, and it was followed by his appointment as assistant superintendent of the Naval Observatory at Washington D.C. He held this post until October 1884. Shortly after taking up his duties there he married Elizabeth Susan Burling of Rochester, with whom he had two sons. It was during this spell at the Naval Observatory that Sampson made an important contribution to the post graduate education of American naval officers, when he served on a board under Rear Admiral Stephen B Luce to consider the setting up of a Naval War College. The board strongly recommended the establishment of such an institution, which Navy Secretary William E Chandler accepted, as a result of which the college was launched in 1885. It was not, however, a decision which was universally accepted, and the future of the Naval College was not by any means assured.

Sampson's next assignment was to serve as one of the US delegates at the International Prime Meridian and Time Conference, held at Washington, intended to resolve the confusion from the existence of two systems of measuring longitude, the Greenwich and the Parisian. To the chagrin of the French, the majority of delegates accepted Sampson's proposal that Greenwich be chosen as the site of the prime meridian. Fresh from his work there, Sampson became inspector of ordnance at the Torpedo Station at Newport, where he was able to apply his scientific experience and enthusiasm to improving the effectiveness of mines and torpedoes. He experimented with developments of the spar torpedo, before concentrating on increasing the explosive power of a torpedo's war head. He also worked on a wide range of other scientific developments, particularly in the use of electricity.

Sampson was also called on to serve on the board of naval officers that was convened to review the design of the so called 'ABCD' cruisers when their construction ran into difficulties with the bankruptcy of John Roach, the shipbuilder. In another indication that Sampson had become the 'go to' officer to serve on boards requiring an intellectual approach to naval problems, he was appointed to the Endicott Board, in May 1885, which undertook a comprehensive examination of the problem of American coastal defence. The Board's report was published in January 1886, with an appendix written by Sampson headed 'Floating Batteries.' In this, he argued that coastal defence must be a joint army and navy responsibility. The immensely long American coastline in the Atlantic, the Gulf and the Pacific would require a large number of forts, equipped with heavy artillery of the latest design, as well as the gunboats, torpedo boats and other vessels to support them. It would also be necessary to subsidise the steel industry if the necessary metal for guns and armour plate was to be sourced domestically.

Sampson left the Torpedo Station in the summer of 1886 to take up a position for which his career to date particularly fitted him. Appointed superintendent of the Naval Academy, his selection by Navy Secretary Whitney was described by the *Army and Navy Journal* as 'a conspicuous instance instance of the office seeking the man,' though Richard West suggests that it was also intended as a less demanding post after his previous work, while keeping him in easy reach of the Navy Department in case of need.[10] As superintendent, Sampson at once embarked on a series of reforms, intended to improve the Academy's retention of its students, and to modernise the buildings, equipment and systems in use there. One change was to reduce the number of examinations that cadets must take during their career there; he claimed that 'no other professional corps and no other body of men in the world except the literati of China is required to pass so many examinations.'[11] He also introduced a new assessment of a cadet's leadership qualities, known as the 'aptitude for the service grade,' intended to identify those with the potential to make good naval officers. This continued to be applied at the Academy throughout the twentieth century.

During his final year at Annapolis, Sampson was promoted to the rank of captain. His term of office had been one of considerable achievement, but it was clearly desirable that he should put in some more sea time. Leaving the Academy in the summer of 1890, he was next assigned to the command of the new protected cruiser *San Francisco*, now fitting out, and he travelled to California to supervise the completion of the process. The *San Francisco* was notable for being constructed entirely to American designs; her engines were based on plans produced by the Bureau of Steam Engineering. She was designed as a flagship, and spacious apartments were provided for both admiral and captain. The engineers were not so fortunate; owing to a miscalculation due to overlapping bureaucratic authority, their quarters could be reached only by crawling on hands and knees through a low passage way.

The *San Francisco*, of 4098 tons, was armed with twelve 6-inch guns; she had a protective steel deck covering the length of the ship and sloping down her sides to about four feet below the waterline. This varied in thickness from one and a half inches on deck to two and a half inches on her sides. On her trials, she attained the entirely satisfactory speed of 19.7 knots. British naval officers visiting California aboard the *Warspite* were reported as saying that she was 'infinitely superior in her fitting and accommodation to her English sisters of the *Galatea* class.' In rough weather, she was found to be a stable gun platform, although water was found to sweep aboard very freely. Her commissioning trials complete, the *San Francisco* stood out from San Francisco on March 31 1891, flying the flag of Rear Admiral George Brown, to take up observation duties off the coast of war-torn Chile.

While there, Brown had to cope with the fall out from the unfortunate incident involving the *Baltimore*, which brought the United States to the brink of war with Chile. Brown's task during this difficult time was to report on the condition of the Chilean fleet, the coastal defences, strategic harbours and significant movements of potentially enemy warships. Sampson's experience in this period amply confirmed his belief that the American navy must be enormously strengthened. It also induced in him a profound distaste for the Press and its methods, having seen the extent of the falsehoods about Brown published in Chilean newspapers. Once the crisis was over, the *San Francisco* sailed to Honolulu. This was a goodwill mission intended to strengthen American control over what was seen as an important coaling base. Hawaii was also the object of such as Mahan, and Theodore Roosevelt, who actively promoted the notion of annexation. President Harrison and Navy Secretary Tracy were also sympathetic to this objective, although accepting that American public opinion was opposed to it. The voyage across the Pacific highlighted another issue of crucial importance to naval activity; Sampson found that her endurance with a full load of coal was not much better than half of that originally estimated.

Sampson's command of the *San Francisco* ended abruptly in June 1892 when he was recalled to Washington for another important administrative assignment. Navy Secretary Benjamin Tracy wanted him to relieve Commander WM Folger, the chief of the Bureau of Ordnance. The responsibilities of this post made Sampson a most suitable appointee, and would have particularly appealed to him. Nevertheless, he insisted that before taking up the role he should serve for a while as Folger's subordinate to enable him to familiarise himself with the current issues of the Bureau, and the advances in naval gunnery since he had last served in the Bureau. This was in spite of the fact that Folger was four years Sampson's junior. Tracy accepted Sampson's condition, and it was arranged that Folger should stay in post for a further three months. Since Sampson had left his family in California, for this period he took up residence in Folger's home. It was an arrangement that Folger, who was unwell and exhausted by his duties, came to regret, writing later of the guest's single minded professional interests:

> We talked of little else than ordnance, its history, and present conditions. He read little but scientific works and periodicals. I do not recall ever seeing him read a novel, and he cared little for historical subjects or general reading. This side of his temperament and taste was often a source of regret to me, as it left us without resource in conversation after discussion of the shop.[12]

Alfred Mahan would have known how Folger felt.

Sampson's new post, which he took up in January 1893 and relinquished in May 1897, was at the heart of the drive to provide the US navy with the modern warships which it desperately needed. When he returned to Washington one of his first tasks was to survey the work of the naval gun factory commissioned to produce the 13-inch guns for the *Kearsarge* and *Kentucky*. He supervised the design and production of the mountings for the guns of the new ships, and reviewed the powder supplied by contractors to the US navy as well as the shell casings. One design caused particular concern. This was the novel plan for double decked turrets superimposing a pair of 8-inch guns on the 13-inch guns below designed for the battleships. Ultimately, in spite of the risks of danger from flash and explosion of ammunition moving on hoists through the turret, Sampson approved the design.[13]

Another of his concerns was the poor quality of nickel-steel armour plate produced by the Carnegie Steel Co. in breach of the terms of its government contract. Allegations of fraud, based on statements by a Pittsburgh informer, led Sampson to carry out an investigation. Other instances of unsatisfactory quality came to light; Sampson recommended that a fine be imposed on Carnegie Steel of 15 per cent of the price of armour plate delivered during 1892-1893;

President Cleveland reduced this to 10 per cent. Sampson's aim was to compel the steel companies to deliver high quality armour plate produced by the 'Harveyised' manufacturing process. He was also involved in the design of the turret turning systems for the new battleships, insisting, not altogether successfully, on the use of electricity for the mechanism. This was a problem that affected not only Ordnance, but also the Bureau of Construction and Repair and the Bureau of Steam Engineering, and the issue led to a considerable controversy among the bureaucrats involved; the three bureau chiefs had to appear before the Navy Secretary to argue their case.

It was characteristic of Sampson's attention to detail that he personally supervised the preparations for a test firing to determine the effect of a direct hit on an armoured turret. The dummy turret was constructed on the lines of the main armament of the *Indiana* class battleships. The 15-inch armour plate was manufactured by the Bethlehem Iron Works of Harveyised nickel steel. The frame of the mock up weighed 67 tons and the armour 157 tons, while inside it 180 tons of pig metal represented the guns and gun carriages. The total structure, of 404 tons, was mounted on twenty radially placed cylindrical steel rollers of 10 inches in diameter and 30 inches in length. As well as testing the strength of the armour, it was desired to ascertain whether the rollers would work satisfactorily under heavy shot, the extent to which the structure would stand up to a direct hit, and the effect on the gun crews inside the turret. Four test rounds were fired, a 10-inch with a powder charge of 178 pounds, a 12-inch with 440 pounds, a 12-inch with 355 pounds and a 12-inch with 440 pounds. Only the last penetrated the armour before it broke up, while the turret structure was unhurt.[14]

The 13-inch guns designed for the *Kearsarge* and *Kentucky* were also to be employed in the *Indiana*, the *Oregon* and the *Massachusetts*. The *Iowa*, however, although larger than her predecessors, was to be equipped with 12-inch guns, and it was suggested by Sampson's eldest son that this was due to international influence. Commander Ralph E Sampson wrote in 1944 to Richard S West with an account of an incident which he recalled when he was aged eleven, which was the only time he saw his normally placid father exhibit any reaction to external provocation:

> It was his last year as Chief of the Bureau of Ordnance just before he took command of the brand new *Iowa*. He came home one evening not at all the man I knew. My mother attempted to find out what the trouble was. His reply was 'the Dutch have taken Holland,' which was his stock reply to all inquiries over the years. But later in the evening he surprised me with this: 'Boy! Always watch the British. They have just objected to the big guns we were going to put on the new battleships. They say they are too big. The White House says we must redesign the ship.'[15]

If this conversation took placed just before Sampson took command of the newly commissioned *Iowa*, it is not clear to which new battleships he was referring. 13-inch guns were fitted to the *Kearsarge* and *Kentucky*, already under construction and launched in March 1898; if these were the ships to which Sampson was referring, it would seem that any British comment was ignored. The *Illinois* class, which were launched later in 1898, and launched in 1901, became the first to revert to 12-inch guns.[16]

Sampson took command of the *Iowa* on June 15 1897. She was the largest vessel so far built for the US Navy; she was 11,410 tons, 360 feet in length and 72 feet in the beam, drawing 24 feet. She was armed with four 12-inch, eight 8-inch and six 4-inch guns. She was also the most expensive ship, her hull and machinery costing over $3 million. The 'hot weather' Secretary was pleased to be able to attend the *Iowa*'s first target practice, which he did on September 7, visiting the fleet on that day. Roosevelt first lunched with Rear Admiral Sicard about the flagship, before being welcomed aboard the *Iowa* and escorted to the bridge amid the sounding of gongs. All was in readiness; the target was under tow 2000 yards off, and earplugs were handed out to Roosevelt and his party. The first salvo from the 8-inch guns was fifty yards short; the second was slightly to one side, but the third, from the 12-inch guns, destroyed the target. Roosevelt was delighted with the exercise, telling journalists that his trip had been more than satisfactory:

> The rapidity and precision of the practice with the rapid fire guns and the extraordinary accuracy with which the huge turret guns were fired were equally noteworthy...At last we are beginning to have a navy fit to uphold the interests of our people, a navy which, though too small in size, need fear comparison with no other as regards the quality of its ships and men.[17]

Although apparently very well at the time he took command of the *Iowa*, it seems that Sampson's health was beginning to deteriorate, although this was not physically apparent until the following year. Meanwhile, as the war clouds gathered, he continued in command of the *Iowa* as part of the North Atlantic Squadron. His responsibilities did not, however, end there. Sampson had long since earned a well deserved reputation as the man to go to as a member of a board of inquiry set a particularly difficult problem to resolve, and Roosevelt had already seen enough of him to form a favourable opinion. In October 1897 he called on Sampson to serve as the senior officer on another special board.

This board was established by Roosevelt to bring to an end the long standing jealousies and resentment that existed between line officers and engineers. Sampson, and the ten other line officers and staff officers that sat with him, reached the conclusion that to end the feud engineer officers should be amalgamated with the line. It was not an easy problem; the issue had been ongoing for half a century. The Personnel Board grasped the nettle firmly: 'Every officer on a modern war vessel in reality has to be an engineer whether he wants to or not. Everything on such a vessel goes by machinery.'[17] The board went further, concluding that reasonable promotion must follow the election of the best fitted officers, as well as the retirement of officers.

5

George Dewey

Of the four admirals who may be taken as defining the era which saw the emergence of the American navy on to the world stage George Dewey was the eldest, born on the day after Christmas 1837 in Vermont, the son of a successful doctor. He was also by some way the luckiest; he was in due course to gain a stellar reputation by winning a battle that was almost impossible for him to lose. The events in Manila Bay were, however, a far cry from September 1854, when his father brought him to the Naval Academy at Annapolis; it had originally been hoped to find a place for him at West Point. Once there, he displayed much the same attitude to his studies as that of Schley, considering that there was far too much of reading, writing and arithmetic, and not nearly enough of sport. Nor was his disciplinary record very good; he picked up a large number of demerits for a range of minor offences. However, although not much enjoying the academic side of life, he looked back in his *Autobiography* with some approval of his time at the Naval Academy:

> The things that we knew we knew well. This has always been the character of Annapolis, which fashions a definite type of man for a definite object in life. The relentless examinations permit of no subterfuge of mental agility and no superficial familiarity with a variety of subjects to take the place of exact knowledge of a limited number of subjects.[1]

After four years, Dewey joined the steam frigate *Wabash*, aboard which as a midshipman he cruised for seventeen months before she returned to Brooklyn Navy Yard. After two more short cruises, Dewey returned to Annapolis in January 1861 to sit his lieutenant's examination, passing third in his class. After receiving his commission, he was on leave in Vermont when news came of the taking of Fort Sumter, and by May 10 he was aboard the elderly side wheeler steam frigate *Mississippi*. She was assigned to the blockade of the Confederacy's Gulf coast.

For Dewey and his fellow officers on both sides of the conflict, the war was going to be very different from what they had been trained to expect, as Dewey mused in his *Autobiography:*

> On the other side were men bred to the same traditions as we were. Officers fought officers with whom they had gone to school, and with whom they had served and messed. The recollection of old comradeship, while softening the amenities of a civil conflict, also touched us the more deeply with the sense of its horrors and waste, and brought to its conduct something of the spirit of professional rivalry. Unlike the officers of volunteer

> infantry who marched south to meet strangers against whom a strong sectional feeling had been aroused, we knew our adversaries well.[2]

Towards the end of 1861 planning began for a naval attack on New Orleans from the mouth of the Mississippi, which would be a major blow at a key commercial centre of the Confederacy. In command of the force to attempt this operation was David Farragut. The *Mississippi* was to form part of his squadron. Dewey's biographer Ronald Spector observes that this was one of the most rewarding periods of his career, noting that the pages of the *Autobiography*, which was ghost written by the journalist Frederick Palmer and frequently is stilted in its effect, 'glow with enthusiasm' when describing this period of Dewey's life.[3] And the events of the Civil War left Dewey with a profound and lasting admiration for David Farragut, writing of him: 'Farragut has always been my ideal of the Naval officer, urbane, decisive, indomitable; valuable as the training at Annapolis was, it was poor schooling beside that of serving under Farragut in time of war.'[4]

Dewey shared with Farragut a profound religious belief. At Annapolis he had conducted Bible classes for local children; aboard the *Wabash* he had been leader of the ship's choir, while all his life he carried a small notebook containing his favourite Bible texts, which he read regularly. He wrote of Farragut that he 'had unswerving belief in Providence as he had faith in the righteousness of the Union cause.'[5] The captain of the *Mississippi* was now Melacthon Smith, who was also strongly religious, and who particularly objected to profanity on the part of his officers and men, threatening that any officer caught swearing would be suspended and any man so doing would be put in irons.

Preparations for the assault on New Orleans required that the heaviest draught vessels in the fleet should be lightened in order to get them over the bar of the Southwest Pass so that they could go up river. The heaviest ships were the *Pensacola* and the *Mississippi*, and it was essential that they form part of the fleet because they carried the heaviest guns. For Dewey, as the *Mississippi*'s executive officer, the work involved was tremendous; it took eight hours for shallow draft mortar boats to tow her over the bar. Once across, and into deeper water, the heavy paddle steamer still struggled, having been designed as an ocean going vessel and never intended to operate in the restricted waters of the river.

The mortar boats were under the command of Commander David D Porter. Once all the fleet, except the frigate *Colorado* which could not be got over the bar, were in the river, Farragut gave the order for the mortars to open fire on April 18. Dewey described the scene:

> All night long, at regular intervals of about ten minutes, a mortar shell would rise, its loop in the air outlined by the burning fuse, and drop into the forts. It must have been pretty hard for the gunners of the fort to get any sleep. We, with the fleet, were too busy to sleep much, but we were soon so accustomed to the noise, and so dog-tired when we had a chance to rest, that we could have slept in an inferno.[6]

Farragut now gave orders for the fleet to try to pass the Confederate forts during the night of April 23/24. Smith, whose night vision was poor, ordered Dewey to take the helm of the *Mississippi*, which was the third ship of the first division. It was an unnerving task; the *Pensacola*, immediately ahead of his ship, stopped twice to allow her gunners to take aim, obliging Dewey each time to reverse engines to stop the *Mississippi*, all the while under fire from the forts. At the height of the engagement the Confederate ram *Manassas* appeared, looking to Dewey 'like the back of an enormous turtle painted lead colour,' and he altered course in an effort to ram her. Warley, the ram's commander, had, before the war, served in the *Mississippi*, and knew how clumsy she was, and evaded the blow before turning back in endeavouring to ram the paddle wheeler. He struck her a glancing blow just abaft the port paddle wheel, ripping off a seven foot section of her planking. Fortunately for the *Mississippi*, the paddle wheel was undamaged, and she was able to continue on past the forts.

As the battle continued, most of Farragut's ships got past the forts, but now the Confederates sent down fire rafts, one of which nearly put paid to the flagship *Hartford.* As dawn broke, the *Manassas*, which had passed all the way through the Union fleet, reappeared to launch a fresh attack. Farragut, in his flagship's rigging, shouted to Smith on the deck of the *Mississippi*, ordering him to run down the ram. Smith asked Dewey if he could turn the ship; he replied that he could, though in fact he was far from sure of this:

> I did not know whether I could turn her or not, but I knew that either I was going to do so or else run her aground. Indeed, the *Mississippi* had not yet made a turn in the narrow part of the river, and it was a question if she could turn under her own steam without assistance. But with so strong an incentive at the first trial we succeeded beautifully.[7]

Warley, aboard the *Manassas*, saw the paddle wheeler bearing down on him, and avoided the blow but drove his vessel into the river bank, where she was wrecked by the broadsides of the *Mississippi*. Later abandoned by her crew, she floated free, drifting downstream to the alarm of the mortar flotilla, before she blew up and sank.

After five hours, the battle was over, and the fleet anchored some fifteen miles below New Orleans. Next day Farragut puhed on to New Orleans, taking up a position off the city with his guns trained on its streets. The taking of New Orleans was a sensational achievement, and Farragut had overnight become a national hero. For Dewey, the aftermath of the victory was an anti-climax. The *Mississippi* was deemed by Farragut to be too heavy to move upstream with the rest of the fleet against Vicksburg, while steamers could not be spared to tow her back over the bar into the open sea to join the blockading fleet, so for the next ten months she lay tied up to a wharf, together with the *Pensacola*. Dewey recalled that his social life ashore 'was limited mostly to the scowls of the people we passed.' He also had from time to time to deal with General Benjamin F Butler, the commander of the army of occupation, who had a well deserved reputation for bloody mindedness, not only towards the civilian population but also towards the sister service of the navy.

In the spring of 1863 Farragut decided to attempt to cut off Vicksburg from supplies from the river side. For this, he must take the fleet up past Port Hudson, which the Confederates had strongly fortified. He now decided that after all the *Mississippi* was not too heavy to operate up river, and on March 14 she rejoined the fleet anchored off Profit's Island, seven miles below Port Hudson, in readiness for the attempt to pass the strongly fortified line of bluffs on the east bank, where the river bent sharply. Farragut ordered that the other large vessels of his fleet, being screw vessels, should attempt the passage of the forts with a gunboat lashed to their port side, so that if the ship went aground she should have assistance in reversing off the bottom. The *Mississippi,* being a paddle wheeler, had to make passage unaided. Leading the line that day was the *Richmond*, which was temporarily commanded by Lieutenant Winfield Schley. At a crucial moment, due to an error by her civilian pilot, the *Mississipi* ran hard aground. While her guns engaged the forts, her engine room force did all they could to keep her paddle wheels turning, but she was hit again and again, before fire broke out in her forward storeroom. Captain Smith ordered that the guns of the port battery be thrown overboard in the hope of lightening the ship, but it was soon apparent that she must be abandoned if the crew was to be saved. In the confusion, there was panic; Dewey, having left the ship, went back in one of the boats, being obliged to threaten his crew with the acting master's revolver before rescuing Smith and those of the crew still on board. The *Mississippi* was set on fire; as her stern filled with water she floated free; some way downstream she grounded again, before blowing up.

Dewey was sent to serve as a prize commissioner at New Orleans before being appointed as executive officer of the sloop *Monongahela,* to which Farragut transferred his flag, while operating south of Port Hudson. Aboard her, Dewey had what he described as the closest call in his career, when the ship was hit by a shell which killed her captain and wounded Farragut's chief of staff, but which left Dewey entirely unscathed.[8]

On July 10 the *Monongahela* was ordered up river to accompany the *Essex* to rescue the *New London*, which had been disabled when a shell hit her boilers. When they reached her, Dewey attached tow lines to the port side of the *Essex*, and the *New London* was then towed down river under fire from the enemy batteries, to the starboard of the two ships. The captain of the *Essex* wrote that Dewey had 'displayed coolness, skill, and judgment' in the operation.[9]

Dewey's remaining postings during the Civil War did not take him again into action. He went first to the *Brooklyn*, on blockade duty off Charleston. She was a wooden vessel, which her officers considered, would stand no chance if asked to operate against the powerful Confederate forts there. To Dewey's relief, she was sent back to New York to be over hauled and he next spent a year aboard the wooden side-wheel steamer *Agawam* in the James River; he described her spell there in support of Butler's attempted advance on Richmond as 'pretty active and trying service.' After an abortive appointment to the *Wabash* class steam frigate *Minnesota*, which ended because her captain thought Dewey too young, he went back to the *Agawam* before being appointed to the *Colorado*. Dewey had had an opportunity to go back to the Gulf, bur he was not keen to do so, telling his father: 'If I go to the Gulf I shall have fighting and I have had quite enough of that.'[10]

The *Colorado* carried the flag of Commodore Thatcher, second in command of the North Atlantic Squadron. Dewey had been sent for to join the squadron by Porter, who took command in September 1864. As executive officer of the *Colorado*, Dewey found that he had joined a ship with exceptionally low morale, which was due not least to his predecessor having been a harsh and erratic martinet. Dewey's hope that he could avoid fighting did not materialise; on December 23 the squadron stood in to commence the assault on Fort Fisher, the *Colorado* being second in line of the first division. Anchored before the forts, she came under heavy fire, and was hit a number of times before withdrawing to follow the rest of the squadron which was now out of range. Thatcher praised Dewey for 'invaluable assistance… in having all departments of the ship in perfect order for battle as well as for the valuable aid in the management of the ship during the action.'[11] Dewey would have liked next to take command of the *Colorado*'s landing party, which went ashore as part of a force of 1,600 sailors and marines, but Thatcher forbade this; if anything should happen to Porter, he would as second in command take over, and Dewey would have to command the ship.

Dewey's final assignment during the Civil War was as executive officer of the *Kearsarge*, renowned in Europe as the ship which had sunk the Confederate raider *Alabama* off Cherbourg.

Dewey took up the post with the rank of lieutenant commander, and sailed with her to Europe to show the flag after the ending of the Civil War. The sort of disciplinary problems that he encountered aboard the *Colorado* were now being repeated across the whole of the American fleet, with a considerable increase in desertions. In various ports Dewey was obliged to publish advertisements locally offering ten dollar rewards for the bringing in of deserters. Years later, there were many anecdotes illustrating the extent to which Dewey was a stern disciplinarian, although some of these may have been apocryphal. One of his fellow officers aboard the *Colorado*, to which Dewey returned in 1866, wrote:

> [Dewey] was smarter than chain lightning, quick, passionate, and always demanded perfect discipline of his men. He never would have a drunkard near him, and any man found in the least bit intoxicated aboard ship was dealt with in the severest manner.[12]

In September 1867 the *Colorado* returned to the Brooklyn Navy Yard, and Dewey was posted to the Naval Academy. Apart from a brief spell ashore in New Orleans, he had been at sea for nine years. It gave him the opportunity to get married to Susan Boardman Goodwin, the daughter of the former Governor of New Hampshire, Ichabod Goodwin, who seems to have approved of his new son in law, remarking: 'George is sort of reckless sometimes, but hang me if I can't help liking him. He's honest and full of grit, and he'll be heard from one of these days.'[13] Vice Admiral David Porter had in the meantime became superintendent of the Naval Academy; Dewey admired him, writing: 'Few men whom I have known had such a buoyantly irrepressible, active temperament as he. His mind seemed equally resourceful in a battle or at a reception.'[14] Porter was succeeded as superintendent by Rear Admiral John L Worden, commander of the *Monitor* in the famous action against the *Merrimac*, who made Dewey his aide. Worden, who tended to burn on a short fuse, was of the old fashioned school of naval officer, sceptical of the value of academic teaching as compared to the benefit of seagoing experience.

Dewey left the Naval Academy after three happy years to take command of the sloop *Narragansett*, which he took to New York Yard to undergo extensive repairs. There she remained for several months, to Dewey's great frustration. At the end of this period he was put temporarily in command of the elderly stores ship *Supply*, taking medicines and food for the relief of the inhabitants of Paris following the end of the Franco Prussian War. When he returned, he was assigned to the torpedo station at Newport Rhode Island. A posting ashore was not unwelcome, as his wife was expecting a baby; on December 23 his son was born, but five days later his wife Susie died. Dewey was shattered by his loss; his mother in law told a friend that he was 'so crushed;' and she remained always in his mind.

At his own request, he left the torpedo station to go to sea again, being assigned once more to the command of the *Narragansett*, She was under orders to survey the Pacific coast of Mexico and Lower California. It was a posting that was to last some two years. Richard West writes that 'surveying and charting these little known coastal waters… in this torrid and enervating region was a job to stifle a man's domestic grief.'[15] Dewey had now reached the rank of commander, but progress up the career ladder was going to be slow, in a navy that was not only run down but which had far more officers than it required. Some lieutenants, for instance in 1881 had held the rank for more than a dozen years, and many were over fifty years old.[16]

The surveying went smoothly enough. Dewey frequently took the *Narragansett* into an anchorage at La Paz, where he made friends with a Mr Brook, the American manager of a silver mine in the interior. On one visit while delayed at La Paz by bad weather, Dewey heard from his friend that he and other Americans were besieged in his compound by angry Mexicans. This followed an incident in which Brook had shot two Mexicans who had, he claimed, insulted him. Realising that his ship's landing party was too small to attempt a rescue, Dewey sent his executive officer to the local governor of La Paz, with a demand that he send troops to relieve Brook; if he did not, he would seize the city. The governor at first demurred, until it was pointed out that the *Narragansett* had changed position in the harbour so that her guns pointed down the city's streets. The governor complied. Months later, the Navy Department got to hear of the incident and called for a report; Dewey, sending this, cheerfully explained that he 'had not considered it of sufficient importance to be made the subject of a report.'[17] It was an entirely characteristic reply.

Dewey was in many ways luckier than many of his contemporaries. He had the advantage of a substantial private income, derived from his share of his father's investment in the National Life Insurance Co. During the depression of 1893, his brother was able to reassure him that most of his investments were still paying dividends, and that his capital was worth the considerable sum of $68,400.[18] In 1875 he came on shore again, serving two years in Boston as a lighthouse inspector before moving to Washington DC as naval secretary of the Lighthouse Board. He was rather bored by his professional responsibilities, telling his brother Charles that he wanted for more occupation. He was, however, content with his personal circumstances:

> I found myself in Washington social life, with its round of dinners and receptions, which were a new and enjoyable experience to me, if exhausting physically. Among statesmen Blaine and Conkling were at the height of their careers; Grant's candidacy for a third term developed and failed; and Admiral Porter and General Sherman, whom I frequently met, were still living.[19]

He was also able to indulge his taste for riding, which was his favourite pastime, while professionally he was able to keep in close touch with colleagues in the Navy Department.

After seven years ashore Dewey was appointed to the elderly steam sloop *Juniata* with orders for the Far East. He was not, however, destined to complete the trip. He was taken ill on the voyage across the Atlantic; in Gibraltar, he was seen by a British doctor but refused to admit the pain from his liver, with the result that when he reached Malta he was rushed to hospital suffering from an abscess on his liver, complicated by typhoid fever. He told his sister that at one time he was expected to die; his convalescence was prolonged, and he travelled extensively in an effort to regain his health. Recovery was achieved in Santa Barbara, California, in 1884; returning to duty that year, he was promoted to the rank of captain, and appointed to command the *Dolphin*. Prolonged delays in her commissioning led him to accept instead the command of the venerable *Pensacola*, which had survived the Civil War and been the subject of repairs in the following years so extensive that they amounted to more than her original cost. She remained, however, a relic of bygone years, of little fighting value. Her wooden sides would not have stood up long against modern guns, while her own armament remained her old muzzle-loading smooth bores.

The *Pensacola* carried 30,000 square feet of sails, and like most of her contemporaries was required to rely on these as her method of propulsion wherever possible. The use of steam power was frowned upon by the Navy Department; it was necessary to conserve the stocks of coal, not only as an economy measure but because the United States had no overseas coaling stations. The coal that American ships carried was required for use in emergencies or in battle.[20]

Dewey served aboard the *Pensacola* for four years. It was a pleasant but undemanding time, involving frequent social encounters with the great and the good of the foreign ports she visited, carrying the flag of the admiral commanding the European Station. Although he found service in European waters 'delightful,' Dewey concluded that maintaining a European squadron was a pointless exercise. The navy's first task, he thought, was the defence of the American coastline, and sending ships abroad deprived officers and men of the chance of becoming acquainted with their own coasts, as he later explained to Navy Secretary Benjamin Tracy:

> Above all, we would be spending the country's money at home and giving our people a chance to see something of the navy, which they can't do when it is scattered all over the world. We don't need to keep ships constantly on foreign stations – we have no interests there for them to protect, and there is really nothing for them to do. But if anything occurs which makes it necessary for ships to visit foreign countries, let us send a squadron of four ships instead of one, for whatever is to be done can be accomplished by four better than by one.[21]

Returning to the United States aboard the *Pensacola*, Dewey observed that it was his last experience aboard a ship that carried sail. Having witnessed one abrupt naval transition during the Civil War, he was, he later wrote, about to witness another:' this time to armoured steel vessels with powerful engines and guns in turrets.' On July 20 1889 Dewey took up the post of Chief of the Bureau of Equipment in succession to and at the suggestion of his old friend Winfield Scott Schley. To secure the post he lobbied hard through the Vermont senators and by direct approaches to senators that were especially influential in naval affairs.[22] He was to remain ashore until 1897, resuming his place in Washington society. He led a comfortable bachelor existence in an apartment only a few blocks from his office in the Navy Department. His was an orderly existence; his housekeeper recalled that he was her neatest tenant:

> He never left a match on the floor, scrap of paper, or any of his clothing scattered about. He even hung up his nightshirt in its proper place, and his clothing for washing was always in the hamper … He was what women would call a very easy man on his clothes.[23]

In his *Autobiography*, Dewey wrote little about the four years he spent as a bureau chief, remarking:

> We were busy with the equipment of the ships of our new navy, which was now entering upon a forward stage with our first battle ships being planned. There was nothing showy about the four years' service that followed. The detail was not exacting, but vitally engrossing and important. In common with every other ambitious officer of the navy, I was feeling the pulse of the new spirit and problems.[24]

Ronald Spector, Dewey's most recent biographer, has pointed out the absurdity of the claims of 'some of his more eulogistic biographers' that his time in the bureau was brilliant and spectacular. He 'had done a creditable job in rather routine assignments', and was no more impressive than some others, including Schley and Sampson, and possibly less so. Administration was not Dewey's first strength, and bearing in mind his pugnacious temperament, it is not surprising that from time to time it bored him.

One achievement of his time in the bureau deserves mention, and that was obtaining an increase in the amount of the annual allowance that Congress permitted for the equipment of the navy's vessels and coal for ships and shore stations. As a result, when the Chilean crisis in 1891 erupted, he was able to supply the ships directly involved with the necessary supplies of coal. It was this that gave rise to an anecdote in Theodore Roosevelt's *Autobiography*, which described an entirely fictitious incident based on the incorrect suggestion that during the Chilean crisis Dewey had been off the Argentine, and had been ordered to prepare to move to Chile:

> If the move became necessary, he would have to have coal, and yet if he did not make the move, the coal would not be needed … In a crisis, the man worth his salt is the man who meets the needs of the situation in whatever way is necessary, Dewey purchased the coal and was ready to move at once if need arose …. I knew that in the event of war [with Spain] Dewey could be slipped like a wolf-hound from a leash; I was sure that given half a chance he would strike instantly and with telling effect; and I made up my mind that all I could do to give him that half chance should be done.[25]

It was a story typical of the legends that were quickly to spring up around Dewey's life after the war of 1898. While completely untrue, it was in its essence consistent both with Dewey's character and Roosevelt's assessment of it.

Dewey's term as Chief of the Bureau of Equipment ended in 1893, and he was next appointed as President of the Lighthouse Board, in which capacity he served for two years before becoming president of the Board of Inspection and Survey. As he wrote in his *Autobiography*:

> This was a very important duty. All the new vessels which were then nearing completion were subject to the board's inspection and approval. Ours was the responsibility that the construction from stern to stern was sound and that the builders kept to the letter of the specifications.[26]

In this capacity Dewey was to oversee the trials of most of the battleships and cruisers that would participate in the war or 1898.

On May 23 1896 Dewey was promoted to the rank of commodore. He continued with the Board of Inspection, but noted that his rank entitled him to the command of a squadron as soon as there was a vacancy. He was not, however, automatically the first in line for such an appointment; there were a number of officers senior to him who must necessarily be considered. He could, though, count on support from the Assistant Secretary of the Navy who took office in April 1897.

6

Roosevelt

The presidential election of 1896 brought a Republican to the White House. William C McKinley was a Civil War veteran and a lawyer in Ohio. He entered politics in the 1870s, and became a Congressman in 1876. He was an advocate of the protective tariff, which was an issue with which he had been identified throughout his political career. He was defeated in the congressional election of 1890, but the following year became governor of Ohio, an office he won again in 1893. After the end of his second term he was an obvious candidate for the Republican nomination, which he duly secured at the convention in 1896. McKinley's Democrat opponent was William Jennings Bryan, hitherto an obscure ex Congressman from Nebraska, who had defeated President Grover Cleveland for the party's nomination. Bryan was nominated on a ticket that was so radical that it caused many members of his party to desert him. Meanwhile McKinley conducted his campaign from his front porch in Canton, Ohio, refusing to do more than receive visitors there, to whom he would read a prepared speech of welcome.

It was necessary, therefore, for the Republican Party to deploy powerful speakers to campaign for McKinley. One of the most energetic of these was the thirty eight year old Theodore Roosevelt, at that time a Police Commissioner in his home state of New York. Roosevelt had always been fascinated with ships and the sea, and at the age of twenty three published *The Naval War of 1812*, a history which has stood the test of time, and which was an important contribution to the burgeoning debate about the future of the country's navy. Roosevelt coveted the job of Assistant Secretary of the Navy, and after McKinley's victory in the election lobbied hard for it. His campaign for this office was led by his lifelong friend and supporter Henry Cabot Lodge; there were many other public figures on whom he could count for support, including John Hay, the future Secretary of State, the Secretary of the Interior Cornelius Bliss, Judge William Howard Taft of Ohio and Vice President elect Garret A Hobart. However, even this impressive array of support, and his tireless campaigning during the election, did not make him a certainty for the post. McKinley, on the eve of his inauguration, told the outgoing President Grover Cleveland that if, at the end of his term he could leave office with the knowledge that he had done all in his power to avert war with Spain over Cuba, he would 'be the happiest man in the world.'[1] It was with this in mind that Lodge summed up the arguments against Roosevelt's appointment by saying that there was a fear that he would want to fight somebody at once.

As Secretary of the Navy McKinley appointed John D Long, described by one of Roosevelt's biographers as 'a comfortable old Yankee, mildly hypochondriac, who liked nothing better than to potter about his country home'.[2] Long was apparently at first doubtful about the wisdom of Roosevelt's appointment, but he came round, and in the end of April 6 1897 Roosevelt duly took office. In his memoirs, published in 1903, Long claimed that it had been he who selected Roosevelt because of his 'hearty interest in the navy.' In this, however, as in other matters, Long is not a reliable reporter.[3]

The appointments to the Navy Department were generally welcomed in the American press. The *Washington Post* welcomed Roosevelt's arrival in Washington:

> Of course he will bring with him… all that machinery of disturbance and upheaval which is as much a part of his entourage as the very air he breathes, but who knows that the [Navy Department] will not be the better for a little dislocation and readjustment.'[4]

Overseas, however, Roosevelt's arrival on the scene was perceived as disquieting. Contemplating the rising tension at this crucial moment in the foreign relations of the United States, *The Times* remarked that 'what now seems ominous is his extreme jingoism.' It was not an unreasonable concern. Less than eighteen months earlier, Roosevelt had expressed himself in a letter to General James Harrison Wilson in astonishingly bellicose terms:

> If I were asked what the greatest boon I could confer on this nation was, I should answer, an immediate war with Great Britain for the conquest of Canada… I will do my very best to bring about the day … I want to drive the Spaniards out of Cuba. I want to stop Great Britain seizing the mouth of the Orinoco. If she does it, then as an offset I want to take the entire valleys of the St Lawrence, the Saskatchewan, and the Columbia.[5]

The relations between Long and Roosevelt would obviously be of critical importance but the Secretary's easy going character ensured that it got off to a smooth start. Long and McKinley had been colleagues in the House of Representatives in the 1880's and Long was popular in New England, a region traditionally supportive of naval expenditure He had been, as a result, one of the first appointments decided on by the President-elect. Roosevelt liked him, calling him a 'perfect dear', and from the outset displayed a proper respect and loyalty, which led Long to comment on his 'generous good nature':

> Indeed, nothing could be pleasanter than our relations. He was heart and soul in his work. His typewriters had no rest. He, like most of us, lacks the rare knack of brevity. He was especially stimulating to the younger officers who gathered about him and made his office as busy as a hive.[6]

Long was entirely happy to leave complex technical questions to Roosevelt, whose appetite for detail meant that he could safely be entrusted with the task of dealing with them.

Roosevelt wasted little time, taking up his duties on April 19, and settling down to master the intricacies of the Navy Department. He brought with him, though, profound convictions about the way forward for the US Navy and on June 2 first took the opportunity to express them when he went to Newport to address the Naval War College. It was what one of his biographers has called 'the first great speech of his career, a fanfare call to arms.'[7] Adopting George Washington's maxim that 'to be prepared for war is the most effectual means to promote peace,' he called unequivocally for the strengthening of the navy. He was nevertheless explicit in emphasising the reality of war:

> No triumph of peace is quite so great as the supreme triumphs of war… It may be that at some time in the dim future of the race the need for war will vanish; but that time is yet ages distant. As yet no nation can hold its place in the world, or can do any work really worth doing, unless it stands ready to guard its rights with an armed hand.[8]

During the course of his speech, Roosevelt moved on from general principles to the specific situation of the United State which, he argued, was more vulnerable than it had been at the beginning of the century. As things stood he contended that it would be six months before the United States could successfully meet a sudden attack, and a further eighteen months before she could begin to return it. He spelled out the need for more ships, and bigger ships, and more and better trained personnel. He rounded off his passionate address with a direct appeal to his listeners:

> There are higher things in this life than the soft and easy enjoyment of material comfort. It is through strife or the readiness for strife, that a nation must win greatness. We ask for a great navy, partly because we feel that no national life is worth having if the nation is not willing, when the need shall arise, to stake everything on the supreme arbitrament of war, and to pour out its blood, its treasure, and its tears like water, rather than submit to the loss of honour and renown.[9]

It might have been supposed that this speech, which created a national sensation, would cause the pacifically minded McKinley extreme disquiet. In fact, however, the President only remarked that he suspected that Roosevelt was right, and that the only difference between them was that his was the great responsibility. Roosevelt's explicit language set the tone for the course of dealing with Spain on which the administration must necessarily embark, and he had made it abundantly clear just how firm he believed must be its policy. Privately, he was still more extreme, writing to Mahan that he believed that the Nicaraguan Canal should be built at once, that a dozen new battleships should be built, and that if he had his way Spain should be turned out of Cuba 'tomorrow'; until then, the United States would always be plagued by trouble there.[10]

The first victory for the expansionists came with McKinley's approval of the treaty of annexation of the Hawaiian Islands on June 16 1897. On the day following this hugely important step, Secretary Long went off on two weeks holiday, leaving Roosevelt in charge as the 'Hot Weather Secretary' which he had promised to be. Long went away with real concern about the extravagance of Roosevelt's speech at the War College, and his Assistant Secretary felt it necessary to suggest to Mahan that he might write to him to explain the need for more battleships, something that Mahan was very ready to do.

Meanwhile Roosevelt enjoyed himself in temporary charge of the Navy Department, although careful not to overstep the mark. He was glad to receive the draft of the department's new war plan just before Long returned from his short break, and to note the terms in which it was written. It contained all the features of previous plans which had previously been deleted because they were thought too aggressive, and it also contained some new expansionist proposals. Essentially it was a plan for war with Spain for the liberation of Cuba, calling for hostilities in the Caribbean and the Philippines and possibly in the Mediterranean as well. All this was of course meat and drink to the Assistant Secretary.

It was about this time that he formed a close acquaintance with George Dewey. A man of action who seemed to have shared Roosevelt's expansionist views was always going to be an attractive colleague; and as Assistant Secretary of the Navy it was in his power to advance the commodore's career. He began to contemplate the possibility that he might be appointed to the command of the Asiatic Squadron when that post fell vacant, for which Dewey had already made application to the Bureau of Navigation.

The potential importance of the post was heightened by the change in what was planned for the operations of the Asiatic Squadron if war broke out. The immediately preceding war plan, of December 1896, had provided for the squadron to reinforce the vessels already in European waters and to join an attack on the Canary Islands. With the addition of further ships from the North Atlantic Squadron, it was believed that the islands could be captured and used as a base for operations in Spanish waters. This plan had been produced in the Navy Department by a group in which Rear Admiral Ramsay played a prominent part. There was a dissenting voice; Captain Henry C Taylor, the president of the War College, opposed such an operation so far away from home bases, arguing that 'all the naval forces at the disposal of the government be concentrated upon Cuba.'[11]

The new plan proposed that the Asiatic Squadron should, instead of sailing to Europe, 'go down and show itself in the neighbourhood of the Philippines.' The object was both strategic and political; an attack on Manila would serve 'the purpose of further engaging the attention of the Spanish Navy[away from the main theatre of operations] and more particularly to improve our position when the time comes for negotiations with a view to peace.'[12] Not surprisingly Roosevelt was a keen supporter of this plan, which he urged on both McKinley and Long as the year went by.

One of Dewey's biographers considers that Roosevelt's strong preference for the appointment of Dewey to the Asiatic Squadron was because of his disapproval of the principal alternative, Commodore John A Howell. He was dismayed to find a letter from Senator William E Chandler to Long supporting Howell's application, which coming from a past Secretary of the Navy must carry a lot of weight. He determined to pre-empt it by writing at once to the senator:

> Before you commit yourself to Howell I wish very much that you would let me have a chance to talk to you. He is an honourable man and a man of great inventive capacity but I have rarely met one who strikes me as less fit for a responsible position… I hardly know of a man of high rank in the Navy whom I would be more reluctant to see entrusted with a squadron or fleet … he is irresolute and he is extremely afraid of responsibility … You and I feel alike not only on foreign policy but on the kind of man who should carry out that foreign policy and if we do take vigorous action … we must have it taken by men with whom there is no chance of failure.[13]

Roosevelt, determined to ensure that Long should not impede Dewey's appointment, pressed the commodore to get Senator Redfield Proctor to take up the matter; in due course on October 16 the Senator reported on a positive meeting with the President. Long later claimed in his memoirs to have made the choice himself, much as he had in Roosevelt's case. At all events, though, he seems to have been irritated by the political intervention.

Meanwhile at the beginning of July Roosevelt had himself taken a brief vacation, in the course of which he delivered a provocative speech about Japan's objections to the American annexation of Hawaii. The United States, he bellowed, was 'not in a position which requires her to ask Japan, or any other foreign power, what territory it shall or shall not acquire.'[14] This got him into trouble with Long when he got back to the office; the Navy Secretary gave him 'a heavy wigging.' Nevertheless, Long still felt able to leave Roosevelt in charge when he set off for an extended vacation through most of August.

That summer Roosevelt thoroughly enjoyed himself, in spite of concerns about his wife's health. It may have been this which in part led to his throwing himself into his duties at the Navy Department with astonishing vigour. Once Long was safely out of the way in his garden in Massachusetts, Roosevelt was free to take effective charge, and he had no intention of letting the grass grow under his feet. Above all other considerations, the worsening relationship between Spain and the United States naturally provided a focus for his activity, since it was evident, at the least, that war was becoming a distinct possibility. He had twenty two days of freedom from superior restraint, and in that time accomplished a huge amount, while regularly writing reports to Long, all the while urging the Navy Secretary to have 'an entire rest'; there was no reason, he told him, to come back before the end of September. Reviewing the political situation, the *New York Sun* on August 23 showed itself fully aware of Roosevelt's activity:

> The liveliest spot in Washington at present is the Navy Department. The decks are cleared for action. Acting Secretary Roosevelt, in the absence of Governor Long, has the whole navy bordering on a war footing. It remains only to sand down the decks and pipe to quarters for action.[15]

While Long was away, Roosevelt had the opportunity of putting his views at first hand before the President, of which he took full advantage. He told McKinley that if war did break out he intended to enlist in the army at once. McKinley assured him that he would have the chance to serve if war did come. In particular, he succeeded in bringing McKinley to his view that Dewey should have the Asiatic Squadron, which presented Long, when he returned to the Navy Department at the end of September, with an effective fait accompli. The Secretary was far from pleased that the decision had thus been taken out of his hands. Roosevelt was unrepentant; his policy was invariably to press on at all costs; the *Boston Sunday Globe* also noted his incessant activity, describing him as the most entertaining performer in public life, though adding that it would never do to permit him to get into the Presidency: 'He would produce national insomnia.'[16]

After the turn of the year, the situation in Cuba deteriorated alarmingly, causing Fitzhugh Lee, the US Consul General in Havana, to fear for the security of American residents, following which the decision was taken to send the battleship *Maine* there. She arrived there on January 25, and her presence in Havana harbour was an unmistakeable demonstration of the extent to which the tension was rising. It was in Washington, however, that the next crisis erupted, with the publication on February 9 by the *New York Journal* of the text of the Spanish Minister's letter. The news of this went straight to Roosevelt's head. In the course of an encounter with Senator Mark Hanna and two other senators, Roosevelt burst out that he hoped to see the Spanish flag and the English flag gone from the map of North America before he was sixty. Hanna told him he was crazy. Roosevelt's belligerence was however very shortly to be further inflamed.

7

Cuba

Cuba had been part of the Spanish empire since the arrival of Christopher Columbus in 1492. It was a significant part of an empire which stretched from Mexico to the Straits of Magellan. Havana, the capital, provided the Spanish with a magnificent deep water harbour as a base for their principal fleet in the Caribbean. From here, Spanish galleons could sail to escort the treasure ships from Vera Cruz and Portobello as they started on their homeward journey to Cadiz. Havana's obvious strategic importance had brought a British expeditionary force to seize the place in 1762. After the end of the Seven Year's War it was returned to Spain as part of the peace settlement and a powerful new fort, the Morro Castle, was constructed to protect the port from any future assault.

The disintegration of the Spanish empire began in 1808, when Napoleon invaded Spain, and replaced her king with his brother Joseph. The governors of the Spanish possessions in the Americas declined to recognise the new regime, and some declared independence. In 1814 King Ferdinand VII was restored to the throne of Spain, but the genie was out of the bottle, and could not be replaced. By 1825, independence movements throughout the empire meant that practically all of it was lost to Spain. Only Cuba and Puerto Rico remained in the Caribbean, together with the Philippines, some groups of islands in the Pacific and some territory in North Africa.

Cuba, therefore, was special. Its loyalty to Spain led to its being termed 'the ever faithful isle,' and its continued possession gave it a special significance in the eyes of Spanish governments and people. Throughout its history as a Spanish possession emigrants arrived from the mother country to settle in Cuba. The new arrivals were known as '*peninsulares*,' having been born in the Iberian Peninsula; their white children born in Cuba, were termed '*creoles*.' *Peninsulares* enjoyed a privileged status in the island, and occupied most of the key positions in government, the military, commerce and the church.

A census taken in 1842 had found that the total population of the island amounted to just over one million. Of these, about 45% were white, 15% free coloured and the remainder were Negro slaves. Early in the nineteenth century, the slave population had grown enormously with the development of the sugar industry, and greatly increased the risk of slave uprisings.[1] This census did not distinguish between *peninsulares* and *creoles*. It did, however, demonstrate the extent to which the island's sugar economy was based on slave labour. Although the Spanish government had in 1817 accepted the international agreement to end the slave trade, the fact was that the flow of slaves from Africa increased rather than diminished after that date. Both the *peninsulares* and *creoles* were opposed to attempts to abolish slavery; while the institution persisted; *creole* discontent with Spanish rule was necessarily muted.

The existence of slavery had been a factor in the attitude of successive American governments to attempts from outside to bring about Cuban independence, since in the first half of the nineteenth century it was feared that the abolition of slavery there would have a pronounced effect on the Southern states. From time to time, though, the project of purchasing Cuba was raised.

The arrival of *peninsulares* throughout the nineteenth century did not slacken; indeed, in the 1880's the Spanish government afforded financial subsidies to unemployed Spaniards wishing to emigrate to Cuba. A census in 1817 identified just under ten per cent of the population of 1.6 million as *peninsulares*, while a further sixty per cent were *creoles*. The remainder of the population, black and mulatto, were descended from the slaves imported to work on the plantations. Slavery persisted in Cuba throughout nearly the whole of the nineteenth century until it was formally abolished in 1886. In the rural areas, slave uprisings, provoked by the severe poverty and poor living conditions, were not unknown, and a military garrison some 20,000 strong was maintained in the island.[2]

While the *creoles* thus benefited from the security provided by Spanish rule, the disproportionate power and influence of the *peninsulares* ensured a continuous discontent. Throughout the century this was stimulated from outside by many in the United States who, unlike their governments, believed that Cuba, like the rest of the Spanish colonies, should be freed from Spanish subjection. Thomas Jefferson had in 1823 put forward directly the proposition that Cuba should be annexed by the United States, while John Quincy Adams, noting the extent of Cuban economic dependence on the United States, believed that in due course, so long as it remained a Spanish possession, Cuba would fall into the lap of the United States. Annexation was a concept which never entirely disappeared from American political consideration. It was supported by many men of influence; Senator Henry Cabot Lodge in 1895 articulated a popular view:

> From the Rio Grande to the Arctic Ocean there should be but one flag and one country … For the sake of our commercial supremacy in the Pacific we should control the Hawaiian Islands and maintain our influence in Samoa. England has studded the West Indies with strong places which are a standing menace to our Atlantic seaboard. We should have among those islands at least one strong naval station and when the Nicaragua Canal is built, the island of Cuba, still sparsely settled and of almost unbounded fertility, will become to us a necessity.[3]

It was a view warmly endorsed by his friend Theodore Roosevelt, and represented an expansionist view of the future of the United States which contributed substantially to the outbreak of war with Spain.

Spain's failure to introduce any sort of a liberal regime in Cuba, which led to the discontent and ultimately to the uprisings against her rule there, was ascribed by a prominent American historian to be principally due to the French invasion of Spain in 1823. Writing in 1909, Rear Admiral French Ensor Chadwick, who had played a prominent part in the naval war of 1898, observed:

> Without this action Spain, with her more liberal forces free to develop, might in some degree at least have advanced politically with the rest of Europe. Cuba might have been

> today a Spanish Canada and the Philippines a Spanish India. But these things were not to be. Racial peculiarities, regionalism, religious bigotry, and the ignorance which went hand in hand with fanatical subservience to priestly rule were possibly sufficient to have prevented such a change; but the French invasion, or to speak more truly, the invasion by the Holy Alliance, made this change impossible, and by its reinstallation of absolutism made certain anarchy at home and loss of empire abroad.[4]

The long narrow island of Cuba stretches for more than seven hundred miles, varying in width from twenty to fifty miles, divided into six provinces. These, from west to east, are Pinar del Rio, Havana, Matanzas, Santa Clara, Camagüey and Oriente. Much of the wealth of the island was concentrated in the westernmost provinces, and it was accordingly in Oriente that was to be found the most fertile soil for insurrection, where the smaller planters particularly resented the burden of Spanish rule. Across the whole of the island, however, there was particular concern about the effect of the abolition of slavery during the American Civil War, which led to mounting demands by the *creoles* for reform, but which hardened the pro Spanish sentiments of the *peninsulares*, who sought to maintain the institution of slavery in Cuba.

A royal decree of November 25 1865 set up an inquiry to consider reforms in Cuba and Puerto Rico, and gave rise to widespread optimism that the islanders' grievances would be resolved. However, the initiative failed entirely; instead of introducing reform, the Spanish government imposed new taxes while maintaining the high customs duties which had been a major source of complaint. This triggered large scale political discontent, particularly in Oriente, and led directly to the proclamation in October 1868 of an insurrection by the 'Grito de Yara,' which ushered in the bitter guerrilla struggle which became known as the Ten Years War. This war for independence faced a number of serious difficulties. The insurgents were ambivalent about the issue of slavery; their leaders frequently quarrelled; troops of one area were apt to refuse to fight elsewhere; and the wealthier inhabitants of the western provinces opposed the revolt entirely.[5]

By the following year the seriousness of the revolt had become apparent, and the incoming administration of President Ulysses S Grant and his Secretary of State Hamilton Fish had to face the issue, as Chadwick explained:

> The Cuban insurrection had by early spring of 1869, taken on so virulent a character, on both sides, that it became a matter of deep concern to the United States government, so many of whose citizens were large proprietors in the island, and so much of whose commercial wellbeing was involved.[6]

It was a concern which no American administration could thereafter avoid, and which was continuously to present great political difficulties. In June 1869, after the shooting of two American citizens, carried to Cuba by a group of armed men who seized possession of the vessel in which they were travelling, a serous crisis arose between the United States and Spain. Full reparation was demanded, and the American consul at Santiago was instructed to 'solemnly protest against any longer carrying on the war in this barbarous way … Our relations with Cuba are so many and so intimate that we cannot regard this struggle in all its details with anything but intense interest.'[7]

Efforts were made to resolve the diplomatic crisis, and to get agreement to US mediation, but these foundered on the rock of Spanish intransigence, and the war continued. Spain continued

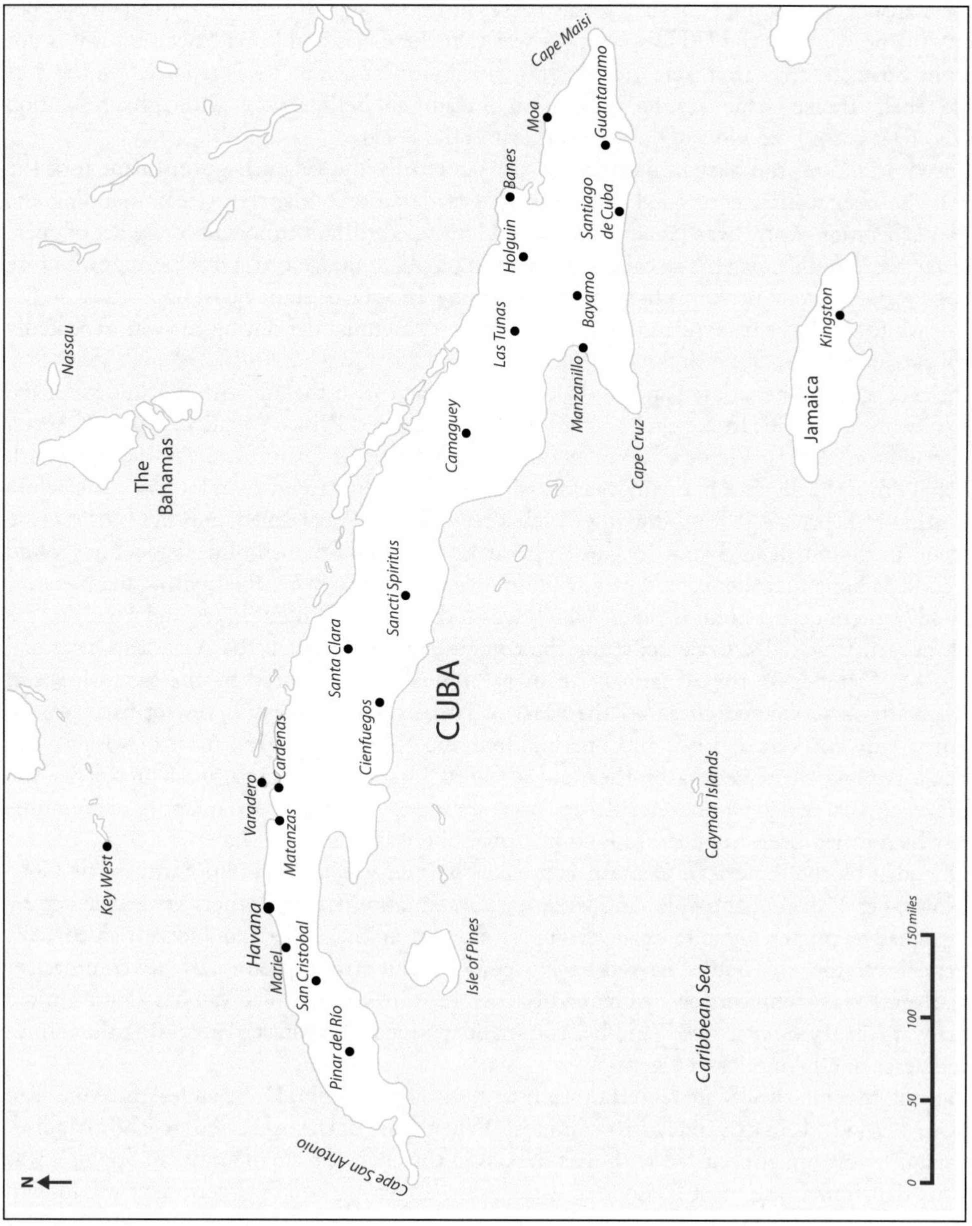
N
Nassau
The Bahamas
Key West
Havana
Mariel
San Cristobal
Pinar del Rio
Cape San Antonio
Varadero
Matanzas
Cardenas
Cienfuegos
Santa Clara
Sancti Spiritus
CUBA
Camaguey
Las Tunas
Holguin
Banes
Moa
Cape Maisi
Guantanamo
Santiago de Cuba
Bayamo
Manzanillo
Cape Cruz
Jamaica
Kingston
Cayman Islands
Isle of Pines
Caribbean Sea
0
50
100
150 miles

1 Cuba.

to build up the army in Cuba; by the end of 1870 this was over 100,000 strong, inclusive of 40,000 volunteers undertaking garrison duty. Only 7,500, however, were cavalry; infantry were of limited value in fighting a guerrilla war. Chadwick observed that 'amazing as was her energy in the transport and support of such great masses of troops, equally amazing was its misdirection.'[8] The problem for the US Government was that there was ample evidence that it was not only the Spanish forces that were guilty of atrocities; similar conduct was reported on the part of the rebels. The key issue was the recognition of insurgent belligerency; although a resolution to this effect passed the House, the vote was lost in the Senate.

Notwithstanding the vast military resources poured by the Spanish government into the island, the insurrection continued. The principal leader of the insurgents, commanding the Cuban Liberation Army, was General Maximo Gomez, a brilliant exponent of the art of guerrilla warfare. Another was the so called 'Bronze Titan,' Antonio Maceo, a black leader who rose to be brigadier general in the Cuban Liberation Army. In spite of some racist opposition on the part of white rebels, he was the most successful military commander during the war, repeatedly defeating much larger Spanish forces.

The prospect of a negotiated end to the war diminished with the effective breakdown of the government in Madrid. In November 1870 the Cortes elected Prince Amadeo, Duke of Aosta, the second son of King Victor Emmanuel of Italy, to be king of Spain. In the following month Marshal Prim, the dictator of Spain was assassinated; Amadeo struggled on for two years before abdicating in February 1873, following which a republic was proclaimed, and the Carlists rose in revolt in the north of Spain. In Cuba, the attitude of the Spanish officials on the ground offered little hope that there could be any useful negotiations to bring the fighting to an end.

In 1873 there occurred an incident which was to bring the United States and Spain to the brink of war. It was also to demonstrate the ruinous state into which the American navy had fallen. On October 31 the American steamer *Virginius* was captured by the Spanish vessel *Tornado* after a prolonged chase off the coast of Jamaica. She carried a crew of fifty two, of whom twenty six were British, and one hundred and three passengers, most of whom were Cubans. Among them were a brother and a son of Cespedes, the insurgent president. The *Virginius* also carried five hundred rifles, a large number of revolvers and a quantity of ammunition, which it had been intended to land in Cuba. She was flying the American flag, and was commanded by the American Captain Fry. The *Virginius* was carried into Santiago de Cuba on November 1; during the following week her captain and fifty two others were executed by firing squad as pirates, in spite of the strongest protests by the American and British consuls. A British warship, the *Niobe*, arrived on November 7, but strong protests by her commander were dismissed contemptuously by General Barriel, the Governor. On November 15 the United States warship *Wyoming* arrived, and her commander added his protest, demanding the immediate release of all American citizens.

Naturally Secretary of State Hamilton Fish sent, through General Dan Sickles, the American minister at Madrid, an extremely strong protest. When news of the executions reached Madrid, the Spanish government reacted with dismay. Given the chaotic state of affairs in Spain, it was realised that something must be done to assuage the anger of the US government if a foreign war was not to be added to all the other problems confronting Spain's leaders. President Castelar told Sickles how deeply he deplored the execution of the first four prisoners, which was all he knew of at that time. Local officials in Cuba did not help matters by seeking to justify what had occurred. In the face of huge popular demonstrations of protest held in New York and elsewhere, the US government was obliged to take a strong line. Fish instructed Sickles to inform the Spanish government that the United States would 'demand the most ample reparation of any wrong which may have been thereby committed upon any of its citizens or its flag.'

The terms of this note changed the attitude of the Spanish government, which it regarded as insulting to its dignity, and the crisis deepened. The Spanish government now sought to justify not only the seizure of a vessel bearing the American flag, but also the executions, claiming that 'the persons shot were rebels seeking to trample the law under foot, enemies of the country and disturbers of the peace and of the rule of a sister republic.'[9] Such a response was, it was made clear by Fish, completely unacceptable, and the Spanish, recognising that the United States was indeed prepared to go to war over the issue, hastily retraced its steps. Rapid exchanges of diplomatic notes followed: the Spanish agreed to restore the *Virginius*, and release her surviving passengers and crew, against an undertaking by the US government to inquire into the whole matter and, if necessary, take proceedings against individuals found to have violated the law. Subsequently, Spain paid the sum of $80,000 to be distributed to those entitled.

The crisis had necessitated the assembly of a United States squadron at Key West under the command of Admiral Porter. It was abundantly clear to him, and all those concerned with the preparation of these warships for war, that they were wholly inadequate to take on a fleet even as weak as that of Spain. It would have meant engaging the relatively modern Spanish cruisers with completely obsolete monitors and vulnerable wooden steamships armed with out of date muzzle loaders. The settlement of the crisis came as a profound relief to all in the American navy. Navy Secretary Long was much later to describe Porter's squadron as having been a collection of 'antiquated and rotting ships,' which in the opinion of Captain A C Rhind could probably have been destroyed by a modern warship 'without serious damage to herself.'[10]

Meanwhile on January 2 1874 the republican government of President Castelar was overthrown, to be replaced by a dictatorship under Marshal Serrano. This, in its turn, was succeeded a year later by a new ministry under Canovas del Castillo, which proclaimed the restoration of the monarchy under King Alfonso XII. The problem of Cuba, however, remained; it could only be resolved if the Madrid government was able to reassert its control over events in the island. Efforts were made to establish a proper legal basis for the trial of American citizens charged with offences against Spain or the government of Cuba, in order to defuse any future incident that might occur. General Martinez Campos was sent to the island as commander in chief, with substantial reinforcements in October 1876. He was a broad minded man, not unsympathetic to the grievances of the Cuban population. He was also a competent commander, who began to get on top of the insurgents in the continuing campaign. As a result of this, on February 10 1878, a peace agreement was signed at Zanjon in Camaguey province by Campos on behalf of the government and by Maximo Gomez and Vicente Garcia on behalf of the rebels, bringing the Ten Years War at last to an end. Its terms included a general pardon for those that had taken part in the insurrection, and the grant to Cuba of the political privileges that had been accorded to Puerto Rico. Antonio Maceo, however, refused to accept the terms of the Treaty of Zanjon, arguing that neither independence nor the abolition of slavery, for which he had fought so long, had been achieved. Whether, in their heart of hearts, the signatories of the treaty regarded it as finally concluding matters is doubtful.

In fact, revolutionary activity did continue, and the final abolition of slavery in 1886 greatly strengthened the hands of those seeking independence. It removed the primary reason for the wealthy sugar planters' commitment to Spain; without it, the possibility that independence would provide greater economic advantages, particularly in terms of unlimited trade with the United States, was a powerful argument. Cuban exiles in the United States worked consistently to promote the idea of Cuban independence. Among the emergent leaders of the revolution, the outstanding personality was José Marti, a poet, writer and passionate orator. Born in 1853, his work in Havana in support of the revolution brought him a spell of imprisonment. In exile in New York, he met Gomez and Maceo in 1884, when they visited the United States to assess support for a fresh revolution, and was dismayed by the former's autocratic views of how it was to be managed. The two men were reconciled, however, and Marti continued his work of organising for the day when the flag of independence would again be raised. In 1892 he founded the Cuban Revolutionary Party, which served as the medium for raising funds. In August that year he visited Gomez in Santo Domingo to offer him the post of commander of the revolutionary forces, inviting him 'without fear of refusal, to undertake this new task although I have no other remuneration to offer you than the pleasure of sacrifice and the probable ingratitude of man.'[11]

Marti also recruited Maceo to the cause, promising him that he would deliver the arms and ammunition that the insurgents required. Maceo, who had settled in Costa Rica, where he had become a successful plantation owner, took at first a lot of persuading, possibly because of the risk of the plans being leaked to the Spanish. By June 1893, however, Marti had overcome his doubts. Steps were now taken to establish contact with groups in the various provinces of Cuba who would provide the local leadership when the revolution broke out, while Marti worked unceasingly to raise the funds necessary for the purchase of supplies. In April 1893, however, Marti had faced a setback, when unauthorised revolt broke out in Holguin, which was quickly suppressed; its failure led for a while to a diminution of support for the Cuban Revolutionary Party, while the economic crisis in the United States which began in May 1893 further reduced contributions to the party's funds. It also provided employers in the tobacco industry in the United States with an excuse at the end of the year to slash their workers' wages, leading to a long running strike. This eventually, was successful, in spite of Spanish efforts, with the help of the larger Cuban employers, to break the strike by recruiting strike breakers in Cuba to go to the United States to work in the factories.

By the end of January 1895, it appeared to Marti and to those organising the revolution in Cuba that the moment had arrived to raise the standard of independence. One factor was the continued groundswell of opinion in the United States that favoured annexation Typical of press comment was a leading article in the *Detroit Free Press* of 1891:

> Cuba would make one of the finest states in the Union, and if American wealth, enterprise and genius once invaded the superb island, it would become a veritable hive of industry in addition to being one of the most fertile gardens of the world. There is a strong party growing up in the island in favour of reciprocity with and annexation to the United States.[12]

It was certainly no part of the insurgents' intentions that they should drive out the Spanish only to become part of the United States; but it was evident to Marti that such an outcome would be favourably received by some of the wealthier population of Cuba, whose undisguised self interest he regarded with contempt.

On January 29 1895 the order went out for the rising to begin, and on February 24 this was signalled by the issue of the 'Grito de Baire.' On March 23, before setting off for Cuba, Marti and Gomez published their manifesto setting out the principles on which the revolution was based. They landed on April 10, after a desperate voyage in a violent gale and heavy rain. On May 2 Marti wrote an article for the *New York Herald* summarising their objects:

> Cuba wishes to be free in order that here Man may fully realise his destiny, that everyone may work here, and that her hidden riches may be sold in the natural markets of America ... The Cubans ask no more of the world than the recognition of and respect for their sacrifices.[13]

The insurgency soon took hold, although there was a significant early casualty when on May 19 Marti was killed in an ambush. The military operations were conducted with great skill and determination by Gomez and Maceo. The Spanish government responded by appointing the competent Martinez Campos as governor general, with wide powers and substantial financial resources. Now aged sixty four, he brought with him his experience of the Ten Years War. But he arrived with the gravest misgivings, saying to Queen Cristina that his heart told him that this would be Spain's last war in America.[14]

He employed the concept of a 'trocha,' a cleared strip of terrain about 200 yards wide, with many forts and block houses, in an effort to confine the insurgents to the province of Oriente. This time around, however, they were better organised, stronger, better equipped and better led, and Gomez ruthlessly employed the economic weapon of destroying the sugar plantations, while the Spanish troops were unable to pin down his nimble guerrilla forces. Martinez Campos, who had concluded that orthodox military operation would not defeat the rebels, and who was unwilling to introduce the policy of *reconcentrado*, sent in his resignation on January 7 1896.

The government turned to the more ruthless General Valeriano Weyler to carry out this policy, which involved forcing the peasant population into towns controlled by the Spanish army. It soon became apparent that the army was incapable of providing the necessary housing, food, sanitation and healthcare for the unfortunate victims of this strategy; the consequent mortality rate was appalling, of the order of 100,000.[15] Weyler conducted the war vigorously and with some success; by now his forces had reached a total of 175,000. The insurgents were now prepared more often to stand and fight, which reflected their growing strength, but which also cost them higher casualties. On December 7 the revolution suffered a serious blow when Maceo was killed outside Havana; Weyler issued triumphant announcements that the insurrection in the province of Pinar del Rio had been crushed. These claims, reported Fitzhugh Lee, the US Consul, were false; and indeed, led by Gomez and Generals Calixto Garcia and Jose Maria Rodiguez, the rebels continued to gain victories over the overstretched and exhausted Spanish troops.

8

The United States and Spain

It had been Martinez Campos who had, in December 1874, ushered in the Bourbon restoration by declaring, with his brigade, for Alfonso XII. It had been the army that had restored the king, and had shown once more that in the nineteenth century 'the existence of any regime in Spain was a function of the loyalty of the army.'[1] But it brought to power a civilian leader who was able to create the stable government which Spain had lacked for so long.

Born in 1825, Antonio Canovas del Castillo, the leader of the Conservative party, was a remarkable man. Raymond Carr has described him as 'the greatest statesman of the Restoration' in these terms:

> Like so many of the political oligarchs, Canovas was a self made provincial, a schoolmaster from Malaga who came to Madrid with nothing but a letter of recommendation to the banker Salamanca, a fellow townsman. Physically tough and a greater eater, he slept only six hours a night. His eminence was that of a hard worker in a lazy society. Unprepossessing in appearance – with his squint, nervous tic, and appalling clothes, he looked like 'a subaltern on half pay' – he possessed intellectual powers that were an essential part of his political capital ... As a speaker he was irresistible and his parliamentary prestige unchallenged. His opponents, half in admiration, called him 'the Monster.'[2]

He was Prime Minister six times. His last administration was formed in March 1895, and thus it at once fell to him to respond to the outbreak of the Cuban revolution, succeeding to the premiership a month later after the 'Grito de Baire.' His decision to appoint Martinez Campos, in spite of the latter's well known liberal views on what to do about Cuba, was logical; he had, after all, ended the previous rising. But Canovas, to an even greater extent than the previous Liberal government, took the same stance as the unionists in Cuba; he was not prepared to negotiate with the rebels, and he was committed to providing all the resources that might be necessary to bring about a military solution.

His policy was generally approved in Spain; Praxedes Mateo Sagasta, the Liberal Prime Minister whom Canovas succeeded, had declared: 'The Spanish nation is disposed to sacrifice to the last peseta of its treasure and to the last drop of blood of the last Spaniard before consenting that anyone snatch from it even one piece of its sacred territory.'[3]

Canovas was not, however, unaware of the danger of intervention by the United States. Successive Spanish governments had had to deal with delicate diplomatic questions arising from the acts of American sympathisers with the aspirations of the Cuban people; a breakdown in relations was avoided by the desire of both governments to avert a situation in which an outbreak of war became inevitable. When, in February 1895, the revolution began, President Grover Cleveland and his Secretary of State Richard Olney were anxious to avoid taking any active steps; but public opinion and the Press in the United States was not going to permit a policy of inaction for long. On June 12 1895 Cleveland proclaimed a policy of neutrality, which recognised the insurgency but did not grant the rebels the nights of belligerents under international law. It was by no means enough to satisfy public opinion, as Chadwick pointed out:

> The tide of popular feeling in the United States was now rapidly rising. A great democracy, the education of whose mass usually ends with the public school, and whose library, later, is the newspaper, does not reason with a volume of international law in its hand or trouble itself, if the question takes form in its mind at all, with what seems to it minor distinctions which weigh not at all with its prejudices and sympathies. For a hundred years the American democracy had been in antagonistic contact with Spanish rule in Louisiana, in Florida, in Mexico, and it knew but one mode of settlement of the difficulties which had thus arisen.[4]

Getting rid of the Spanish, therefore, was the desirable end against which US government policy would be judged by public opinion.

Not surprisingly, therefore, prominent politicians began to put before Congress resolutions designed to force the President's hand. On December 3 1895 Senator Call offered a resolution calling for the recognition of Cuban belligerency; Senator Allen demanded the independence and annexation of Cuba, and Senator Kyle, on January 13 1896 asked that the President be authorised to receive accredited representatives of the rebel government. On February 28 the Senate passed a resolution 'that the friendly offices of the United States should be offered by the President to the Spanish government for the recognition of the independence of Cuba.' On March 2 the House of Representatives more directly called for intervention if necessary. On April 6 the House and the Senate passed a joint resolution calling for recognition of the Cuban revolution.

The violent language of American politicians, and the passing of these resolutions, provoked public demonstrations against the United States in Madrid and Barcelona. The Spanish minister in Washington, Dupuy de Lome, expressed in strong terms in the *New York Herald* on February 23 the view of his government and people, complaining that there was a conspiracy not to present to the American people the Spanish side of the question. He denied the existence of a genuine desire for independence on the part of the mass of the Cuban people:

> All the representative leaders were and have been abroad, and have obeyed the junta which has been established in New York and which had more than one hundred and fifty revolutionary clubs, the greater part of them being in the United States. The revolution is not the popular uprising of a discontented nation. It is a filibustering movement, principally of demagogues without standing in the island, who have nothing to lose and are trying their chances.[5]

Cleveland and Olney, notwithstanding the resolutions adopted by Congress, were still determined to follow a pacific line. On April 7 Olney sent a note, which he carefully backdated in order not to appear to be responding to the congressional resolutions, asking that Spain should consider making 'an authentic declaration of the organic changes that are meditated in the administration of the island with a view to remove all just grounds of complaint.' His note was, he said, 'prompted by the friendliest feeling toward Spain and the Spanish people.'[6] A more reasonable expression of American concern to bring the civil war to an end can scarcely be imagined, and in forwarding it Dupuy de Lome justly acknowledged the respect shown to the legitimate rights of Spain.

Given his concern to avoid complications with the United States, it was surprising that Canovas did not at once respond to Olney's approach. But he did not. In the event six weeks were allowed to pass before the Spanish Foreign Minister, the Duke of Tetuan, replied. When he did so, on June 4, it was to reject all of the reforms which had been proposed, and restated, in appropriately diplomatic but unmistakeably adamant terms the policy which Canovas had been pursuing. This response was profoundly alarming to Cleveland, who correctly saw the need for extreme caution because 'the public mind seemed to be in an inflammable state, and a spark might kindle a conflagration … There seemed to be an epidemic of insanity in the country just at this time.'[7] The rejection of Olney's very moderate proposal meant that sooner rather than later the intervention that Canovas was so anxious to avoid had become almost inevitable.

There were two particular matters which may have played some part in influencing Canovas. First, there was an initiative which he planned in order to attract support for the Spanish position from the six Great Powers of Europe. A note was drafted, and was unofficially circulated to the relevant Spanish ambassadors. Before, however, it could be formally presented to the Great Powers, its contents became known to Hannis Taylor, the US minister in Madrid, in August 1896. His protests were immediate and strongly expressed; he made clear to Tetuan that if it was presented it would be treated in Washington as an unfriendly act. The consequences would be serious, and would be immediate. Tetuan backed down, although making sure that the Great Powers were aware of its contents. It produced little save formal expressions of sympathy. A typical comment was that of Bülow in Germany: 'I admire the courage Spain has shown but I would admire more a display of common sense.'[8]

The second factor was the decision to name General Valeriano Weyler y Nicolau as Governor General of Cuba. In choosing him Canovas could not have made a clearer statement of his intention to stop at nothing to crush the revolution. Weyler was born in 1838. He had fought in Cuba during the Ten Years' War; during this time, and later in campaigns against the Carlists he had gained a reputation for ruthlessness. He was Governor General of the Phillipines in 1888 until returning to Spain to take command in 1892 of the 6th Army Corps, and he then became Captain General in Barcelona. Although by no means the monster that he was painted by the American press, he believed that he knew what must be done to win the war, and he arrived with a firm determination to do just that. The war, he thought, could be won in two years.

Weyler had been a military attaché in Washington during the American Civil War and understood and admired the conduct of Sherman in his march through Georgia. He arrived in Havana on February 10, to be greeted with almost universal detestation by the American press: the *New York Journal,* for instance, called him a 'fiendish despot' and a 'brute,' who was a pitiless, cold exterminator; 'there is nothing to prevent his carnal, animal brain from running riot with itself in inventing tortures and infamies of bloody debauchery.'[9] To comments such as this Weyler retorted: 'How do they want me to wage war? With bishops' pastorals and presents of sweets and money?'

1896 was a presidential election year, so Cleveland's annual message to Congress of December 7 was his last. In it he traced in considerable detail the course of the war and the policy of the United States. While opposing recognition of the rebel Cuban government, he referred to various ways in which the conflict might be brought to an end, and the forbearance which his government had shown. He observed that the United States had, in its own domains, enough to satisfy all possible longing for territory' which precluded all dreams of conquest. 'No other great power, it may safely be said, under circumstances of similar perplexity, would have manifested the same restraint and the same patient endurance.' He spelled out, however, a warning which, coming from a President who had been so careful to avoid a confrontation, should have had a profound significance for Canovas and his government:

> It should be added that it cannot be reasonably assumed that the hitherto expectant attitude of the United Spates will be definitely maintained. While we are anxious to accord all due respect to the sovereignty of Spain we cannot view the impending conflict in all its features, and properly apprehend our inevitable close relations to it and its possible results, without considering that by the course of events we may be drawn into such an unusual and unprecedented condition as will fix a limit to our patient waiting for Spain to end the contest, either alone and in her own way or with our friendly cooperation.[10]

By then, of course, the election had taken place, and the Republican William McKinley had been elected after a campaign in which Cuba had not been the leading issue. Domestic concerns had been at the centre of the debate, and foreign policy questions played little part in the outcome of the election. Nevertheless McKinley, as his remark to Cleveland before his inauguration showed, was very much aware that the problem of Cuba was one which he would have to tackle very soon.

It was surprising; therefore, that he should have allowed his choice as Secretary of State to be determined by what amounted to a piece of political jobbery. The appointment of the 74 year old Senator John Sherman, in poor health, was prompted by a desire to create a vacancy in the Senate for Mark Hanna. Chadwick, observing that Sherman had been one of the senators most hostile to Spain, carefully understated the case on describing the appointment as a mistaken one, given the critical international situation, going on to remark: 'That the appointment was a concession to certain political adjustments in his state of a decidedly personal nature, did not add to the political morality of the appointment.'[11] Fortunately, the Assistant Secretary of State, the able William R Day appointed in April 1897, was soon able to take charge of much of the day to day management of the Cuban crisis. McKinley himself angrily rejected claims that he had known of Sherman's poor physical health and declining intelligence, asserting that when he had seen him last he was 'convinced both of his perfect health, physically and mentally, and that his prospects of life were remarkably good.'

The approach which McKinley would bring to key foreign policy issues was not entirely clear. Henry Cabot Lodge visited him in Canton in December 1896, and was relieved to be able to report to Theodore Roosevelt that 'his whole attitude of mind struck me as serious, broad in view, and just what we all ought to desire.'[12] He viewed foreign policy from the standpoint of its effect on American trade, and would decide the issues in a manner best calculated to benefit American economic influence. He was entirely ready to add to the territory of the United States; from the outset of his presidency he was determined on the acquisition of Hawaii. So far as

Cuba was concerned, McKinley came to office after Weyler had been in command there for a year and the consequences of his policies had been increasingly the subject of political protest in the United States. In addition, the commercial consequences of the insurgents' policy of devastation of the sugar industry were now making themselves felt. Sugar production in 1894-1895 had been 1,004,264 tons; it fell in the following year to 225,251 tons. The scale of the destruction wreaked by the insurgents necessarily affected the value of the holdings in Cuba invested by Americans, estimated at $50 million. The reaction of such investors to the ongoing situation was varied; some called for intervention as a means of protecting their assets, while others concerned about the possibility of war with Spain wished to see a speedy peaceful settlement to enable the economy to recover from the depression.

McKinley's biographer Lewis L Gould has pointed out that the widely held view that the President's policy was a continuation of that pursued by his predecessor is incorrect. Cleveland had, on the whole, been pro-Spanish, preferring to see Spain's sovereignty maintained as a means of avoiding the turmoil that might result from Cuban independence, which in its turn might lead to European intervention.[13] McKinley, on the other hand, was inclined to favour the insurgents. It was, however, some time before the line he would take became clear. His wish to avoid war remained absolute, as he had told Cleveland. He expressed it in similar terms to another listener, saying at the outset of his presidency: 'We want no wars of conquest, [and] we must avoid the temptation of territorial aggression. War should never be entered upon until every agency for peace has failed; peace is preferable to war in almost every contingency.'[14] His hope that the Cuban question might have been resolved before he took office was disappointed, but was inevitable in all the circumstances; it remained to be seen how he could bring about a peaceful solution.

9

The Road to War

In the summer of 1897, as the Cuban insurrection ground remorselessly on, with its bitter harvest of destruction and death, there occurred an event which just might have provided an opportunity to avert Spain's further descent into the maelstrom. On August 8 1897 as he sat reading a newspaper after Sunday Mass, Antonio Canovas was shot dead by an Italian anarchist named Miguel Angiolillo. The assassination was an act of revenge for the torture and death of Spanish anarchists, and was unrelated to the Cuban insurrection.

After an interim government led by the War Minister General Marcelo Azcarraga had briefly taken over, a Liberal government under Praxedes Mateo Sagasta took office on October 5. The common front of the Conservative and Liberal parties over the right policy to pursue over Cuba had began to crumble some months earlier. Segismundo Moret y Prendergast, a prominent Liberal spokesman, indicated on July 19 that a Liberal government would at once adopt a policy of home rule for Cuba: 'Military force will tear the flesh of Cuba, but autonomy will staunch the blood that gushes from wounds opened by steel.'[1] Sagasta himself had condemned the government's policy on May 19 when he said: 'After having sent 200,000 men, and having spilt so much blood, we are masters in the island only of the territory on which our soldiers stand.' He had seen autonomy as naturally following from the reforms contemplated by Canovas; now, when he took office he was aided by the fact that the leading hawks in his party had refused to join the government. Moret was appointed as Colonial Minister, and Sagasta was hopeful that his new government might be able to keep thte United Stastes from intervening, while negotiating a settlement with the insurgents. He took an important step towards this by recalling Weyler and replacing him with the former Government General of the Philippines, General Ramon Blanco y Erenas.

The situation in Cuba that Sagasta's ministry had inherited was desperate, as a report to the government from the embattled island made all too clear:

> The administration has reached the last stage of disarray and disorder; the army, exhausted and bloodless, filling the hospitals, without the power to fight or hardly even to lift their arms; more than three hundred thousand *concentrados* suffering or starving, dying of hunger and misery all around the towns; the people frightened, in the grip of real terror, obliged to abandon their homes and properties in order to suffer under even more terrible tyranny, with no opportunity to escape this fearful situation except by going and joining the ranks of the rebels.[2]

Additionally, the country's financial situation was desperate. The lack of funds, which had resulted in the troops fighting in Cuba being six months in arrears in their pay, had also seriously handicapped the efforts of the Spanish navy for a war which it dreaded. In spite of all this, however, Sagasta still felt obliged in a newspaper interview to assert that 'no Spanish party, certainly not the liberals, could assent to foreign interference in our domestic affairs or with our colonies.'[3]

Sagasta's Foreign Minister was Pio Gullon Iglesias. On October 23 he announced to the new American Minister in Madrid, General Stewart Lyndon Woodford, that Spain would grant to Cuba an autonomy which would give the Cubans 'their own local government, whereby they shall be at one and the same time the initiators and regulators of their life, but always forming part of the integral nationality of Spain.' Foreign affairs, justice and the armed forces would remain the prerogative of Madrid. In return, Gullon expected the United States to prevent military resources reaching the insurgents and avoid behaving as if sympathetic to them. In his statement of Spanish policy Gullon reflected the complete inability of his government and its predecessors to recognise either just how much restraint had been shown by the United States government in endeavouring to enforce neutrality on the part of its citizens, or the extent to which, in a free society, it had to permit free speech and discussion of the issues.

It was not a promising start for Woodford's mission to Madrid. He had arrived on July 28, accompanied by the new military attaché, Captain Tasker Howard Bliss, and the new naval attaché, Lieutenant George Leland Dyer. The two attachés did not have a high opinion of Woodford, regarding him as too weak in the face of the Spaniards, and not altogether trustworthy; Dyer described him as 'a bald, blond tabby of a man who holds girls' hands and brags horribly.'[4]

Woodford had arrived in Madrid with instructions from his government which should have left Sagasta and his colleagues in no doubt that the end game in Cuba was approaching, and that it would not be possible to fill McKinley's glass with false promises. Spain had, the letter of instructions affirmed, already had a reasonable time to restore peace and been unable to do so, in spite of 'measures of unparalleled severity.' Spain could not expect the United States government to sit idle, 'letting vast interests suffer, our political elements disturbed, and the country perpetually embroiled, while no progress is being made in the settlement of the Cuban question.'[5]

Weyler left Cuba on October 31. Before he left he gave vent to a bitter expression of his views in terms which brought him close to a court martial:

> I had expected my release from the time of the death of Senor Canovas, not believing that any political leader would be strong enough to sustain me when the United States and the rebels were together constantly demanding that Spain should come to a settlement.[6]

His successor almost at once endeavoured to alleviate the suffering of the *concentrados,* but to little effect; his order that they be supplied with daily rations, and medical help, while the agricultural and industrial labour forces should be reorganised, was described by the American consul at Matanzas as 'inoperative and of no effect,'

In Havana, the US Consul General was General Fitzhugh Lee, a Democratic politician from Virginia and a veteran of the Confederate army. Appointed by the Cleveland administration, he made no secret of his sympathy for the insurgents. In his reports to Washington he made clear that in his opinion Spain could not suppress the insurrection by force; as to autonomy, he flatly stated that the insurgents would not accept this, while the Spanish property owners would prefer to see the island annexed by the United Sates.

President McKinley still hoped that the reforms promulgated by the Spanish government might be the basis for a settlement. His annual message to Congress reviewed a number of the courses of action open to the US government and rejected them. Neither recognition of the insurgents as belligerents, nor the recognition of Cuban independence, nor active American intervention were at this stage appropriate. He wished to give Sagasta sufficient time to bring about a peaceful solution. Sufficient time meant, however, a finite limit to the process:

> The near future will demonstrate whether the indispensable condition of a righteous peace, just alike to the Cubans and to Spain as well as equitable to all our interests so intimately involved in the welfare of Cuba, is likely to be attained. If not, the exigency of further and other action by the United States will remain to be taken.[7]

McKinley did, however, rule out forcible annexation, which would, he said be 'criminal aggression.'

Looking on the positive side, Sagasta and his Cabinet read McKinley's message to Congress with something approaching relief. Captain Bliss, however, recorded that popular opinion in Spain took a very different view, reacting badly to the warning note sounded by the President:

> The President's message has been received in a spirit of intense hostility by everyone except the Cabinet of Sagasta, and the unofficial expressions of some of its members are by no means friendly. They see in it a veiled threat of intervention unless war in Cuba stops. And against that all Spain is one.[8]

As Woodford noted, everything now depended on the success or failure of the programme of reform introduced by the Spanish government. It was not long before Fitzhugh Lee's reports confirmed the views he had previously expressed that the grant of autonomy would not bring peace to Cuba, and the information which he gave as to the situation of the civilian population demonstrated how little time was left. Out of about 101,000 *reconcentrados* in Havana province, it was estimated that 52,000 had died; the resources available for relief were virtually non existent. This information prompted McKinley to issue calls for donations to a relief fund for the population on December 24 and January 8, to be administered by the Red Cross; Spain agreed to permit the import into Cuba free of duty of supplies of clothing, food and medicine. The President anonymously made a contribution of his own of $5,000. At the same time, in a decision that was to have a fearful consequence, the battleship *Maine* was ordered to sail from Port Royal to Key West, where she would be conveniently placed if it was thought necessary to send an American warship to Cuba in support of American citizens there. It was a precaution for which Fitzhugh Lee had been calling for some time.

For a while, the situation in Cuba appeared somewhat stabilised. This was not the case on Capitol Hill, where the Democrat leadership in the House had reacted badly to McKinley's message, with its rejection of the suggested recognition of Cuban belligerency. A resolution was passed calling for the recognition that 'a condition of war exists in the island of Cuba between the Government of Spain and the Cuban people.' Public opinion, though, seemed inclined, with McKinley, to give Spain a chance to resolve matters peaceably.

On January 12, however, matters took a sharp turn for the worse when, as Fitzhugh Lee reported from Havana, rioting mobs, apparently led by Spanish officers, attacked the offices of the newspapers there which had been advocating autonomy. On the following day he sent a more detailed report:

> After a day and night of excitement all business suspended, and rioting. Everything quiet at this hour. City heavily guarded. Soldiers protect public square and threatened points. Mobs shouted yesterday. 'Death to Blanco, and death to autonomy,' while 'Viva Weyler' was frequently heard. Contest between Spanish factions. Attention has not been directed to other issues. Heard once yesterday of a few rioters shouting a proposal to march to our consulate. Presence of ships may be necessary, but not now.[9]

Later, he added a warning that if Blanco could not maintain order, or if American and their interests were in danger, ships must be sent.

These reports caused serious anxiety at Washington, as the Spanish Minister Dupuy de Lome reported to his government on January 14. Although no ships were to be sent immediately, the change of sentiment 'has been so abrupt, and our enemies, influenced by it, so numerous, that any sensational occurrence might produce a change and disturb the situation.' Two days later, after a meeting with the 'head of staff' of the *New York Herald*, he told Gullon that McKinley appeared to think that the autonomy proposal had 'come to nothing.', and that he was prepared to land troops from warships to protect the consulate. Dupuy de Lome had replied that this would mean fighting; the Foreign Minister agreed with him that it would be 'intolerable.' Later in the month, the Spanish minister reported that the President had decided to send the *Maine* to Havana, but that this 'must be taken as an act of friendly courtesy, and not looked upon in any other aspect.'

Navy Secretary Long issued a press statement announcing the decision to send the *Maine*, stressing that this was a reflection of the cordiality of relations between Spain and the United States. Told of the decision, Lee advised that the visit be postponed to allow the situation in Havana to cool down, but Assistant Secretary of State Day merely confirmed the vessel's probable arrival on January 25. Before she entered Havana harbour, Lee reported that the authorities there believed that the sending of the ship was with an ulterior purpose. From Madrid, however, Gullon was prepared to take the *Maine*'s visit at face value, and said that Spanish vessels would likewise visit US ports. McKinley took the opportunity of a diplomatic dinner on January 28 to tell Dupuy de Lome how much better the position was, saying 'You have no occasion to be other than satisfied and confident.'

Somewhat surprisingly, however, Gullon now sent a note to Woodford on February 1, the effect of which could not fail to increase tension, as he reproached the US government for its suggestions as to what its attitude might be in the future:

> It is certainly not the time for the United States government to substitute for its former offers of its good offices hints of a change of conduct in the event of more or less remote contingencies, and to base this notification of its change not only upon the contingency of a material success … but upon its own estimate of the success itself.[10]

Gullon was skating on thin ice; no formal reply was made to his note, and Woodford told him that it was a serious mistake.

This it certainly was; but its significance was almost immediately lost when a major diplomatic incident exploded on February 9, with the publication in the *New York Journal* of the text of a letter which Dupuy de Lome had sent to the editor of a Madrid newspaper, who was visiting Havana. The letter had apparently been stolen by a spy for the insurgents, and sent by them to the Cuban junta in New York, where its propaganda value was immediately realised. In his letter, the Spanish minister commented on the President's message to Congress:

> It once more shows what McKinley is, weak and a bidder for the admiration of the crowd, besides being a would-be politician who tries to leave a door open behind himself while keeping on good terms with the jingoes of his party … It would be very advantageous to take up, even if only for effect, the question of commercial relations, and to have a man of some prominence sent hither in order that I may make use of him here to carry on a propaganda among the senators and others in opposition to the junta and to try and win over the refugees.[11]

In the same letter Dupuy de Lome also remarked that not sufficient attention had been paid 'to the part England is playing,' suggesting that 'England's only object is that the Americans should amuse themselves with us and leave her alone;' English journalists were, for this reason, stirring up anti Spanish feeling in the United States.

Dupuy de Lome at once sent in his resignation and Gullon at once accepted it, hoping that in this way to avoid any possibility that 'any manifestation on the part of the United States government could be provoked.' Day told Woodford that 'the publication of the letter had created a good deal of feeling among Americans,' but he was anxious that too much should not be made of it. Within a very few days there was a much more significant crisis with which the Spanish and America governments had to deal.

At about 2:00 a.m. on the morning of February 16, Long was woken to read a telegram that had just arrived at the Navy Department:

> *Maine* blown up in Havana Harbour at 9:40 tonight, and destroyed. Many wounded and doubtless more killed or drowned. Wounded and others on board Spanish man-of-war and Ward Line steamer. Send lighthouse tenders from Key West for crew and the few pieces of equipment above. No one has clothing other than that upon him. Public opinion should be suspended until further report. All officials believed to be saved. Jenkins and Merritt not yet accounted for. Many Spanish officers, including representatives of General Blanco, now with me to express sympathy.[12]

Long at once sent Commander Dickens to the White House with the telegram. McKinley read it several times, understandably shocked by the news. His first public reactions were deliberately low key; on his instructions Long told the press that judgment should be suspended until a full investigation had been made, but it was apparent to every one that this must not be long delayed. Inevitably the response of Press and public was violently hostile to Spain; the French ambassador reported that 'a sort of bellicose fury has seized the American nation.' The loss of two officers and two hundred and fifty eight men was a blow from which McKinley's efforts to achieve a negotiated peace in Cuba would be hard put to recover.

Orders went at once to Rear Admiral Montgomery Sicard to convene a court of inquiry from among the officers of the North Atlantic Squadron; the officers selected were Captain William T Sampson and French E Chadwick, and Lieutenant Commander WE Potter; Lieutenant Commander Adolph Marix was appointed judge advocate. They set off for Havana aboard the lighthouse steamer *Mangrove* on February 20 amid a continuing uproar from the yellow press. Not all newspaper editors reacted in the manner of Hearst and Pulitzer; a leading article in *The Nation* of February 24 was sharply critical:

> The admirable conduct of the government officials at Washington renders the course of the sensational press in this city [New York] the more shameful by contrast ... It speaks well for the good sense of the masses that so little effect has been produced by all this stuff. It is evident that a large proportion of the public refuses to take the sensational newspapers seriously.[13]

The members of the Court of Inquiry, based on the *Mangrove*, started work as soon as they arrived at Havana. Chadwick, the captain of the *New York*, had all his professional life had a profound admiration for Sampson, who was four years his senior. He graduated from the Naval Academy in November 1864; his service at sea aboard the *Susquehanna* came too late to see action in the Civil war. Thereafter, he had a wide range of experience in the peacetime navy, both at sea and ashore, including a trip to Europe to study training methods in other navies. He went back to Europe in 1882, becoming the first naval attaché permanently appointed to an American embassy. Based in London, he travelled extensively in Europe, reporting on many technical questions arising from his survey of foreign navies. In 1889 he returned to the United States to commission the new gunboat *Yorktown*. He already had a sufficient reputation for Benjamin Tracy to consult him about the organisation of the Navy Department, about which he delivered an outspoken opinion:

> I believe no such example of defective organisation exists in any civilised country as that which has existed for many years in ours of the Navy, nor has there in this generation at least been anything approaching it in badness outside of Turkey, Spain or Russia. We have ... established a system the like of which exists nowhere else, and... which had the result (and necessarily) of reducing the service to a painful exhibition of worthless vessels and decaying navy yards.[14]

Chadwick's growing reputation was such that Mahan suggested that he should succeed him as President of the Naval War College, but he was not keen to do so, and Mahan stayed on. Chadwick, in 1892, became head of the Office of Naval Intelligence, and in the following year became Chief of the Bureau of Equipment, serving until November 1897, when he took command of the new armoured cruiser *New York*. When appointed to the *Maine* Court of Inquiry, he considered at first that it was very probable that the cause of the explosion was internal, but in the course of a painstaking investigation he came to the opposite conclusion.

In its report, dated March 21, the Court of Inquiry unanimously concluded that the explosion was caused by a submarine mine, set off outside the *Maine* by a person or persons unknown, which had resulted in the ship's forward magazines exploding, as a result of which she had sunk. On the following day the inquiry instituted by the Spanish authorities reported, but not surprisingly found that the *Maine*'s forward magazines had exploded as a result of internal causes. This conclusion was supported by various circumstances; there was no geyser of water shooting up, which would normally occur with an explosion below the surface, there were no dead fish near the wreck, and there was no convincing opportunity for a mine to be placed beneath the *Maine* or near her mooring.[15]

The questions of the motive for anyone placing a submarine mine beneath the *Maine*, and the opportunity and the means to do so, rendered the conclusion of the American inquiry dubious, and a debate began in later years as to the cause of the explosion which was never finally resolved, and perhaps never will be. In 1900 the British naval historian HW Wilson set out exhaustively the factors which had led to the outcome of the American inquiry that the explosion was caused externally, and concluded:

> It will readily be acknowledged that the evidence of the American inquiry is far from being absolutely conclusive. Still it does seem to the author to have established the probability that the *Maine* was destroyed by a mine.[16]

In 1976, however, Admiral Hyman G Rickover, the US Navy's nuclear submarine expert, became interested in the question of the *Maine*'s destruction, and commissioned a study into the causes of the explosion from Ib S Hansen and Robert S Price. Their conclusion, which is almost certainly the nearest that it would be possible to get to certainty, came down on the side of the Spanish inquiry. They found that the initial explosion, which then triggered off the explosion in the forward magazines, was internal and accidental, caused by spontaneous combustion in the soft, bituminous coal which generated enough heat to ignite power in one of the magazines, leading to the second and more severe explosion. Admiral Rickover, accepting the findings of Hansen and Price, wrote that there was no evidence that a mine destroyed the *Maine*. He was inclined to attach some blame to Captain Sigsbee: 'There is no evidence that he took more than routine measures in Havana to safeguard his ship from an accident.' He added that it was perhaps significant that 'the *Kearsarge* and *Texas* while under his command were inspected and found dirty.' This last observation Michael Blow found harsh, pointing to the steps that Sigsbee had in fact taken, and concluding that in the end the Hansen-Price study had proved conjectural and inconclusive: 'A bunker fire was likely, but could not be proved; a mine was unlikely, but possible.'[17]

In the fevered atmosphere of 1898, the American Press and public had heard quite enough; no one was going to second guess the conclusions of the Sampson inquiry, as McKinley well knew. He delayed sending the report to Congress for a week, hoping that Woodford, in Madrid, would be able to make some headway in discussions with Gullon. The latter was now showing a greater sense of urgency in the search for some kind of peace formula; Woodford reported a conversation between them on March 25, in the course of which Gullon

> was very earnest in his desire that the report ... on the subject of the *Maine* should not be sent to Congress but should be held as the subject of diplomatic adjustment between the two governments. He assured me that Spain would do in the matter whatever was just and right.[18]

On March 26 Woodford was sent a statement outlining in full the position of the United States, and a specific proposal which he was to put to the Spanish government. As to the possibility of the United States purchasing Cuba, Day, the author of the instructions, said firmly: 'We do not want the island.' Woodford was told to put McKinley's proposal in these terms:

> If Spain will revoke the reconcentration order and maintain the people until they can support themselves, and offer the Cubans full self-government with reasonable indemnity, the President will gladly assist in its consummation. If Spain should invite the United States to mediate for peace and the insurgents would make like request, the President might undertake such office of friendship.[19]

Woodford, who on the same day had been sent a summary of the report of the *Maine* inquiry, telegraphed Day for clarification of the meaning of 'full self-government with reasonable indemnity;' Day's reply would leave the Spanish government in no doubt that the end game had been reached: 'Full self government would mean Cuban independence.' Woodford was now to negotiate with Spain on the basis of an end to reconcentration, an armistice to last until October 1 and a commitment by Spain to accept Cuban independence.

McKinley's line was hardening, which came as a relief to those who, like Roosevelt, were becoming impatient for action. It was an awareness that feelings were rising to the point at which he might lose control of the situation that now prompted the President's policy, although he risked inspiring outrage on the part of Congress when forwarding the report of the *Maine* inquiry without comment. He had previously, in early March, taken one essential step without which he could not have contemplated the possibility of war, when he put to Congress a bill authorising the expenditure of $50 million for national defence, telling congressmen: 'I must have money to get ready for war. I am doing everything possible to prevent war but it must come, and we are not prepared for war.' The unanimous approval on March 8 by both houses of Congress of the bill had sent a strong message of the determination of the United States to see matters through to a conclusion, but in Madrid it was taking some time for it to sink in.[20]

On March 29 Woodford had a meeting with Sagasta, Gullon andd Moret. He read a prepared statement setting out in the clearest terms the policy of the United States. Sagasta, in reply, gave an explanation of what the authorities were doing for the *reconcentrados*. He explained that in the existing situation in Spain his government could not offer an armistice, but if sought by the insurgents it would at once be granted.

The Cuban Congress would meet on May 4, when it could ask for an armistice. Woodford said that only the immediate cessation of hostilities would be acceptable, coupled with a revocation of the reconcentration order. They agreed to meet again in March 31; meanwhile Blanco issued an immediate order ending the reconcentration. Woodford reported to Day, who said that there could be no delay beyond March 31; Woodford, who was optimistic about the progress made, replied that if no definite result was obtained on that day's meeting, he would terminate negotiation. He had however, chosen to avoid reference to the question of full self government, evidently feeling that to do so might lead to a breakdown of negotiations

In Washington, the hope that even at this late hour the Spanish government might make some decisive concessions left McKinley to postpone sending his war message to Congress, which prompted Roosevelt's insulting comment that: 'McKinley has no more back bone than a chocolate éclair.'[21]

On March 31, however, Woodford's hopes were dashed. Gullon handed him a document outlining the Spanish response. As to the *Maine*, Spain would submit to arbitration. As to reconcentration, Blanco had revoked the order in the western provinces, and a sum of $600,000 dollars had been placed at his disposal for relief operations. However, as to the restoration of peace, this was to left to the Cuban Congress, 'it being understood that the powers reserved by the constitution to the central government are not lessened and diminished.' A truce would be granted as soon as the insurgents asked for it. Taken overall, as Woodford pointed out to the Spanish, it did not meet McKinley's demands, though as he observed to McKinley Spain had made concessions that would have been out of the question a month before As Trask points out, however, a settlement on American terms was probably never possible; on the American side it was never appreciated that to the Spanish people 'the loss of Cuba represented a repudiation of Spain's most pervasive and emotional national myth.'[22]

There was one last momentary flicker of hope that war might be averted, which originated in Europe. The worsening situation between Spain and United States had naturally been monitored closely by all of the Great Powers. In Germany Kaiser William II had for a time cherished the idea of a joint European initiative which might save Cuba for Spain. His motivation was to uphold the monarchical principle, believing that if Cuba was lost, the monarchy in Spain would fall. Bülow, his Chancellor, was extremely dubious about any step of this kind, and advised caution. William, who always had a penchant for fishing in troubled waters, did not give up on the idea, and continued to prod Bülow to do something about it. The latter remained unenthusiastic, being perfectly aware that without British and French participation no joint initiative stood any chance of success. He did, however, see some mileage in getting the Pope to arbitrate, reckoning that Papal authority, ' which is recognised nowhere in the world more unquestionably than in Spain, would then cover the Regent's responsibility and minimise the dangers threatening the Monarchy.'[23] The Vatican was prepared to do what it could, and put out feelers in Washington and Madrid to see if Papal arbitration would be acceptable. However, the Nuncio in Madrid was told flatly that it would 'be impossible to accept arbitration on the basis of the cession of Cuba.' So that was that. The Kaiser endorsed the telegram from Bülow reporting this:'Then there is no way of helping, then! They will lose Cuba all the same.'[24]

Queen Maria Cristina made her own last ditch attempt on April 5 to stave off war by authorising Woodford to ask Washington if an immediate ceasefire which she would proclaim at the Pope's request would prevent hostile action by Congress. To this request Woodford next day received a response which suggested that it was now too late:

> The President highly appreciates the Queen's desire for peace. He cannot assume to influence the action of the American Congress beyond a discharge of his constitutional duty in transmitting the whole matter to them with such recommendation as he deems necessary and expedient. The repose and welfare of the American people require restoration of peace and stable government in Cuba.[25]

On April 6 also the representatives of the six Great Powers in Washington presented a joint note appealing to 'the feelings of humanity and moderation of the President and of the American people,' hoping that further negotiations would lead to an agreement. This, which in the circumstances was no more than a formality, was unlikely to cut much ice in Washington; McKinley's reply merely hoped that the Great Powers would show equal appreciation for the US government's 'earnest and unselfish endeavours to fulfil a duty to humanity' by ending a situation that had become insufferable.

On April 9 Woodford, who had still not given up all hope, reported that Blanco had been given authority to proclaim an immediate armistice; he thought that if Congress gave McKinley a free hand, a final settlement could be achieved by August 1, the possible terms of which if necessary would include independence or annexation to the United States. Where he got that from is not clear, but there is no evidence that Sagasta and his government even now were prepared to contemplate independence, and McKinley, now believing that war was inevitable, sat down to review his message to Congress, which was sent on April 11. It set out at length the history of all that the United States had done to address the intolerable situation in Cuba, and concluded:

> I ask the Congress to authorise and empower the President to take measures to secure a full and final termination of hostilities between the government of Spain and the people of Cuba, and to secure in the island the establishment of a stable government… and to use the military and naval forces of the United States as may be necessary for these purposes.[26]

He added, as a postscript, the news of the armistice proclaimed by Blanco, which he was sure would have the 'just and careful attention' of Congress.

The debate in the Senate continued until 1:20 a.m. on April 19, when by 42 votes to 35 the joint resolution, as finally amended, was passed; at 2:40 the House passed it by 311 to 6. The President was granted the war powers for which he asked; the resolution also included a disclaimer on the part of the United States of any 'intention to exercise sovereignty, jurisdiction or control' over the island of Cuba. When news of the resolution was received in Madrid, diplomatic relations were broken off at once. On April 25 Congress declared that a state of war had existed since April 21. It had been a long and circuitous route which the United States government had taken; but the hawks had finally got their way.

10

The Spanish Navy

Rear Admiral Pascual Cervera y Topete took command of the Spanish naval forces at Cadiz in October 30 1897, soon after leaving his post as Minister of Marine in the Liberal Cabinet of Praxedes Sagasta. He had held that office only briefly, before resigning on the grounds that his colleagues in government seemed to him to be prepared to put political expediency before the interests of the nation. He was in no doubt that Spain's international situation was of the utmost gravity and that it was all too likely that in the event of war with the United States the Spanish navy would be hopelessly unprepared. He soon began a correspondence with his old friend and successor as Minister of Marine, Rear Admiral Segismundo Bermejo y Merelo in which he pointed out the inadequacies of the ships under his command, and the huge discrepancy in their fighting power when compared to the United State navy.

One of the first problems confronting Cervera when he assumed command was the fact that the most powerful unit of his squadron, the *Cristobal Colon*, lacked her main armament of 10-inch guns. Those supplied by Ansaldo, the Italian shipbuilders, had proved to be unsatisfactory, and had been rejected by the Spanish Admiralty's experts. The issue of whether to take them in any case ran like a thread throughout Cervera's correspondence, both official and personal, with Bermejo; he set out his views in a letter February 9:

> It is very much to be regretted that there is always so much underhand work about everything, and that there should be so much of it now regarding the acceptance of the 9.6-inch guns … it seems to me that we should accept, as the proverb says, 'hard bread rather than none;' and if we have no other guns, and these can fire even 25 or 30 shots, we should take them anyhow, even though they are expensive and inefficient, and we should lose no time about it, in order that the vessel may be armed and supplied with ammunition as soon as possible.[1]

The lengthy exchange of correspondence between Cervera and Bermejo contained many such instances of the extraordinary failure to prepare for a war that had been threatening for many months.

Cervera had written an official letter to the minister to set out bluntly the present state of the fleet:

> Although I am sure that I am telling you nothing new, I think it is not idle, in these critical times, to make a study of the condition of the fleet. We must discount the *Alfonso XIII*,

> so many years under trials that it appears we shall not have the pleasure ever to count it among our vessels of war. The fleet is reduced to the three Bilbao cruisers, the *Colon*, the *Destructor* and the torpedo destroyers *Furor* and *Terror*. The three Bilbao cruisers are practically complete. But the 5-inch guns, the main power of these vessels, is practically useless, on account of the bad system of their breech mechanism, and the bad quality of the cartridge cases, of which there are only those on board. The *Colon*, which is undoubtedly the best of all our ships from a military point of view, has not received her guns.[2]

The reference to the Bilbao cruisers was to the three armoured cruisers *Infanta Maria Teresa*, *Almirante Oquendo* and *Vizcaya*. These were of 7,000 tons, carrying two 11-inch guns and ten 5-5-inch guns and had a design speed of 20.25 knots. The *Cristobal Colon* was slightly smaller at 6,840 tons; lacking her main armament of two 10-inch Armstrong guns, she was armed with ten 5.2-inch guns, and six 4.7-inch guns, and she also had a design speed of 20.25 knots. Wilson calls her 'incomparably the finest' Spanish armoured cruiser, 'in which extraordinary qualities of offence and defence are obtained upon a very moderate displacement…The Americans had no cruiser to compare with the *Colon*.'[3] The mixture of different calibre guns among the ships of the Spanish fleet was characteristic of the hand to mouth policies pursued for many years, due principally to the impoverishment of the national treasury.

Apart from the *Alfonso XIII* referred to in Cervera's letter to Bermejo, which was incomplete, as was the *Lepanto*, there were two other major units which were manifestly not ready for a combat role, although they were taken account of in American naval circles and in international press comments. These were the battleship *Pelayo* and the armoured cruiser *Carlos V*. The *Pelayo* displaced 9,900 tons; her main armament consisting of four 12.5-inch guns and two 11-inch guns, in armoured barbettes. She also carried nine 5-5-inch quick firers, eighteen smaller guns and seven torpedo tubes. The quick firers were, however, exposed, and work was in hand to construct an armoured redoubt to protect them; this was not completed until some weeks after the outbreak of war. Her armoured deck was three and a half inches thick; on the waterline she had a narrow belt of armour from twelve to seventeen inches thick. On trial she had attained a speed of 16.7 knots. She had been refitted just before the war. Wilson rates her as being 'decidedly superior to the *Texas*, and as decidedly inferior to the *Indiana* class, which was just about as fast, and infinitely better armed and armoured.'[4] Nonetheless, had she been ready, she would have been a valuable addition to Cervera's squadron. As Spain's only battleship, she was known by the sad nickname of *el solitario*.

The armoured cruiser *Carlos V* would also have been useful had she been ready, although Wilson describes her as being 'large but feebly armed and ill protected.' Her armour was, he thought, 'so thin as to be positively dangerous.' She carried fore and aft two 11-inch guns, with a secondary battery of the usual Spanish heterogeneous character of ten 5.5-inch quick firers, four 3.9-inch and some smaller guns. Her design speed was 20.5 knots.

The only other armoured vessel which the Spanish attempted to get ready for combat after the outbreak of war was the aged ironclad *Numancia*. She had been built in 1863, but subsequently refitted, re-boilered and rearmed. He speed was low, and she was not of great fighting value.

There was also the elderly ironclad *Vitoria*, which Cervera had hoped might prove serviceable, but she was not, and no serious attempt seemed to have been made put her in a combat ready condition.

In addition to these vessels the Spanish navy possessed twelve old cruisers. Of these, seven were based in Manila, under the command of Rear Admiral Montojo; these were the *Reina Cristina*, *Castilla*, *Isla de Cuba*, *Isla de Luzon*, *Don Antonio de Ulloa*, *Don Juan de Austria* and *Velasco*, in varying degrees of decrepitude and of little or no fighting value. There were also the *Marques de Ensenada*, *Reina Mercedes*, *Conde de Venadito*, *Alfonso XII* and *Isabel II*, all of which were entirely useless.

There were five torpedo gunboats: *Filipinas*, *Nueva Espana*, *Marques de Molins*, *Martin Alonzo Pinzon* and *Temerario*; armed with two 4.7-inch guns, they were slow, with poor coal endurance and lacking protection. More useful were the seven destroyers; *Destructor*, *Audaz*, *Osado*, *Proserpina*, *Furor*, *Terror* and *Pluton*. All except the *Destructor* were of the most recent type, built in England and displacing 370 to 400 tons. *Terror* and *Furor* were theoretically capable of 28 knots and the others 30 knots, although in service they did not exceed 22 knots. They all carried two 14-inch torpedo tubes. Of the seven listed, only the last three were ready at the outbreak of war. There were three seagoing torpedo boats, *Ariete*, *Azor* and *Rayo*, capable of up to 26 knots; *Azor* carried three torpedo tubes and the others two. Finally there were four elderly and almost completely useless gunboats.

The relative strength of the American and Spanish fleets was set out in a table by HW Wilson, to demonstrate the considerable discrepancy between the apparent and the actual strength at the moment of the outbreak of war:

	Apparent		**Actual**	
	United States	**Spain**	**United States**	**Spain**
Battleships	5	1	5	0
Monitors	6	0	5	0
Armoured cruisers	2	7	2	4
Old ironclad	0	1	0	0
Protected cruisers	14	3	8	0
Other cruisers	9	14	9	12
Torpedo gunboats	1	11	1	5
Destroyers	0	7	0	3
Torpedo boats	6	12	6	3

The figures set out in the columns of apparent strengths were bandied about in the United States before the outbreak of war, and contributed to the anxiety of communities on the east coast of America about the risk of attacks from the sea. In fact, as the figures of actual strength demonstrate, the Spanish navy was hopelessly unready for war; and even if it had been, their fleet was far outmatched in modern warships; only nine of the American vessels had been launched before 1890, compared with thirty two of the Spanish.[5]

There was a similar discrepancy between the paper strength of the personnel of the Spanish fleet and the men actually engaged. In theory, after allowing for about 1,500 men in the Philippines and a similar number in Cuba manning the vessels stationed there, there should have been about 11,000 seamen available in Spain. However, the squadron with which Cervera finally sailed to the Caribbean (four armoured cruisers and three destroyers) was not properly manned, and later in the war the greatest difficulty was experienced in finding sufficient men for the crews of other vessels such as the *Pelayo* and *Carlos V* then coming into service. The American navy had, on the other hand, an effective strength in excess of the nominal strength, due to the vigorous recruitment embarked on when war was seen as a distinct possibility.

Cervera had taken up his command with no great hope that the Spanish navy could put up much of a fight against its opponent; but as he laboured to overcome the legacy of years of neglect, his pessimism steadily deepened. By January 30 he was writing again to his cousin Juan Spottorno to record for posterity his opinion of the situation which he faced:

> Today we find ourselves again in one of those critical periods which seem to be the beginning of the end, and I write to you again to express my point of view and to explain my action in this matter, and I beg you to put this letter with the other one, so that the two may be my military testament. The relative military positions of Spain and the United States have grown worse for us, because we are reduced, absolutely penniless, and they are very rich, and also because we have increased our naval power only with the *Colon* and the torpedo boat destroyers, and they have increased theirs much more.

He went on mournfully to record the deficiencies of his other ships, and of the slow procedure of the Spanish system of administration:

> But my purpose is not to accuse, but to explain why we may and must expect a disaster. But as it is necessary to go to the bitter end, and as it would be a crime to say that publicly today, I hold my tongue, and go forth resignedly to face the trials which God may be pleased to send me. I am sure that we will do our duty, for the spirit of the Navy is excellent; but I pray God that the troubles may be arranged without coming to a conflict, which, in any way, I believe would be disastrous to us.[6]

Meanwhile his correspondence with the minister continued; Bermejo wrote to Cervera on February 8 to instruct him to get the *Oquendo* ready for sea, as she was to proceed to the Caribbean to join the *Vizcaya* which was already there; he went on to write soothingly of the steps he was taking to deal with Cervera's concerns. To this, Cervera replied in the letter of February 9 quoted above that he would use his best efforts to comply with Bermejo's instructions, and went on to express his concerns about the *Colon*'s guns. What was particularly exercising his mind was the lack of information about the American navy, its bases and the distribution and movements of its ships, and he asked a number of pertinent questions:

> What will be the objective of the operations of the squadron – the defence of the peninsula and the Balearic Islands, that of the Canaries or Cuba, or, finally, could their objective be the coasts of the United States, which would seem possible only if we had some powerful ally? What plans of campaign does the government have in either event? I should like also to know the points where the squadron will find some resources and the nature of these; for, strange to say, here, for instance, we have not even found four inch rope, nor boiler tubes, nor other things equally simple.[7]

As he pointed out, without knowing these things, he could not work out what was best to be done. He pointed out that the American forces were three or four times as strong as his own, and would have access to all the harbours of Cuba that were occupied by the insurgents. The best thing, he added, would be to avoid the war at any price; 'but, on the other hand, it is necessary to put an end to the present situation, because this nervous strain cannot be borne much longer.'

Bermejo's reply, dated February 15, came on the day of the destruction of the *Maine*. The plan of operations which he proposed was evidence that he had only a tenuous grip on reality:

> As to the war with the United States, I will tell you my ideas about it. A division composed of the *Numancia, Vitoria, Alphonso XIII* (or *Lepanto*), the destroyers *Audaz, Osado* and *Proserpina*, and three torpedo boats would remain in Spain in the vicinity of Cadiz. In Cuba the *Carlos V, Pelayo, Colon, Vizcaya, Oquendo, Maria Teresa*, three destroyers and three torpedo boats, in conjunction with the eight larger vessels of the Havana Navy Yard, would take up a position to cover the channels between the Gulf of Mexico and the Atlantic, and try to destroy Key West, where the United States has established its principal base of provisions, ammunition and coal. If we succeed in this, and the season is favourable, the blockade could be extended to the Atlantic coast, so as to cut off communications and commerce with Europe – all this subject to the contingencies which may arise from your becoming engaged in battles in which it will be decided who is to hold empire of the sea. For your guidance in these matters, you are acquainted with the preliminary plans of the staff of this ministry, which I placed at your disposal, including the attack upon Key West. I will advise you as to the location of the United States ships and other data for which you ask.[8]

As Chadwick observes, these views could not be more inaccurate and futile. Cervera responded next day, pointing out the glaring defects in Bermejo's plan:

> I do not know when the *Pelayo* and the *Carlos V* will be able to join the fleet, but I suspect that they will not arrive in time… It seems to me that there is a mistake in the calculation of forces we may count upon in the sad event of a war with the United States. In the Cadiz division I believe the *Numancia* will be lacking. I do not think we can count on the *Lepanto*. Of the *Carlos V* and the *Pelayo* I have already spoken. The *Colon* has not yet received her artillery, and if war comes will be caught without her heavy guns. The eight principal vessels of the Havana station, to which you refer, have no military value whatever, and, besides, are badly worn out; therefore they can be a very little use. In saying this I am not moved by a fault finding spirit, but only by a desire to avoid illusions that may cost us very dear. Taking things as they are, however sad it may be, it is seen that our naval force when compared with that of the United States is approximately in the proportion of one to three. It therefore seems to me a dream, almost a feverish fancy, to think that with this force, attenuated by our long wars, we can establish the blockade of any part of the United States. A campaign against that country will have to be, at least for the present, a defensive or a disastrous one, unless we have some alliances, in which case the tables may be turned.[9]

Blunt though this was, it did not serve its purpose; Bermejo, although conceding that his idea was 'perhaps somewhat optimistic,' did not alter his view or submit any more sensible plan of operation.

In his prolonged correspondence with Bermejo, Cervera had concentrated on the immense superiority of the Americans in terms of the ships which would oppose his squadron, and the many practical and material difficulties which he faced in preparing it for combat. He did not directly address the issue of the personnel of his command; their shortcomings were pointed out by HW Wilson, who commented adversely on the low professional capacity of the officers and the want of discipline. He went on:

> The Spanish engineer was of poor quality; Scotchmen had kept the machinery in order before the outbreak of war, and it does not appear that their place was properly filled. As for the Spanish seaman he displayed heroic courage, but he was unintelligent, awkward, and in many instances of bad physique. The war training of the Spanish Navy was thoroughly defective. Gunnery was an almost unknown art; manoeuvres were never held; even drill and evolutions were neglected, as Captain Sigsbee of the *Maine* records that during some weeks' stay in Havana harbour he saw 'very little drilling of any kind on board the Spanish men of war.' The *Vizcaya* and *Oquendo*, two crack ships, when they reached Havana and lay there after the *Maine*'s destruction, did not drill their crews, though war was then imminent.[10]

Cervera kept up the pressure on Bermejo, trying again on February 26 to get the minister to see reason, when he wrote a carefully detailed official report pointing out the massive American superiority in ships and more particularly in guns. He calculated that the offensive power of the artillery of the Spanish ships would be less than two fifths of that of the enemy:

> Now, to carry out any serious operations in a naval war, the first thing necessary is to secure control of the sea, which can only be done by defeating the enemy's fleet, or rendering them powerless by blockading them in their military ports. Can we do this with the United States? It is evident to me that we can not. And even if God should grant us a great victory, against what may be reasonably expected, where and how would we repair the damages sustained? Undoubtedly the port would be Havana, but with what resources? I am not aware of the resources existing there, but judging by this *departamento*, where there is absolutely nothing of all that we may need, it is to be assumed that the same condition exists everywhere.[11]

In other words, whatever was the outcome of the battle, a large part of the Spanish fleet would be *hors de combat* for the rest of the campaign, while the Americans had limitless resources to repair damaged ships. It was a further statement of the obvious, but neither Bermejo nor his cabinet colleagues were ready to accept the obvious, then or later.

Bermejo was, however, sufficient sufficiently shaken by the force of Cervera's letters to need time to respond; on February 28 he acknowledged them but said that he wanted to wait until he had 'somewhat recovered from the painful impression caused by the reading of your letters before answering them.' To this Cervera replied, regretting the painful impression he had caused; but he did not back down, saying that he was not surprised, 'because they are truly sad, and still, perhaps, they fall beneath the mark, judging from everything one sees.' He concluded:

> I have deemed it my duty to express my opinions to the proper authorities – that is, to you and to the whole Government through you – clearly and without beating around the bush.

> Now, let orders be given to me; I will carry them out with energy and decision. I am ready for the worst.[12]

Cervera might have hoped that the painful impression he had caused would serve to jolt Bermejo in the direction of reality. The minister's response, however, when it came dated March 4, disclosed that he simply did not accept the grim arithmetic set out by Cervera to display the inferiority of the Spanish fleet. He produced his own table listing the comparative tonnage of the warships of Spain and the United States that he considered would be available for the campaign in the west. He excluded the *Oregon*, as being on the Pacific coast; but, predictably, included the *Pelayo*, *Carlos V*, *Alfonso XIII* and the five largest vessels that were quietly rotting in Havana harbour. This enabled him to come up with comparative figures of tonnage of 66,537 to 62,818, a difference 'not so excessive' as appeared from Cervera's calculations. He gave a pretty clear indication to Cervera that he was wasting his time urging the government to ensure that peace was maintained, when he said of Cuba that the Spanish flag was still flying there, and that the government 'to meet the sentiments of the people, even at the cost of many sacrifices, desires that this Spanish colony should not be separated from our territory.'[13]

Throughout March the correspondence continued, Cervera showing enormous patience as he pointed out the reality of the situation in the most explicit terms. He still had no sensible directions as to how he should proceed, and was particularly concerned about the security of the Canary Islands as well as a suggestion that the torpedo boat flotilla should set off across the Atlantic. On March 16 he made another attempt to get through to Bermejo the consequences of going to war:

> As clear as daylight to me, it appears that since we cannot not go to war without meeting with a certain and frightful disaster, and since we can not treat directly with the United States, whose bad faith is notorious, perhaps there is nothing left to do but to settle the dispute through arbitration or mediation, provided the enemy accepts.[14]

Cervera accepted that all this was outside his sphere of duty, which was to inform the government of the true situation; as to this he wondered whether it would not be best for him to address the members of the Cabinet in person. This suggestion was not taken up.

He tried again on April 4, sending a telegram to Bermejo:

> I believe it very dangerous for torpedo boat flotilla to continue voyage. As I have no instructions, deem it expedient to go to Madrid to receive them and form plans of campaign. The Canaries trouble me; they are in dangerous situation. If during my absence it should be necessary for squadron to go out, it could do so under second-in-command.

To this he received the absurd reply:'Your cipher telegram received. In these moments of international crisis no definite plans can be formulated.'[15]

Bermejo, who appears by now to have completely lost the plot, also sent a letter to the same effect. To this Cervera replied on April 6 in terms which, as Chadwick pointed out, were dictated by the simplest common sense:

> It is precisely on account of the general anxiety prevailing that it is very important to think of what is to be done, so that, if the case arises, we may act rapidly and with some chance

> of efficiency and not be groping about in the dark, or like Don Quixote, go out to fight windmills and come back with broken heads. If our naval forces were superior to those of the United States the question would be an easy one; all we would have to do would be to bar their way. But as our forces, on the contrary, are very inferior to theirs, it would be the greatest of follies to attempt to bar their way, which could only be done by giving them a decisive naval battle. That would simply mean a sure defeat, which would leave us at the mercy of the enemy, who could easily take a good position in the Canaries, and by establishing there a base of operations, crush our commerce and safely bombard our maritime cities.[16]

Cervera's long and despairing correspondence was now to end. A telegram from the Governor General in Cuba of April 7, expressing concern for the security of the island's coastline as a result of the torpedo flotilla remaining in the Cape Verde Islands, spurred Bermejo into action. That day he telegraphed Cervera to the effect that the squadron should sail on April 8 to St Vincent, Cape Verde, where it was to take on coal and water. The torpedo boats under Villaamil were placed under his orders. Cervera, confirming that his ships were ready for duty, insisted on being given a general plan of campaign. Bizarrely, his instructions were entrusted to a slow steaming collier which was to follow him to Cape Verde, but which would not arrive for several days. Cervera sailed at 5:00 p.m. on April 8 with the *Maria Teresa* and the *Colon*, though not before writing a final letter to Bermejo, restating once again a demand for 'some plan, even on general lines' for which purpose he had repeatedly asked permission to go to Madrid. He again pointed out the folly of exposing the Spanish fleet to a defeat, which he believed would simply bring about the ultimate loss of Cuba.

Cervera arrived at Porto Grande, the principal port of the Cape Verde Islands, at 10:00 a.m. on April 14, having made the passage at a speed of 12 knots. This resulted in the consumption of about half the coal on board his two cruisers; the *Colon* had 550 tons remaining and the *Maria Teresa* 570 tons. At this period of naval history the availability of sufficient supplies of coal, and the opportunity to take it in, were major considerations in the minds of fleet commanders, and the coming campaign was to prove no exception to this. Cervera now called for the supply of at least 1000 tons of coal.

When he arrived at Porto Grande, Cervera learned that the *Oquendo* and *Vizcaya,* which had been at Puerto Rico, were now on the way to join him; their arrival merely increased the problem of coal supplies, but it was of course welcome that the four major ships of his squadron were now to be concentrated. In due course the collier *San Francisco* arrived, bearing 1000 tons of coal, as well as the promised orders. The captain of the *Maria Teresa*, Victor M Concas y Palau, an old friend of Cervera, wrote angrily of the foolishness of communicating the squadron's orders in this way:

> To send instructions to a modern squadron by means of a steamer of eight knots speed, which was to stop at the Canaries for the purpose of coaling, in place of giving them to the admiral himself, is a proceeding which before the tribunal of history will stand as one of the gravest charges of this period.[17]

Concas also thought it absurd that Cervera's squadron had been ordered direct to Cape Verde, rather than to stop at the Canaries, where all the necessary facilities and supplies were to be found. As it was, Cervera had to pay through the nose to purchase such quantities of coal as were available at Porto Grande. The fact of being sent there had strongly suggested that the purpose of the move was to escort the torpedo flotilla back to mainland Spain. The orders which now arrived put paid to this belief. Written before Cervera had sailed from Cadiz, they anticipated that further orders would be forthcoming but in the meantime set out Cervera's strategic objective:

> As far as the contingencies feared make it possible to determine the objective of the expedition, it will be the defence of island of Puerto Rico. In this operation you will take charge of the naval part, in cooperation with the army, with the concurrence of the Governor General of the island, without forgetting, however, that the plan rests with you alone, in view of your ability, in your capacity as admiral, to measure the forces of our probable enemy, estimate the significance of their movements, as well as the best purposes to which the ships under your command can be put.[18]

Bermejo went on to restate a number of elementary principles of naval warfare, in which Cervera certainly required no tuition.

Reading these orders, it seemed to Cervera that the plan to send the squadron to Cuba had been abandoned, which he thought a wise decision. He was not sure, however, whether the port of San Juan in Puerto Rico would provide adequate protection for the fleet. If not, and if the port of Mayaguez could not be effectively closed, he would find himself in 'a most unfavourable position,' as he pointed out in a letter to Bermejo of April 19. He was really doubtful about the plan to send the squadron to Puerto Rico, observing: 'If Puerto Rico is loyal, it will not be such an easy task for the Yankees; and if it is not loyal, it will inevitably follow the fate of Cuba, at least as far at least as far as we are concerned.' Since Bermejo had suggested that Cervera should convene a council of war of his captains, this was called for April 20.

It was attended by Cervera, Commodore José de Paredes, his second in command, Captains Juan Lazaga. Emilio Diaz Moreu, Victor Concas and Antonio Eulate, of the *Oquendo*, *Colon Maria Teresa* and *Vizcaya* respectively, Captain Joaquin Bustamente, the chief of staff and Captain Fernando Villaamil, commanding the destroyers and torpedo boats. Cervera submitted the following question for consideration: 'Under the present circumstances of the mother country, is it expedient that this fleet should go at once to America, or should it stay to protect our coasts and the Canaries and provide from here for any contingency.' The latter course was firmly held by Concas and Cervera to be the correct decision but the admiral kept his opinion to himself and let his captains reach their own conclusion. The council agreed unanimously to send a telegram to the Minister of Marine proposing that the squadron should move at once to the Canaries. Concas later wrote that it was 'impossible to describe the impression which the reading of the instructions made upon us.' All agreed that for the squadron to go to the West Indies meant the foredooming of its destruction. San Juan had no military protection for the ships. It would be impossible to reach Havana, with the Americans based at Key West and Dry Tortugas; it was not known if Cienfuegos was fortified but in any case it would be closely watched by the enemy, since it was connected by rail to Havana and could easily be blockaded. After crossing the Atlantic, the engines of the squadron would be the worse for wear, and would need at once to coal ship. Concas went on:

> In view of these considerations, which are rigorously exact and have since been repeated by all naval writers of the world, with the exception of a few English publications in bad taste,

> we all agreed that it would be mad, criminal and absurd to go out to surrender the country to the mercy of the enemy, for there was no doubt that the less difficulties the campaign presented to them the more exorbitant would be their demands.[19]

The telegram setting out the council's view was, as first drafted, seen to be too vehement, so a very much milder version was sent in Cervera's name: 'In agreement with the second in command and the commanders of the vessels, I suggest going to the Canaries … all the forces would be in a position, if necessary, to hasten to the defence of the mother country.' When returning to the *Maria Teresa*, Concas told Cervera that this telegram 'hardly expressed what had occurred at the meeting and suggested that everyone at the council should have put their views in a signed statement.'

> The admiral thought a moment, placed his right hand on his forehead, closing his eyes for an instant, then laying his hand on my shoulder, he turned to Bustamente, who was writing, but listening at the same time, and said to him: 'Victor is right!' and shaking me affectionately, as I was still absorbed in profound meditation, he added 'You write it out then.'[20]

Concas demurred, saying that if he did so it would appear to be his own personal views, but Cervera told him to do it, as all were of the same opinion. Accordingly, Concas wrote out a statement setting out the grounds of his opinion, which included a protest at the division of the fleet, a dismissal of the plan of defending Puerto Rico as 'absolutely impracticable,' and an explanation on the way in which, from the Canaries, that point, the coast of mainland and the Balearic Islands could be covered. Cervera sent this to Bermejo next day with a full report of the four hour discussion of which he said the spirit was 'of purest discipline, characterised by the high spirit which animates the whole fleet, and especially the distinguished commanders, who are an honour to Spain and the navy.' In enclosing the statement which Concas had prepared, he added that it represented the average opinion prevailing in the council. Later that day he followed it up with a telegram: 'The more I think about it the more I am convinced that to continue voyage to Puerto Rico would be disastrous. The captains of the ships are of same opinion as I, some more emphatically.'

On April 22 Cervera repeated his view in a further telegram, insisting 'that the result of our voyage to America must be disastrous for the future of our country,' and asking that this telegram and the whole of his correspondence be read to Sagasta. Meanwhile Villaamil, who was himself a deputy, sent a personal telegram that day to Sagasta contending that the sacrifice of the squadron was 'as certain as it was useless and disastrous.'

There was one last chance to avert the inevitable catastrophe; on April 23, the day of Spain's declaration of war, Bermejo convened in Madrid a council of leading naval officers to consider the orders to go to Cervera. In addition to the minister, the meeting was attended by one admiral, four vice admirals, eight rear admirals and five captains. They were not told in advance of the object of the meeting, and hence could not properly prepare for it. Bermejo introduced his own ideas; there followed a vigorous debate before, one by one in reverse order of seniority, each gave his opinion. Captain Ramon Aunon, the most junior, supported the proposal that Cervera should sail at once as did all but five of those present; of these, three favoured waiting for the *Pelayo, Carlos V, Lepanto* and *Alfonso XIII* to be made ready for sea; the other two, while of this view, submitted to the will of the majority.

Thus the die was cast. On April 24 Cervera received his final and explicit orders to complete the coaling of ships and put to sea for San Juan. The process of coaling in fact occupied a further five days, and it was April 29 before the squadron was able to put to sea. Certain it was that Cervera seemed outstandingly the best man to lead the Spanish fleet into battle, admired and implicitly trusted by the men under his command. Wilson wrote of him, however:

> His valour, as subsequent events showed, was above all reproach, while his chivalry and tenderness of heart won the regard of his enemies. In warning the Spanish government persistently and strenuously of the weakness of the navy, he displayed a high degree of moral courage. But it is quite evident that he was by nature despondent and a pessimist, of much the same mental temper as Villeneuve or McClellan, who always saw the defects of the forces they commanded and never those of the enemy; who forgot that, as Abraham Lincoln once said, 'God sends his rain upon the unjust as well as the just.[21]

Wilson goes on to say that Cervera lacked energy and initiative, and was 'crushed by the terrible circumstances in which he found the Spanish navy,' and concludes that 'he was obviously unfit to command upon a desperately dangerous and risky enterprise.' Well, that is one opinion; but given those 'terrible circumstances,' it is hard to conceive of anyone who could have done better.

11

American Preparations

Unlike the Spanish navy, the United States navy had examined the possibility of war with Spain on a number of occasions in the years before 1898, producing a series of outline plans. In 1894 students at the Naval War College looked at the issue as a training exercise, while Lieutenant Commander Charles J Train produced a scheme in which he assumed that Spain would send a fleet across the Atlantic. To meet it, he proposed the occupation of Nipe Bay on Cuba's north-east coast as a base, while the navy would blockade the principal ports. He thought it possible that the enemy might approach Cuba from the south, and head for Santiago de Cuba. In the following year the Naval War College produced a plan which the Navy Department reviewed in 1896. This looked at three options: to attack mainland Spain, to attack Spanish possessions in the Pacific, or to attack Cuba and Puerto Rico. The third option was seen as preferable, with the American forces based at Key West.

This early work was followed by the production of a full-scale war plan drafted by Lieutenant William W Kimball. This assumed a strictly naval war for the liberation of Cuba. The objective would be to gain control of the Florida Straits to facilitate the seizure of Matanzas and Havana. In addition a raiding squadron would harass the commerce of mainland Spain, while another squadron would capture Manila. The Naval War College did not accept Kimball's plan, and revived Train's plan which also allowed for the possibility that Britain might join Spain. Captain Henry C Taylor, the college president, next submitted a synopsis of a plan that called for maximum preparation before launching a campaign against Cuba, with a subsidiary operation in the Philippines. The basis of the plan was to complete the seizure of Havana in thirty days, before the arrival of the main Spanish fleet.[1]

The Navy Department now embarked on a planning process of its own, putting together a group of officers led by Rear Admiral Francis M Ramsay, then Chief of the Bureau of Navigation. This completed its work in December 1896. It proposed a blockade of Cuba and Puerto Rico, and called for military forces to operate alongside the Cuban insurgents. Instead of operating against Manila, the Asiatic Squadron was to proceed to Europe, joining with the squadron there to seize a base in the Canaries and to operate against commerce and the Spanish mainland. This aspect of the plan was heavily criticised by Captain Taylor, who argued for a concentration of effort in the Caribbean. A fresh planning board was set up in June 1897, which extensively revised the plan. The Asiatic Squadron would now attack Manila. The European Squadron would still operate in Spanish waters, but no attempt was to be made to attack the Canaries. The operations in the Caribbean would include the taking of Puerto Rico. Later that summer the Naval War College produced a fresh plan, which made provision to counter any Spanish attack on the Delaware and Chesapeake Bays by concentrating a force there. One feature of all these plans was the basic assumption that the principal war aim was autonomy or independence for Cuba. Apart from a passing suggestion of acquiring the Isle of Pines, there was no proposal for annexations.[2]

These exercises were of course largely academic at a time when the United States government was doing all it could to avert war. For Theodore Roosevelt, though, they were a crucially important activity for a navy that, come what may, must be made ready for war – a war which he devoutly believed would and should come. His bellicose opinions were in sharp contrast not only with those of the president, but also his superior in the Navy Department. Secretary Long had to put up with constant badgering from Roosevelt to put in hand preparations for war. The Assistant Secretary set out the necessity for these:

> If we drift into it, if we do not prepare in advance, and suddenly have to go into hostilities without taking the necessary steps beforehand, we may have to encounter one or two bitter humiliations, and we shall certainly be forced to spend the first three or four most important weeks not in striking, but in making those preparations to strike which we should have made long before.[3]

Long's reaction to Roosevelt's campaign was recorded in his diary: 'He bores me with plans of naval and military movements and the necessity of having some schemes of attack arranged for instant execution in case of an emergency.'[4]

During the period before the destruction of the *Maine* on February 15 1898, Roosevelt's optimism that war would come about waxed and waned, as his correspondence with such as Kimball and Mahan demonstrated. In December, for instance, he had expressed to the former a concern that 'our hopes as to the Spanish business are a dream.' However, with the loss of the *Maine* the situation was totally changed. Perhaps surprisingly, Long rashly left Roosevelt in charge of the Department on February 25. It was an opportunity not to be missed, and Roosevelt grasped it with both hands, as Long's diary recorded:

> Having the authority for that time of Acting Secretary, he immediately began to launch peremptory orders: distributing ships, ordering ammunition, which there is no means to move, to places where there is no means to store it; sending for Captain Barker to come in about the guns of the *Vesuvius*, which is a matter that might have been perfectly arranged by correspondence; sending messages to Congress for immediate legislation, authorising the enlistment of an unlimited number of seamen; and ordering guns from the Navy Yard at Washington to New York, with a view to arming auxiliary cruisers which are now in peaceful commercial pursuit... He has gone at things like a bull in a china shop, and with the best purposes in the world has really taken what, if he could have thought, he would not for a moment have taken; and that is the one course that is most discourteous to me, because it suggests that there has been a lack of attention which he was applying. It shows how the best fellow in the world – and with splendid capacities – is worse than no use if he lacks a cool head and careful discretion.[5]

Some of Roosevelt's orders Long felt obliged to revoke; one that he did not was the famous message of that day to Dewey, ordering him to Hong Kong and keep full of coal, and identifying his ultimate objective as being 'offensive operations in Philippine Islands.' This was not, as David Trask points out, inconsistent with the planning that had taken place within the Department; 'it was no surprise, but rather a logical step at the time… Roosevelt did not originate the order; he simply decided the timing of its transmission.'[6] Roosevelt, of course, was quite unrepentant, telling Henry Cabot Lodge that he had 'continually meddled in what was not my business, because I was willing to jeopardise my position in a way that a naval officer could not.'

The superiority of the American fleet to that of Spain, so painfully apparent to Admiral Cervera, was unquestionable. Its principal strength lay in the five battleships previously described: these were the *Texas, Indiana, Massachusetts, Oregon* and *Iowa*. In addition there were the two armoured cruisers *Brooklyn* and *New York*, somewhat larger than the Spanish armoured cruisers. The *New York*, laid down in 1892, was of 8,150 tons displacement, mounting six 8-inch guns, with twelve 4-inch quickfirers and some lesser guns. She had a waterline armoured belt of four inches, and a protective deck of six inches on the slope and four inches on the flat. Her trial speed was 21 knots. The *Brooklyn* represented an improvement; laid down in 1893, she displaced 9,100 tons, and carried eight 8-inch guns with twelve six pounders and some smaller guns. She was armoured similarly to the *New York*, save that her waterline belt was three inches. Her trial speed was 21.9 knots.

Among the 14 protected cruisers, the *Olympia*, flagship of Dewey's Asiatic Squadron, was certainly the best. Laid down in 1890, she displaced 5,800 tons, and carried four 8-inch guns and ten 5-inch quickfirers. Her trial speed was 21.25 knots. The remaining cruisers of the Asiatic Squadron were the protected cruisers *Boston* (3,000 tons) *Raleigh* (3,213 tons) and *Baltimore* (4,313 tons) and the unprotected cruisers *Concord* (1,710 tons) and Petrel (892 tons). The other protected cruisers were the *Charleston* (3,730 tons) based in San Francisco, *Columbia* and *Minneapolis* (both of 7,375 tons) *Newark* and *San Francisco* (4,098 tons). The *New Orleans* (3,437 tons) was purchased in Britain where she was being built for Brazil; her sister ship, named *Albany*, was also purchased, but was not released in time to take part in hostilities. There was also the *Cincinnati*, of 3,213 tons. There were 20 unprotected cruisers, of which two as described above were with the Asiatic Squadron. The US navy also possessed six unwieldy monitors, which were essentially coast defence vessels and unsuited to any sort of fleet action. There were eight torpedo boats, all based in the Atlantic.

Both Spain and the United States sought to strengthen their naval forces by purchases abroad. The Spanish navy took over fourteen ships of the Compania Transatlantica to serve as transports and in some cases as armed merchant cruisers, and also purchased three large German merchant vessels, the *Normannia*, *Columbia* and *Havel*, which were renamed *Patriota*, *Rapido* and *Meteor* respectively. Capable of 19 knots, they were armed with four 6.4-inch and four 4.7-inch guns; they were not available before the middle of May. The Americans also pressed into service a large number of merchant vessels, including four large steamships of the American Line, *St Paul*, *St Louis*, *New York* (renamed *Harvard*) and the *Paris* (renamed *Yale*); in due course they were armed with between four and eight 5-inch guns. They were capable of 22 knots, and had a high coal capacity, enabling them to remain at sea for long periods.[7] It has been calculated that the Navy Department spent a total of over $21 million. The acquisitions included not only warships from Europe, and merchant vessels purchased or chartered from various sources, but also revenue cutters, lighthouse tenders and, oddly, vessels of the Fish Commission, and amounted in all to 131 additional vessels.[8]

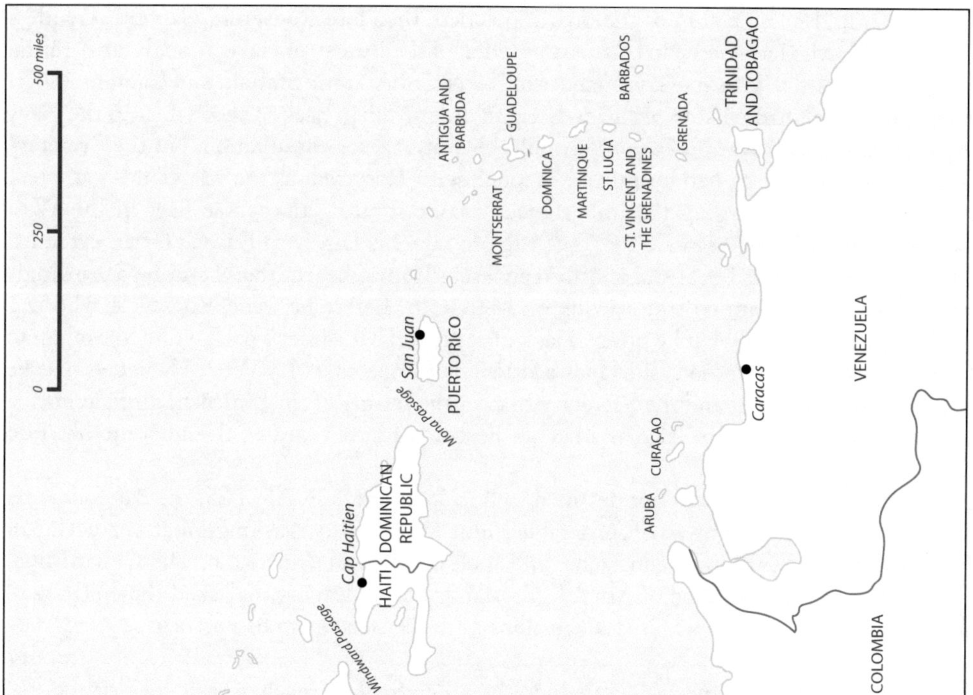

2 General Map of the West Indies.

Until the loss of the *Maine*, the work of the Navy Department in devising the strategy to be adopted and in the preparation of war plans was left to a number of ad hoc groups assembled for the purpose. In March, however, Long set up a permanent group known as the Naval War Board. The initial membership of the board included Theodore Roosevelt, Captain Arendt S Crowninshield, who had succeeded Ramsay as Chief of the Bureau of Navigation, Rear Admiral Montgomery Sicard, the former commander of the North Atlantic Station, and Captain Albert S Barker. Roosevelt had tried to persuade Long to order Mahan back to active duty in the Navy Department, so that if war broke out he would be available for consultation, but the Secretary declined to do so. Mahan had been in close touch with Roosevelt as the war clouds gathered, and had been strongly urging the importance of concentrating the whole fleet in the West Indies. He had, however, planned for some time to take his family to Europe for an extended vacation, to enable his 15-year-old son to recuperate from a heart attack, and he accordingly went ahead with his planned trip, leaving on March 26. Before he went, Roosevelt, who was increasingly dismayed by what he saw as a lack of action on McKinley's part, wrote to Mahan to tell him that he had forwarded all Mahan's letters to Sampson at Key West. He added that he had 'advised the President and the Secretary to treat the sailing of the [Spanish] torpedo flotilla from the Canaries for Puerto Rico as an act of hostility. I have repeated the advice today. I do not think it will be regarded.'[9]

Mahan's visit to Europe was not destined to be a long one. On April 25, the day following Spain's formal declaration of war, Long cabled him to return to Washington at once. Mahan duly shaved off his beard and moustache, and took passage for America on the Cunard liner *Etruria*, travelling in the name of Mr AT Maitland. Before leaving, he asked the embassy to cable the Navy Department with his suggestions as to the strategy to be pursued:

> First, if two or three enemy's battleships enter Puerto Rico or elsewhere, they should at once be blocked by a force superior to any combination possible by the enemy at the moment. Second, in such case, and in existing conditions, it seems probable that Havana could be left to light vessels swift enough to escape if unfortunately surprised by superior force. Third, it is improbable enemy fleet would seek to enter Havana adding to the burden of food subsistence, unless meaning to fight, which of course we wish. Fourth, M does not think any enemy large ship would venture to enter any of our Atlantic ports. Torpedo vessels might, but they can be handled. Fifth, M heartily approves naval strategy up to date, especially refusing to oppose ships to their Havana forts. He would not favour any dispersal of battleships, as he is reported to have done, to guard ports against attack. Sixth, M requests secrecy as to his movements till his return.[10]

One of Mahan's biographers, Robert W Seager, suggests that this message may not have reached the Navy Department, and in any case had little or no effect on subsequent events. Nevertheless, his recommendations contained several points of interest. There is no suggestion that operations in European waters should be pursued, and he added his voice to those opposed to dispersing units of the fleet to protect America's eastern coastline. This last was becoming a considerable problem for the administration, since the prospect of the sailing of Cervera's squadron for an unknown destination had aroused very considerable public anxiety in the United States. It was an issue with which Long, politically speaking, had to deal; and it had led to the division of the fleet which Mahan so strenuously opposed.

On March 20 Schley had received a telephone call from the Navy Secretary asking him to come to the Department. He assumed that it was in connection with the offer which he had made, as chairman of the Lighthouse Board, of a number of vessels for service with the navy. When he got there, Long told him that the president had selected him to command the Flying Squadron which was being assembled, and wanted to know how soon he would be ready to assume command. Schley said that he would be ready next day. It was the first that he knew of the possibility, as he recounted in his memoirs, but then and later he was sensitive to the possible suggestion of any undue influence having been applied to obtain the post. He was careful in his memoirs to address the point:

> He had not intimated, or suggested, or authorised the suggestion of his name in connection with this matter to anyone. The assignment came to him without solicitation in any form on his part. If it was made in deference to the wishes of his friends, it was without his knowledge.[11]

Harold M Langley suggests that the choice of Schley for this high-profile post was probably due to Roosevelt's influence. It was one which was widely acclaimed in the press, and it was this that Long had in his mind when inducing the president to follow his recommendations.[12] The Navy Secretary, when he came to write his own memoirs, had by then become heavily involved in the controversies that followed the ending of the war, and explained his selection of Schley in somewhat qualified terms:

> Among his naval associates Schley was not credited with as high a measure of professional ability as Sampson and some other officers. Nevertheless his career was filled with stirring incidents which had their scenes in the War of the Rebellion, in the frozen North, where he voluntarily went in search of Greely and his daring companions, and in other parts of the world where American interests demanded protection. He had been Chief of the Bureau of Equipment, had commanded a vessel of the New Navy, and appeared to be an officer of skill, judgement, and resource.[13]

Long also had to address the question of the command of the North Atlantic Squadron, in effect America's principal battle fleet. The commander on that station, Rear Admiral Montgomery Sicard, had been suffering from ill health, and retired from the post on March 26. As had been the case in the appointment of Schley over the heads of several officers senior to him in the Navy List, Long was prepared to make the crucially important appointment without regard to seniority. In choosing Sampson he was confident that he had picked the officer best qualified for the post. Sampson had been serving as Captain of the *Iowa* and as chief of staff to Rear Admiral Sicard, and of course had most recently been chairing the court of inquiry into the sinking of the *Maine*. Long, in his memoirs, recorded his reasons for his choice:

> The moment required a man of splendid judgement, quick decision, possessing intimate knowledge of the characteristics of the vessels he would have to use, and the officers and men manning them, and enjoying the esteem and confidence of his subordinates. The consensus of naval opinion was that Sampson had these qualifications. He had graduated number one in his class at the Naval Academy, and this without social prestige. He had

> maintained this superiority throughout his naval career. He had been a dominant voice in important boards which had considered the development of the material and personnel of the new navy. He was the senior captain of the North Atlantic Squadron, and in command of it during Sicard's incapacity. He enjoyed the full confidence not only of the officers and men of his own ship, but of the officers and men of the entire navy. There was no political demand for Sampson. He had no friends in Congress to speak to him, nor did he directly or indirectly indicate to the Department that he desired to succeed Rear Admiral Sicard.[14]

Chadwick, who was devoted to Sampson, serving throughout the war as his flag captain and chief of staff, recorded that the appointment was a great surprise to Sampson: 'He felt no elation in it; he felt too deeply the great responsibility to which he had been elected.' Chadwick went on to describe Sampson as 'the hero by nature, for nature made him good without thought of self; of incomparable simplicity and truthfulness; quiet and reserved, though most kindly; with never a harsh word; with absolute courage both physical and moral.'[15] There were moments in the days and months to come when Sampson did not altogether live up to this character study but there is no doubt that he was greatly respected by his captains in particular. Perhaps HW Wilson's assessment is a little more dispassionate: 'His judgement, perhaps, was never very severely tested, owing to the amazing mistakes of the enemy. But all that he planned and did seems to have been sound and judicious, with the possible exception of his wish to bombard Havana.'[16]

Schley received his formal orders from Long on March 24; four days later he proceeded to Hampton Roads and thence to Newport News, where he assumed command of the Flying Squadron, hoisting his broad pennant on the *Brooklyn*. When he arrived, he found that work was being done to renew the elevating gear of her turret guns, while the ship was being painted drab grey in readiness for war. The battleship *Massachusetts* was at the same anchorage undergoing some repairs. As soon as both vessels had completed the repairs they moved to an anchorage off Fortress Monroe, where the battleship *Texas* was already anchored. Schley was soon joined by the cruisers *Minneapolis* and *Columbia*, but these were then detached and sent to cruise off the north-east coast, where the appearance of isolated Spanish ships, which had been feared would launch an attack there, had already been reported, albeit quite incorrectly. In due course they were replaced as part of the Flying Squadron by the *New Orleans*, the brand-new cruiser purchased from Brazil which had just been completed in England, and the *Scorpion*, a newly purchased steam yacht.

It was the loudly expressed alarm for the security of her eastern seaboard which led the United States to establish the Flying Squadron, and which resulted in that squadron being retained at Hampton Roads rather than at any anchorage further south. Indeed, the division of the fleet was a serious strategic error, as Wilson pointed out:

> When war came, every town and village on the seaboard wanted fortifications or ships to defend it. A few guns of moderate calibre might no doubt have been needed to protect important places on the coast against the raids of cruisers. But these inordinate demands, to which, in a democracy, some concession had to be made, hampered the American strategists grievously... Theoretically, it may be the soundest policy to place every ship in the foremost line, close up to or watching the enemy. Practically, it is impossible unless the public has thoroughly grasped and understood the principles of naval war. As the Press

> guides and directs opinion, the importance of censorship not only upon war news, but also upon the comments on war news, is very evident.[17]

The decision to form the Flying Squadron had been taken on March 17, two days after Roosevelt's strategy meeting, as a response to the recommendations that had been made. It was a step derided by the responsible leaders of the U.S. navy, all of whom saw perfectly clearly that the fleet should be concentrated for operations off the Cuban coast; but for the reasons noted by Wilson, the Navy Department felt obliged to defer to public opinion. Typical of naval opinion was the scathing comment of Captain Robley Evans: 'the Flying Squadron was the badge of democracy, the sop to the quaking laymen whose knowledge of strategy derived solely from their terror of a sudden attack by Cervera.'[18]

The delay while the Flying Squadron was held at Hampton Roads at least gave Schley the opportunity to prepare it for what lay ahead:

> Time was taken to organise the squadron and put it upon a war footing. Pickets and patrols were thrown out towards the capes of Virginia; lights were masked, officers were required to be on board at sundown; leaves of absence beyond signal distance were withdrawn; sea watches were ordered and the surveillance maintained day and night. Gun practice with the sub-calibre guns was ordered and was maintained every day regardless of the weather, leading up to very great precision and skill, as attested later in action. A short cruise for a few days off the capes was made to exercise the squadron in technical manoeuvres, to inculcate alertness, quick signalling and to hold their places in battle order near each other for mutual support or attack.[19]

On March 23 orders were issued by the Navy Department to prepare for a blockade of Cuba, in accordance with the long held opinions of Mahan. It would close the western half of Cuba's northern coastline, including both Havana and Matanzas. Outside Havana, the first line of the blockade would be a screen of torpedo boats and revenue cutters, with the second line of protected cruisers and a third line of armoured vessels. When they received the details of this plan Sampson and Chadwick demurred. While accepting the importance of preserving the major units of the fleet all the time that the enemy forces remained intact, Sampson wrote to Long on April 9 to set out an alternative proposal, which was immediately the war broke out to launch an attack directly on Havana. He listed the batteries protecting the port, which he conceded were 'well calculated to keep off a fleet from seaward, which approaches to within a moderate distance of a few thousand yards.' However, he went on:

> I do not think they are well-placed to resist an attack (for instance, the western batteries) from the westward and close inshore where the batteries would be exposed to a flank fire, or to the fire of our big ships at short range, where the secondary batteries would have full effect. Even under these circumstances the ships must have such a heavy fire that the men in the batteries would be overwhelmed by its volume. Before the *Puritan* and *Amphitrite* arrived I was not entirely sanguine of the success of such an attack. Since their arrival yesterday I have little doubt of its success. Although the monitors are weak in secondary fire I expected to put a cruiser with heavy secondary fire between each two of them. In this way I do not think the Spaniards would be able to fire. They would be driven away from

> their guns and kept away, while the fire of the ships would so injure the guns or mountings that they would be unserviceable… Having silenced the western batteries, it would be quite practicable to shell the city, which I would do only after warning given 24 hours in advance.[20]

Sampson added that all his captains united with him that a direct attack was sufficiently promising to justify the attempt. He was in little doubt that the operation would result in the speedy surrender of the city with little resistance.

The Navy Department was not, however, convinced and forbade the operation; anticipating that a major fleet action and eventually take place, it was felt that the risks to Sampson's armoured ships from the land batteries and mines were too great to be accepted in the meantime. Mahan later endorsed this view: 'no merely possible success justified risk, unless it gave a fair promise of diminishing the enemy's naval force, and so of deciding the control of the sea, upon which the issue of the war depended.'[21] Wilson was of an even more decided opinion: 'It must be doubtful whether there was any real prospect of success against Havana.' He went on to list examples of bombardments of fortified positions such as Charleston, Lissa, Alexandria and, during this war, at San Juan and Santiago which 'have shown that ships can rarely be trusted to silence even weak and ill constructed batteries.'[22] In launching such an attack, Wilson thought, the American fleet would have had to suffer severely at a time when Cervera might at any moment appear.

Chadwick, when he came to write his history of the war, was unrepentant. He reviewed in detail the batteries defending the harbour at Havana, and concluded that had the attack been made it was 'scarcely supposable' that the city would not have surrendered, 'with the guns of the fleet but a few hundred yards distant pointing up its streets and also directly into the harbour.' And he also dismissed any humanitarian objections to the making of such an attack, with an argument that has considerable resonance in the context of later wars:

> War is war. Its results are of such stupendous importance that they take on somewhat the character of the convulsions of nature, which destroys and constructs without reference, so far as we can see, to questions of humanity. Man is doing in this last what he can, but his efforts must ever be of slight effect in face of the overpowering necessity of success. The rules of war allow the bombardment of fortified places even to their destruction. Only seventeen years before were Strasbourg and Paris bombarded until they yielded, without reference to the extent of destruction, whether of life or property.[23]

On April 18 Sampson issued preparatory orders for the blockade of Cuba, providing for detachments of his squadron to cover respectively Havana, Mariel, Matanzas and Cardenas. When war broke out, he intended to approach within sight of Havana with his entire force, before detaching the vessels assigned to blockade the other ports. Now, all the squadron could do was wait. On April 21, however, Sampson, marooned at Key West, received a telegram from Long formally assigning him to his command with the rank of rear admiral. This was quickly followed by instructions to implement the blockade forthwith:

> Blockade coast of Cuba immediately from Cardenas to Bahia Honda. Blockade Cardenas if it is considered advisable. Issue a proclamation of blockade covering the blockaded ports

> according to terms contained in my letter of April 6. Do not bombard. Permit neutrals now loading to come out.[24]

Schley, meanwhile, remained at Hampton Roads, awaiting the formal outbreak of war. Although he had been deprived of the *Minneapolis* and *Columbia*, his squadron was reinforced by the arrival of the *New Orleans*. Meanwhile the North Atlantic Squadron was about to be reinforced by the battleship *Oregon*, which had been based on the Pacific coast and which was ordered to sail around South America to join the fleet. It was a remarkable venture, which exposed the vessel to the theoretical risk of being attacked by the Spanish as she made her lone way up through the South Atlantic. She had left Puget Sound on March 6, reaching San Francisco by March 19. After rounding the Horn, she reached Rio de Janeiro on April 30, where Captain Clark learned that Cervera's squadron was at sea. He later wrote:

> I felt that the chances were that Cervera was bound to the West Indies, and that the need of the *Oregon* there was so great that the risk of his turning south to meet me should be run; so I hurried to Bahia, and cabled to the Department my opinion of what the *Oregon* might do alone and in a running fight… My object was to add the *Oregon* to our fleet, and not to meet the Spaniards if it could be avoided.[25]

The *Oregon* left Rio on May 4 with the gunboat *Marietta* and the merchant vessel *Nictheroy* in company, but they slowed her so much that Clark went on alone. After several alarms he finally reached the coast of Florida on May 24, and proceeded to join Sampson after taking on coal and water. She had covered 14,700 nautical miles in 79 days, averaging a speed of 11.6 knots.

While the more or less entirely professional navy was thus in an advanced state of preparedness, the same could not be said for the army, which would have to depend to a large extent on the raising of volunteer forces. The professional peacetime army of the United States was miniscule; a total of some 28,183 men were scattered in small units across half a continent. By an act of Congress of April 22 the army was constituted in two branches, the first being the regular army and the second the volunteer army. The regular army was to be increased by August to 56,365; the president called for a volunteer army of 125,000 men, in accordance with the act of Congress; this was increased in May by a further 75,000. There were also to be three volunteer cavalry regiments, one of which became Theodore Roosevelt's Rough Riders. His friend Colonel Leonard Wood was the first commander of the regiment, Roosevelt being second-in-command. Later he was to take command when Wood was promoted. Eight army corps were to be established, under Major Generals John R Brooke, William R Graham, James I Wade, John J Coppinger, William R Shafter, James H Wilson, Fitzhugh Lee and Wesley Merritt. The sixth of these, under Wilson, was finally not organised. The Secretary of the War Department, Russell A Alger, had a difficult personal relationship with the commanding general of the army, Major General Nelson A Miles. Both men were vain; but where Alger was cautious and slow to take decisions, Miles was impulsive. The latter had a high national reputation earned in campaigns against Indian fighters; Roosevelt, however, dismissed him as a 'brave Peacock.'[26]

Predictably, there had been little work done in advance of the war to define the military strategy to be adopted. Nor had proper consideration been given to the equipment of the large number of volunteer forces that were being raised. Historians have been virtually unanimous in their criticism of Alger for his complacent approach to the preparations that needed to be made. He did, however, make a start on assembling an expeditionary force when he ordered the concentration of twenty two infantry regiments at the Gulf ports of New Orleans, Mobile and Tampa, and six cavalry regiments at Chickamauga in Tennessee. For his part, Miles was doubtful about launching a full-scale invasion of Cuba; the troops would face a very substantial Spanish army, would be threatened by disease, and could not be transported to Cuba until the Spanish naval forces had been destroyed. He wrote to Alger on April 18:

> By using such force as might be necessary to harass the enemy, and doing them the greatest injury with the least possible loss to ourselves, if our Navy is superior to theirs, we can compel the surrender of the army on the island of Cuba with very little loss of life.[27]

The scale of the problem faced by the American army can be shown by the numerical superiority of its opponents. The official strength of the whole Spanish army in 1898 was 492,067. Of this figure, 152,284 were based in Spain and the adjacent islands; 51,331 (both regulars and volunteers) were in the Philippines; 10,005 (both regulars and volunteers) were in Puerto Rico; and the rest were in Cuba. Again including regulars and volunteers, this left 278,457 men in Cuba for the defence of the island. However, the army there was fully occupied in dealing with the insurgents and it was undoubtedly the case that the actual number of troops available there was well below the official figure. The regular troops were probably of the order of 150,000, supported by perhaps 80,000 volunteers, many of whom were of doubtful fighting value.[28]

12

'You May Fire When You Are Ready, Gridley'

Commodore George Dewey had been ordered on October 21, 1897 to relieve Acting Rear Admiral McNair in command of the Asiatic Squadron. As a recent biographer has pointed out, he was somewhat fortunate to have been selected for such a desirable command; he had not been to sea for eight years, and had had only four years sea duty in the previous twenty. He had got the job largely through political influence, mainly due to the efforts of Theodore Roosevelt.[1]

Dewey set off for the Far East bearing a considerable grudge. Unlike his predecessors as commander-in-chief of the Asiatic Squadron, he had not been raised to the rank of acting rear admiral, a custom intended to put them on the same level as the local commanders of European squadrons. This slight appears to have been due to Navy Secretary Long's disapproval of the use of political influence to gain appointment, although the latter, in his memoirs, claimed that his selection of Dewey had nothing to do with political or personal influence, and was entirely his own decision. Of course, by the time that Long came to write his memoirs, Dewey had become a national hero, and Long was not averse to claiming credit where he could. In his own memoirs Dewey himself candidly admitted the efforts which Roosevelt and Senator Proctor had made on his behalf, observing that Rear Admiral Arendt S Crowninshield, the chief of the Bureau of Navigation, would hardly have recommended him to any command. He added, with some satisfaction, that when he saw Crowninshield after his appointment, the bureau chief seemed none too pleased about it.[2] Indeed, Dewey was inclined to think that it was Crowninshield who decided that he should not be made acting rear admiral.

Dewey was to leave San Francisco for Japan on December 7, so had time to do something about preparing for a war that few people in Washington really expected:

> Whether there was likelihood of war or not, it was my duty to make sure that the squadron was properly prepared for any emergency and that not a single precaution was left to chance. Enquiry about the quantity of ammunition in the squadron developed the fact that there was not even a peace allowance. Although a further supply had been ordered, no one had seemed to think it necessary to facilitate its shipment, thanks largely to the red tape of official conservatism.[3]

Discovering that further delays in shipping the ammunition were expected, Dewey, with Roosevelt's help, arranged for the small gunboat *Concord*, then fitting out for far Eastern service, to take half the ammunition required, while the rest was carried by the cruiser *Baltimore*.

Dewey took up his new command at Nagasaki on January 3, when he hoisted his broad pennant on his flagship, the protected cruiser *Olympia*, resplendent in her peacetime white and buff livery. The rest of the squadron consisted of the small cruiser *Boston*, the gunboat *Petrel* and the extremely ancient *Monocacy*, a paddle steamer dating from the Civil War. The *Monocacy* was destined to play no part in the war; she was in harbour at Shanghai, and when hostilities broke out she was laid up, and her crew employed on other duties. When Dewey arrived in Japan, the *Boston* was on duty at Chemulpo in Korea, ready to land marines to protect the American Embassy at Seoul if the unsettled situation necessitated it, while the *Petrel* was en route to Canton where she was to observe the Chinese New Year celebrations, which sometimes led to anti-foreign demonstrations.

On January 15 Dewey sailed for Yokohama, taking a train to Tokyo on February 1 for an audience with the Emperor, which greatly impressed him. Ten days later, the *Concord* having joined him with her vital cargo of ammunition, Dewey sailed for Hong Kong, arriving on February 17. On the following day he received news of the destruction of the *Maine*. Then, on February 25, he received Roosevelt's historic cable:

> Order the squadron except the *Monocacy* to Hong Kong. Keep full of coal. In the event of declaration of war Spain, your duty will be to see that the Spanish squadron does not leave the Asiatic coast, and then offensive operations in Philippine Islands. Keep *Olympia* until further orders.[4]

Roosevelt had sent this message, and a number of others, to squadron commanders all over the world, to put the navy in a state of readiness for war, in the absence of Long, who was undergoing medical treatment that day. The Navy Secretary was apparently far from pleased at this initiative; he wrote in his diary: 'During my short absence I find that Roosevelt, in his precipitate way, has come very near causing more of an explosion than happened to the *Maine*... The very devil seemed to possess him yesterday afternoon.'[5] In point of fact, however, the instruction to Dewey was perfectly consistent with the strategy agreed upon by the Navy Department, and Long made no complaint about it in his memoirs.

In Hong Kong, Dewey had been joined by the *Petrel*. The cruiser *Raleigh* was expected soon from the Mediterranean, and orders had gone to the *Boston* to join the squadron. It was also to be reinforced by the cruiser *Baltimore* and the revenue cutter *McCulloch*; the first of these was bringing the rest of the reserve ammunition ordered for the squadron. Dewey found the harbour at Hong Kong crowded with men of war of different nationalities, and noted that ' there was a feeling of restlessness and uncertainty in the air.' Among the foreign officers there was Prince Henry, the Kaiser's brother; after a period of coolness due to a misunderstanding over the American national anthem, Dewey got on rather well with the prince, whom he found 'a charming companion and a thorough sailor... Although brought up in the strict forms of court etiquette, he was delighted to cut adrift from conventionalism whenever circumstances would permit.'[6]

Long had been keeping Dewey informed of the deteriorating diplomatic situation, and the latter used his time in Hong Kong to complete his preparations for war, purchasing the British collier *Nanshan* with its supply of coal, and the steamer *Zafiro* as a supply ship. He also secretly took steps to ensure future supplies of coal when needed, and mindful of the neutrality laws selected Mirs Bay, on the Chinese mainland, as a place for receiving supplies or making repairs to any damaged ship. Dewey did not suppose that the Chinese government could effectively uphold the international law of neutrality, unlike the British Crown Colony of Hong Kong.

On April 17 the *McCulloch* arrived, followed on April 22 by the *Baltimore*. In the meantime the squadron was painted a dull grey in readiness for battle. Another arrival was Commander Benjamin Lamberton, who had been assigned to take command of the *Boston*. The latter's captain, Frank Wildes, was extremely reluctant to give up his command, and Dewey made Lamberton his chief of staff. He also made an important change of senior officers of the *Olympia*, invaliding home her executive officer and replacing him with Lieutenant Rees, from the *Monocacy*. The flagship's captain, Charles Gridley, was also unwell, but Dewey had not the heart to send him away at such a moment.

News that war was imminent led Dewey to send the *Boston*, *Concord*, *McCulloch*, *Nanshan* and *Zafiro* to Mirs Bay on April 24; the governor of Hong Kong had formally notified Dewey of the war neutrality proclamation, and he sailed next day with the rest of the squadron, consisting of the *Olympia, Raleigh* and *Baltimore*. Meanwhile Dewey had gained a valuable public relations adjunct. Accompanying Lamberton on a steamer from Yokohama was the journalist Joseph L Stickney, who recorded that when they arrived at Hong Kong they saw the squadron still in the harbour: 'and simultaneously the same thought flashed through our minds, and together we cried 'They're grey! They're grey! This means war!"[7] Stickney, a former naval officer, asked if he might come aboard the *Olympia* for the campaign, promising to send only news approved by the commodore, and Dewey appointed him as his aide.

In Mirs Bay Dewey was anxiously awaiting the arrival of Consul Williams from Manila, from whom he hoped to learn the latest intelligence of the Spanish preparations. Williams had been sending a stream of important reports about the situation there. At 12:15 p.m. on April 25 Dewey received the momentous cable from Navy Secretary Long:

> War has commenced between the United States and Spain. Proceed at once to Philippine Islands. Commence operations particularly against the Spanish fleet. You must capture vessels or destroy. Use utmost endeavours.[8]

Believing that Williams would soon arrive, Dewey delayed his departure from Mirs Bay, and was rewarded on the morning of April 27 by the sight of the tugboat *Fame* bringing the consul to join the squadron with important news, which Dewey found 'anything but encouraging:'

> It upset my preconceived ideas, as I had counted upon fighting in Manila Bay. Just as the consul was leaving Manila he had learned of the sailing of the Spanish squadron for Subig Bay. Thus Admiral Montojo at the last moment seemed to have realised the strategic advantage of Subig over Manila, which we had hoped he would fail to do.[9]

Nevertheless, Dewey set off from Mirs Bay at 2 p.m. on April 27, full of confidence; he had written to his son on April 7 that his squadron would be far superior to the Spanish, adding: 'I think it will be short work for us.' However, in December 1899, perhaps unnecessarily anxious that his achievements should not be belittled, Dewey was to write to the journalist LA Pradt, firmly but unconvincingly stating the opposite:

> The enemy's force was unquestionably superior to ours. Once you are inside the bay the fleet had guns to its front and rear. It would have been possible for those guns, properly served,

> to disable all our ships. The defences of Manila can't be fairly estimated without considering these guns and the mines in the bay and the channels.[10]

Dewey similarly talked up the potential strength of the Spanish position in his autobiography; but as HW Wilson pointed out in his account of the battle of Manila Bay it was unnecessary to do so. Observing that the information brought by Consul Williams of the disorganisation and lack of preparation by the Spanish in Manila may have 'contributed in no small degree to the bold and decided course adopted by the American commander,' he remarked that this would not derogate from his high reputation.

Dewey enjoyed one particular advantage over Montojo, quite apart from the massive fighting superiority of his squadron, and that was in the captains of the ships, upon whom he knew he could rely absolutely. In the weeks before the outbreak of war he had ensured that they were entirely familiar with the tactics which he intended to pursue. In particular, he had assured them that the threat of mines could be discounted; the depth of water and the strong current in the approaches to Manila Bay would render mining operations extremely difficult, even if the Spanish had sufficient expertise, which they had not. In any case mines would deteriorate quickly in warm tropical waters.[11]

The Spanish plan to transfer their squadron to Subig Bay derived from the report of a commission headed by Capt Julio del Rio, which had in 1891 produced a report on the subject of the defence of the Philippines. This asserted that it was impossible to prevent any enemy squadron from entering Manila Bay unless it was opposed by one of at least equal strength. It went on to propose that the Spanish squadron should be based on Subig Bay which should be turned into a fortified harbour. There, the narrow main channel was only a mile wide, and the Spanish squadron could be deployed so as to envelop the enemy squadron with its fire. The attackers could not risk entering Manila Bay with an undefeated squadron in their rear. Del Rio had concluded his report in ominous terms: 'if the voice of reason is heard, we await the enemy at Subig. If certain material interests prevail, we await him off Manila.'[12]

Montojo himself had entirely accepted the logic of del Rio's suggestions. Although not much had been done to carry these into effect, he had made his position clear to the governor general on March 15, when he told him that his 'poor squadron would not be able to withstand the onslaught of the American ships'and that it would be destroyed. Asked what steps should be taken, he replied:

> Considering that I have heard your Excellency say repeatedly that the port of Subig would have to be the refuge of our ships in extreme cases and that said port possessed exceptional qualifications as a military port, I suggest that it be fortified, if only temporarily, at the earliest possible moment, so that our fleet may repair to it and there await the enemy, provided they come at all, keeping the fleet in readiness, in case Manila should be assaulted, to hasten there at night and attack the Americans unexpectedly.[13]

Del Rio, who was serving as the naval commandant of Subig Bay, supervised the preparations there, including the sinking of three vessels to close the eastern entrance. However, the erection of fortifications on the island of Isla Grande, two fifths of the way up Subig Bay, was not taken in hand, and nor had the four 5.9-inch guns, which had been taken to Subig Bay, been mounted.

Montojo sailed from Manila Bay to Subig Bay on the night of April 25/26 with the cruisers *Reina Cristina*, *Don Juan de Austria*, *Isla de Cuba*, *Isla de Luzon*, the dispatch vessel *Marques del Duero* and the old wooden cruiser *Castillo*. On the morning of April 26 he met with del Rio, who endeavoured to reassure him that although the defensive works were not yet complete, they soon would be. The *Castillo* was found to be taking on water heavily, and although the leaks were patched up with cement, it meant that her engines could not be used, so on April 27 Montojo had her towed to a position on the east side of the Isla Grande to cover the western entrance to the bay. He then made an unpalatable discovery:

> With much disgust I found that the guns which should have been mounted on that island still needed a month and a half to be got in position. This surprised me, as the shore batteries that the Navy had installed (with no little difficulty) at the entrance of the Bay of Manila, under the intelligent direction of Colonel of naval artillery Señor Garces and Lieutenant Commander Benevento, were ready to fire twenty four days after the commencement of the work. I was also disgusted that so little confidence was to be placed in the efficacy of the few torpedoes which they had found feasible to put there.[14]

This meant that Subig Bay, instead of being a readily defensible base for the Spanish squadron, would effectively become a trap in which it would almost certainly be destroyed. Montojo, by now aware that Dewey had sailed from Mirs Bay, convened a council of war. All those present, except for del Rio, accepted Montojo's conviction that the situation was 'unsustainable,' and it was agreed that the squadron should return to Manila Bay and fight there under less unfavourable conditions. The location in which it was agreed to accept battle was Canacao Bay, from which the squadron would be able to combine its fire with that of the batteries of Point Sangley and Ulloa.

In making this decision the unfortunate Montojo and his captains were in no doubt of the outcome of the conflict that lay immediately ahead of them. In considering what to do next, Montojo had three possible courses of action. The first of these, which is apparently the option which he was inclined to favour, was to recognise the inevitable in terms of his squadron's inability to defend itself against overwhelming odds, to land his crews, their guns and ammunition, and fight the invaders from onshore leaving his ships to be scuttled or blown up when Dewey's squadron appeared. But Montojo was subject to the orders of the military governor of the Philippines, General Basilio Augustin Davila, who would not countenance this. Secondly, Montojo might confront Dewey with his four serviceable warships, and perhaps by a sudden assault in the darkness while the Americans were passing Corregidor, inflict serious damage on the enemy, possibly with the use of the ram. Finally there was the option actually chosen, which was to anchor the ships under the guns of the land batteries, and fight the enemy from there.[15]

There remained the question of where the Spanish squadron should anchor to receive the coming assault. It was decided to locate the ships in position off Cavite, rather than off Manila itself, in order to spare the civilian population of the city. As Wilson points out, this was a seriously mistaken policy:

> Had the Spanish vessels drawn up in front of the latter place, projectiles from the American squadron must have exploded in the city. But though few will blame Montojo for his anxiety to save the civilian population from suffering and injury, it was a military mistake

> not to take position under the far more powerful batteries of Manila, when the issue of the engagement might have been different. The general or admiral must in war steel his heart and neglect no advantage.[16]

Montojo's largest vessel was the wooden *Castillo*, of no fighting value save as a floating battery. Getting her to and from Subig Bay had proved extremely difficult. Now, she was moored with lighters filled with sand on her seaward side. Only her port battery could be brought into action, and some of her remaining guns had been removed. The *Ulloa* was moored just behind Sangley Point, in Canacao Bay, in her case with her starboard battery bearing; her port side guns had been removed to strengthen the land batteries. The *Velasco* was moored off Cavite arsenal; she had neither her guns nor boilers aboard. The rest of the Spanish squadron took up a position in line to the east of Sangley Point. The total weight of the Spanish broadside was about one third of that of Dewey's squadron. The latter possessed ten 8-inch, twenty three 6-inch and twenty 5-inch guns; the Spaniards had seven 6.3-inch, four 5.9-inch, twenty 4.7-inch and 11 smaller guns.[17]

By April 30 Dewey's squadron, steaming at eight knots, had arrived off Bolinao Point, where it paused to land a Filipino insurgent leader. In its passage from Mirs Bay the squadron rehearsed the battle drills and built barricades of canvas and iron to shield the gun crews; all surplus woodwork (except, apparently, aboard the flagship) was stripped out and thrown overboard. At night the squadron steamed without lights. Early in the morning Dewey sent on the *Boston* and *Concord* to reconnoitre Subig Bay; when some of his officers declared that they could hear gunfire, he ordered the *Baltimore* to follow them in support, and to await the arrival of the rest of the squadron when it reached the entrance to the bay. This it did at 3:30 p.m.; the three ships sent ahead were sighted at the opening of the bay. When they signalled that no enemy vessels had been found in the bay, Dewey was deeply relieved, saying to Lamberton: 'Now we have them.'[18] The squadron now turned south heading for the entrance to Manila Bay, and at 5:30 Dewey signalled for all captains to come aboard the flagship.

The meeting was brief. Dewey told them that he had decided to enter the bay that evening, the ships steaming in single file, led by the *Olympia*. Lieutenant William Winder, his nephew, suggested that one of the supply ships should lead the way to set off any mines that might have been sown in the channel. Dewey would have none of this: 'Billy, I have waited sixty years for this opportunity. Mines or no mines, I am leading the squadron in myself.'[19] As the squadron steamed through the darkness, it was scarcely visible; only a small stern light was showing on each vessel. Lieutenant Bradley A Fisk, aboard the *Petrel*, remembered the approach to the Boca Grande:

> There was nothing to see except for the dim outlines of a few ships and the vague outlines of a coast two or three miles distant and there was nothing to hear except the sound of the engine and the swish of the water along the sides.[20]

The entrance to Manila Bay was some ten miles across. The two channels entering the bay, the Boca Chica and the Boca Grande, were separated by the island of Corregidor; in the Boca Grande there lay the islands of Caballo and El Fraile. Beyond the entrance, the bay opened out to a width of over thirty miles. Gun emplacements hastily erected on Corregidor covered the Boca Chica, while those on Caballo and El Fraile protected the Boca Grande. Dewey's

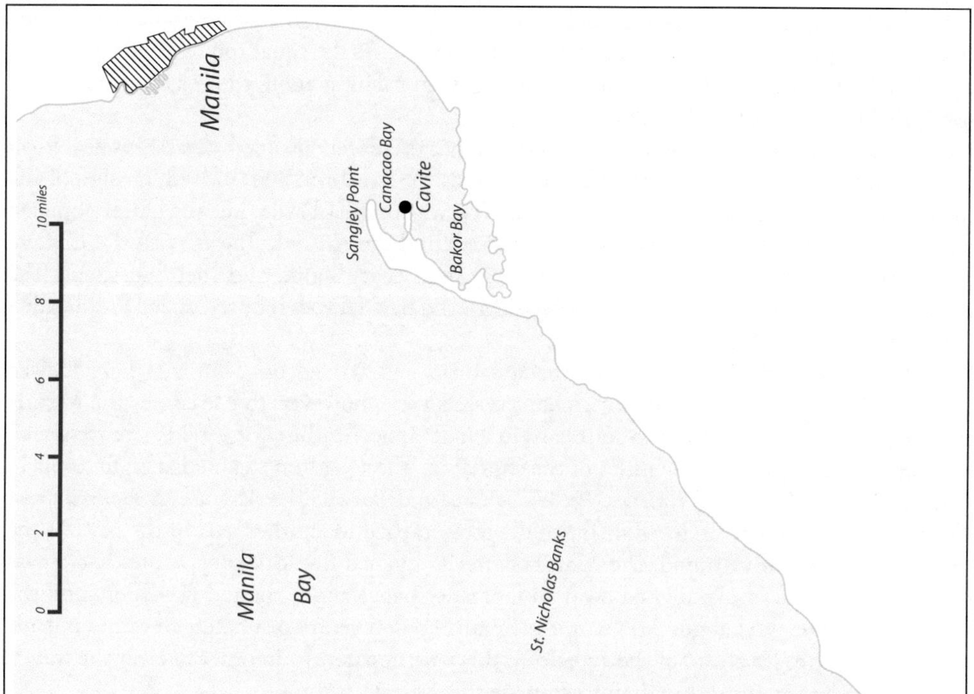
Manila
10 miles
0
2
4
6
8
10
Sangley Point
Canacao Bay
Cavite
Bakor Bay
Manila
Bay
St. Nicholas Banks
Caballo Island
Corregidor Island
Boca Grande Passage
El Fraile Rock
Boca Chica Passage
Bataan
Punta Gorda
N

3 Manila Bay.

intention was to steam through the Boca Grande, reasonably confident that the great depth of water there meant that there was a negligible risk from mines. It was the relatively heavy guns of the batteries on Caballo and El Fraile that represented the first danger faced by Dewey's squadron; certainly, the gunners should have been well prepared, since the news of the squadron's arrival off Bolinao Point had been reported to Manila. As the squadron reached a point ten miles from the Boca Grande, signal lights could be seen flashing along the coastline of Luzon, suggesting that the squadron had been sighted.

As it entered the Boca Grande, tension was high; but there were no enemy warships visible off the entrance, no torpedo boats boats dashing towards the squadron and, indeed, no sign of life until about 12:10 a.m. By now most of the squadron was past El Fraile, but the battery opened with the single round that passed between the *Petrel* and the *Raleigh*. These, with the *Concord* and the *McCulloch*, returned the fire. The battery fired twice more, and then fell silent. The battery on Caballo did not open fire. Safely within the bay, Dewey reduced speed and headed for Manila, to look for Montojo's squadron.

By 5:00 a.m. as dawn was breaking, the squadron had arrived off Manila, where Dewey expected to find his adversary. Only merchant vessels were, however, to be seen in the Manila anchorage, and Dewey led round to starboard in a half circle, heading for Cavite, a move which brought him within two or three miles of the shoreline. The squadron steamed at eight knots in the order *Olympia, Baltimore, Raleigh, Petrel, Concord* and *Boston*. The *McCulloch*, *Nanshan* and *Zafiro* were to take no part in the fighting and were detached to another part of the bay. As the squadron steamed slowly around, the Manila batteries opened fire; Stickney wrote that 'it was a pretty sight, for the smoke floated away in fantastic shapes above the red clay shore and the bright green foliage.'[21] At about 5:06 a.m. the Spanish detonated two submerged mines outside Cavite, about four miles ahead of the squadron; this was, apparently, in order to clear the waters for their own manoeuvres rather than to damage the American ships.

Dewey stood on the *Olympia*'s bridge as she headed for Cavite, while Captain Gridley was below him in the armoured conning tower behind the forward turret. For once, Dewey was not the figure of sartorial elegance to which he normally aspired, and as he was subsequently depicted. His uniform hat had been lost the day before when a wooden bulkhead had been torn down in his quarters for the better operation of a secondary gun. He wore instead a casual civilian golfer's cap, which rather spoilt the effect of his immaculate white uniform.[22]

The first shot from a heavy gun battery on Sangley Point was fired at about 5:15, but Dewey continued to hold fire as the squadron neared its objective. Lieutenant Calkins, the navigator of the *Olympia*, called out the range as she approached the enemy. At a range of about 5,000 yards, Dewey altered course to starboard to steam on a course roughly in parallel to Montojo's line. Then, leaning over the rail of his flying bridge, he called down: 'You may fire when you are ready, Gridley.' The first shot was from one of the forward 8-inch guns; as the squadron turned into line on a westward bearing, firing became general at a range of about 4,000 yards. When the column reached Sangley Point the range was down to about 2,500 yards. Soon after the squadron began its cannonade there was an alarm when a small steam launch was seen emerging from the cove behind the point; it was assumed that this must be a torpedo boat intending to attack the *Olympia*, as she crossed the flagship's bows and then turned back towards the shore. Concentrated fire from secondary batteries was poured upon the hapless vessel, which was driven ashore under the guns at Sangley Point, where she was abandoned by her crew. It turned out that this was a market boat heading for Manila at the behest of an English family living at Canacao. Although entirely a false alarm, there were two lessons that could be learned from the incident. First, it showed just how much of a threat even a lone torpedo boat might be, and secondly, that the fierce gunfire which was aimed at the boat had failed to destroy her, while her crew escaped unhurt.

The American column turned 180° when off Sangley Point, and retraced its course parallel with the Spanish line, passing it altogether five times, three times to the west and twice to the east, each turn made with port helm. Lieutenant Calkins described the battering of the Spanish squadron:

> Animated by desperate counsels, Spanish vessels had made one or two attempts to meet us in front of their line. Only one of these was persistent or significant enough to be remembered. As we stood to the eastward on our third passage along the zone of fire, the *Reina Cristina*, bearing the flag of Admiral Montojo, was seen to detach herself from her consorts and to approach a gap in the line, with the apparent purpose of coming to close quarters with the *Olympia*, which had just changed her course 60° to the southward of her previous tracks towards the turning point. The two flagships seemed closing rapidly, but the Spaniard had only advanced a ship's length or so beyond his line before his progress was arrested by a hail of concentrated fire which produced immediate and visible results. His speed slackened; smoke puffed out forward and aft; a white plume of escaping steam showed that his motive power was crippled, and an awkward turn, exposing the unprotected stern, suggested that his steering gear had met the same fate. The beaten flagship crept toward the arsenal, where she grounded, burned and blew up during the morning.[23]

The shooting of the Spanish squadron was not good, but the American vessels sustained several hits. Stickney, aboard the *Olympia*, described one shell which struck her close by a gun in the wardroom, while another, seeming to head for the bridge, exploded a hundred feet away. Another hit the bridge railings and still another, 'about as large as a flatiron' gouged a hole in the deck a few feet from where Dewey stood.[24] Both the *Baltimore* and the *Boston* sustained hits, causing casualties but which, fortunately for them, did less damage than might have been expected.

At 7:35 a.m. Gridley reported to Dewey that ammunition was running low; there remained only fifteen rounds per gun for the *Olympia*'s 5-inch battery. At the current rate of fire, these guns could not keep up their bombardment very much longer. This came as a fearful shock to Dewey:

> It was a most anxious moment for me. So far as I could see, the Spanish squadron was as intact as ours. I had reason to believe that their supply of ammunition was as ample as ours was limited. Therefore, I decided to withdraw temporarily from action for a redistribution of ammunition if necessary. For I knew that fifteen rounds of 5-inch ammunition could be shot away in five minutes.[25]

As Dewey broke off the action and led the squadron out towards the middle of the bay, there was, according to Stickney, a pronounced sense of disappointment aboard the flagship where, he wrote, 'the gloom on the bridge of the *Olympia* was thicker than a London fog in November.' After two and a half hours hours of fighting, the intensity of the Spanish fire seemed not to have slackened:

> Our projectiles seemed to go too high or too low – just as had been the case with those fired by the Spaniards. Several times the commodore had expressed dissatisfaction with the failure of our gunners to hit the enemy. We had begun the firing at too great a distance, but we had gradually worked in further on each of the turns, until we were within about 2,500 yards at the close of the fifth round. At this distance, in a smooth sea, we ought to have made a large percentage of hits; yet so far as we could judge, we had not sensibly crippled the foe.[26]

Although at first it seemed that the Spanish squadron was still more or less intact, it quickly became clear that this was not the case. In fact, Montojo's ships had taken a terrific pounding. The *Reina Cristina* in particular had suffered extensive damage, as Lieutenant Calkins had noted. Her foremast was smashed when a shell hit the pilothouse; another hit destroyed her steering gear. A shell exploded in the hospital, killing most of the wounded and medical personnel there, while another hit the ship's after magazine, which had to be flooded. By the time the American squadron withdrew, the *Reina Cristina* was a total wreck, with half her crew out of action, and although the few guns still undamaged continued to fire at the retreating enemy, at 7:40 a.m. Montojo gave the order to abandon ship. Both he and Captain Cadarso had been wounded; the latter, endeavouring to save as many of his crew as he could, was killed by one of the last shells to hit the ship before the Americans were out of range. Montojo went aboard the *Isla de Cuba*, and was taken to the convent of Santo Domingo de Cavite for treatment to his leg wound.

The *Castillo* had also been hit many times and was ablaze, with all her guns out of action save one. Her forward moorings had been shot away, and she swung round to expose her defenceless starboard side. Captain Algado continued to fight as best he could, but soon was obliged to abandon ship; the survivors were rescued by boats putting off from shore and by the *Don Juan de Austria*. This ship, too, had been badly damaged and was on fire. The *Isla de Luzon*, though not seriously damaged, had had three of her guns put out of action; the *Marques de Duero* had been hit in the engine room and had only two guns still serviceable. When he saw the American squadron withdrawing, Montojo gave orders that the ships that were capable of movement should retire inside Bakoor Bay. If the Americans attacked again, they should resist to the last, but then be scuttled if no more could be done.

Aboard the *Olympia* Dewey learned to his relief that the report about the shortage of ammunition had been a false alarm. He took advantage of the lull in the fighting to order that the crews should have their breakfast. Stickney, with an eye to the public relations effect, suggested that it should be made known that it was this that had led to the breaking off of the action, and this went down well in the American Press. Dewey wrote in his autobiography that this suggested a nonchalance that had never occurred to him. While the squadron remained out of action he took the opportunity to summon his captains, expecting them to have both damages and casualties to report:

> To my gratification not a single life had been lost, and considering that we would rather measure the importance of an action by the scale of its conduct than by the number of casualties we were immensely happy. The concentration of our fire immediately we were in telling range had given us an early advantage in demoralising the enemy, which has ever been the prime factor in naval battles.[27]

The lull continued for three and a half hours. It could now be seen that both the *Reina Cristina* and the *Castillo* were heavily afire, and the sound of exploding ammunition could be heard. There was no doubt that victory had been won, and Dewey at 11 a.m. ordered the squadron to return to finish off what remained of Montojo's squadron. The *Baltimore* led the line, followed by the *Olympia, Raleigh, Boston, Concord* and *Petrel.* They were met with fire from the shore batteries and from the *Don Antonio de Ulloa*, the only Spanish vessel that was still battleworthy. Upon her was concentrated the fire of the American ships, and although she bravely fought back as long as she could, by 12:30 she was in the sinking condition, and she went down just behind Sangley Point, resting on the bottom with her upperworks showing. Meanwhile Montojo, upon the approach of the American squadron, had given orders that the remaining Spanish ships should be scuttled.

Dewey now ordered the *Petrel*, with the lightest draught of all his ships, to enter Cavite harbour to destroy any ships that had taken refuge there. As she entered the harbour, she fired a number of shots into the arsenal, as a result of which the white flag was displayed on the government buildings. Commander Wood, the *Petrel*'s captain, reported to Dewey:

> Lieutenant Hughes was sent with a whale-boat's crew of seven men, this whale-boat being the only one on the ship which would float, and set fire to the *Don Juan de Austria, Isla de Cuba, Isla de Luzon, General Lezo* and *Marques del Duero.* Afterward Ensign Fermier was sent to set fire to the *Velasco* and *Elcano.* The *Isla de Cuba*, *Isla de Luzon* and *Don Juan de Austria* were aground and full of water when they were fired. Their outboard valves were opened and the ships allowed to fill. The breech plugs of the 4.7-inch guns had been taken off and could not be found… The *Don Antonio de Ulloa* was sunk, and the *Reina Cristina* and *Castillo* were burning in the outer harbour. Lieutenant Fiske was sent ashore and brought off two tugboats, the *Rapido* and *Hercules*, and three steam launches.[28]

Once the *Ulloa* had been sunk, and the Sangley Point batteries silenced, at 2 p.m. Dewey sent Consul Williams to board a British ship moored near the mouth of the Pasig River to ask her captain to deliver a message via the British consul to the governor general. This was to the effect that if the Manila batteries fired on the American ships, he would destroy the city. Any torpedo boats in the Pasig River must be surrendered; and provided that he was allowed to send messages to Hong Kong by the undersea cable, the Spanish would also be permitted to use it. The response was immediate; unless it was clear that the American squadron was manoeuvring to bombard the city, the batteries would remain silent. Augustin added that he knew of no torpedo boats on the river, but if there were, 'his honour would not allow him to surrender them.' In fact, there were none. He refused Dewey's request to use the cable, so next morning the *Zafiro* was ordered to cut it.[29]

On the morning of May 2, the Spanish flag was again flying over Cavite arsenal. Dewey sent Lamberton in the *Petrel* to go ashore and find out what this meant. When he reached the arsenal, the commandant, Captain Sostoa, said that the colours had been lowered on the previous day to mark a temporary truce. Lamberton's reply was brusque; if the white flag was not hoisted by noon, he would open fire. Sostoa temporised, saying that he must seek instructions from Madrid; when Lamberton refused this, Sostoa asked for time to refer it to the governor general. Lamberton told him that only an unconditional surrender would be accepted. His bluff called, Sostoa hoisted the white flag at 11:35 a.m. on the express order of Admiral Montojo.

Dewey was now in complete control of Manila, and the bay. He did not, however, have the ground troops to occupy the city, as he made clear in his reports to Washington.

With the cutting of the cable from Manila to Hong Kong, the only way Dewey could communicate with the outside world was to send a ship to Hong Kong; only the *McCulloch* could be spared for this purpose, and she sailed from Manila on May 5. She arrived in Hong Kong with Flag Lieutenant Brumby and other officers, together with three journalists. Brumby despatched two telegrams from Dewey to the Navy Department; the first of these, composed on May 1, reported the destruction of the Spanish squadron, and asked for fresh supplies of ammunition. The second, dated May 4, announced the taking of Cavite arsenal, and the destruction of the fortifications there and at the entrance to the bay. Dewey went on: 'Have cut cable to mainland. I control bay completely and can take city at any time, but I have not sufficient men to hold.'[30]

McKinley, as soon as the news of the victory had begun to arrive, had been swift to telegraph his congratulations. On May 7, after reading Dewey's second telegram, he thanked the commodore, his officers and men, in the name of the American people for their 'splendid achievement and overwhelming victory,' and promoted Dewey to the rank of rear admiral. On May 10 Dewey received the official thanks of Congress, (by which he was in the following March raised to the rank of Admiral of the Navy), while Lamberton, Brumby and the commanding officers of the squadron all received promotions. Gridley, who was by now a very sick man, was invalided home, but died in Japan while en route. The congratulations, by cable and letter, which began to arrive for Dewey were the start of the outpouring of public adulation unprecedented since the end of the Civil War. Theodore Roosevelt, by now with his volunteer cavalry regiment, was predictably not to be outdone in hyperbole, writing:

> Admiral Dewey has won a victory greater than any since Trafalgar, with the exception of Farragut's. It is one of the great sea fights of all time, and every American is his debtor.[31]

Dewey was of course entitled to the credit for his victory, although it was a battle that he could not really have possibly lost; the outcome was entirely inevitable. The extravagant praise which he received, so obviously over the top, was due to the craving of the American public for an early victory. To get it so soon, and so convincingly, allowed the American Press to indulge in the most extravagant overstatements of the merits of his achievement. A more moderate assessment is perhaps that of one of his admirers, Nathan Sargent, who wrote:

> Admiral Dewey's success was due to his exhaustive preliminary studies of the situation, to his careful foresight and preparations at Hong Kong, to his wise consultations with his captains, and their mutual consideration of every contingency which might arise, to his analytical diagnosis of all the ominous rumours of Spanish preparation, and finally to his celerity and virtual surprise of their position at an hour when he was least expected.[32]

Dewey made no real mistakes in the course of the campaign, but even if he had done so, he must necessarily have emerged the victor over a Spanish squadron that was miserably inadequate for the task it had to perform.

The unfortunate Admiral Montojo was, predictably enough, made a scapegoat for the defeat. On his return to Spain he was brought before a court martial, in the course of which he vigorously defended himself, pointing out the desperate weakness of his squadron when compared to that of Dewey. His decision to offer battle at Cavite was, he contended, justified by the fact that Subig Bay had not been adequately prepared for defence, and it was important not to subject the city of Manila to bombardment, which it would have suffered had he taken up a position under the batteries there. As to the option of taking the fleet out of Manila Bay, and conducting operations from elsewhere in the Philippine Islands, (and which Chadwick, among others, considered was his best course), which might have delayed the outcome, he pointed out that Augustin, to whose orders he was subject, would not have permitted it. On the other hand, Montojo has been criticised for allowing the badly needed work of repair to some of his ships to proceed so slowly at a time when the international situation so obviously indicated the possibility of war. Edward L Beach is one of those suggesting that responsibility for this should be laid at Montojo's door.[33] In fact, no amount of repairs could have rendered Montojo's small and elderly ships fit to stand up to Dewey's squadron, by which it was heavily outgunned. A much greater share of responsibility was that of the Spanish government, which made no effective attempt to reinforce the feeble squadron which it assigned to the defence of the Philippines, in spite of the appeals of Augustin, his predecessor Primo de Rivera, and Montojo.

More justified, perhaps, was Dewey's criticism of the failure of the batteries at Boca Grande to fire on his squadron as it entered Manila Bay, and the failure to mount a torpedo attack. Dewey was however generous in victory, sending a message shortly after the battle to Montojo: 'I have pleasure in clasping your hand and offering my congratulations on the gallant manner in which you fought.'[34] Neither this, nor the letter which Dewey wrote at Montojo's request to give his 'testimony to a gallant foe,' cut any ice with the Spanish authorities. Montojo and Captain Sostoa were arrested on March 4, 1899, and held in deeply unpleasant conditions in prison until their trial was completed six months later. Thereafter the Queen Regent ordered Montojo's retirement from the service, with a ban on his holding any public office in the future. Sostoa, on the other hand, was acquitted; but General Jaudenes, who had signed the subsequent capitulation of the city of Manila, was also convicted and subjected to the same penalty as Montojo. Chadwick commented:

> Such treatment of honourable and brave men, who had done their duty and who, in the circumstances in which they were placed, succumbed but to the inevitable is a stain upon the honour of Spain. Certainly Montojo's gallant conduct deserved a better fate. His sentence… was from an American standpoint, of extreme rigour and injustice.[35]

Justice demanded that his court-martial should have led to Montojo's acquittal, recognising the extent to which both Madrid and the governor general were responsible for the situation. The tactical course of pulling out of Manila Bay was not available to the admiral, as William R Braisted has noted: 'Distracted by internal unrest and by the irresolute government in Madrid, the Spanish authorities in Manila were perhaps too weak to order a retreat.'[36]

The casualties sustained on each side during the course of the one-sided battle were as disproportionate as the damage to the ships engaged. The total number of Americans engaged was 1,743; of these, only eight were wounded, all aboard the *Baltimore*. Their wounds were all caused by splinters. The Spanish, who according to Montojo's account had 1,134 men engaged, lost 75 killed and 281 wounded. An analysis of the effectiveness of the American shooting revealed that out of a total of 5,859 shots fired from all guns, from 8-inch to 1 pounder, 142 hits on the Spanish squadron were noted, a percentage of 2.43. The bulk of the hits were sustained by the

Reina Cristina, *Castillo* and *Don Antonio de Ulloa*. Lieutenant Ellicott, the officer who compiled the statistics, reckoned that the hits noted on these three ships were probably less than half the actual total.[37] It was noteworthy, however, that the proportion of hits scored by the 8-inch guns was considerably higher than the rest, amounting to 9%; these guns fired very much less often, the bulk of the firing being from 6-inch, 5-inch, six pounder and three pounder guns. The ships of Dewey's quadron sustained only 23 hits, the most significant being suffered by the *Baltimore*. After the battle it was noted that the American vessels showed little sign of the engagement, due to the fact that the Spanish mainly used shrapnel, less effective at long ranges.[38]

Wilson summed up the engagement in these terms:

> The battle was thus a military execution rather than a real contest. It must be placed on the same plane with the destruction of the Chinese fleet at Foochow by Admiral Courbet, or with the bombardment of Alexandria. The odds, as we have seen, were against the Spaniards, but their miserable shooting rendered their defeat more terrible and crushing than might have been expected.[39]

13

San Juan

The news that Cervera had sailed from Cape Verde meant that, apart from instituting the blockade of Cuba, locating him was the most urgent task for the American Navy. National morale was high, and it was soon further enhanced when news came of Dewey's crushing victory at Manila. The uncertainty about Cervera's movements remained a serious threat, however, and for defensive purposes the east coast of the United States was divided into eight districts. Available for each of these was a handful of armed steamers, tugs or yachts. Their presence was to serve as a reassurance to the local communities, though in truth they would have served little purpose if Cervera had descended upon them. Roosevelt was derisive, observing that they stood as much chance against a modern warship as a Carthaginian galley would have done. There was, though, one squadron which was of real fighting value. This was the Northern Patrol Squadron under Commodore John A Howell, which consisted of the cruiser *San Francisco* and four armed mail steamers.

For the moment Schley's Flying Squadron was still detained at Hampton Roads, and at the time of Cervera's sailing consisted of two battleships, an armoured cruiser and a protected cruiser. Schley continued to spend the time waiting for orders to move in constant exercising of his ships, but it was a frustrating period for him. Meanwhile Sampson's squadron, with which he was to maintain the blockade of Cuba and to watch for Cervera's arrival, was a very mixed bunch. Not all of them were of great value, as Wilson explained:

> The composition of Admiral Sampson's Squadron was very heterogeneous. It had only two armoured ships of any speed and this pair – the *New York* and *Iowa* – could not be reckoned as fast as Cervera's squadron, as was to be seen when the *Iowa* could not keep up with the Spanish cruisers when they dashed out of Santiago. The monitors were very slow and defective, unable to steam more than eight or 9 knots in the seaway, and carrying very little coal.[1]

The monitors were not, therefore, going to be of much use to Sampson in any engagement with Cervera, not least because they were such poor gun platforms that accurate shooting from them, in any sort of the sea, was impossible.

Sampson's total force amounted to two battleships, an armoured cruiser, four monitors, five cruisers, six gunboats, a yacht and six torpedo boats. He was reinforced, by mid-May, by four fast armed liners, a gunboat, a torpedo boat, a yacht, and a large number of other armed vessels of variable utility. He was also joined by the so-called 'dynamite gunboat' *Vesuvius*, a remarkable experimental vessel of 929 tons, capable of 21 knots. Unarmoured, her main armament consisted of three 15-inch pneumatic guns, mounted parallel to each other on the keel line, with a fixed elevation of 18°. Shells were fired at the rate of one minute or less, the propellant being compressed air. In target practice the *Vesuvius* apparently achieved very considerable accuracy; but although it was claimed that further progress in developing the concept was achieved during the war, the fact that no other vessels of the type were ordered tells its own story.

Sampson sailed from Key West on April 22 to commence the blockade, arriving off Havana at 5:00 p.m. The vessels earmarked for the blockade of Matanzas, Mariel and Cardenas were detached, and with the rest of the squadron Sampson settled down to the blockade. In the days that followed a number of prizes attempting to enter Havana were taken, although the Spanish liner *Montserrat*, carrying troops, provisions and a large quantity of gold, which had unsuccessfully attempted to get into Havana, succeeded in delivering her cargo to Cienfuegos. There were no Spanish warships in Havana remotely capable of interfering with the blockade; such as it was, the squadron consisted of the old cruisers *Alfonso XII*, *Conde de Venadito* and *Marques de la Ensenada*. The first of these was incapable of movement under her own steam, and the others were capable of no more than 10 knots. There were also two torpedo gunboats, *Nueva Espana* and *Molins*. Elsewhere, there was the old cruiser *Reina Mercedes*, at Santiago, also immobile, and the torpedo gunboats *Galicia* and *V Y Pinzon* based at Cienfuegos and Cardenas respectively.

Central to all operations was the need constantly to recoal the ships. On May 2 the *New York*, *Indiana*, *Iowa*, *Amphitrite* and *Puritan* returned to Key West, and coaled there for extended operations. The problem of keeping his ships supplied with coal was a constant problem for Sampson, even though Key West lay only 80 miles from Havana. In particular, the torpedo boats and monitors, with a very limited fuel capacity, were continually needing to recoal. Attempts were made to coal them from colliers or from the battleships at sea, but it was a risky business, while the monitors frequently broke down. To conduct the blockade, Sampson had barely sufficient ships, but his smaller vessels were soon in action along the coast. On May 8 the torpedo boat *Winslow* entered Cardenas Bay, and fired on three very small Spanish gunboats before withdrawing. It was a bold move; her commander was unaware of the existence of a masked battery, and when the *Winslow* repeated her exploit on May 11, accompanied by two gunboats (*Wilmington* and *Machias*) and a revenue cutter (*Hudson*), she was hit a number of times, and only avoided destruction when the *Hudson* got a towline aboard her. Other skirmishes took place, of which the most significant was an attempt to cut the telegraph cable at Cienfuegos. This was carried out by the cruiser *Marblehead*, with the gunboat *Nashville* and the revenue cutter *Windom*. Two steam launches and two sailing launches were sent in, covered by fire from the *Marblehead* and *Nashville*. Heavy Spanish fire inflicted a growing number of casualties as two of the three cables were cut, at which point the operation was abandoned.[2]

Meanwhile Sampson continued to be hampered by the problem of coaling his ships, reporting that although he had begun the blockade of Cienfuegos, it could not continue unless colliers were sent to resupply the vessels there before their stocks approached exhaustion. This was not the only difficulty which he was experiencing; his ships were very deficient in supplies of fresh water, while his torpedo boats were, as Chadwick noted, 'wholly unfit for the rough service to which they were being applied'. He described the effect on them:

> They had been holding their own with hearty goodwill along the shore, doing scouting work close in, which would have been admirable had there been anything to look after, but

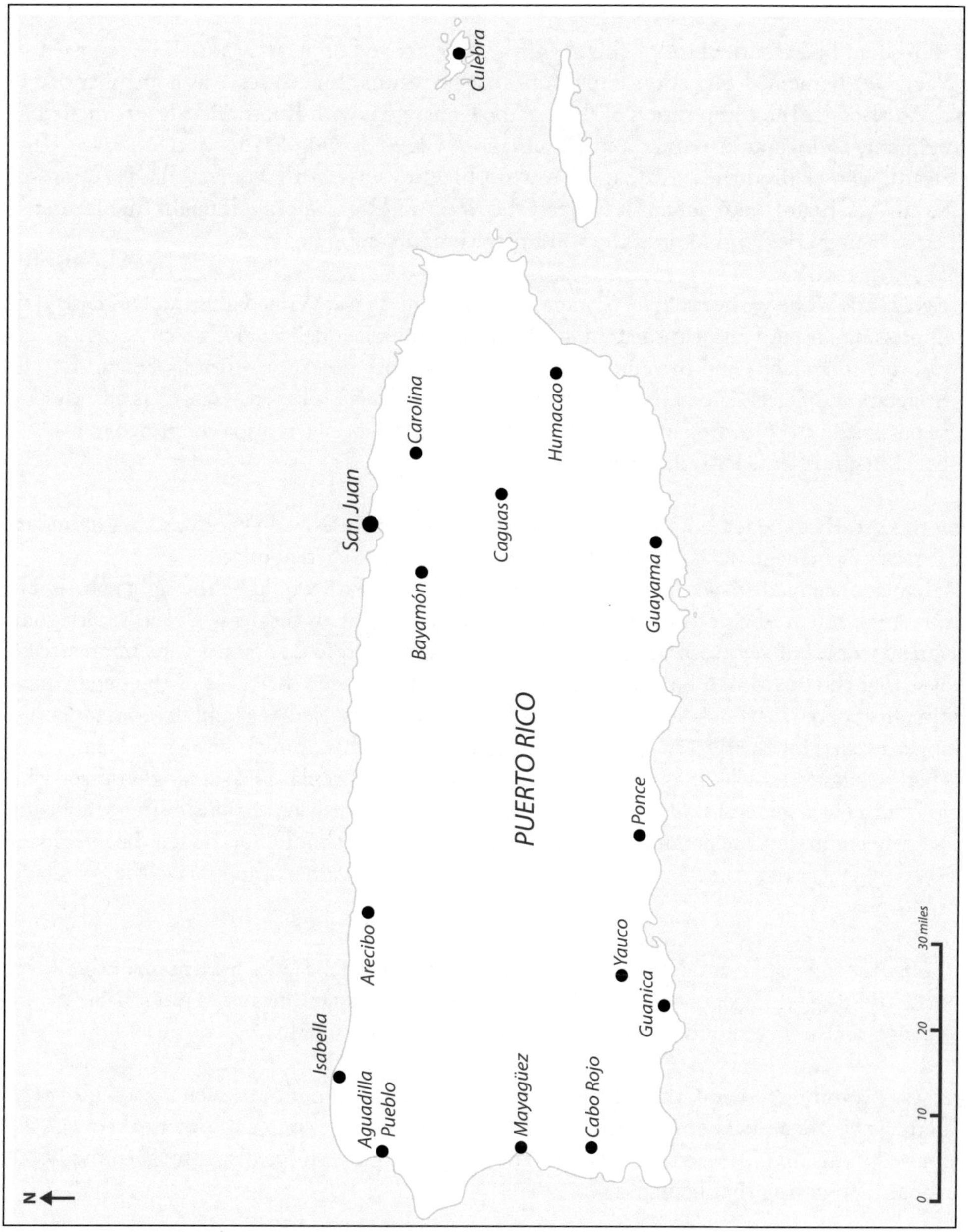

4 Puerto Rico.

> the short heavy sea produced by a strong trade blowing east at 2 to 3 knots an hour knocked them about in a way which called for much greater strength of structure, and which must have made life almost unendurable to those aboard.[3]

Alfred Mahan had returned to Washington where he arrived on May 9. When he reported to the Navy Department, Long at once told him that he wanted him to serve as a member of the Naval War Board. The composition of this had now changed, with Roosevelt's departure to join his regiment, and Captain Barker and Commander Clover having left for active service. This left Sicard, who chaired the board, and Crowninshield to serve with Mahan. The functions of the Naval War Board were not entirely clear; the *Army and Navy Journal* thought that it existed to utter 'warning cries' and to prod the administration into action:

> Every little while we hear of one or more of them going to the White House and urgently impressing on the President something which they think he ought to do, which he seems to listen to amiably, and then does not do. Then at other times they turn up before the Secretary and fiercely prod him, the result of which is he gets his hat and escapes as quickly as possible in the direction of the Executive Mansion, whence he returns confirmed in his belief that further delay is indispensable.[4]

What was greatly to be feared, the *Journal* thought, was that the Naval War Board might undertake directly to manage fleets, in which case it should be abolished at once.

Mahan at once made clear his view that abolition of the board would be the right course. He did not think much of Sicard's fitness to chair it, observing that 'Sicard is a clearheaded man for Bureau work, but very second or third rate for what we had to do'. Nor was he impressed to discover that the board had been allotted accommodation 'under the eaves of the department building in a room with one window which had heretofore been used as a lumber room for books no longer needed for the library'.[5] Mahan immediately made his opinion known to Long.

What he suggested was that the board be disbanded, and replaced by a single officer who would head a naval general staff, and upon whom would alone rest the responsibility for advising the Navy Secretary on the conduct of naval warfare. The navy should not, he felt, be effectively governed by a 'majority vote'. A committee was not the proper source of support to the Secretary. He told Long:

> I offer the suggestion at once before any difference with my colleagues has arisen, or could arise. Resting, as my opinion does, upon a wide study of military history, it is not liable to change, and at present it has the advantage of absolute impersonality.[6]

Long was beginning to think that perhaps recalling Mahan had not been such a good idea after all. Perhaps his theoretical eminence did not make him the best source of practical advice. He soon noted in his diary that Mahan was 'on the rampage again' in his disapproval of the Naval War Board, observing that he had

> achieved great distinction as a writer of naval history and has made a very thorough study of naval strategy; no naval officer stands higher today. Yet I doubt very much whether he will be of much value practically. He may be or he may not. That remains to be seen.[7]

Mahan's biographers have speculated whether he saw himself as the right person to fill the post which he was suggesting. There was some newspaper speculation that this might be the case, but it has been concluded that there was no evidence that it was in his mind. He had no doubt that his years of study and research gave him the necessary qualifications to lay down the law as to what should be done. The *New York Sun*, apparently a newspaper that had been unenthusiastic about the establishment of the Naval War Board, suggested that however great might be the strategic attainments of Crowninshield or Sicard, 'it is undeniable that they are eclipsed in the public eye by the capacities ascribed to Captain Mahan, who now gets the opportunity of his life to demonstrate whether he be the consummate strategist which the English have been insisting for years that he is.'[8] Not everyone was impressed by the capacities of the membership of the board, retired Rear Admiral Belknap writing in the *New York Times* on May 11 to describe the board as 'a body of men not celebrated as sea fighters, sitting in the comfortable retirement and reposeful comfort of the capital.'[9] It was an observation that no doubt riled Mahan, and his colleagues, but he was now very much in the public eye and had to get used to the outspoken comments of the press.

Long defended stoutly his decision to reject Mahan's opinions about the utility of the Naval War Board, setting out his position thus:

> The War Board is not a formal body. It has no set rules and regulations, and is not composed of a certain number of men. Its members are officers in whose judgement and ability the Secretary of the Navy has confidence, and they act merely as advisers. The function of the board is to collect information about the enemy and furnish it to the commanders of American squadrons or single vessels. The Secretary of the Navy is not bound by its advice, and there has never been any intention to have the Board determine what Adml. Sampson for example, should do in certain cases.[10]

It was an argument which some newspapers found unconvincing, and the subject of the Naval War Board and its activities was one which frequently raised its head in the columns of the Press, where a great deal of strident advice was offered to the Navy Department on a daily basis. And it was not only the newspapers which were critical; Senator Samuel Pascoe, for instance, had a lot to say on the subject:

> It is generally understood that both Sampson and Schley have little, if any, freedom of action and are held in check by all the authorities in Washington. It was a good thing that Dewey cut the cables. Both Schley and Sampson ought to take a hint in this respect.[11]

Long, who was more than a little vain, was nettled by the constant attacks in the newspapers, and the suggestions that he was not competent to direct the operations of the fleet. Insinuations that he was indecisive were repeated throughout the Press, and in London *The Times* observed that 'despite official denials, the proceedings of the United States Board of Strategy unquestionably indicate diversity and even conflict of councils and the absence of a strong directing hand.'[12]

When he returned to take up his duties on the Naval War Board, Mahan was not at all happy that the division of the fleet, which he had for so long argued against, had taken place. Nor was he pleased to find that Schley had been appointed to command the Flying Squadron, and could not have concealed his jaundiced view of Schley's abilities. Inevitably, therefore, when concerns arose about Schley's handling of the ships under his command, the board will have been influenced by Mahan's extremely negative opinions. These will have been sympathetically received by Crowninshield in particular; as had been the case with Dewey's appointment, Schley had got his job in the teeth of his disapproval.

Political considerations made it impossible for the Navy Department to release the Flying Squadron from its detention at Hampton Roads all the time that Cervera's whereabouts were unknown. Mahan also concurred in the decision of May 12 not to detach any ships from Schley, or from Sampson, to go in support of the *Oregon*, which was by then approaching the West Indies after its long voyage around Cape Horn. The Naval War Board correctly concluded that it was unlikely that she would be intercepted by Cervera's squadron, and that in any case her armament was such that she ought to be able to take care of herself.

It was on May 1 that Sampson had first received the news that Cervera had put to sea. The telegram from Washington correctly identified the Spanish Squadron as consisting of the *Maria Teresa*, *Oquendo*, *Vizcaya*, *Cristobal Colon*, *Terror*, *Furor* and *Pluton*. Notwithstanding the obvious superiority of the American fleet in the numbers and quality of its ships and the training of its men, there was a real concern in the United States about the threat that Cervera posed. And *The Times* described his squadron as 'a real fighting force, fast, modern and formidable of its kind.'[13] It would be Sampson's responsibility to deal with it, and he at once called his captains aboard to discuss what should be done.

The outcome of the meeting was a decision to move to the eastwards with part of the fleet, another division of force of which Mahan would not approve. Sampson reported this in a telegram to Long:

> The *New York*, *Iowa*, *Indiana*, *Amphitrite*, and *Terror*, after coaling, will sail immediately Windward Passage Cuba and await developments. Request you to communicate through consul at Cape Haitien, Turks Island, Nicolas Mole. Duplicate dispatches should be sent to all of them. Request the *Massachusetts* and *Texas* may meet me leeward of Tortugas islands, Haiti, May 6.[14]

In making this move Sampson had it in his mind to go on to San Juan in Puerto Rico if no other news was received of Cervera's movements, believing that this would be the objective of the Spanish squadron.

Sampson completed the coaling of his force by May 3, though not until 4:00 p.m., and he repeated his request for the *Massachusetts* and *Texas*; the reply, when it came, was in the negative. It was, Long said, considered undesirable to detach them at present. This was almost at once followed by further news:

> Large army movement cannot take place two weeks, and small movement will not take place until after we know whereabouts four Spanish armoured vessels, three destroyers. If objective San Juan, Puerto Rico, they should arrive about May 8 and action against them and San Juan is then authorised. In this case Flying Squadron will reinforce you.[15]

Chadwick irritably commented on the reference to the Flying Squadron: 'it is hardly possible to grasp the logic of this reinforcement, unless it was supposed that Sampson would await for four or five days the arrival of the squadron before attacking. He certainly had no intention of any such

Rear-Admiral Sampson.

Admiral Montojo.

Admiral Cervera.

Isidor Rayner.

US Navy Secretary John D. Long.

Captain Francis A Cook.

Admiral George Dewey.

Rear-Admiral Schley.

USS *Concord* & USS *Boston* in action 1 May 1898.

USS *Raleigh* in action 1 May 1898 & USS *Petrel* in action 1 May 1898.

The *Gloucester* bombarding Guanica, Puerto Rico.

Explosion of the *Vizcaya*.

Starboard quarter view of the *Almirante Oquendo*.

Rear Admiral Sampson on Board the *New York*.

Rear Admiral Alfred Thayer Mahan.

Commodore W.S Schley, making an announcement to his men.

Rear Admiral Sampson (left) with Captain Chadwick and an aide on board the *New York*.

The *Oquendo*, destroyed and run on the beach west of Santiago.

Sampson's Fleet steams into New York Harbour on its return from Cuba.

Commodore Schley's flagship, *Brooklyn*.

Commodore Schley in his cabin.

Captain Cook and his officers of the *Brooklyn*.

The *Vizcaya* had been raked by the *Oregon*.

The *Colon* turned over in the surf.

The *Infanta Maria Teresa*.

USS *New York*.

USS *Iowa*.

Vizcaya.

USS *Oregon*.

USS *Porter*.

USS *Ericsson*.

USS *Cushing*.

USS *Massachusetts*.

USS *Minneapolis*.

USS *Katahdin*.

USS *Vesuvius*.

USS *Miantonomah*.

USS *Cincinnati*.

USS *Marblehead*.

USS *St Paul*.

delay.'Meanwhile just as the fleet was putting to sea, a further telegram arrived to the effect that further important instructions were about to be telegraphed, causing Sampson to put off his departure for several hours. When no further orders had come, he gave up waiting, and put to sea, heading in the first instance to Havana to pick up the vessels sent there, before setting off for San Juan.

It was not an easy journey; the best speed the squadron as a whole could manage was eight knots. To economise on fuel, the *Iowa* towed the *Amphitrite*, the *New York* the *Terror* and the cruiser *Montgomery* the *Porter*. Towlines frequently broke, causing endless trouble and delay, while on May 5 *Indiana* disappeared when sustaining an accident to one of her cylinders, not rejoining the squadron until the following day. That afternoon the crown of one of her boilers came down, and she could not steam more than 8 knots, while the *Terror*'s steering gear failed. Off Cape Haitien the sea was so smooth that it was possible to coal the monitors and cruisers at sea, but these delays meant that it would certainly not be possible to reach San Juan by May 8 as had been intended.

On May 7 the *Porter* was sent into Cape Haitien for news, returning with a clutch of telegrams from Washington. The most important of these, dated May 6, imposed a severe restraint on Sampson, in the light of further information which appeared to have reached Long as to the composition of the Spanish squadron:

> Do not risk so crippling your vessels against fortifications as to prevent from soon afterward successfully fighting Spanish fleet composed of *Pelayo*, *Carlos V*, *Oquendo*, *Maria Teresa*, *Vizcaya*, *Cristobal Colon*, four destroyers if they should appear this side.[16]

Long's thinking was set out in a letter of the same date, which Sampson was not however to read until he next returned to Key West on May 18. Sampson was enjoined not to risk his ships by exposing them 'to the fire of heavy guns mounted on shore which are not protecting or assisting formidable Spanish ships', though he could do so if there were 'Spanish vessels of sufficient military importance protected by these guns'. He was writing the letter, said Long, 'to guard against any probable misconception' on Sampson's part. Since the only Spanish vessels of sufficient importance were Cervera's armoured cruisers, and he was unlikely to have divided his force, this could only refer to Sampson's finding that that Cervera was already at San Juan.

Sampson called another conference of his captains on May 8, at which it was agreed to continue the mission to San Juan in the hope of finding Cervera there, and to capture Culebra Island if a blockade became necessary. Chadwick explained Sampson's reasoning:

> He was... well aware that in making this decision he was running the risk of traversing the sound rule of holding the interior line, but he felt the risk was worth taking; that he was not warranted in giving Cervera the chance to coal at San Juan, overhaul his machinery, and get away uninterfered with.[17]

Chadwick went on to explain that in determining to attack the batteries at San Juan, Sampson had decided that if the city was ready to fall he would take it, rather than leave it available to Cervera's ships, if they should not already have reached it:

> Its seizure would take from them a stepping stone toward the true seat of conflict of distinct advantage, which it was his duty, if conditions favoured, to annul. It was his intention, if

> successful, to leave the monitors in possession, and transport the garrison north in the *Yale*, or nearest scout, either of which could have carried the whole.[18]

There was nothing in his instructions from the Navy Department which called for an occupation of San Juan; but on the other hand there was nothing forbidding it.

The presence with the fleet of many war correspondents, and of the steamers chartered by newspapers to follow the events of the naval war, meant that secrecy of the naval movements was impossible, and Sampson had to ban one correspondent in particular on account of the information which he was telegraphing home. On the other hand, he was able to make use of the Press vessels on occasion; on May 8, for instance, the *Dauntless* brought out a further telegram from Long, which left Sampson uncertain as to whether he would have to face the *Pelayo* and *Carlos V*; these, Long said, could not leave Cadiz for two weeks. On the other hand, there was a report that Cervera had been seen off Martinique, which might mean a threat to the blockade: 'Therefore you should be quick in your operations at Puerto Rico. In everything the Department has the utmost confidence in your discretion. The Department does not wish to hamper you'.

Sampson continued his course towards San Juan, although still plagued by the problem of breaking towlines, by problems with the engines of the monitors, and by the leaky boilers of the *Indiana* which limited her speed to 7 knots. As the squadron finally neared San Juan, Sampson shifted his flag at 5:00 p.m. on May 11 to the *Iowa*, as being the most powerful and best armoured of the ships. He had issued detailed battle orders as to the conduct of the expected engagement, as Wilson described:

> Early on the 12th the lights of the city came into sight, and the American crews were called. The fleet approached warily, expecting at each moment to see Cervera's ships putting to sea. The *Detroit* led 1000 yards in advance of the flagship; then, in line ahead, at intervals of two cables, came the *Iowa*, *Indiana*, *New York*, *Amphitrite* and *Terror*. The *Wompatuck*, 500 yards off on the flagship's starboard bow, towed a boat which was to be anchored as soon as the water shoaled to 10 fathoms, as a mark to the fleet.[19]

The *Porter* had orders to take station close in under the bluffs to the east of the Morro to lie in wait for and torpedo any Spanish vessels emerging from the harbour. Her position, unexpectedly, was exposed to a heavy fire from the shore batteries. The *Detroit*, and the *Montgomery*, which brought up the rear of the line, were ordered to be on the lookout for Spanish torpedo boats. It was soon apparent however, that Cervera was not in port.

The *Iowa* opened fire at 5:16 a.m. with a shot from a six pounder, which was the signal to the squadron to commence the bombardment, which immediately opened up on the Spanish batteries. These were mounted on the ancient fortifications, at the extreme north-west of which was the castle of the Morro, built on a cliff rising almost vertically for a hundred feet above the water. For half a mile facing west, and for a mile facing north, there was a line of lofty fortifications in which were mounted twenty five 5.9-inch rifled guns and sixteen howitzers. Their failure immediately to respond seems to be due to their having been taken by surprise as the American squadron approached from a north-westerly direction. It was eight minutes before the first of the shore batteries opened fire, concentrating at first on the *Detroit*. Thereafter the batteries fired constantly as the column turned in a half circle to the north-west and ceased fire. At 5:59 Sampson again ordered the ships to get into column, and in the *Iowa* led them back into the attack. At 6:09 he signalled 'use only large guns', partly to avoid wasting ammunition of the small guns that could not have much effect on the thick stone walls, and partly to reduce the thick pall of smoke which the squadron had raised in the windless calm of the early morning.

Sampson led the column around on the same course as before after having begun firing at the range of 1500 yards, withdrawing again before returning at 7:16 on a third run. This ended at 7:45, the *Terror* lingering inshore for a prolonged final exchange with the shore batteries before firing a last shot at a range of 5000 yards. The Americans could not however feel very proud of their gunnery this day. One correspondent, JR Spears, wrote that 'the aim of the big guns was particularly bad, for many shots intended for the Morro, built upon a hill sixty feet above the sea, really splashed in the water at the foot of the bluff.'[20] Allowance had evidently not been made for the height of the fortifications, and accuracy was impeded by a heavy swell and by the dense clouds of smoke. Goode wrote: 'Accurate aim was almost out of the question, and the keeping of distances between ships became a matter of great difficulty, hence made collisions hard to avoid.'[21] On the other hand the shore batteries had not been very effective either. The *New York* was hit once by 5.9-inch shell which hit her port side near the 8-inch waist gun, killing one and wounding four of its crew. The *Iowa* was hit by a 5.9-inch shell abreast of the after 8-inch turret, wounding three men and destroying one of the ships' boats; fragments narrowly missed Sampson, Evans and Lieutenant Commander Rogers on the bridge. The only other casualty was a gunner's mate aboard the *Amphitrite*, who succumbed to the heat in the turret.[22] In San Juan, two or three guns were dismounted; Spanish casualties amounted to eight killed and 20 wounded. The Spanish protested that the Americans had, without warning, bombarded the city itself, but the damage to a number of houses was inadvertent, and was due only to poor shooting. All in all the bombardment of San Juan had not been a very effective performance.

Sampson now had to decide what to do next. Notwithstanding his previous confident intention to take possession of the city if Cervera had not arrived, he began to have second thoughts as to the wisdom of that course:

> The mere credit of the reduction of the place weighed not at all in his mind, and his occupancy, unless immediate, could have no weight in comparison with a meeting with the Spanish fleet. It seemed clear that the news of his being in Puerto Rican waters would cause a divergence of the Spanish admiral elsewhere. Was it wise, even with the certainty of surrender of the port, to risk further any danger of injury to his most important ships? None of importance, except to the monitors from concussion of their own guns, had yet occurred.[23]

Pondering this with his captains Sampson decided that the answer to the question must be that it would indeed not be wise. In fact, nothing had changed; quite simply, Sampson had thought better of what had not been a good idea in the first place. His subsequent report explained his reasons for withdrawing from San Juan, but none of these offered anything new:

> It was clear to my mind that the squadron would not have any great difficulty in forcing the surrender of the place, but the fact that we should be held several days in completing arrangements for holding it; that part of our force would have to be left to await the arrival of troops to garrison it; that the movements of the Spanish squadron, our main objective, were still unknown; that the flying squadron was still north and not in a position to render

> aid; that Havana, Cervera's natural objective, was then open to entry by such a force as his, while we were 1000 miles distant, made our immediate move toward Havana imperative. I thus reluctantly gave up the project against San Juan and stood westward for Havana.[24]

All of these arguments were of course a pretty convincing reason for not attempting the movement to San Juan in the first place, which had achieved little if anything constructive. Wilson comments that 'the affair was really nothing more than a reconnaissance', but goes on to observe that 'the retreat of the fleet conveyed to the Spaniards that they had defeated Admiral Sampson and his ships'.[25] If a reconnaissance was all that was required, and that would certainly seem to be the case, it would have been more sensible to send a fast scout to check on whether Cervera had arrived at San Juan and, if he had not, to continue to watch the port thereafter.

The operation had, however demonstrated one thing, and that was the pronounced limitations of the monitor as a warship type. Wilson summarised some of the defects which had become manifest:

> At San Juan their quick rolling had led to very bad shooting. When underway, they had to be towed, and thus retarded the squadron, and placed it in a very disadvantageous position to meet the enemy. In fact, the experiences of this 2000 mile voyage were conclusive against the type, and have resulted in its complete condemnation.[26]

Chadwick was of a similar view:

> However excellent in harbours (and in smooth waters they have most valuable qualities), the strongest advocates of the monitor had to yield to the experience of the campaign in the Caribbean, and grant to the battleship, which is but the logical development of the monitor, far higher qualities as a sea fighting machine. The battleship, besides having the general good qualities of the monitor, has also those of habitability and comfort... The monitor is a floating hell in discomfort in such operations as those in the West Indies, and no government is justified in subjecting its servants to the torture which their crews must have undergone in such waters.[27]

That, so far as the monitor was concerned, would appear to be that; but nonetheless a not inconsiderable use was to be made of the type during the First World War.

14

Cervera in the West Indies

As Cervera made his way across the Atlantic he too suffered difficulty and delay from broken towlines. He had permitted the destroyers to be towed in order to avoid the necessity of coaling at sea, and to spare their delicate machinery. This had not, however, been anticipated when the squadron left Cadiz and the proper equipment had not been fitted to the destroyers. As a result it became extremely difficult to tow them because of a tendency to yaw considerably, resulting in frequent parting of the towlines. Each of the armoured cruisers towed a destroyer except the *Vizcaya*; her speed was much reduced in any case because her bottom had not been cleaned for a year. Two days out from the West Indies the towing was discontinued, and the cruisers steamed in line ahead, with the destroyers on their beam.[1]

On May 10 Cervera sent Villaamil into Martinique with the *Terror* and *Furor* to find out if coal was available there, and to pick up any intelligence that was to be had about American movements. It had been intended that Villaamil should steam in at 20 knots, but a few hours after leaving the squadron the *Terror*'s boilers gave out. Eventually one of them was repaired, but Villaamil decided to go on in the *Furor* without her. He found that the Spanish consul was away from Fort de France, and the governor was unhelpful, prohibiting the *Furor* from leaving at once because the *USS Harvard* had just sailed from another port in the island. In addition, the collier promised by the Spanish government had not turned up, and there was no other coal to be had. However, Villaamil was able to get some information from Captain Antonio Genis, of the merchant ship *Alicante*, who passed on all he had managed to find out from the newspapers.

Villaamil decided to ignore the governor's prohibition on leaving, and with the help of Captain Genis, who with his boats illuminated the exit from the harbour, he was able to make his way to sea, proceeding at full speed in search of Cervera and the squadron. By 3:00 a.m. on May 11 Villaamil was alongside the flagship, bringing Cervera news of the disastrous battle of Manila Bay, and that a powerful American squadron was off San Juan. For the rest of the day Cervera stood on and off in the hope that one of the colliers might appear, but on the morning of May 12 he gave up on this, and sent the *Terror* in alone to Fort de France to get her boilers repaired. He then called his captains to him to discuss the next move.

The option of going to St Thomas was ruled out, as it was believed that the Americans had stationed a steamer there. San Juan was for the moment out of the question. Havana was blockaded, and it would be risky to try to force an entry into that port. Cienfuegos would also, it was thought, be blockaded, since a force off this port would be best placed to intercept the squadron if it made for Havana. In any case, as Concas observed, 'this harbour, situated at the head of

Cazones Bay, is a veritable rat trap, very easy to blockade, and from which escape is more difficult than from any other harbour of the island.' The entrance was also difficult to defend. Concas went on to explain:

> On the other hand, we were 1250 miles distant from the latter harbour, while from Havana, or Dry Tortugas and Key West, the enemy's base of operations, they had to make a run of only 500 miles to cut us off. For these reasons Cienfuegos harbour was not seriously considered by us at that time. Later when starvation stared us in the face at Santiago de Cuba, the former harbour was thought of as a possible solution, but not on the day of our arrival at Martinique.[2]

That left only Santiago de Cuba, which Cervera and his captains supposed was well supplied with provisions and artillery. Its location on the southern coast 'offered chances of sortie on stormy days and an open sea for operations' once the squadron had been repaired and refitted. Before going there, however coal must be found; a collier was expected at Curaçao, which would add only 200 miles to the journey to Cuba. With this in mind the captains reached a decision:

> It was decided to proceed to Curaçao, because, if we had a collier with us, we could have disappeared in the Caribbean Sea and, though at great risk, reached Havana, and our entering the harbour, though we might have to suffer more or less in the attempt, would not have been prevented by anyone, provided always that the battle had taken place within sight of the forts.[3]

Although Cervera had been unwise to show himself off Martinique and thereby to lose for the moment his cloak of invisibility, the move to Curaçao might help him to regain it, as Mahan wrote after the war when reviewing the Spanish options:

> It may very well be, also, that Cervera, not caring to meet Sampson, whose force, counting the monitors, was superior to his own, thought best to disappear once again from our knowledge. He did, indeed, prolong his journey to Santiago, if that were his original destination, by nearly 200 miles, through going to Curaçao, not to speak of the delay in coaling. But, if the Dutch allowed him to take all that he wanted, he would in his final start be much nearer to Cuba than at Martinique, and he would be able, as far as fuel went, to reach either Santiago, Cienfuegos, Puerto Rico, or even Havana itself – all which possibilities would tend to perplex us. It is scarcely probable, however, that he would have attempted the last named port.[4]

The question of coal dominated Cervera's thinking, as it did Sampson's. The arrangements which had been made for colliers to reach him were not working out well. Three vessels were in the West Indies, with the coal which Cervera so badly needed; the *Roath* was at San Juan, the *Twickenham*, with 2800 tons, only reached Martinique some days after Cervera had left the area; thus all depended on the *Restormel*, which he hoped to find at Curaçao. In this he was disappointed; she had not reached the place due to an engine breakdown, and Cervera had to make do with what he found when he arrived at Willemstad harbour at 8:00 a.m. on May 14. Only two of his ships were permitted to enter the harbour, where he found only 500 tons of poor quality coal available. This was loaded aboard the *Maria Teresa* and *Vizcaya*. The opportunity was also taken to purchase provisions and fresh meat, and carry out some work on the *Vizcaya*'s engines, which had been giving trouble. The *Oquendo* and *Cristobal Colon* remained outside the harbour, with the two destroyers; the *Furor* took on 34 tonnes of coal from the *Colon*.

Cervera had taken the opportunity of his pause at Martinique to report to Bermejo his safe arrival in the West Indies, and the minister sent a number of telegrams in reply, which the admiral did not read until after the war had ended. The content of one was ironic:

> Situation changed since your departure. Your instructions amplified so that if you do not believe that your squadron can operate there successfully may return to Peninsula, choosing route and destination, preferably Cadiz. Acknowledge receipt and indicate decision.[5]

When he reached Curaçao, Cervera reported his arrival to Bermejo, and the fact that the *Restormel* had not arrived, as well as the problems he was having with the Dutch. Bermejo replied that the *Alicante*, carrying coal, had been ordered to leave immediately for Curaçao; if Cervera could not wait, he was to leave orders as to where she should go. Cervera also sent Bermejo a lengthy report of his proceedings. He was evidently deeply affected by the news of Manila Bay, observing that 'there is not the least doubt that the sacrifice, such as made by our comrades in the Philippines, is worthy of the highest honour, and I take pleasure in expressing to them from here my enthusiasm and admiration.' He questioned however whether there were any practical results from such a sacrifice. He went on:

> This painful result therefore justifies the crude ideas I have addressed in my correspondence above referred to, upon which I insist no further, as I do not want to be a bore, which is always a bad thing, especially when addressing a superior.[6]

He found time before leaving Curaçao to send a further report to Bermejo, listing once again the various deficiencies of the ships in his squadron, including the lack of sufficient reliable 5.5-inch ammunition. He also noted that two of the *Vizcaya*'s 5.5-inch guns and one of the *Oquendo*'s could not be relied on. None of the torpedoes promised had been delivered before the squadron sailed from Cadiz. The best speed that the *Vizcaya* could make was no more than 13 or 14 knots, a fact that critically reduced the one advantage he might have had over the enemy, since he certainly could not abandon her. It was Cervera's last report to Bermejo; by the time he was next in communication with Madrid, the minister had been succeeded by Captain Ramon Aunon.

Cervera's failure to get adequate supplies of coal was to be of decisive significance for the outcome of his campaign in the Caribbean. If the *Restormel* had joined him he could have coaled without difficulty in a harbour on the Venezuelan coast. He could then have sailed for Cienfuegos, and would have had two days to coal again and leave the port before Schley arrived on the night of May 21/22, and, as Wilson says, 'with moderate luck he might have got away east to San Juan and recoaled there, thus indefinitely protracting the game of hide and seek and seriously embarrassing the American Navy Department.'[7] As it was, he set off to Santiago de Cuba on the evening of May 15, steaming at the most economical speed possible in order to husband the coal supplies of the *Oquendo* and the *Colon*, which were at a dangerously low level. There was a minor alarm when the squadron was off Jamaica during the night of May 18, when two transatlantic steamers were sighted, which it was feared might be armed merchant cruisers. In the event, the squadron was not seen, but it was a warning of what might lie ahead, as Concas noted:

> We paid no attention to these cruisers or merchant vessels, for as their presence seemed to indicate that there were hostile forces at Santiago it was necessary for us to reach that harbour before daylight, whether to fight at the entrance, or whether to force our way through before being defeated in case the enemy was superior. The admiral did not have the least information as to whether there were hostile forces there, and if so, what they consisted of. At dawn on May 19 the squadron was off Santiago, without having seen a hostile ship.[8]

After the destroyers had made a brief reconnaissance of the coast, by 8:00 a.m. the squadron was safely anchored in the harbour. It was just in time for the *Oquendo* and the *Colon*, which had almost exhausted their coal. Although the enemy had not been sighted, it was a close run thing. At the moment the squadron was anchoring in Santiago, the fast scout *St Louis* and the tug *Wompatuck* were at Guantánamo Bay, 40 miles to the east engaged in an effort to cut the cables leading to the coast of Haiti. On the previous day they had been off Santiago, engaged on a similar task under heavy fire from the shore batteries at the harbour entrance.

Cervera duly reported his safe arrival to Aunon, the new Minister of Marine: 'The squadron entered the harbour this morning. Imperative to clean engines and boilers, which will make it necessary for me to remain here several days. Moreover I need more coal than I have.'[9] Aunon replied at once, congratulating Cervera and the squadron on their 'skilful manoeuvre,' instructing him to cooperate with the governor general. Next day Cervera reported to Aunon that he intended to refit his ships in the shortest possible time, because in his opinion Santiago would soon be in a difficult position if it did not get help. He was still not getting much reliable information about American movements, which sharpened his anxiety to get on with the work of refitting, as he explained in a telegram to Admiral Manterola, the chief of the Navy Yard at Havana on May 20:

> These ships must have engines repaired. I do not know composition of hostile squadrons nor distribution of their other naval forces. Would be grateful to you for this information. Also beg you will advise me whether 5.5-inch ammunition and other stores have been received for the squadron and whether Cienfuegos has resources and communication by land with Havana. Deem it absolutely necessary to send coal and large quantity provisions here at once. We are very grateful to your Excellency and personnel of Navy Yard for congratulations.[10]

Cervera was clearly contemplating the possibility that he might have to be on the move again as soon as his ships were in a fit condition and had been fully coaled, but he was not for the moment getting any instructions about the action which he should take. In a telegram to Aunon May 21 he spelled out his situation:

> Congratulate your Excellency on elevation to ministry, of which we hope great results. Santiago de Cuba very short of provisions, and if it does not receive any it must succumb.

> As the squadron is greatly inferior to American, we can not accept decisive battle, which would mean certain defeat, and if we are blockaded before we finish taking coal, which is difficult, we shall succumb with the city. If provisions are received, resistance will be possible as long as they last.[11]

Concas, meanwhile, had been dismayed by what the squadron had found when it reached Santiago:

> Nothing can be compared with the disastrous condition of Santiago the day of our arrival, and the stupendous ignorance of the Spanish residing there must be counted among the most disastrous features, for they had no conception whatever of the true condition of things... But the city, which like all those of Cuba depended upon imports for its principal supplies, was feeling the effect of being closed in, and the poorer classes that of hunger a month before any hostile ship had appeared off the entrance to the harbour.[12]

Given the difficult military situation facing the city, Concas thought that 'nothing was wanting in these circumstances to induce the admiral to leave the harbour as early as possible.' However, the *Vizcaya* and *Oquendo* had just been twice across the Atlantic, and it was essential to put out their fires and refit their engines, while the other ships needed a general cleaning and their boilers needed their water renewing. This last was due to the ships having been in a state of constant readiness for six months subject to an endless stream of 'movements, alarms and orders.' The task of renewing the water of the boilers was put in hand, but it was slow work. So was the effort to recoal the ships, which Concas graphically described:

> The coal supply of the six ships also had to be renewed, and this work was undertaken with frenzy. What coal there was belonged to the state, and was on a quay belonging to the naval station, where it was difficult for the lighters to come alongside, and where with all the means at our command, and with all that we could hire for their weight in gold, and in spite of the energetic aid of the army, we were not able to ship more than 150 tonnes of coal daily, an insignificant amount for six ships which even before relighting the fires of the engines, which was almost immediately, consumed 45 tonnes of coal per day solely for lighting, winches, cooking and steam launches. Everything which was required for rapid coaling – lighters, tugs, and even baskets – was lacking.[13]

All this while Schley and his squadron had continued in their detention at Hampton Roads. The real purpose that it served there was to act as a tranquilliser for the anxieties of congressmen and others who feared the sudden descent of Cervera on the vulnerable eastern seaboard of the United States. The Flying Squadron would, however, have found it difficult to live up to its name if it had been required suddenly to dash out from its base at Hampton Roads in response to any attack by Cervera on Boston, New York, or Charleston, since rather than being equipped with fast steaming cruisers, it was slowed down by the powerful but slow-moving battleships *Massachusetts* and *Texas*. The news of Cervera's appearance off Martinique at last allowed the Navy Department to release Schley from his imprisonment, and on May 13 he moved out from Hampton Roads with the *Brooklyn*, *Massachusetts* and *Texas* and the armed yacht Scorpion. The collier *Sterling* was left behind, and Schley proceeded to Charleston, and lay off the bar there until he received further orders. He was followed on May 14 by the *Minneapolis* and on May 15 by the *St Paul*, which had orders to scout independently. Finally the *New Orleans* left on May 17, heading directly to Key West. It was to that port that Schley was now directed with his squadron, where he arrived on May 18.

Sampson, meanwhile, had returned from his pointless and ineffective attack on San Juan. The intention now was for his squadron to bar the eastern approaches to Havana, while Schley covered the port from the west. En route to Key West Sampson had sent instructions to the commandant there, Commodore Remey, to have all coal lighters filled with coal ready for the arrival of his squadron on May 18. During the night of May 16/17 Sampson had received news via the *Porter*, which had gone to Cape Haitien to send and receive telegrams, that the US consul in Curaçao had accurately reported Cervera's presence there, and his intended departure. This was confirmed by the Navy Department, which also notified Sampson of Schley's departure from Hampton Roads. The latest intelligence made necessary a redeployment of the various American scouting vessels, the orders for which Sampson set out in a telegram of May 16 to the Navy Department and to the *Harvard*, which was now at St Thomas. The *Yale* was to assist the *St Paul* between Morant Point, Jamaica, Nicolas Mole and Cuba; the *Harvard* was to cover the Mona passage and the north side of Puerto Rico, while the *St Louis* was to await further orders at St Thomas.[14]

Chadwick grumbled that 'Sampson's foresightful orders of May 16 failed of execution', when the Navy Department, having on May 14 ordered all scouts to Key West to watch the Yucatán Channel, changed its mind and sent the *Yale*, *St Paul* and *Minneapolis* to the Venezuelan coast because of information that Spanish colliers had been sent there. This was not the first time that intelligence reaching the Navy Department had proved to be faulty, whereas on the whole the information gathered by the Spanish was at least as accurate, sometimes remarkably so. While Cervera was at sea, however, such intelligence did not reach him, and in general Sampson was more promptly, if not more reliably, informed. Chadwick was also unhappy with the imperative orders sent by the Navy Department that he should return to Key West, arguing that 'with the Flying Squadron now probably in a situation to watch Havana, there can be little doubt that Sampson, left to his own judgement, would himself have gone by the south side of Cuba'.[15] This would presumably have entailed arranging for colliers to meet him there and coal his ships at sea, weather permitting.

In the days immediately following the news of Cervera's appearance off Martinique, the Navy Department was extremely active; as Chadwick remarked, 'telegrams came and went with painful frequency.' This activity demonstrated just how far the Navy Department intended to go in managing Sampson and Schley during this critical phase of the operations around the Cuban coast. An example of this is to be found in the telegram which Long sent to Sampson on May 17:

> Armoured vessels and monitors and flying squadron must be coaled immediately upon arrival at Key West, also four gunboats of the force of the *Marblehead*. Flying squadron, after being increased by the armoured vessels Commander-in-Chief North Atlantic station considers most suitable, proceed with dispatch (utmost) off Cienfuegos, accompanied by the smaller vessels above-mentioned and such torpedo boats, if any, as the Commander-in-Chief will choose to send. The remainder of the naval force on the North Atlantic station and the monitors will blockade Havana closely, remembering the importance of having

> current in their favour. Sampson have choice the command of Havana or at Cienfuegos, Schley in either case to remain with his own squadron. Commander-in-Chief is authorised to make such changes of detail in this plan as he may think proper. In general, the object is to engage and capture the enemy off Cienfuegos if possible, or otherwise blockade him in that port.[16]

This order has very much the look of one drafted by a committee, and it is perhaps not unreasonable to assume that the Naval War Board had a considerable input into its contents.

Sampson arrived in the *New York* at Key West at 4:00 p.m. on May 18, and found Schley, who had arrived at 1:00 a.m. that morning, anchored outside the reef with the *Brooklyn*, *Massachusetts* and *Texas*. The Flying Squadron had been coaling since its arrival. By the following day no less than thirty five warships had been concentrated at Key West, an overwhelming force when compared to Cervera's squadron. As soon as the *New York* dropped anchor, Schley came on board for a discussion with Sampson in the light of the orders received from the Navy Department. These appeared to be based on the belief that Cervera must be heading for Cienfuegos or Havana. Sampson had already decided to remain off Havana himself, sending Schley to Cienfuegos. He added the *Iowa* to Schley's command, as the most powerful unit in the fleet, together with the cruiser *Marblehead*, the torpedo boat *Dupont*, and the smaller vessels *Castine*, a gunboat, and *Eagle*, an armed merchant ship. This force should should certainly be powerful enough to deal with Cervera, if Schley should be fortunate enough to encounter the Spanish squadron. Next morning, at 8:00 a.m., Sampson wrote to Schley with his orders, reflecting Long's telegrams. This was Letter No 5. Schley was to sail without waiting for the *Iowa*, which was still coaling, and which would follow on. Sampson went on:

> It is unnecessary for me to say that you should establish a blockade at Cienfuegos with the least possible delay, and that it should be maintained as close as possible. Should the Spanish vessels show themselves in that vicinity, and, finding you on the lookout, attempt to come around the island, either east or west, please send me notice by the best vessel you have for that purpose, as to their direction, that I may be prepared for them at Havana. I will try and increase the number of light vessels at your disposal, in order that you may have them to send with messages to me in case you should desire to do so. After I have the situation more in hand I will write to you and give you any information that suggests itself.[17]

Armed with these instructions, Schley sailed that morning at 9:00 a.m., bound for Cienfuegos. For him, after a long period of suspended animation, things were now beginning to hot up.

15

Cienfuegos

Schley's proceedings off Cienfuegos and immediately thereafter were to be the subject of bitter controversy and ultimately of legal argument. He steamed towards his destination via the Yucatán Channel at no more than 10 knots, with lights out and guns loaded, expecting at any moment to encounter Cervera's Squadron.

The speed of Schley's passage to Cienfuegos was not directly the subject of a specification in the Court of Inquiry precept, but it proved to be a subject which occupied a lot of the court's attention. Schley was cross-examined about this at some length. His attention was drawn to the order in Letter No 5 that he should 'establish a blockade at Cienfuegos with the least possible delay.' To this he replied that the squadron's speed was about as much as it was capable of making as a unit, having regard to the Gulf Stream current. Subsequently there was a brisk dispute between counsel at the inquiry about the matter, which Schley's lawyers contended was an attempt in effect to add a fresh specification about which they had not had the opportunity to call evidence. The court, however, permitted cross-examination of Schley on the subject, on the basis that everything that occurred from May 19 to June 1, when he was in command of the Flying Squadron, relating to the organisation, management and control of the squadron was admissible. In the event however the point was not laboured by the Judge Advocate, who merely noted the difference in speed between the passage from Charleston to Key West, and from Key West to Cienfuegos, and did not challenge Schley's evidence that the speed 'had some reference, probably, to the greater use of coal.'[1]

Several times during the voyage, on both May 19 and 20, Schley cleared for action when suspicious ships were sighted. He gave Cape San Antonio a wide berth before, at noon on May 21, setting a course direct for Cienfuegos, which he reached at dawn the next day, after pausing during the night about a dozen miles off the port. The *Iowa*, although her coaling at Key West had not been completed, followed the Flying Squadron, which she joined off Cienfuegos about seven hours later.

She brought with her a further letter from Sampson to Schley, written after the receipt at 12:30 a.m. on May 20 of a telegram from Long which had caused the commander-in-chief a great deal of anxiety:

> The report of the Spanish fleet being at Santiago de Cuba might very well be correct, so the Department strongly advises that you send immediately by the *Iowa* to Schley to proceed off Santiago de Cuba with his whole command, leaving one small vessel off Cienfuegos.

> And meanwhile the Department will send the *Minneapolis*, now at St Thomas, *St Paul* proceed at once off Santiago to join Schley, who could keep up communication via Mole, Haiti or Cape Haitien, Haiti. If the *Iowa* has gone, send order to Schley by the fastest dispatch vessel.[2]

The terms of this instruction were clear, but Sampson hesitated to carry it out. Chadwick excused this, saying that 'it was vital to a proper understanding of such a telegram that the source of the report should be mentioned.' He was much influenced by the fact that the department's previous telegrams about Cervera's movements had explicitly stated that the Spanish squadron must come within reach of Havana. There seemed to Sampson, and no doubt to Chadwick as well, that these earlier telegrams should not be ignored if there existed some doubt about Cervera's presence at Santiago. Accordingly, he replied to Long that he had decided to follow the plan previously adopted, with Schley continuing to cover Cienfuegos, while he covered Havana with what was left, which amounted to the *New York*, *Indiana* and the monitors *Puritan* and and *Miantonomoh*. Accordingly, he wrote to Schley, sending copies of his letter (No 7) both by the *Iowa* and by the torpedo boat *Dupont*, which reached Cienfuegos five hours before the battleship. In this letter he enclosed a copy of Long's telegram, and told him that he had 'decided to make no change in the present plan: that is that you should hold your present position of Cienfuegos.' Based on his understanding that Cervera was carrying essential war material for Havana (which was quite wrong) he believed that the Spanish squadron must go either to Havana or Cienfuegos, and that the best bet was to hold those places as strongly as possible. If later it was found that Cervera was at Santiago, they could then assemble all their forces off that port.

This was clear enough, and Schley, as he began his blockade of Cienfuegos, was in no doubt that he was in the right place. However, the nature of that harbour made it difficult to see exactly what vessels lay within:

> The harbour of Cienfuegos is of a type common in Cuba. There is a narrow long channel, bordered by high ground, and giving access to an extensive bay. The length of the channel is 2 miles and the widtht at the narrowest point about 400 yards. There is a bend halfway up, and this coupled with a strong current, renders navigation very difficult. The sheltered sheet of water inside measures about 10 miles long by four wide. It is evident that there was abundant space here for a large fleet, whilst close reconnaissance would be necessary to determine exactly what ships were inside. The masts of vessels in the harbour could just be seen from the sea.[3]

Schley made a couple of passes in front of the entrance at a distance of 4000 yards to see if there would be any response from shore batteries, but there was none. He himself believed that he could see the masts of Cervera's ships; others in the Flying Squadron were very doubtful, noting only one steamer and two schooners there. Generally, however, it was thought that the Spanish squadron had been run to earth. At night, while the big ships cruised 3 miles out at sea, the *Dupont* ran in, and reported several ships in the harbour.

Schley would have been better informed if before leaving Key West he had been told of the arrangements for contacting the insurgents, whose signal fires indicating a wish to communicate were seen to the west, but not understood. These secret arrangements had been made by Commanderr McCalla of the *Marblehead*, who had mentioned them to Chadwick in a conversation when he handed over his report of contacts made with the insurgents. He did not, however, set them out in his report, supposing that he would in any case be shortly seeing Schley at Cienfuegos, and wishing to maintain security. Thus when Schley got a copy of the report containing the information about Spanish positions which McCalla had collected which accompanied Sampson's Letter No 6, he was unaware of the contact arrangements.

On May 20, evidently by now convinced that instructions to Schley to go to Santiago would already be en route to him, the Department ordered Sampson to send some light vessels to Cienfuegos, and to reinforce Schley with two unarmoured cruisers. This did not change the position as far as Sampson was concerned; but later in the day a meeting between Lieutenant Staunton, his assistant chief of staff, and Captain Allen of the Army Signal Corps, revealed that positive confirmation had now been received of Cervera's arrival at Santiago. Sampson learned of this at 6:00 p.m., and prepared a fresh letter to Schley (No 8) to go by the *Marblehead*. It was dated May 21. Even now, however, Sampson did not give an entirely strict instruction to Schley, with unfortunate consequences:

> Spanish squadron probably at Santiago de Cuba – four ships and three torpedo boat destroyers. If you are satisfied that they are not at Cienfuegos proceed with all dispatch, but cautiously, to Santiago de Cuba, and, if the enemy is there blockade him in port. You will probably find it necessary to establish communication with some of the inhabitants, fishermen or others, to learn definitely that the ships are in port, it being impossible to see into it from outside.[4]

Chadwick says that both he and Sampson supposed, 'judging from the chart, that the hills were low enough to permit Cienfuegos to be observed,' a supposition which, he says, was partially correct.

Throughout May 23 Schley's squadron lay off Cienfuegos with engines stopped. During the day the collier *Merrimac* arrived with the gunboat *Castine* and the armed yacht *Hawk*, and the *Iowa*, *Castine* and *Dupont* coaled on the open sea. While the squadron was engaged in this task Schley pondered his next move. In addition to Letter No 8, Sampson had also sent with the *Marblehead* a memorandum which appeared to assume that Schley would have satisfied himself that Cervera was not at Cienfuegos, since it did not repeat that qualification, but said:

> It is thought that the enclosed instructions will reach you by 2:00 a.m., May 23. This will enable you to leave before daylight (regarded as very important), so that your direction will not be noticed, and be at Santiago a.m. 24th. It is thought that the Spanish squadron will probably still be at Santiago, as they must have some repairs to make and coal to take.[5]

The memorandum went on to give instructions about the deployment of the ships scouting off Santiago. There was also, as Schley noted, a manuscript addition to the margin 'written in ink … in an unknown hand' an additional comment with regard to the masking of Schley's direction:

> Our experience has been that ships can be traced by their smoke from 20 to 30 miles, and it is suggested in case you leave in the daytime, to stand a good distance to the westward before turning southward.[6]

Schley, not unreasonably, observed that 'one who reads these dispatches impartially today can not but be impressed by them as uncertain in tone and undecided in information.' Set against his firm conviction that Cervera almost certainly was in Cienfuegos, it is not difficult to see why Schley decided not to move.

That conviction had been strengthened during the day by the arrival off Cienfuegos of the British steamer *Adula,* bound there from Jamaica, and authorised to enter the port for the purpose of carrying away neutrals. She also brought news that the Spanish squadron had arrived at Santiago on May 19 and had sailed on the following day. This, Schley thought, was 'strongly presumptive of the presence of the fleet in Cienfuegos,' and was of course consistent with Long's telegram to Sampson that Cervera's orders, to reach Havana, Cienfuegos or another port linked by rail to the capital, were imperative. Schley allowed the *Adula* to proceed into the port, exacting a promise that she come out next day, so he could get definitive information about whether Cervera was there.

It was in this state of mind that Schley reported to Sampson in two letters dated May 23. He thought that Cervera was in Cienfuegos. In his first letter he expressed this by saying that he was 'by no means satisfied that the Spanish squadron is not at Cienfuegos,' and considered it extremely unwise to chase up a probability at Santiago de Cuba, reported via Havana, no doubt as a ruse. He considered that 'the large amount of smoke seen in the harbour would indicate the presence of a number of vessels.' He would therefore, he said, remain off Cienfuegos. In his second letter he reported his dealings with the steamer *Adula;* that he had heard gunfire towards Cienfuegos, which he took to be a salute welcoming Cervera; and that the news from Jamaica was to the effect that the Spanish had left Santiago. He concluded: 'I think them here, almost to a certainty.'[7]

It was suggested by Wilson, and by others such as William Goode, the Associated Press correspondent, that Schley was in this way disobeying a direct order. Wilson wrote that 'it would seem that these orders left Schley no discretion, unlike those sent by the *Marblehead* which arrived on the 24th.'[8] He was wrong about the arrival of the latter, which reached Schley on May 23, but that hardly changes the case. On May 23 Schley had all the orders he was going to get about Cienfuegos. Sampson indeed cabled Long: 'Schley has been ordered to Santiago,' being satisfied that the total effect of his various orders left no discretion in the matter. Goode also regards the effect of the memorandum which accompanied Letter No 8 as 'in the nature of a direct order for Schley to proceed instantly to Santiago.'[9] Explaining the somewhat tentative wording of Sampson's instructions to Schley, Goode observed:

> Sampson was particularly loath as to adopt any measures when dealing with Schley that could possibly be taken as needless usurpation of authority. He then looked upon Schley more in the light of a joint commander than as a subordinate... The fact that Schley at this point period actually ranked Sampson and also commanded a squadron of his own made the situation somewhat delicate.[10]

If Sampson really supposed that Schley was conscious of his seniority, he might have concluded that this was all the more reason to put his orders to move at once to Santiago completely unequivocally, rather than allow Schley to feel that that seniority gave him some freedom in the matter. In fact, when considering the text of the first of Schley's two letters of May 23, it is possible to see that he did suppose himself to have the discretion that his critics deny. Of course, his judgment that Cervera was to be found at Cienfuegos was quite wrong; but in his defence it has been argued that it was in any case his responsibility, and that had the Spanish squadron actually been there, and he had left without satisfying himself, he would have been justly condemned if they had then emerged and got into Havana.

Schley's letters did not reach Sampson until May 26, being carried at first by the *Hawk* and then by the *Dolphin*. Parker, whose book on the campaign is as partisan as one would expect from one of Schley's lawyers, introduced a possibly significant element into the debate when setting out a statement 'from an officer of high rank (whose declarations import, in the Navy, absolute verity)' describing the reception of Schley's letters aboard the flagship:

> There were present, besides myself, Admiral Sampson, Captain Chadwick, chief of staff, and perhaps others. Chadwick was animadverting upon Schley's proposed delay at Cienfuegos. I said: 'Let us see the orders that have been sent to him.' These were brought in, and as they were read aloud I saw a surprised look come into Chadwick's face, and he said to the Admiral, 'I didn't know that you had sent such orders to Commodore Schley.' 'Yes,' replied the Admiral, 'he is only obeying his orders.'[11]

The 'officer of high rank' was almost certainly Commodore John C Watson. Parker finds some confirmation of this statement in the evidence which Chadwick subsequently gave to the Court of Inquiry, when he said: 'I did not read the original dispatch until the answer was brought by the *Hawk*. That was on May 26, when the ship (*New York*) was at a point between Havana and Cay Francis, and in the vicinity of Cay Pedros.'[12]

Goode, one of the most partisan of Sampson's supporters, described the reaction of the admiral and his staff to Schley's report in very different terms:

> Sampson and his commanding officers and his staff read this letter over and over again, searching for some intelligent reason for Schley's action. All they found was the smoke seen by Schley in the harbour. Comparing this with the definite information regarding Cervera's arrival at Santiago, it was only too evident that Schley had allowed himself to be cruelly deceived.[13]

Schley's second letter, suggesting that he had drawn conclusions from hearing the sound of gunfire at the remarkable distance of 40 miles was, thought Goode, 'past all comprehension.' Schley's reasoning was such, he argued, that both at Washington and aboard the flagship there was serious alarm and a consequent loss of confidence in his judgement and professional capability.

Schley's conviction that Cervera was at Cienfuegos did not long survive his discussion with Commander McCalla on May 24 after his arrival to join the squadron off the port. Schley told him of the signal lights that had been observed on the shore at night. George Graham, another Associated Press correspondent, was quite as partisan as his colleague William Goode, though in his case it was an as an ardent supporter of Commodore Schley. He recounted the conversation:

> McCalla said in an evidently very much surprised way, 'Why, those were signals from the insurgents who desired to communicate with you. Didn't you know about that?' 'No,'

said Schley shortly. And for a few moments I thought his temper would get the better of him and that he would say something ugly. He stamped up and down the quarterdeck, twitching nervously at his little imperial and grinding his heels savagely down on the deck. 'Why in the world didn't you tell me about this?' he said to McCalla. 'Here I have been waiting two or three days to get definite information from the shore.' McCalla said something about the matter having slipped his mind when he passed Schley Sunday morning.[14]

Schley ordered McCalla to proceed at once to contact the insurgents; a few hours later, McCalla returned with the news that the insurgents needed arms, provisions and ammunition and, more importantly, that Cervera's squadron was not in Cienfuegos. During the afternoon, supplies of ammunition, clothing and food were transferred from the *Brooklyn* to the *Marblehead* for delivery to the insurgents. At 7:00 p.m. on May 24 the squadron, leaving behind the *Castine* to watch the entrance to the port, sailed for Santiago, steering at first south-east and then, after an hour, altering course eastwards.

The squadron's speed at first was about 9 knots. However, once away from the lee of the land, both wind and sea increased, and soon the weather was so heavy that the squadron had to slow down, first for the *Eagle* and then for the *Marblehead*. The ships steamed in column, the *Brooklyn* leading, followed by the *Massachusetts*, *Texas*, *Iowa*, *Marblehead*, *Vixen*, *Eagle* and the collier *Merrimac*. The *Eagle* was running short of coal, and Schley detached her, sending her first to Jamaica with orders to go on to Key West. Before sailing, Schley drafted two telegrams to the Navy Department, carried by the *Dupont* with orders to take them to Key West for transmission to Washington. The first commented on the difficulties experienced in coaling off Cienfuegos, made recommendations about coaling in future, and concluded:

Have ascertained that the Spanish fleet is not here, and I will move eastward tomorrow communicating with you from Nicolas Mole. On account of short coal supply in ships, cannot blockade them in Santiago.[15]

The second, mentioning the coal shortage of the *Texas* in particular, repeated that he would not be able to remain off Santiago 'on account of general short coal supply of squadron;' he would proceed to Nicolas Mole, where the water was smooth and he could coal his ships.

When the squadron set off to Santiago the weather was beginning to deteriorate. Captain Francis S Cook, the captain of the *Brooklyn*, who served as Schley's chief of staff, subsequently gave evidence to the inquiry as to the conditions encountered:

We had a fair run the night of the 24th. The weather gathered during the night, and the next day it was squally, stormy; and there was from a moderate to rough sea. The 25th was a bad day. On the 26th the weather had moderated so far as the wind was concerned, but there was a long, nasty sort of sea and the ships rolled a good deal.[16]

The logbooks of the ships in the squadron confirmed Cook's recollection. The weather was not such as to inconvenience the *Brooklyn* or the battleships, but the smaller vessels suffered considerably.

The squadron arrived off Santiago on May 26, though squally rain prevented visibility of the land until afternoon. The average speed of the squadron during its passage of about 315 miles had been about 7 knots. Later in the afternoon contact was made with the scouts *St Paul* and *Yale*, and Schley ordered the squadron to heave to, only to learn that nothing had been seen of Cervera's squadron. Later, the *Minneapolis* joined the squadron, but also reported that there had been no sign of the Spanish warships. The *St Paul* had, however, at 6:00 a.m. on the previous day captured the British collier *Restormel* which, having missed Cervera at Curaçao, had been ordered to Santiago. This was an indicator that the Spanish squadron had been bound for that place.

Captain Charles Sigsbee, the erstwhile captain of the *Maine*, came aboard the *Brooklyn* to report what he knew to Schley. He brought with him a letter which he had drafted to Captain Jewell of the *Minneapolis* but which he now addressed to Schley. This concluded: 'I have seen absolutely nothing of the Spanish fleet.' The only information that he or any of the captains of the scouts had relating to Cervera derived from the telegrams from the Navy Department. To Captain Jewell the Navy Department had telegraphed on May 19 the following:

> Proceed at once off Santiago de Cuba; the Spanish fleet reported there; Schley ordered there; find *Harvard*, if practicable, she is somewhere off the north coast of Puerto Rico; proceed with off Santiago; her orders same as yours; keep touch with Spanish fleet: communicate occasionally.[17]

It was no easier for a blockading fleet to be sure what ships were at Santiago than Cienfuegos. There was considerable difficulty in entering the harbour, the narrow channel zigzagging first one way and then another, so that it was impossible for two ships to be navigated abreast, as Chadwick described, explaining the difficulty experienced by the scouts:

> The narrow and twisting canyon of the entrance and the high bluff bordering it, forbidding any view of the harbour beyond the river like reaches stretching in for about a mile, with several turns before opening into a beautiful bay three and a half miles long and nearly a mile in its broadest part... Nothing, however, as just said, could be seen by the *Yale* and *St Paul* of the Spanish squadron in the inner harbour, though the former was near enough to the entrance for a close inspection.[18]

It was at this point that the collier *Merrimac* signalled that her intermediate valve stem had broken off, and that it would take two or three hours to repair, while Captain Wise in the *Minneapolis* reported his vessel to be short of coal and that her engines were in a bad condition. In answer to an enquiry from the *Brooklyn*, he said that he had just enough coal to get to Key West. Meanwhile it took the *Yale* until 10:30 a.m. the following morning before she finally got a towline aboard the hapless *Merrimac* after several unsuccessful attempts.

Captain Cotton of the *Harvard* had reached St Nicolas Mole early on May 25, and sent off Schley's dispatch of May 22 from Cienfuegos which had reached him via the *Scorpion*. This of course had been overtaken by events with Schley's move to Santiago. Copying these to Sampson, Cotton explained the coaling situation of the various scouts, and reported that the *Yale* had reconnoitred Santiago on May 21, and saw nothing in the harbour. Nor had he or Wise any news to report of the Spanish squadron. On May 26 the *Dolphin* reached Sampson with Schley's two dispatches of May 23 to the effect that he was remaining off Cienfuegos, which caused Sampson serious anxiety. He at once sent off orders to Schley which, at last, were in unequivocal terms; they, too, however, had been overtaken by events, but were sent by the armed yacht *Wasp*, the fastest vessel available:

> Every report, and particularly daily confidential reports received at Key West from Havana, state Spanish squadron has been in Santiago de Cuba from the 19th to the 25th instant inclusive, the 25th being the date of the last report received. You will please proceed, with all possible dispatch, to Santiago to blockade that port. If, on arrival there, you receive positive information of the Spanish ships having left, you will follow them in pursuit.[19]

Sampson reported all this to the Navy Department, pointing out that Schley should, in the circumstances, be able to reach Santiago before he could.

Meanwhile Schley's two dispatches of May 24, sent after discovering that the Spanish squadron had not been in Cienfuegos at all, had reached the Navy Department; copies of these reached Sampson, and caused still greater alarm, since although the Flying Squadron was now said to be en route to Santiago, Schley had announced his inability to remain off the port on account of the general short coal supply of his ships. Sampson convened a meeting with Commodore Watson and his flag captain, Commander Converse of the *Montgomery*, Captain Folger of the *New Orleans*, and Chadwick, to discuss what should be done. It was concluded that an attempt should be made to block the entrance to the harbour at Santiago, and thus bottle up the Spanish squadron. Commander Converse suggested that the unfortunate *Merrimac*, by reason of her great length and full cargo of coal, would be suitable for the purpose. Folger was therefore sent off in the *New Orleans*; he was to communicate with Schley, 'directing him to remain on the blockade of Santiago at all hazards, assuming that the Spanish vessels are in that port.' He was also to outline the blocking plan, although Schley could use his own judgment as to the details. In the meantime, Schley was to use the utmost care to ensure that none of Cervera's squadron was to be allowed to escape.[20] Folger left for Santiago at 6:55 p.m. on May 27, accompanied by the collier *Sterling*, which was to replace the *Merrimac*; he was, however, to leave her to proceed at her own pace to Santiago, while he steamed there at full speed.

16

Schley at Santiago

Schley's conviction that Cervera was at Cienfuegos had led him to disregard the admittedly tentative instructions that he had had from Sampson to move to Santiago. He was mistaken; but the reason for his actions was clear enough. The same cannot be said of his explanation for the movements of his squadron after it arrived off Santiago de Cuba. It was a matter which formed the subject of three of the specifications of the precept that was before the Court of Inquiry, and he was pressed hard to explain his actions.

When the Flying Squadron reached the area of Santiago, the three ships that had been watching the entrance to the harbour had joined it, leaving it uncovered from 6:00 p.m. on May 26 until the *St Paul* returned to the station at 5:00 p.m. on the following day. According to Schley, he had asked Sigsbee directly, when he came aboard the *Brooklyn*: 'Have you got the Dons here, or in here?' To this Sigsbee replied: 'No! They are not in here, they are only reported here.' He added that he had been close in the day before and had seen nothing unusual, and that the Captains of the *Yale* and the *Minneapolis* had assured him that they had not either.[1] Schley talked also to Eduardo Nunez, a pilot who had arrived with Sigsbee and who was very familiar with Santiago, who did not believe that Cervera's squadron had entered the harbour.

These conversations appear to have fixed in Schley's mind that the Spanish squadron was at sea. He gave several accounts of his reasoning. In point of time, the first was a narrative which he provided for George Graham's first-hand history of the Santiago campaign, when he wrote:

> I did not call any council of war. The information which these people gave me led me to infer that my impression was correct, that the telegraphic information was a ruse precisely similar to that which was telegraphed from Cadiz that the squadron had returned from the Cape de Verdes. It is precisely what I would have done if I had been militarily managing their situation – to have attracted the squadrons in the direction of either one of these ports and then gone in behind them.[2]

Cross-examined during the hearings of the Court of Inquiry, Schley was asked by Lemly if after the receipt of instructions he had nevertheless left his station. He replied:

> Yes, I did, and for these reasons. First, Captain Sigsbee, who commanded a scout placed in front of that harbour, declared that he did not believe the squadron was there. Secondly, Eduardo Nunez, the pilot, stated that he did not believe that that squadron could enter that

> harbour. Thirdly, on account of dispatch No 7 with the accompanying memorandum, in which Admiral Sampson minimised the importance of the squadron being there, and that the fact that the department's telegram, which reached me on May 27, was so ambiguous in its terms. It authorised me to coal at Gonaives, Haiti, or Cape Cruz. Gonaives, under the circumstances, being to the eastward, and knowing that Admiral Sampson was at Cay Francis, in the Bahama channel, to the north, it occurred to me that if the Spanish squadron were extant the proper strategic move was to go to the westward and not to the eastward... Those were the influencing and operating motives. I felt that the move west was, strategically, the proper one, with the determination to coal as rapidly or as quickly as possible, and I felt the efficiency of my squadron was only equal to the efficiency of the coal supply of the lowest one that composed it. Those were the motives which influenced that movement.[3]

Three years after the Court of Inquiry, when Schley published his memoirs, he repeated his reliance on the information, or non-information, from the scouts; added the 'strong possibility of the truth of the Jamaica bulletins;' repeated his concern that the Santiago telegrams might be Spanish ruses; and emphasised again 'the implied doubts'in Sampson's orders and 'the uncertainty of Mr Long's information.' These factors, taken with the fact that Sampson was at Cay Francis, suggested his westward move at 9:50 p.m. on May 26, the purpose of which was to block 'the passage to the westward to bar any effort of the enemy to reach Havana by a dash through the Yucatán passage in Sampson's rear.'[4]

When he gave the order at 7:45 p.m. on May 26 to the squadron to steam westwards via the south side of Cuba and the Yucatán Channel to Key West as soon as the squadron was ready, it occasioned some surprise. Robley Evans, aboard the *Iowa*, was amazed; he later recounted a megaphone exchange with John Philip, the captain of the *Texas*. Evans is not always to be depended on for an entirely truthful account of matters about which he held a strong opinion, and by the time he came to give his account of this incident he was extremely hostile to Schley; but he can hardly have invented the exchange with Philip. After receipt of the order to move to the west he hailed him:

> 'Say, Jack, what the devil does it mean?'
> 'Beats me. What do you think?'
> 'Damned if I know, but I know one thing – I'm the most disgusted man afloat.'[5]

The *Merrimac*'s engine failure, and the subsequent problems experienced in getting a towline securely aboard her meant that the squadron could not set off in accordance with Schley's order until 10:30 a.m. on May 27. In the meantime Schley had sent the *Harvard* to Jamaica with a telegram in response to that from the Navy Department which, when it reached its destination on May 28, caused dismay in Washington. In this telegram Schley reported the problems with the *Merrimac*, and the impossibility of coaling the ships due 'to very rough seas and boisterous weather since leaving Key West.' He went on to say that it was 'impossible to remain off Santiago in present state of coal account of the squadron... It is also regretted that the department's orders cannot be obeyed earnestly as we have all striven to that end. I am forced to return to Key West via Yucatán passage for coal.' He added that he could ascertain nothing certain with regard to Cervera's squadron.[6]

Long, in his memoirs, described Schley's message as 'one of the most infelicitous in history.' He went on:

> I remember well the receipt of this dispatch. I was with President McKinley at the Army review at Camp Alger. His face fell when I showed it to him. It was incomprehensible – the first flinching of the campaign. It was the darkest day of the war. It was the lack, not of personal courage, but of that unswerving steadiness of purpose and nerve which is the essence of supreme command, and of which Farragut is an example.[7]

Long set out in some detail the official view of the actual state of the coal supply of the ships in Schley's squadron, commenting on the facts presented to the Court of Inquiry. The Department contended that at noon on May 27 his vessels had coal sufficient to remain on blockade duty of Santiago, 'the *Brooklyn* for 26 days, the *Iowa* for 16 days, the *Massachusetts* for 20 days, the *Texas* for 10 days, the *Marblehead* for 5 days and the *Vixen* for 23 days,' and that after that each ship would have had enough fuel to get to Gonaives or Cape Cruz, where they could have been coaled from the *Merrimac*. The *Texas* and *Marblehead* both coaled at sea from the *Merrimac* on May 27 and May 28, and the rest of the squadron over the ensuing three days.[8]

Sampson had reached Key West on May 28 at 2:00 a.m., resolved to go on to Santiago himself if the situation remained uncertain. From Key West he updated Washington as to the situation as he understood it. At 8:00 a.m. he learned that, if Cervera was proved to be in harbour at Santiago, it was 'the intention of the Department to make a descent immediately upon that port with 10,000 men, United States troops, landing eight nautical miles east of that port.' Sampson's task was to convoy the transports carrying the invasion force, probably 15 or 20 in number. That afternoon Sampson told the Department of his orders to Schley to blockade Santiago, and to sink a collier across the entrance to the port. After the consequences of Schley's message had sunk in, the Department at midnight asked Sampson how long it would take him to reach Santiago with the *New York*, *Oregon*, *Indiana* and some light vessels, and how long he could remain on blockade there. Sampson's response at 3:00 a.m. on May 29 was that he could be there in three days, and could blockade indefinitely, and that he would like to start at once. At 2:00 p.m. the tension was eased when a despatch was received from Schley dated May 28, which had been carried by the *Yale* to Jamaica:

> Collier now having been temporarily repaired and able to make six knots or seven will endeavour to coal *Texas* and *Marblehead* in open sea and hold position off Santiago until coal supply of larger ships is reduced to lowest safe limit. Will then go to Gonaives or coast near or in vicinity of Port-au-Prince to coal.[9]

Schley, it appeared, had changed his mind about proceeding to the westward. What had happened? From the evening of May 26 until 3:40 p.m. on the following day the squadron had been lying to, waiting for the *Yale* to get a secure towline aboard the *Merrimac*. That afternoon Schley had an indication from the press boat that Sampson was on his way to Santiago; Chadwick reckons that this information 'may have had influence in the decision, shortly reached, to turn for Santiago.' This is hardly fair, since it was after hearing about Sampson's movements that Schley set off with his squadron to the west, and it seems reasonable to accept Schley's explanation that it was a gradual improvement in the weather that led to his decision. At 7:00 p.m. he signalled Philip in the *Texas*: 'If collier is cast off do you think you could coal tonight?' To this, Philip replied: 'We can try.' Asked the same question, the *Marblehead* replied: 'Yes, if collier stops'. Thereupon, Schley immediately ordered the squadron to stop, and the work of coaling got under way. Next morning, Schley signalled the *Minneapolis*: 'We are going to hold on here as long as coal lasts. Proceed to Key West and coal.' At 1:20 p.m., at which time the squadron was some 37 miles west of the entrance to Santiago harbour, he ordered it to steam towards the entrance at 6 knots. En route, he confirmed to all ships his intention to remain off the port as long as the coal lasted, and at 8 p.m. arrived at a point ten miles south of Santiago, where he stopped for the night.[10] If in this way he had repaired his original error of judgement, he cannot avoid the criticism that it was based purely on hearsay evidence.

In Santiago, Cervera had found the local military commander, Lieutenant General Arsenio Linares, to be extremely cooperative, although grimly aware that the situation of his troops was extremely grave; Concas described them as 'completely exhausted by three years of warfare in that horrible climate, with arrears in pay amounting to thirteen months, and impossible food, the result of this lack of pay.'[11] Although some of the guns installed to cover the entrance to the harbour were antique in the extreme, the guns of the elderly cruiser *Reina Mercedes* were disembarked and installed on the Socapa and at Punta Gorda, although the work was incomplete at the date of the squadron's arrival. The *Mercedes* herself was immobile and in any case of no fighting value.

Cervera now convened a council of war to consider the squadron's next step. It assembled in his cabin on May 24. He reported the outcome of their discussion in a telegram to Aunon:

> Squadron being ready to leave anchorage in search of stores it needs, have assembled captains of ships, which are unanimously of following opinion: In view maximum speed this squadron reduced to 14 knots, account of *Vizcaya* bottom fouled, lack of coal, location of hostile fleets, and condition of harbour, certain danger of sortie greater than advantages gained by reaching San Juan, only harbour where we could go. Proceedings drawn up and signed by me. Shall await more favourable opportunity. Meanwhile will get all possible supplies, and in conjunction with commander-in-chief of army division aid in defence of harbour and city. To supply city, necessary to run blockade with fast vessels 20 knots at night, after agreeing on day and hour to send out of harbour pilot and keep channel clear. Have instructed transatlantic steamers Havana and Martinique not to go out because would certainly be captured.[12]

This was certainly an opportunity missed; the squadron could have got out unmolested, and could almost certainly have reached San Juan, and there taken on more coal. Although the squadron's departure would have been noted by the scouts stationed off the harbour, they could not have delayed it, and Cervera would have had a decisive lead over any armoured ships that set off in pursuit, whether from Schley's squadron or that of Sampson. The problem for the Spanish, however, was where then to go. Cienfuegos was a rat trap, and Schley was watching that port. From San Juan, a journey to Havana would be to incur the risk of an encounter with part at least of the American fleet and the considerable probability of the squadron's destruction. The only remaining alternative was to return to Europe, and thus end the Navy's contribution to the defence of Cuba.

Information from the governor general suggested that the chance of escape might have already gone. On May 24 Blanco informed Cervera that the *Oregon* had reached Key West, and that the Flying Squadron was proceeding to Santiago 'where Sampson also intends to arrive tomorrow, unless notified of departure of Cervera's squadron. If latter does not go out, may be closed in.' In a separate telegram Blanco wrote of news from the United States of an intention to blockade Santiago. This information, together with the appearance of the *Minneapolis* and the three scouts off the port, convinced Cervera, and he telegraphed Aunon on May 25:

> We are blockaded. I qualified our coming here as disastrous for interests of country. Events begin to show I was right. With disparity of forces any effective operations absolutely impossible. We have provisions for one month.[13]

Perhaps conscious that he had missed a chance to escape, the admiral wrote to Linares to tell him of what of what had transpired, remarking that 'it is much to be regretted that the squadron did not go out yesterday while it had all the fires lighted.' He went on to say that his ships needed a number of hours to get up steam, and hence they could not be ready before night, which would be too late. Accordingly, he would take up positions to defend the harbour and city against any American attempt to force the entrance. The *Colon* was already in place; she was moored three quarters of a mile inside the entrance, and broadside to it, with lines running from her stern to the eastern bank. The rest of the squadron was moored at intervals further within the harbour.

From Madrid, Aunon sent an encouraging response to Cervera's gloomy telegram of May 25, approving the admiral's determination and reiterating his freedom of action, as well as the government's confidence in him. The squadron must not, however be sacrificed in vain, a direction which Cervera took to heart. As he had said to Linares, it was bad luck which had brought him to a harbour so ill supplied with provisions, coal and stores of every kind. He had expected to be blockaded in due course, but reckoned that he could keep the greater part of the American fleet occupied there, 'which was the only effective service that can be expected of this small and poorly equipped squadron.'[14] When Schley's squadron, having made its way from Cienfuegos, appeared off Santiago on the morning of May 26, it was clear that the door was about to be bolted, and Cervera convened another council of war for that morning. He was not to know it, but the movements of Schley's squadron consequent on the latter's decision to return to Key West had given him a final opportunity to escape.

Although the ships' bunkers were not full, the *Infanta Maria Teresa* had 300 tons of coal, the *Cristobal Colon* 700 tons and the *Oquendo* and *Vizcaya* 500 tons each. On this occasion there was unanimous agreement that the squadron should go out, and make for San Juan, and orders were issued for the ships to be ready to leave at 5:00 p.m. At 2:00 p.m., however, the watchers reported to Cervera the presence of three ships off the entrance; these were the *Minneapolis*, *St Paul* and *Yale*, and he began to have second thoughts. He called another council of war, and this time opinion was divided, as Concas recorded:

> Some thought we should go out in any event, directing our course towards San Juan, and that if we should perish there it would be by will of the government, and if we succeeded in getting to sea with all or part of the squadron it would be safe. Others thought that, as it was quite possible and even probable that the *Colon* would be lost at the mouth of the harbour, for which reason she must be the last to make the sortie, the squadron would be reduced to nothing.[15]

During the course of the discussion doubts about whether the prevailing swell would prevent the ships going out had grown since the earlier meeting, and Cervera called in the pilot Miguel, who had piloted the flagship in when the squadron arrived. He was emphatically of the opinion that there would be no trouble taking out any of the cruisers, with the exception of the *Colon*. The others drew only 23.3 to 23.6 feet; but he advised that 'the going out of the *Colon*, whose draft is 24.9 feet, might present difficulties on account of a flat rock in the water off Point Morrillo, where the water is only 27.5 English feet deep.' The pilot was sent out to form a more exact opinion on the state of the sea, and returned saying that owing to the swell, the *Colon* might touch bottom on the flat rock. Cervera then put a question for the council of war: 'is it expedient to risk the *Colon* being injured, or should the sortie not be effected, awaiting more favourable circumstances?'

To this question, five of those present replied that they were not in favour of going out; these were the second in command, Commodore Paredes, and Captains Eulate, Lezaga, Moreu and Villaamil. Two took the opposite view – Concas and the chief of staff, Joaquin Bustamente. Each of these annexed their dissenting opinions to the record of proceedings. Bustamente, reviewing the situation in which the squadron found itself, was sceptical about the risk to the *Colon*. He summed up his detailed argument:

> Within the range of possibilities, I believe it preferable for the *Colon* (which in my mind should be the last to go out) to remain disabled at the harbour entrance than for us to await what I fear is in store for us. This is my opinion. I sincerely hope that I may be mistaken, but my current conscience dictates it to me, and I can not hold it back.

Concas was of the same view; he did not think that the loss of the *Colon* was at all probable, and in any case 'circumstances demand our running the risk even of total loss, which I consider very remote.' He had no hope that a more favourable opportunity would present itself.[16]

Confronted with these conflicting opinions, Cervera took the fatal decision to support the majority, saying that he 'did not consider the circumstances so extreme as to make it necessary to risk the loss of the *Colon*.' He hoped that the sea would calm down, and that they would have another chance. It was a decision that many in Santiago, and elsewhere, found puzzling. Concas, ever loyal to Cervera, wrote subsequently of his 'terrible dilemmas' and added that although he had been one of those who voted for the sortie he thought that 'Admiral Cervera was very wise in deciding to have the fires extinguished under eight boilers of each ship and remain at Santiago in expectation of whatever opportunity fortune might offer us.' It had been his opinion that the squadron's destruction had been what the government wanted; and as for hoping for a better opportunity, it never came, 'as it never does when the disproportion of forces is so great and when all the fundamental principles of naval strategy have been disregarded.'[17]

Wilson was not so kind to Cervera, using language which was extremely severe, particularly with regard to the failure to prevent the capture of the *Restormel* by the *St Paul* at 6:00 p.m. on May 26. At that time the *Colon* was in position to see the *Restormel*, smoke belching from her funnel as she sought the safety of the harbour:

> Whilst still some distance away the merchant man was overhauled and captured: a little later she vanished with her captor towards the south. No condemnation for the apathy or positive cowardice which allowed such an incident to take place can be too strong. The

> *Colon* had ample coal to run out and save the collier; her mere appearance must have driven off the *St Paul*. With the *Restormel* a large quantity of excellent coal and some coaling appliances would have been at Cervera's disposal.[18]

With Schley's return to the vicinity of Santiago on the evening of May 28, Cervera's last chance of escape was gone. On the following morning, as the American squadron stood in towards Santiago, the *Colon* was sighted. The *Massachusetts* signalled to the flagship: 'a vessel inside of harbour looks like a man-of-war.' A more detailed report came from the *St Paul* at 8:00 p.m: 'in the entrance, apparently coming out, two men of war resembling armoured cruisers with flags at each masthead, also two smaller vessels.' The identity of the *Colon* could not be in doubt, having only a single mast unlike the other ships of Cervera's squadron. Since the *Colon* had been moored in her position since May 26, Sigsbee was pressed during the Court of Inquiry to know how it could be that he had not sighted her on that day. He told the court that during May 26 he went in to four miles, or a little less, from the harbour:

> I think she warped ahead (i.e. after mooring). I have no doubt that she was lying in that entrance on this day, but unless she warped into sight I could not have seen her in there. There is plenty of room for her there. You will see that the log shows that she did shift her fasts – did shorten them in at different times.[19]

The failure to detect the *Colon* was, however, more than a little surprising.

With the news that Cervera's squadron had been definitively identified, Schley called a meeting of his captains aboard the *Brooklyn*, at 8:30 a.m., when he explained how he would attack the Spanish should they attempt a sortie. The squadron was now in line of battle, steaming slowly east and west before the harbour entrance at a distance of about six miles. If the Spanish emerged, Schley proposed to attack them as they filed out, concentrating his fire in the first instance on the leading ship. Evans asked if it was Schley's intention to remain immobile as they came out, or to steam directly at them. Schley was emphatic in his response: 'Certainly. What do you think I'd do? We'll just get as close to that entrance as we possibly can, the instant we see them making a move to come out, and I don't think they'll get very far.'[20]

During the day the *Massachusetts* and the *Vixen* coaled from the *Merrimac*. Schley sent off Sigsbee in the *St Paul* to Key West, with a telegram to the Navy Department and Sampson announcing the discovery of Cervera's squadron and the identification of the *Colon* and *Maria Teresa*; which was to be sent from St Nicholas Mole. During the night of May 29/30 the squadron steamed very slowly back and forth across the harbour entrance. At 9:30 a.m. next day HMS *Indefatigable* arrived from Jamaica, requesting permission to enter Santiago, but although this was granted she departed without doing so. The weather was fair, and the sea smooth, and throughout the day and the following night Schley maintained his vigil of the port. Coaling at sea continued. On the morning of May 31 the *Harvard* arrived from Jamaica, with a number of telegrams to Schley from the Navy Department. These required him to remain off Santiago unless it was unsafe to do so, and if he must leave, to block the entrance; asked about the other two armoured cruisers; told him that Sampson was on the way with the *New York*, *Oregon* and *New Orleans*; and identified Sagua, 25 miles east of Santiago, as a good place for landing, and which was held by the insurgents.

Schley had decided during May 30 to attack the *Colon*, which had not moved, and at 9:55 a.m. on May 31 transferred his flag to the *Massachusetts*. At 11:10 he signalled that the *Massachusetts, New Orleans* and *Iowa* were to approach the Spanish cruiser to a distance of 7000 yards and fire at the *Colon* with their main armament. At 1:25 the *Massachusetts* led the other two in, opening fire at 1:50. It was not a particularly effective exercise. The heavy guns concentrated on the *Colon*, while the 8-inch guns fired on the fortifications. There were no hits on the armoured cruiser, and the damage to the fortifications was minimal. The American ships fired only for 10 minutes; the *Colon* and the forts replied, continuing to fire until 3:00 p.m. without hitting anything. Wilson condemned the firing of a few shots at long range as 'utter futility;' Schley argued that the operation was successful in locating the batteries and testing their strength. Responding to criticism, he described as an anomaly that he should be censured for 'not risking his ships or the lives of his men in such operations, when the purpose to be reached could be accomplished without doing either.'[21]

In retrospect, it seems rather surprising that Cervera should have stationed the *Colon* at the harbour entrance. Concas records that she was moved there 'with her broadside bearing on the harbour entrance,' which suggests that she was there to reinforce the batteries in the forts. After the bombardment of May 31, conducted by Schley at a range of 7,000 yards, to which the *Colon* could reply only with her 6-inch guns, it was seen as 'advisable to recall her into the harbour, and Admiral Cervera did so in order not to expose her to no purpose.'[22] Since Cervera cannot have supposed that the *Colon* enjoyed much protection from the batteries at the harbour entrance, the ineffectiveness of which must been obvious to him, it is odd that he left the *Colon* there after the Flying Squadron appeared. Schley was later criticised for not having done enough to destroy the armoured cruiser; Cervera's actions seem to suggest that this was not as easy as was supposed.

During the day Schley received two more telegrams from Long which were evidently intended to put backbone into him. In the first, the Secretary stressed that the most urgent thing was to know positively that Cervera was in Santiago, so that a military assault might be launched. It went on:

> You must surmount difficulty regarding coaling by your ingenuity and perseverance. This is a crucial time and the department relies on you to give information quickly as to the presence of Cervera to be ready for concentrated action with the army... Sampson coming around by Windward Passage... Cervera must not be allowed to escape.

The second telegram read:

> It is your duty to ascertain immediately the Spanish fleet if they be at Santiago de Cuba and report. Would be discreditable to the navy if that fact was not ascertained immediately. All naval and military movements depend on that point.[23]

Cervera's squadron was safe enough inside the harbour of Santiago de Cuba, but only until an American expeditionary force brushed aside the enfeebled troops of General Linares or until provisions ran out. Wilson described the city and its environs:

> The town of Santiago, which at this time counted about 30,000 inhabitants, lies at the northern end of the landlocked harbour, one of the finest and safest in the West Indies. The

> distance from the city to the harbour mouth is just about 4 miles. The mouth is narrow with high ground on either side: to the east rises Punta Morilla, on which is the Morro Castle, 200 feet above sea level, an old masonry structure; to the west is Socopa Point, of about the same elevation. The cliffs fall precipitously on their seaward face, and just under the Morro are great caverns. Just opposite the Morro the width of the channel is 300 yards, but the rocks of the Diamante Bank, extending 180 yards out from Socapa, reduce the fairway to 120 yards.[24]

Even after Sampson's arrival it would be impossible to force the entrance without a colossal risk to the attackers, a risk that had been increased by the laying of two rows of mines, the first of seven between Estrella and Socapa Points, and the second of six a little higher up. On the heights either side of the entrance the Spanish continued to mount additional guns; the artillery strength of the forts reached a total of 30 guns. Considerable difficulties had to be overcome, including the building of a pier to land the guns and a road made to the top of the hill where they were to be installed.

Cervera had reported the decision not to attempt a sortie on May 26. Two days later he assured Aunon that he was on the lookout for an opportunity to run the blockade: 'meanwhile we are vigilant to frustrate enemy's plans. Under these conditions the battle would be unequal. Shall therefore try to elude it if possible. Coal is being shipped slowly.'[25] The Spanish seemed to be collecting remarkably accurate and up-to-date information, no doubt by monitoring the American press; Aunon told Cervera on May 28 of the American intention to sink hulks in the entrance to the harbour, while Blanco informed Correa, the Minister of War in Madrid that 'United States and their admirals are being charged with lack of ability.' Watching the movements of the American ships, Concas thought that all the luck was on their side:

> We do want to mention their good fortune, for the sea, in general so rough to the south of Cuba, was so smooth in this instance that the cruisers were able to coal, sometimes having a steamer on each side, which could not be done even in the majority of the harbours. As for the rest, the communication with Jamaica, the real base of operations, was so manifest and barefaced that if any doubt as to the complicity of England had existed, an ascent to the Morro would have been sufficient to convince anyone of the contrary.[26]

17

The *Merrimac*

Sampson arrived off Santiago de Cuba at 6:30 a.m. on June 1 aboard the *New York*, accompanied by the *Oregon*, the torpedo boat *Porter* and the auxiliary *Mayflower*. Before leaving Key West he had had a meeting with Naval Constructor Richmond Pearson Hobson, who had prepared a plan for clearing the entrance channels of Havana harbour of mines. After hearing what Hobson had to say, Sampson told him that an entirely different operation was what he had in mind, which was the sinking of a block ship to close the entrance to the harbour of Santiago. During the course of their passage there, Hobson worked upon the scheme. Sampson asked how an iron ship could be scuttled, and made to sink quickly. Hobson considered this carefully:

> After thinking over the question for some time I replied, in effect, that there seemed to be two effective methods, one to drive bottom plates from the inside, and the other to explode a series of torpedoes placed advantageously on the outside. We examined the chart of the harbour together, and I expressed full confidence in the practicability of putting the vessel into the channel, and stated that I should be happy to be allowed to endeavour to carry out the work.[1]

The term 'torpedoes' as used here was still employed to describe all explosive devices, static or otherwise, designed to sink or damage vessels, and not merely those launched from afar with that objective; these were quaintly known as 'automobile torpedoes.'

Sampson directed Hobson to prepare the details of the scheme, for which he had selected the collier *Merrimac*, which had caused such difficulty as a result of her propensity to break down, and Hobson set to work, while the squadron made its way towards Santiago. By the morning of May 30 he was able to present Sampson with an outline of his scheme, which was duly approved. His first thought was that the *Merrimac* should approach the entrance to the harbour at night; when about 5 miles off she would be 'discovered' by blockading ships, eliminated by searchlights, and fired upon (with great care) (to give the illusion that she was a blockade runner. As she entered the channel, making heavy smoke, she would sound blasts on her whistle, showing a Spanish flag upon which the searchlights would play. When, as was to be hoped, the shore batteries opened fire on the *Merrimac*'s pursuers, they would be replied to and thus kept occupied. However, the more he examined the chart the more Hobson became convinced that this would not work; the difficulties of navigating the channel at night were far too great, and for the captain of a collier to appear to attempt it would not be convincing.

Instead, Hobson proposed going in alone by moonlight, just before the moon set. A floodtide was essential, so that if the anchor gear broke the *Merrimac* would be set into the channel with ample time to sink before the ebb could take her back out. He calculated that he would have enough time after the squadron's arrival off Santiago to carry out the necessary preparations aboard the *Merrimac* in orderto launch the operation on the night of June 1/2; the moon was approaching full and would set at about 3:30 a.m. on June 2. To meet that deadline, however, there would only be time to prepare the explosives to be placed along the port side of the vessel about twelve feet below the waterline. There would be ten of these, each consisting of seventy eight pounds of brown prismatic powder, each to be detonated by its own electric primer. Hobson gave his design for these charges to Gunner Morgan of the *New York*, and he and his men started work on them immediately. As a backup, Hobson asked Sampson if he could take two warheads from the *New York*'s torpedoes and locate them abreast of the *Merrimac*'s most important bulkheads. Sampson thought about this, but then said: 'No, I cannot let you have them; two hundred pounds of gun cotton on the inside would blow everything to the devil.'[2] Sampson had been doubtful whether it would be possible to improvise the necessary charges, but Hobson was confident that it could be done.

After Sampson's arrival off Santiago, Schley went on board the *New York* at 8:00 a.m. to report the situation. To him, Sampson explained his plan for sinking the collier in the harbour entrance. Schley was opposed to this; in his view every inducement should be offered to the enemy to come out, where they could certainly be destroyed. On the other hand, while they remained in the harbour they were a threat to the army. When given the details of Hobson's proposal, Schley remained unconvinced:

> He still further objected on the ground that it was a sacrifice of human life, with the chances ninety to a hundred that it would not succeed, and, finally, that the collier would prove as much of a menace to us if we attempted to go in as to the Spaniards if they attempted to come out.[3]

Sampson, however, was firm that the operation should proceed. If Cervera could not get out, his ships would be captured when the army took the city. If he did emerge, it would be to escape rather than fight, and there was always a chance one or more of his ships might get away. Forcing the entrance was theoretically an option, but Sampson was concerned that mines might have been laid, while he was also subject to the Navy Department's instruction not to risk his ships against fortifications. The sinking of the collier was in any case a temporary expedient, pending the arrival of the army, while leaving Sampson free to deal with Spanish reinforcements. Once the forts had been taken, the *Merrimac* could be removed. The plan had been approved by the Naval War Board.[4] Chadwick, responding to subsequent criticism of the attempt, observed that from the point of view of the time, it was sound strategy. He developed his justification in a letter to Long of June 10:

> Were the entrance to Santiago of a different character, i.e. with low-lying land, we could easily force our way in, but it is extraordinarily narrow, commanded by bluffs two hundred feet in height, and these bluffs occupied by an active enemy would render our action in this narrow inlet, but three hundred and fifty feet broad, planted with mines, very difficult and disaster there would be irretrievable. If we were sure to be left alone, we should of course try it at whatever risk; with the hope of the arrival of the army we of course wait.[5]

Whatever Schley might think, it was of course Sampson's decision. Long had sent a telegram to Sampson on May 24: 'till further orders flying squadron is under your command; Schley so informed.'[6] This was scarcely necessary, since when originally appointing Schley to the command of the Flying Squadron he had made it clear that he would be subordinate to Sampson as commander of the north Atlantic fleet, to which Schley 'cheerfully agreed.' Perhaps it was intended to give Sampson confidence in issuing firm directions to Schley at a time when the latter's movements seemed uncertain.

Immediately after his meeting with Schley, Sampson took the *New York* close into the entrance to Santiago in order to give Hobson the opportunity of reconnoitring at first hand. Schley had pointed out the location of the Spanish batteries, but it was desired to get the bearing based on Estrella Point for the course to enter the channel. It was only when the *New York*'s steam launch was lowered that the actual shape of the land was identified, and Hobson was able to fix in his mind the points by reference to which the channel could safely be entered. This done he returned to the *New York* before crossing to the *Merrimac*, from which the *Massachusetts* was at this time coaling. He found the collier's officers at lunch; they were amazed when he told them what was planned for their ship that night.

Hobson signalled to the *New York* to send over half her deck force, and 40 coal heavers, to assist in preparing the *Merrimac*. While waiting for them, he employed the *Merrimac*'s crew in locating the anchors and chains that would be an essential part of the process of sinking her in the required position. He also began considering the question of the *Merrimac*'s crew for her last journey. He reckoned only six were needed. A call for volunteers had been made by signal to the fleet, and hundreds of men put their name forward. It was decided that only one per ship could be accepted. Hobson had assumed that he would be in command, but during the afternoon Sampson sent to him to tell him that Commander Miller, the captain of the *Merrimac*, claimed the right to go, and that he did not see how he could refuse him. Hobson was a forceful and persuasive young man (he was 28) and Sampson had a high opinion of him, and he now urged the admiral that if Miller went, he would only be a passenger, even if nominally in command, since he was wholly unfamiliar with the scheme. Hobson was ready to serve in any capacity, he said, but go he must. He had limited the crew to the bare minimum, all of whom were young and athletic; no one, he argued, of Miller's age could stand the physical strain, and if there should be a chance of escape Miller's presence would endanger them all. Miller would, he said, understand all this when it was explained to him. Sampson, considering Hobson's submission, finally agreed that he should be in command, and that Miller should not go.[7]

As the day wore on Hobson encountered a number of problems. There was no electric charger in the fleet, so each of the explosives would have to be fired by individual batteries. There were serious difficulties with the anchor chains. There were no tackles with which to haul them to the stern. The hogging lines to hold the explosives in place became entangled. Hobson was able to make good a shortage of wire by getting some from a Norwegian cable steamer that lay nearby, while he went back and forth to the *New York* to collect all manner of items of equipment which he needed to complete the collier's fitting out. He was particularly anxious to obtain a large national flag, which he wished to hoist as the *Merrimac* sank.

While all this was going on, the *Merrimac* and the *New York* had drifted eastwards for twelve or fifteen miles, and it became necessary to get under way to be in position to make the attempt on time. By 12:30 a.m. the two ships began to move, but it was 3 a.m. before the *New York* joined the *Merrimac* some 6 miles off the entrance, and Sampson came aboard to make a final inspection, and to bid Hobson and his crew farewell. As he left the ship aboard his launch, it fouled one of the *Merrimac*'s lines, causing a further delay before the collier could get under way, which she was obliged to do at a higher speed than planned. However as she made her way towards the entrance, in the early light of dawn, the torpedo boat *Porter* came up with Sampson's orders for the *Merrimac* to return. Hobson begged her commander to go back to the *New York* and seek permission to proceed, but his great regret that was refused.[8]

Aboard the *New York* it was Chadwick who was the prime mover in the decision to abort the mission. His concern was not only the delayed start, but the fact that the *Merrimac* was further out than intended, so that it would be fully daylight by the time she reached the entrance. Sampson had first been inclined to let Hobson go on, but Chadwick persuaded him against this. Hobson thought this a mistake; later, when writing his history of the war, Chadwick confessed that this was so and that it would have been better to let him go. He also thought then that the scheme of a feigned pursuit should have been adopted.[9]

The sun rose on June 3 in a cloudless sky; no wind disturbed the surface of the glassy sea as the *Merrimac* made her way towards the *New York*, and lay within hail. Almost at once, however, the flagship got under way, and set off in pursuit of a strange vessel that had been sighted in the south-west. It took three hours to overhaul the chase, which proved to be the steamer *Hampstead*, on passage from St Vincent to Mobile, which had approached Santiago purely out of curiosity. Sampson was, understandably, extremely angry with the master of the vessel before heading back to rejoin his fleet. By the time he did so Hobson and his men had used the day's grace that they had been given to make good some of the defects aboard the *Merrimac*, but as night fell all was ready for another attempt to be made. In the late afternoon Hobson went to see Sampson, suggesting that it should be made at sunset. The admiral and Chadwick listened to his reasoning, but after due consideration rejected the proposal; they also concluded that Hobson's second idea, that the whole fleet should approach as if intending bombardment and thereby distracting the Spanish gunners, would simply give them enough time to concentrate all their fire on the *Merrimac* before she entered the channel. They reluctantly allowed that Hobson, who regarded some light as essential to success, could wait until the last hours of the moon, and that if he needed he could go in after daybreak. Hobson had also been brooding on the risk of his steering gear being shot away; he was anxious, too, about the effectiveness of the charges, and made a further attempt to persuade Sampson to let him take two torpedo warheads in case they were needed to sink the vessel. Sampson again refused.[10]

At 3 a.m. on June 3 Hobson, having added one more to his crew, set off again for the entrance to the harbour. The *Merrimac* made good progress, entering the channel before being spotted by the Spanish lookouts. A picket boat was moored on the western side of the entrance, and was the first to open fire; it seemed to Hobson that she was aiming at the collier's rudder. Hobson stopped her engines at the point he had planned, relying on her momentum to carry her to the point where she was to be scuttled, and she passed within thirty feet of the Morro rock. Just before he changed course, a shot hit the *Merrimac*'s steering gear, and she was unable to answer her helm. She drove on, deeper into the channel, under a hail of fire from artillery and small arms; in addition, the Spanish exploded several mines. Hobson ordered the explosive charges detonated, but only two went off, which meant that it would take some time for the vessel to sink, and all the time the flood tide was carrying her beyond the chosen location towards Estrella Point, off which the *Merrimac* finally began to sink. The *Reina Mercedes* was moored behind Socapa; she launched a torpedo, as did the *Pluton*, on the other side of the channel, but both missed. The *Merrimac* finally went down at a point where she was not a serious obstacle. Hobson and all his crew escaped unhurt, hanging onto a catamaran carried by the collier until they were rescued by a steam launch, from which a Spanish officer leant over to haul them in board. Only later did Hobson learn that the officer was Admiral Cervera himself.[11]

They were taken on board the *Reina Mercedes* before subsequently being transferred to Morro Castle, where Cervera came to visit Hobson. He courteously enquired as to Hobson's welfare, and avoided asking any embarrassing questions; he said that he would arrange to send out a flag of truce in order that Sampson might know of the rescue of Hobson and his crew. After about 10 minutes conversation, Cervera withdrew, leaving Hobson profoundly impressed by his kindness:

> Ah, I thought, this Admiral commanding the Spanish naval forces has taken the pains to put on the uniform for official visits, and has come at the earliest moment to visit a young lieutenant of the enemy in prison! Surely chivalry is not yet dead.[12]

Cervera was as good as his word, sending Captain Bustamente out to give Sampson the news of the safety of Hobson and his men. The silence which had followed the sinking of the *Merrimac* had left the watchers in the American fleet profoundly anxious for the safety of her crew. A steam cutter had been sent in to pick up any survivors, but as the sun came up she returned having sighted none. It was soon clear from the position of the collier's masts which could be seen far up the channel that her mission had not been completely successful, but the extent to which it might have been was not apparent. The fears for the lives of her crew continued until Bustamente arrived under a flag of truce, with a kindly note from Cervera announcing their safety and expressing his admiration for their courage. Chadwick described his visit:

> Captain Bustamente remained aboard some little time answering Sampson's questions regarding the prisoners and awaiting the preparation of packages to go to them. He smilingly remarked during the conversation:'you have made it much more difficult for us to come out.'[13]

When the news of Hobson's exploit broke in the national press, he became overnight a national hero. To the New York Journal, 'the name of Hobson has gone on the list of American heroes, with Lawrence, Paul Jones, Perry, Cushing, and the rest.' William Goode wrote that 'the *Merrimac*'s failure to fulfil her purpose does not in the slightest dim the glory that must ever cling to the men who took her in.' It was what the American public had been waiting for. Dewey's success at Manila had whetted the national appetite for glorious news, but a month had gone by, and the Press avidly seized on this latest evidence of American courage and inventiveness, even though it had failed to be of significant military effect.

For Sampson, it meant that he must now impose an extremely close blockade to ensure that the Spanish did not emerge from Santiago or, if they did, that they would be destroyed. Aware that military operations would soon commence, he saw these as being conducted to assist the Navy, rather than the other way about. As matters developed, the latent distrust between the Army and the Navy soon began to be apparent.

18

Blockade

Once he had arrived at Santiago Sampson wasted no time in issuing orders to regulate the fleet's operations there. It would be organised into two squadrons. The first of these, under his direct command, consisted of the *New York*, *Iowa*, *Oregon*, *New Orleans*, *Mayflower* and *Porter*; the second, under Schley's command, was composed of the *Brooklyn*, *Massachusetts*, *Texas*, *Marblehead* and *Vixen*. The blockade would be maintained in a half circle some six miles from the Morro in daytime, closing in at night, with the first squadron to the east and the second squadron to the West. The order went on:

> If the enemy tries to escape, the ships must close and engage as soon as possible, and endeavour to sink his vessels pr force them to run ashore in the channel. It is not considered that the shore batteries are of sufficient power to do any material injury to battleships.[1]

Sampson had of course been strictly instructed that he was not to risk injury to his battleships in engaging fortifications, so the opinion he here expressed would justify vigorous action against the Spanish batteries at the entrance.

On June 3 the *St Louis*, accompanied by the armed auxiliary *Yankee* and the collier *Justin* arrived. She brought a number of telegrams, of which the most important carried news that the army's expeditionary force of 18,000 to 20,000 men, under the command of General Shafter, was expected to leave Tampa in Florida on June 4. The hastening of military action in Cuba was due in large part to McKinley's desire to conduct as vigorous a campaign as possible in order to bring Spain to recognise the inevitable need to make an early peace. It was also a result of pressure from the Navy for military action at Santiago as soon as possible, due to the difficulties of maintaining a close blockade there while the threat of Spanish naval reinforcements existed. Long had much to say about the plans for military action, writing to McKinley on May 31 with suggestions about the points at which the troops should be landed. He also firmly opposed the suggestion that there should be naval landings:

> The primary object of the expedition is the capture or destruction of the enemy's fleet in this port, which would be most decisive of the war. Therefore the US squadron should not be weakened by the loss of skilled men in view of so important a possible naval action.[2]

On June 4 Sampson convened a council of war to consider the arrangements for a bombardment of the forts. It was suggested that since the following day was a Sunday, it should be put off until the Monday.[3] Next day Sampson issued an order of battle to engage the Spanish shore batteries at 7:00 a.m. on June 6. It was something that the Spanish had been warned from Havana to expect and the large and menacing fleet of ships deployed in front of the port suggested that a bombardment was imminent. On the evening of June 4, Lieutenant Muller, a Spanish naval officer, described the scene:

> The evening was most beautiful; the sea was smooth as a lake; there was hardly any wind, and the sky was perfectly clear. At a distance of about five miles seventeen ships could be seen, among them seven battleships and one torpedo boat. The other nine were merchant ships, the nearest about six miles from the harbour. They formed a large arc, one extremity of which was at Aguadores and the other at Punta Cabrera. The largest and most powerful ships were in the centre. All had their engines stopped, and their bows in different directions according to the current. From time to time one of them would move a short distance forward, and then return again to her place.[4]

At 6:30 a.m. on June 6 the fleet formed into columns and stood in towards the entrance. The eastern column was led by the *New York*, followed by the *Iowa*, *Oregon*, *Yankee* and *Dolphin*; the western column was headed by the *Brooklyn*, followed by the *Massachusetts*, *Texas*, *Vixen* and the armed yacht *Suwannee*. Anticipating the bombardment, the Spanish had reinforced the batteries with 120 men, but the disproportion of force was immense. Only three of their guns, 6.3 inches in calibre, were reliable; a number of the other guns were of eighteenth century vintage. Against these the Americans were now bringing eight 13-inch, six 12-inch, thirty eight 8-inch, twenty four 6-inch, twelve 5-inch, twenty 4-inch and many smaller guns. The armour of the battleships and armoured cruisers was quite strong enough to resist even a direct hit, while the batteries were of a simple and makeshift construction.

The flagship opened fire at 7:41 a.m. at a range of about 6000 yards, followed by the other ships. They steamed slowly in until they got within 1900 yards of the Morro; closer than this, it would be difficult to elevate the guns against the battery on the 200 foot high cliffs. Sampson, mindful of the fact that Hobson and his men were held prisoner within Morro Castle, had ordered that it should not be fired on. The general bombardment continued only until 8:05, but a slow and deliberate fire was maintained until 9:40; at 10:08 Sampson considered that he had done enough, and ordered the fleet to resume its blockading stations. The operation had confirmed the weakness of the batteries, and he reckoned that a force on shore, supported by the guns of the fleet, could carry them without difficulty, as he reported by telegram to the Navy Department:

> Bombarded forts at Santiago today, 7:30 to 10:00 a.m., June 6, and have silenced works quickly without injury of any kind, though stationary within 2,000 yards. If 10,000 men were here, city and fleet would be ours within 48 hours. Every consideration demands immediate army movement. If delayed city will be defended more strongly by guns taken from fleet.[5]

To the watching journalists the bombardment was, as William Goode wrote, 'undramatic;' he wrote that he ' lost interest in the affair after finding that when only a little over a mile away it was still utterly impossible to tell what your own guns were effecting,' and thereafter paid more attention to what was happening around him. George Graham observed: 'for three quarters of an hour this fleet of 13 vessels fired almost continuously at the earthworks, but with the exception of a couple of good shots from the *Texas*, seemed to do very little harm.'[6] The experience was, though, very different on shore, as Lieutenant Muller described:

> When the American fleet opened fire, it was so intense and the shots followed each other in such quick succession that it might have seemed like a fusillade if the mighty thunder of guns can be compared with the crackling of small arms. By 9 o'clock it became somewhat slower, shortly after reaching again the same intensity, then decreasing once more at 10:15, and again becoming terribly intense at 10:30. At 11:02 it ceased. Punta Gorda battery fired only seven shots. During the first moments the firing was so intense that it resembled one prolonged thunder. In fact, I had no idea that any firing could be so terrific as that of these ten ships.[7]

Muller exaggerated the length of the bombardment, but it must have been terrifying to the Spanish gunners. In spite of its ferocity, however, their casualties were relatively light; the *Reina Mercedes* lost six men killed and 12 wounded, while in the batteries three were killed and 51 wounded.

Cervera reported the bombardment to Aunon; reporting the Spanish casualties, he said that he did not know the enemy's loss; '*Reina Mercedes* has suffered much. *Vizcaya* received two shells, *Furor* one shell in the bunker without serious injury. Works of defence have suffered slight injuries of no military importance.'[8] He followed this up with a further telegram, strikingly feeble in its terms: 'Fear enemy will succeed in obstructing harbour entrance. Beg your Excellency to give me instructions.' To this, Aunon sent a soothing but not particularly helpful reply on June 8:

> As it is impossible to foresee and properly solve from here all cases that may arise in the campaign, the government, which knows the means at your disposal, your own high qualities, and the wide scope given you, is confident that you will make of them best possible use in every case, and will consider that you have fulfilled your difficult mission if you satisfy the letter and spirit of our ordinances.[9]

Cervera's reaction to this, not unreasonably, was to convene another council of war. Those present divided much as they had done in previous discussions, with only Bustamente and Concas arguing for a sortie. The chief of staff believed that the squadron should take advantage of the dark of the moon, and undertake a sortie after a few days' rest. The destroyers should go out first, and at top speed pass the four American battleships. Then the *Colon* should go out heading west south-west straight for the *Brooklyn*, and the *Maria Teresa,* heading east south-east, and finally the *Vizcaya* and the *Oquendo.* In the confusion caused to the enemy fleet he thought that at least half of the squadron could be saved. Concas considered that if the *Brooklyn* or *New York*, the fastest of the enemy vessels, left the blockade, a sortie should be attempted at once; if not it should be attempted at the time of the new moon. Paredes, Lazaga, Moreu, Eulate and Villaamil were of the opinion that, as long as the existing situation continued, the sortie

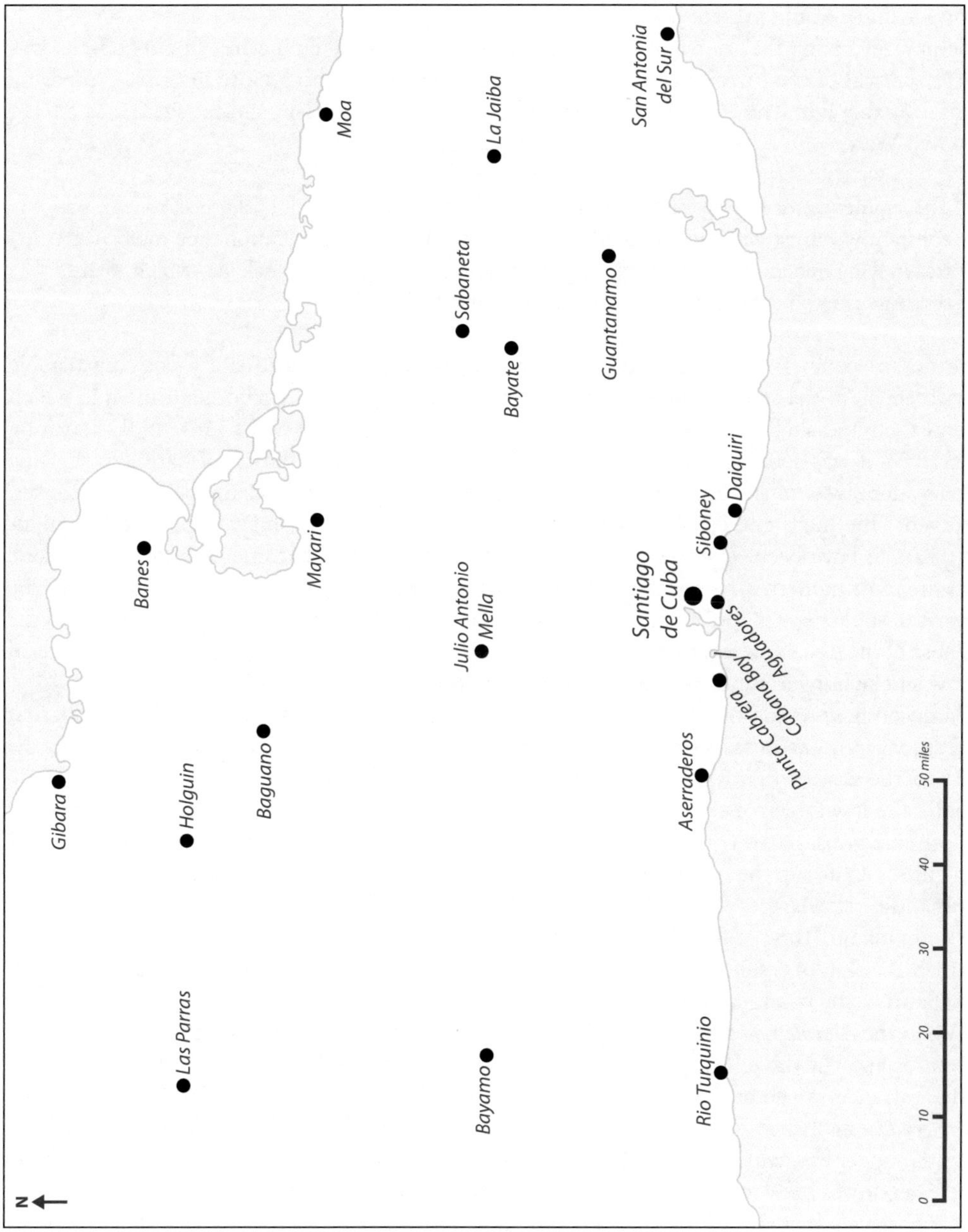

5 South Eastern Cuba.

should not be attempted. Reporting these discussions next day to Aunon. Cervera told him that the 'fires of the ships remained lighted so as to take advantage of the first opportunity'; but he added that since the blockade was very strict and the enemy four times superior, he doubted that an opportunity would present itself.[10]

Schley, reviewing the course of the blockade and the steps taken by the American fleet, was sharply critical of the Spanish failure to prevent it from approaching close inshore, comparing it unfavourably with the effectiveness of the Confederate batteries in similar situations during the Civil War:

> The supineness of the Spanish in this respect, as well as their lack of aggressiveness, was constantly commented upon, and, owing to this, the blockading squadron took many liberties in lying generally within easy range to maintain a more rigid blockade, which made a sortie all the more dangerous for the squadron inside.[11]

Sampson's conviction that he had silenced the forts by the bombardment was a considerable overstatement of the case. In spite of the immediate effect of enduring a bombardment in which several thousand shells were expended, which as Muller described was a profoundly alarming experience, it was soon apparent to the garrison and the civil population of Santiago that the damage done was much less than had been feared. Frederick Ramsden, the British consul, observed: 'The more one considers the bombardment matter of Monday, the more ridiculous it appears to have been. It was probably one of the heaviest bombardments known, and done with the most modern artillery, and yet the result has been comparatively small.[12] In truth, the American shooting was indifferent, as had been the case at San Juan. This was partly due to the stillness of the day; rain began to fall heavily after the bombardment began, and dense clouds of yellow smoke hung around the American ships, making accuracy very difficult

Sampson now took a number of steps to tighten the effectiveness of the blockade. The first of these was to take possession of the excellent harbour at Guantánamo Bay, 40 miles up the coast to the east of Santiago. He sent the *Marblehead* and the *Yankee* there at midnight on June 6. The lower part of the bay was defended only by an ancient fort, mounting a battery of smoothbore guns, halfway up the bay, and by the *Sandoval*, a small gunboat mounting two 57 mm guns. Farther up the bay, Fort Toro mounted a further six elderly smoothbore bronze guns, commanding the narrow passage leading to the small port of Caimanera, which served the town of Guantánamo. This, of 8,000 inhabitants, lay a dozen miles further inland; it was held by a Spanish division of 6,000 men under General Pareja, but was effectively cut off from contact with Santiago by insurgent forces.

When the *Marblehead* and *Yankee* arrived they found the *St Louis* already there, intending to sweep for and cut the telegraph cables, which ran both east and west from Fisherman's Point at the entrance to the bay. This work was soon completed, and Commander McCalla of the *Marblehead* established contact with the insurgent General Perez. No attempt was made to enter the upper bay, which was shallow; the *Sandoval,* which had made a brief attempt to intervene, was driven back to Caimanera, and the Americans now comfortably possessed an excellent anchorage. Thereafter Guantánamo Bay served as the fleet's general base; Pareja reported mournfully to Linares that the Americans occupied it 'as if for a harbour of rest, they having anchored as if in one of their own ports.' Pareja, completely cut off from events at Santiago, was reduced to serving half rations of everything to his troops.[13]

Bustamente's proposal that the squadron should make a break for it at night was a possibility that was much in Sampson's mind, and on June 7 he reorganised the blockade, ordering three picket launches to be located close in, about a mile from the Morro. Behind them would come a line of three small warships, the *Vixen*, *Suwannee* and *Dolphin*. The rest of the fleet would be disposed on an arc around the entrance at a distance of about 4 miles. He was aware that this exposed his ships to the risk of a torpedo attack, but everything possible must be done to prevent Cervera's squadron from escaping, which he considered would be 'a serious blow to our prestige, and to a speedy end to the war.' Next day he modified the arrangements still further, posting the *Iowa*, *Oregon* and *Massachusetts* in turn for two hours each night about 2 miles from the entrance, training their searchlights up the channel. To the west, the *Brooklyn* and the *Texas*, and to the east the *New York* and the *New Orleans* would also take turns either side of the entrance sweeping the coastline with their searchlights.[14]

Sampson's orders with regard to the searchlights were at first not fully appreciated by the captains of the ships, and it was necessary for him to issue a peremptory order overriding all objections and making his intentions entirely clear. In this order, he wrote: 'it is absolutely necessary that the beam of light should be held steadily up the channel into the harbour,' adding that he believed it to be 'absolutely impossible for a vessel to escape detection in any attempt to come out.' What was vital was that the lights should be held as nearly stationary as possible, 'and that no discretion be left to the person holding the light.' Chadwick, rightly, regarded this order as 'among the most important of the war:'

> To it more than to any other one circumstance is due the capture of the Spanish squadron. It made it, in the opinion of the Spanish commander, out of the question for the ships to leave the harbour at night with the entrance lighted so brilliantly that it was impossible for any movement to be made in it which would not be noticed. This action removed, too, any fear whatever of torpedo attack.[15]

Cervera took up with Linares the possibility that the guns in the shore batteries, or at least the 6.3-inch Hontoria guns, could shoot out the searchlights; to this, the general replied that as it was the searchlights reached into the city, a distance of nearly 5 miles. This meant that the American vessels could still illuminate the entrance from a distance beyond the range of his artillery. It was this that explained what Schley thought was a supine failure on the part of the Spanish to interfere with the American operations.

Meanwhile Cervera had offered Linares the services of men of his squadron to serve ashore in the event of a landing of American troops being followed by an assault on Santiago. Blanco, from Havana, suggested this to Linares, but was told that Cervera had already offered the landing forces. The general asked the admiral, if the need arose, for one landing company to be stationed at the Socapa, one at Punta Gorda, one at Laz Cruces pier and one at Punta Blanca, 'all with such number of suitable guns as you may deem necessary.'[16]

In order to ensure the security of the base at Guantánamo, a battalion of 646 marines with four guns arrived there from Key West and landed near Caimanera, where they dug in. Their entrenched position was attacked by troops from Pareja's division, which were beaten off with a loss of four killed and 11 wounded. The marines were soon reinforced by the arrival of a large number of Cuban insurgents, and on June 14 they went over to the offensive, advancing under the gunfire of the *Dolphin*, which heavily shelled the Spanish positions. The marines stormed the blockhouse with a loss of two wounded; the Cubans lost six men killed and wounded. Spanish casualties were high; forty bodies were found and seventeen soldiers taken prisoner. Next day the *Texas*, which had arrived from Santiago, with the *Dolphin*, *Suwannee* and *Marblehead* bombarded and destroyed Fort Toro.

Back at Santiago, to where the *Texas* at once returned, there had been a further bombardment of the forts on June 14, when the *New Orleans* at close range shelled a new earthwork that was being constructed to the east of the Morro. Captain Folger took his ship within 2,000 yards of the battery, at which he fired some 200 shells before retiring. The shore batteries replied sufficiently heavily to leave onlookers thinking that the cruiser must certainly be hit; but in spite of the close range she suffered no hits.

Two days later Sampson decided to undertake a fresh bombardment of the shore batteries, believing that the Spanish had been adding to the defences on either side of the entrance to the harbour. He ordered that, in all guns of 8-inch and larger calibre, reduced charges should be used. It was hoped that by reducing the velocity of the shells fired in this way the angle of fall of the shot might be increased. The fleet again approached in two columns, that on the east consisting of the *New York, New Orleans. Oregon* and *Iowa*, and that on the west of the *Brooklyn, Texas* and *Massachusetts*. The bombardment was carried out much as on the previous occasions, and the watching journalists found little to write about, as before devoting themselves to recording events aboard ship. Goode, for instance, was watching Sampson:

> The admiral, on this occasion, was particularly anxious to have slow and accurate firing. Frequently he leaned over the bridge and asked, 'Can the men see the guns?' meaning that he wished the gun captains to fire not at the batteries, but at the guns themselves. As the *New York* that morning went within two hundred yards of the shore and within about 1500 yards from Morro Castle the men had every chance to aim.[17]

Schley noted that the batteries replied vigorously for about 10 or 15 minutes, 'after which the gunners again fled to the protection of their traverse ditches, to remain until the squadron withdrew'. After this they returned to their guns, firing several shots, but without causing any damage to the ships. Nor, in fact, had the bombardment done much damage to the fortifications, but it did at least give the fleet's gunners some useful practice.[18]

The arrival off Santiago on June 14 of the so-called 'dynamite cruiser' *Vesuvius* lent a new dimension to the blockade. Its armament consisted of three tubes that fired charges of gun cotton each weighing over one hundred pounds, the propellant being pneumatic pressure. She was unarmoured and theoretically capable of 18.5 knots. The problem with this vessel was that the tubes were fixed in position, and thus could only be aimed by steering in the direction in which it was desired to fire the shell. As an experiment it cannot be said to have been successful, but it certainly added to the feelings of insecurity of those onshore, as Schley explained:

> The nights were enlivened now and then by the *Vesuvius* going in close to the shore under the cover of darkness, to throw into the works two or three aerial torpedoes from her pneumatic guns. The detonation of these charges was terrific and their effect on shore must have suggested to the defenders something of an earthquake, as the concussion was sensibly felt on the *Brooklyn*. While the effect was not known at the time, there must have been a widespread demoralisation among the enemy, and this is worth a great deal in war.[19]

Cervera continued to keep Aunon informed of the events of the blockade, noting the contribution of the *Vesuvius* in a telegram of June 16: 'During night projectile, apparently dynamite, burst on the water near *Pluton*, causing injuries which are being examined. At daybreak enemy kept up galling fire for an hour and slower fire thirty minutes, then withdrawing.' This bombardment appears to have inflicted no damage on any of the ships of his squadron, but later that day Cervera was reporting a new anxiety:

> I have a suspicion that the enemy has planted torpedoes in the entrance to the harbour. Have therefore ordered careful investigation in charge of Bustamente. Have purchased provisions, though expensive and bad which will last until the end of July at least.[20]

In Washington the Navy Department, and the Naval War Board, could as far as the blockade of Santiago was concerned, do little except ensure that the logistics of supporting Sampson's fleet were efficiently managed. Mahan wrote later that during this period he remembered no suggestions on the subject of the blockade being sent to Sampson. He did, however, remember how closely he watched the size of the moon, which was new on June 18, and the anxiety with which he greeted each morning lest news arrived of a successful sortie of Cervera's squadron. There was a continuing belief that the Spanish ships could steam faster than most of Sampson's ships. What Mahan and those in Washington did not know, however, was that Sampson's use of searchlights had effectively made it harder for Cervera to get away at night than was the case in daylight.[21]

19

Shafter

While the cat was thus assiduously watching the hole from which at any time the mouse might emerge, there had been a great deal of activity at Tampa, where the first part of the military component of America's war against Spain was being created. There were considerable divisions of opinion among the leaders of the United States Army as to the operations to be conducted against the Spanish in Cuba, some of which envisaged very close cooperation with the insurgents.

What was very soon apparent was that the readiness of the US Army to fight a war was a long way behind that of the Navy, which presented a considerable problem to President McKinley. His priority was to win the war in the shortest possible time, and he opted to support those proposals put before him which appeared most likely to achieve this object. While the assembly of an expeditionary force was approaching completion, Miles put forward a plan on May 27 for an immediate attack on Santiago de Cuba, followed by an assault on Puerto Rico. Thereafter, he proposed that the army be landed on the northern coast of Cuba, in order to operate against Havana in conjunction with insurgent forces.

McKinley adopted the first elements of the plan, but was much less interested in the later proposals for operations against Havana. What he wanted was to see the troops massed at Tampa, principally consisting of regular army units, landing near Santiago as soon as possible. Once Schley had confirmed that Cervera was blockaded at Santiago, McKinley insisted on immediate action, and orders went to Major General William R Shafter, the commander of the expeditionary force, to embark his troops at once. Shafter was another Civil War veteran who had gone on to take part in several Indian wars, but it was seniority as much as any outstanding ability that led to his being appointed to command at Tampa. He was described by one observer as a '63-year-old fat and gouty veteran who looked like three men rolled into one – or, as a quip said, a floating tent.' His physical attributes were, in a sense, indirectly to play a part in the subsequent controversy over the naval battle at Santiago.

Shafter's detailed instructions reached him on May 31. He was to land his troops to the east or west of Santiago, and cover Sampson's forces as they dealt with Cervera's squadron. Thereafter, his objective would be Puerto Rico. By June 4 Shafter was reporting that he had not yet been able to move due to the late arrival of troops from Chattanooga and Mobile, and to loading difficulties: 'every effort is being made to bring order out of confusion... Notwithstanding these difficulties this expedition will soon be ready to sail.'[2] Alger was unimpressed, replying that there was 'much criticism'about the delay. By June 7 Washington's patience was exhausted, and peremptory orders went to Shafter to move immediately, with the troops he had in hand. Time, he was told, was of the essence. By the morning of June 8 Shafter had 16,988 officers and men embarked on 29 transports and six supply vessels, after a chaotic process of embarkation that had seen Colonel Leonard Wood and Lieutenant-Colonel Theodore Roosevelt get their regiment of volunteer cavalry, the Rough Riders, aboard a transport by effectively hijacking it.

The convoy was to sail under the protection of a large naval escort, headed by the battleship *Indiana*, whose captain, Henry Taylor, was in overall command. There were also the unprotected cruisers *Detroit* and *Castine* and a large number of smaller vessels. However, just as the convoy was in the process of clearing the harbour of Tampa, an urgent message reached Shafter from Alger: 'wait until you get further orders before you sail. Answer quick.' The reason for this panic attack was a completely unexpected telegram from the *Dolphin*, reporting that the *Eagle* had sightted enemy vessels in the St Nicholas Channel; the force appeared to consist of an armoured cruiser, a protected cruiser and two torpedo boats. The Spanish identity of these vessels had been 'ascertained,' though only at 9:45 p.m. On the other hand the sighting had been confirmed by the *Resolute*.

In fact, the four ships sighted were almost certainly the British cruiser *Talbot*, the appearance of which was very similar to the Spanish armoured cruisers, and, separately, the American armed yacht *Scorpion* and two supply ships. The Navy Department reported the *Dolphin*'s telegram to Sampson, following it up with news that the sailing of the expeditionary force had been stopped temporarily. It anxiously enquired if Sampson was sure that all four of Cervera's armoured cruisers were still at Santiago. Sampson was critical of the decision to delay the convoy, replying:

> Have no confidence in the report of *Eagle* as to nationality or character of the vessels, and consider very unwise to suspend operations on this account, but even if it is found correct there is sufficient force to furnish convoy. Armoured vessel was probably *Talbot*, which was sighted Thursday 9:00 p.m. by the *Scorpion* standing to the east. Am confident no large ship could have escaped from here.[3]

The apprehension in Washington, as it prepared to commit its expeditionary force to its passage to Cuba, is understandable. Sampson was requested to check with certainty the presence of all Cervera's ships in Santiago harbour, and he did this by setting ashore Lieutenant Victor Blue at Aserrados, with orders to go to Santiago to see for himself. Although assisted by the insurgents, it was a dangerous journey for the young officer, riding in full uniform. In the meantime Sampson made no attempt to comply with the Navy Department's request that he send two armoured vessels to reinforce the convoy's escort.

By June 15 Blue had carried out his mission, and Sampson was able to report that after a detour of 70 miles he had been able to observe inside Santiago harbour; all the ships of Cervera's squadron were still there. Chadwick reflected the irritation felt in the fleet at the abrupt postponement of Shafter's sailing, writing to Long, asking that they be allowed to do their work without paying attention to 'rumours and loose talk.' If they struck energetically and decisively, there would be nothing to fear from possible raids or phantom squadrons. Trask, however, finds it difficult to criticise the War Department for holding the convoy until all doubt was removed, which seems a fair comment.[4]

For the troops aboard the convoy, however, the enforced wait was an extremely disagreeable experience; Theodore Roosevelt likened the condition of his men in the lower hold of the transport *Yucatán* as 'unpleasantly suggestive of the black hole of Calcutta.' While this was going on, Miles began attempting to tamper with the plans for the army, sending a number of messages to Alger, who sharply replied that he was directed by the President 'to say that no change of plan will be made.' McKinley was implacably determined to press on towards his objective of an early peace; George Cortelyou, one of his secretaries, wrote that he was 'solicitous to the last degree for the welfare of our troops and sailors, but he is determined not to delay the prosecution of the war a day longer than necessary.'

The convoy finally sailed from Tampa on the morning of June 14. For the naval escort, the task of keeping the ships together in formation was almost impossible; their speed, and the professional competence of their crews were so variable that stragglers tended to fall further and further behind. If there had been an alert and well-managed Spanish cruiser at sea within range of the convoy, the escorts might have had considerable difficulty in protecting every vessel in their charge. The convoy sailed along the northern coast of Cuba and through the Windward Passage, covering in all about 1000 miles. The correspondent of the *Manchester Guardian* wrote of the voyage:

> It is notable that so large a fleet should have been brought without injury, either from attack by the enemy of from collision among its own vessels... Perhaps no nation but Spain would have allowed us a passage unmolested.[5]

Mahan, who was extremely critical of allowing the army to have the conduct of the transport service, arguing that it was 'radically vicious in theory and directly contrary to the practice of the most experienced nation, Great Britain,' reviewed the extremely cautious policy adopted by the Navy Department. He commented that 'while the man is unfit for command who, in emergency, is unable to run a very great risk for the sake of decisive advantage, he, on the other hand, is only less culpable who takes even a small risk of serious harm against which reasonable precaution can provide.' The unforeseen was ever happening in war:

> Here or there a young Spanish officer might unexpectedly prove, not merely brave, as they all are, but enterprising, which few of them seem to be. The transport fleet had no habit of manoeuvring together; the captains, many of them, were without interest in the war, and with much interest in their owners, upon whom they commonly depended for employment; straggling, and panic in case of attack, could be surely predicted; and finally, as we scarcely had men enough for their work before them, why incur the hazard of sacrificing even one ship load of our most efficient but all too small regular army?[6]

After pausing for several hours on June 18 to allow the stragglers to catch up with the convoy, it finally rounded the easternmost point of Cuba on the following day, and set a course towards Santiago. Meanwhile Sampson had been taking steps to establish cooperation with the insurgents, sending Chadwick on June 19 in the *Vixen* to Aserrados, 15 miles west of Santiago, to examine possible landing places, and to meet with General Calixto Garcia. Chadwick returned to the flagship bringing with him Garcia and a number of members of his staff. Garcia, 'a large kindly faced man,' made a very favourable impression on Sampson, who uncharacteristically immediately took to him. Garcia, unfortunately, was prone to seasickness, and was obliged to cut short his visit, most of which he spent lying stretched out on a sofa in the cabin. When

Sampson raised the possibility that the Spanish might attack his forces, Garcia lifted himself onto his elbow, and replied emphatically: 'the Spaniards never attack; they never attack.'

While the convoy had been making its way around the north coast of Cuba, Sampson had conducted another bombardment of the forts at the entrance to Santiago harbour. He had by now begun the practice of circulating to the fleet a regular bulletin outlining the fleet's activities and containing any relevant news. In that published on June 16 he described the bombardment, albeit in rather over optimistic terms:

> At early dawn the squadron bombarded the forts at the entrance of Santiago. The forts were quickly silenced, and the fire was continued for half an hour and probably did much damage, as no shots were fired at the ships while they were withdrawing. A heavy explosion was observed in one of the batteries. The firing was deliberate, and was very accurate, especially that of the *Texas*. None of the ships was struck.[7]

In fact, not a great deal of damage was done by the bombardment, but as Chadwick remarked, the experience was valuable, and 'gave a confidence and coolness' to the gunners which practice firing to target would not achieve.

While awaiting the arrival of the expeditionary force, Sampson conducted a reconnaissance of Cabanas Bay, which was seen as a possible landing place for an attack at the western side of Santiago. Like so many of the Cuban harbours, it was a bottle shaped pocket of water, protected at its entrance by an ancient fort. The steam cutters sent in to reconnoitre came under such heavy fire that they were obliged to retreat.

At Washington there was mounting concern that, apart from the operations at Santiago and at Guantánamo Bay, the blockade of Cuba was becoming overstretched. On June 14 Sampson had been told that the Navy Department attached 'the utmost importance' to this, and he was directed to send at once some auxiliaries and other cruisers, unless they could not possibly be spared. The request was repeated in a telegram dated June 17, when Sampson was advised of the vessels comprising the escort of the convoy; it went on: 'as soon as possible after their arrival you will send every vessel that can be spared from the operations at Santiago to reinforce the blockade, which is suffering from the want of vessels.' It was, he was told, the President's intention to establish a blockade covering the ports of Cuba from Batabano to Cape Cruz, as soon as it could be maintained effectively. Given the length of the coastline in question, it was not surprising that more ships were required to cover it.[8]

Next day came a warning which resulted from news of a new threat. This was the departure of Admiral Manuel de la Camara, from Cadiz on June 16 with the *Pelayo*, the *Carlos V* and two recently purchased merchant ships which had been armed as exhibit auxiliary cruisers, the *Patriota* and *Rapido*. In addition there were three destroyers, the *Audaz*, *Proserpina* and *Osado*, with two transports carrying 4,000 troops, and four colliers carrying 20,000 tons of coal. It was an awareness of the possible appearance of such a squadron in the West Indies that had originally prompted Sampson's attempt to shut Cervera into Santiago by the scuttling of the *Merrimac*. When that operation failed, Sampson, and the Navy Department, were constantly alert to the possible intervention of Camara's squadron, which was why it was so urgently necessary to take Santiago before he could arrive. Camara's objective was in fact the Philippines; the news that he had passed the Straits of Gibraltar and entered the Mediterranean prompted a counter move which was outlined in Long's telegram to Sampson of June 18:

> Detail *Iowa*, *Oregon* and *Brooklyn* full of coal and ammunition. They will be sent to coast of Spain in the event of Cadiz division passing Suez, Egypt, and *Harvard, Yale, Yosemite, Dixie* same service. If in your opinion these armoured vessels are not in repair to make the above-mentioned cruise, which should you recommend?[9]

The Spanish efforts to get Camara's squadron ready for sea had been monitored by the US naval attachés in Paris and London, Lieutenants William S Sims and John C Colwell, who recruited an extensive network of agents. These enabled the two attachés to report by the end of May that Camara's destination was the Philippines. The Navy Department planted the story in Spain that Sampson would move to Spain after completing the operations at Santiago, hoping thereby to deter the dispatch of Camara's squadron; on June 11 a further leak was planted to the effect that Sampson's vessels had been issued with maps and charts of the Spanish coast. The American intelligence network did not, however, discover the fact that neither of Camara's armoured vessels had been made fully ready for a campaign against Dewey's squadron.[10]

The concern about Camara, and the desire to strengthen the effectiveness of the blockade of Cuba continued to figure largely in the stream of instructions that flowed to Sampson for the rest of June. At Santiago, however, his most immediate concern was with the arrival of the convoy bearing the expeditionary force, and the arrangements that must be made for the landing of troops. This would demand the closest co-operation between army and navy, but it was soon to become apparent that fundamental misunderstandings existed between them

Shafter was travelling with his staff in the transport *Seguranca*, and as soon as news reached the *New York* of her imminent arrival Chadwick went off in the *Gloucester* for a conference with the military, and to convey Sampson's views. These were that the batteries at the entrance should be taken at once, so that the channel could be cleared of mines for the entry of the fleet. Chadwick understood that Shafter agreed that this was the priority. When the *Seguranca* reached the fleet, Sampson went aboard her, and escorted by the *Gloucester* she made her way to Aserrados for talks with the Cuban leaders. Shafter, with his ADC Lieutenant Miley, and Sampson with Lieutenant Staunton, his Assistant Chief of Staff, went ashore, riding for a mile or so to the headquarters of General Rabi; Generals Garcia and Castillo were also in attendance. Chadwick, who had been on duty for 48 hours, did not accompany them, desperately needing some sleep.

Although Garcia had previously been of the view that a landing to the west of Santiago would be the best place, he now considered it impracticable, and he and Shafter agreed that Daiquiri should be selected. Even more important was the question of what the army should do once it was ashore. Shafter seems from the outset to have been dubious about Sampson's desire that the forts at the entrance the harbour should be his first objective. It was his view that he should attack the city of Santiago from the east, taking a route which was relatively far inland and hence out of the range of effective artillery support from the navy. It also, incidentally, ensured that most of the credit for the capture of Santiago should go to the army, unlike Sampson's proposal for an immediate attack on the forts. Shafter subsequently insisted that this was 'the only feasible plan,' and that the result of following it confirmed that this was so: 'these movements committed me to approaching Santiago from the east over a narrow road, at first in some places not better than a trail, running from Daiquiri through Siboney and Sevilla, and making attack from that quarter.'[11]

It was in this way that profound misunderstandings began to occur. Sampson and Chadwick believed that Shafter still accepted the need to attack the forts at the entrance first. Trask suggests that this belief was based on an assumption that the city could not be attacked until Cervera had been dealt with, since otherwise he could ensure the successful defence of the city with naval gunfire. He goes on to say that 'careful army-navy planning would have permitted the invaders to attack the entrance and the city both.' Chadwick, in his history of the war, concluded that Shafter had changed his mind because of the 'misinformation' sent to him by the War Department and confirmed by Garcia. However, at the time, he and Sampson were confident that Shafter would stick to the plan of attacking the forts.[12] Shafter later explained that it was the nature of the terrain which led to his rejection of Sampson's plan, observing that between Daiquiri and the Morro there lay:

> a rugged piece of country, devoid of water, covered with a poisonous undergrowth, and so impenetrable that the railroad running obliquely from Aguadores towards Santiago, and a trail would have been the only means of reaching it.[13]

Shafter also maintained that speed was essential; the area through which he must move was known as yellow-fever country and the sooner the campaign could be completed, the better. This, too, accorded with the urgent messages from Washington requiring him to strike as soon as he could.

The commander of Shafter's cavalry division was the former Confederate Major General Joseph Wheeler, deliberately selected by McKinley as a gesture of reconciliation to the South. He had had the same thing in mind in appointing Fitzhugh Lee as one of the proposed corps commanders. Wheeler examined the shoreline as the convoy approached the Cuban coast:

> With the aid of our glasses we could see the town of Daiquiri, the place selected for a landing. The place has no harbour, but as it was a shipping point for iron ore, General Shafter and the naval officers concluded we could safely land the army by the use of the small boats belonging to the fleet and the transports. There is a strongly built iron pier extending out some distance from the shore but we readily saw this could not be used by us. It extended very high above the water, it being constructed for the purposes of dumping iron ore from the cars into lighters. It was, therefore, evident that we would be obliged to land on the beach, or else at the end of a small dock that extended some 20 yards from the shore.[14]

Before the troops went ashore it was agreed that there should be a naval bombardment of Spanish positions all the way from Cabanas in the west to Daiquiri. At 9:00 p.m. on June 22 this began, with the *Scorpion, Vixen* and *Texas* shelling Cabanas; the *Eagle* and the *Gloucester* at Aguadores; the *Hornet, Helena* and *Bancroft* at Siboney; and at Daiquiri the *Detroit, Christine, Wasp* and *New Orleans*. It lasted 20 minutes in each case, with little response save at Cabanas, where the *Texas* was struck by a 6-inch shell, which killed one man and wounded eight others. The landings began immediately, but the operation was by no means straightforward, as Chadwick recorded:

> The difficulties of getting the troops ashore were greatly accentuated by the reluctance of the masters to come near shore. Many wandered off to great distances, some were found as

> many as 12 miles to the westward. This trouble would have been avoided had a naval officer been aboard each ship to direct movements, the masters being apparently heedless of directions given them by the army officers aboard.[15]

Chadwick records that even three days after the disembarkation two transports, carrying 2,000 men, had gone astray, and Shafter sought the fleet's assistance in finding them.

Inside Santiago the arrival of the expeditionary force made everyone aware that the endgame was approaching. Concas observed that 'a vigorous blockade followed the landing of the army, as was to be expected, and the weather gave us no hope that the hostile squadron would be forced to abandon its position.'[16] Cervera reported to Aunon that he was sending ashore a force from the crews of the squadron; and on June 23 gloomily confirmed to the minister the gravity of the situation:

> As it is absolutely impossible for the squadron to escape, under these circumstances, intend to resist as long as possible and destroy ships as last extreme. Although others are responsible for this untenable situation into which we were forced in spite of my opposition, it is very painful to be a shackled actor therein.[17]

Next day, having belatedly received from Aunon approval to his previous suggestion that the squadron should go out at the first favourable opportunity, Cervera convened another council of war. Bustamente was not present, having gone ashore in command of the force landed from the squadron; but on this occasion those present were entirely unanimous in their conclusion that the sortie was now, and had been since June 8, absolutely impossible. The responsibility for any such decision was now, however, to be taken from Cervera. On the same day he was formally placed under the orders of the governor general, in order 'to give perfect unity to conduct of war in island.' Blanco wasted no time in demonstrating his intention to exercise the overall command, writing to Linares next day to ask him to tell Cervera that he wanted to know his opinion and plans. As for his own opinion, he said that the squadron 'should go out from Santiago as early as possible whenever he may deem best, for the situation in that harbour is, in my judgement, the most dangerous of all.' After summarising (incorrectly) the number of ships off Santiago, Cienfuegos, and Havana, he added that if they should lose the squadron without fighting, the moral effect would be terrible, both in Spain and abroad.[18]

Cervera at once replied to Linares, wearily recording the history of his squadron, and the lamentable situation in which it was placed. To the suggestion that his ships could run the blockade, as two vessels had done from Havana, he pointed out that the situation was entirely different:

> The sortie from here must be made by the ships one by one. There is no possibility of stratagem nor disguise, and the absolutely certain result will be the ruin of each and all of the ships and the death of the greater part of their crews. If I had thought there was even the remotest chance of success I should have made the attempt, although, as I have said before, it would only have amounted to a change of the scene of action unless we had gone to Havana, where things might, perhaps, have been different... As far as I am concerned, the situation has been changed today from a moral standpoint, for I received a telegram this morning which places me under the orders of the captain general in everything related to

> the operations of the war. It is therefore for him to decide whether I am to go out to suicide, dragging along with me those 2,000 sons of Spain.[19]

He also sent a telegram direct to Blanco, pointing out that the six principal ships of the enemy represented more than three times the power of his force. He would not take the step of ordering a sortie on his own account, he said, but if Blanco ordered it, he would carry it out.

Neither Blanco nor Aunon would accept this, both emphasising to Cervera their view that it would be preferable to lose the squadron in a doomed bid to escape than by tamely destroying the ships in harbour as the American ground forces closed in. For Blanco, writing on June 26, it was better 'for the honour of arms to succumb in battle, where there may be many chances of safety;' while Aunon, recalling the minority opinions of Concas and Bustamente at previous councils of war, told Cervera that the government's view was that attempts should be made to save the squadron, in whole or in part, by a sortie by night. To this last, Cervera replied that a sortie by night would be more perilous than in the daytime, as the enemy ships were closer inshore.

On June 27 Cervera replied to both Aunon and Blanco. To the minister he wrote that he was very sorry that he had incurred the government's displeasure by the opinions that he expressed. He had, he said, asked for his landing force to be re-embarked, but doubted if this was possible before reinforcements arrived. He added that Aunon's instructions were of benefit to him 'because I will not be the one to decide upon the useless hecatomb which is being prepared.' His response to Blanco carried more than a hint of irony:

> I have to respect your Excellency's opinions without discussing them, especially after having given you my own opinion formed after mature consideration. I have always believed that there are many sailors more able than I am, and it is a pity that one of them cannot come to take command of the squadron, and under whose orders I would be placed. I construe your Excellency's telegram as an order to go out, and therefore ask General Linares for re-embarkation of forces which were landed at your Excellency's suggestion. I beg that you will confirm the order of sortie, because it is not explicit, and I should feel very sorry if I did not interpret your Excellency's orders correctly.[20]

By now, both in Madrid and Havana, Cervera's pessimism and defeatism had led to a loss of confidence in his judgement. His competence as a naval commander was of course not in question, but not much attention was any longer being paid to his opinions as to what should be done. Blanco privately asked Linares for his candid opinion as to whether the squadron could go out, and what solution seemed best to him. This was on June 27; Linares, who still maintained an excellent relationship with Cervera, seems not to have replied. He did, though, tell the admiral that he did not believe it possible to re-embark the naval landing force until hoped for reinforcements arrived from Manzanillo. On June 28 Blanco definitively set out his instructions to Cervera in a personal and confidential telegram:

> My plan, which I desire your Excellency to carry out, is as follows: the squadron will remain in harbour, and without precipitation, provided it has provisions left, it will watch for a favourable opportunity to go out in whatever direction your Excellency may deem best. But in case the situation should become aggravated, so that the fall of Santiago is

> believed near, the squadron will go out immediately as best it can, entrusting its fate to the valour and ability of your Excellency and the distinguished captains commanding it, who no doubt will confirm by their actions the reputation they enjoy.[21]

By the afternoon of June 22 Shafter had got about half his troops ashore at Daiquiri, when it was learned that the Spanish had pulled out from Siboney. General Lawton, whose division was the first ashore, was ordered to occupy the place, which he did on the following morning; it was a better place for landing, protected by a headland and with an easy shelving beach, and use was immediately made of it to continue the disembarkation. Shafter told Sampson explicitly on June 22 that he was going to advance from to Daiquiri to Santiago as soon as he could. The advance was led by Wheeler's dismounted cavalry division, which on June 24 ran into a Spanish position at Las Guasimas, which it took after a brisk fight, in which the Rough Riders had their first taste of action. Wheeler had 1,141 men engaged; his casualties were 18 killed and 50 wounded. The Spanish force, some 1,500 strong, was officially stated to have lost 12 killed and 24 wounded.[22] Linares ordered a retreat to San Juan Hill, since any more advanced position was exposed to the gunfire of the American fleet.

On June 25 Shafter wrote to Sampson asking that the fleet should bombard the Spanish positions at Aguadores, but not to destroy the bridge there, as he proposed to use it to send Garcia towards the Morro. On June 27, however, the Spanish blew it up. Shafter insisted that Wheeler, who was still inclined to press further forward than he wanted, should not become engaged with the enemy. On June 26 Lawton's division took up a position a mile and a half from San Juan Hill. Having reached this position there was no longer much likelihood of Shafter making an attack on the entrance heights, if indeed there ever had been.[23]

Shafter remained aboard the *Seguranca* while planning his next move, which left Wheeler as the most senior officer ashore. The plan was to get between the principal Spanish force and Santiago, in order to be able to seize the city, and drive Linares towards the Morro. On his side Linares unwisely attempted to cover every option, with the result that his forces were scattered too thinly. He was still hoping for the promised reinforcements from Manzanillo under Colonel Escario, and these were, by now, approaching. It had been hoped that Garcia would intercept them, but he failed to do so. Escario had 3,700 troops, but was reported as having more than twice as many, and this prompted Shafter to launch an attack sooner than originally intended. The attack would go in on San Juan Hill and Kettle Hill, with secondary attacks at El Caney and Aguadores. The attack on El Caney would be made by Lawton's division, while Duffield, with the Michigan volunteers, would feint at Aguadores. The main attack would be made by the divisions of Kent and Wheeler.

The assault began at dawn on July 1, when Duffield moved towards Aguadores; when reaching the bridge he found that the Spanish had blown up the western end and after a few hours he retired to Siboney. At El Caney, Lawton advanced at 7:00 p.m. The Spanish position there was ultimately untenable, but General Vara del Rey held out there for eight hours with just over 500 men. He was killed around noon; when his force finally retreated it had lost more than 80% of its strength but it had inflicted heavy casualties on Lawton's troops.

Meanwhile Linares had strengthened his force on San Juan Hill, upon which the main attack of 8,000 men now fell. It was led by Wheeler's cavalry division, now under the command of Sumner; Wheeler had been taken ill. The Spanish artillery overcame the American gunners, so that the troops had to advance without support under heavy fire. As the troops moved forward the strength of the Spanish position became clear. A British observer, John Black Atkins, commented:

> But this hill – the look of it was enough to stagger any man. Was this to be taken practically without the aid of artillery? Artillery should have battered, and battered, and battered the position, and then the infantry might have swept up at the run.[24]

As it was, there was no help for it, and Kent's division moved forward to storm San Juan Hill. At the same time, Sumner advanced on Kettle Hill. Two regular regiments led the way, with Roosevelt at the head of the Rough Riders close behind. His dismounted cavalry charged up Kettle Hill, in an assault that would make Theodore Roosevelt a national hero; they then turned to support the infantry attacking San Juan Hill; heavily outnumbered, its defenders fell back to strong positions on the outskirts of Santiago. The Spanish troops were now commanded by General Toral, Linares having been seriously wounded. The American victories had been dearly bought. At El Caney, Lawton lost 81 killed and 360 wounded; at San Juan Hill, Kent's casualties were 89 killed and 489 wounded, and Sumner's were 35 killed and 328 wounded, a total of 1,382.[25] Spanish losses were 215 killed, 376 wounded and two taken prisoner. Among the casualties was Captain Bustamente, fatally wounded when leading the naval landing force. When the battle ended, Shafter set about strengthening his position, but no further assault was immediately contemplated. Shafter had gone ashore and was encamped a mile and a half behind the front, but was suffering from both gout and malaria. He had had the stuffing knocked out of him by the extent of his losses, and was not about to order another attack. Lieutenant Muller commented on the failure to follow up the capture of San Juan Hill:

> On July 1 the Americans fought... without protection and with truly admirable courage, but they did not fight again as they did that day... Did they think on that first day that all they had to do was to attack our soldiers en masse and put them to flight?[26]

Shafter spent the next two days profoundly anxious about his position. He believed his flanks to be insecure, and was concerned about the imminent arrival of Escario's column. His reports to Washington indicated that he was contemplating a retreat, which he discussed at a council of war at 7:00 p.m. on July 2. His four generals, Wheeler, Lawton, Kent and Bates all disagreed, and Shafter did not immediately pursue it. Chadwick had been to see Shafter that afternoon; the general told him that his health did not permit him to go on board ship, or even to travel to Siboney, so it was arranged that Sampson should visit him in camp on July 3. It was a decision that was to have momentous consequences.

It was always likely to be a rather testy meeting. Shafter had written to Sampson earlier on July 2 urging him to make an effort immediately to force the entrance to the harbour to avoid further losses to the army, adding: 'you can now operate with less loss of life than I can.' To this, Sampson replied through Staunton that this was impossible until the mines were cleared, 'a work of some time after forts are taken possession of by your troops.'[27]

This went down badly with Shafter. Clearly very rattled now, he replied:

> It is impossible for me to say when I can take batteries at entrance to harbour. If they are as difficult to take as those which we have been pitted against it will be some time and a great loss of life. I am at a loss to see why the navy cannot work as well as the army.

Sampson's patient response to this did him credit. He pointed out, once again, that the channel to the harbour was strewn with mines, 'which would certainly result in the sinking of one or more of our ships if we attempt to enter the harbour.' If this happened, there could be no further progress. He went on:

> If it is your earnest desire that we should force our entrance, I will at once prepare to undertake it. I think, however, that our position and yours would be made more difficult if, as is possible, we fail in our attempt... It is not so much the loss of men as it is the loss of ships which has, until now, deterred me from making a direct attack on the ships within the port.[28]

Although his subordinate commanders had opposed the idea of a retreat, Shafter evidently had not given up on this. In Washington, McKinley and Alger had been anxiously awaiting news all through July 2. At noon on the following day Alger reproachfully asked Shafter to report at the end of each day, or at once if there was anything of special importance. He was dismayed to receive at 12:45 p.m. a message from Shafter that he was 'seriously considering withdrawing about 5 miles and taking up a new position on the high ground between the San Juan River and Siboney.' This was a thunderclap; although the decision was left to Shafter, he was urged to remain on the San Juan Heights, and he was promised whatever reinforcements he wanted. McKinley and Alger began to wonder if Shafter should be replaced.[29] The idea that reinforcements were needed was the subject of an urgent letter from Theodore Roosevelt to Henry Cabot Lodge:

> Tell the president for Heaven's sake to send us every regiment and above all every battery possible. We have won so far at a heavy cost, but the Spaniards fight hard and charging these entrenchments against modern rifles is terrible. We are in measurable distance of a terrible military disaster... Our general is poor; he is too unwieldy to get to the front.[30]

However, in the meantime there had come from Havana messages to Cervera which now changed everything.

20

Santiago: Cervera Comes Out

Cervera had replied to Blanco's 'plan' for the squadron by explaining, on June 29, that it took twelve hours for his ships to get up steam; to keep the fires going so as to be ready to seize an opportunity used fifteen tons of coal a day. He said that he understood Blanco to mean that he should take advantage of any favourable opportunity, but otherwise to go out at the last hour, even though this meant the certain loss of the squadron. With this in mind, the admiral next day asked Linares when that moment might arise, since he would need to re-embark his landing force. On July 1 Linares promised to keep him informed, while warning that 'if the battle should be unfavourable, the moment might not be propitious for effecting the re-embarkation of your forces.'[1] In the light of this Cervera summoned a fresh council of war for 7:00 p.m.

The outcome of the discussion was a unanimous opinion that the situation contemplated by Blanco had arisen; that sortie was impossible without re-embarking the crews on shore, but that they were regarded by Linares as an essential part of his reserve; and that in that case the only thing to do would be to obstruct the harbour entrance. By now Linares had been seriously injured; it was his successor, Toral, who insisted that the squadron's landing force was essential to the defence of the city, as Cervera explained that night in a telegram to Blanco: 'My opinion is the same as Toral's, and our sortie would look like flight, which is repugnant to all. My captains are of the same opinion. I entreat you will send instructions I have asked for.'[2]

Cervera knew of course what those instructions would be, and they came in a telegram from Blanco at 10:30 p.m. that night:

> In view of hostile progress in spite of heroic defence garrison, and in conformity with opinion government, you will re-embark crews, take advantage of first opportunity, and go out with the ships of your squadron, following route you deem best. You are authorised to leave behind any which on account of slow speed or circumstances have no chance of escaping. I will tell your Excellency for your information, not in the nature of instructions, that there are only three ships at Cienfuegos and nine here, none of them of great power.[3]

He followed this up with another telegram fifteen minutes later, telling Cervera to hasten the sortie before the Americans could take possession of the entrance forts. Ten minutes later, he was telegraphing Toral to prolong the defence as long as possible, preventing the seizure of the forts before the squadron's sortie. To Madrid, Blanco reported his instructions to Cervera, still referring to the order that advantage be taken of the first opportunity to leave the harbour. As he well knew, there was no such opportunity nor would there be, and the reference was presumably an attempt to shift some of the responsibility for the impending disaster onto Cervera. Only at 5:10 p.m. on the morning of July 2 did Blanco finally give an unqualified instruction: 'In view of exhausted and serious condition of Santiago, as stated by General Toral, your Excellency will re-embark landing troops of squadron as fast as possible, and go out immediately.[4]

Cervera called his captains together to tell them of this unequivocal order, as Concas records:

> He stated to us that the time for discussion had passed, that we had done all that was within human power to avoid the catastrophe, and that nothing was left now but to obey, to which we all agreed. The learned and beloved Bustamente, who fell wounded in the battle of the previous day never to rise again, was absent, in consequence of which I performed the duties of chief of staff from the day of his landing.[5]

Toral, to whom Cervera had reported Blanco's instructions, was cooperative, telling him that he had given orders to each of the four companies of seamen to proceed to embarkation points. This operation proceeded swiftly, except in the case of the men of the company from the *Vizcaya*, who only rejoined their ship at 4:00 p.m., and arrived completely exhausted. In view of this, Cervera postponed the sortie until the following morning, to give all his crews a much needed rest.

In one respect Blanco's belief that there was a chance that some at any rate of the ships of the squadron might escape was not without justification. It was, though, a remote chance, and it arose as a result of the major vessels of Sampson's fleet having taken steps to conserve fuel by reducing the number of boilers connected for steaming, leaving the others banked or cold. By the beginning of July, for instance, the *New York* had only three boilers connected, with one banked and two cold. Sampson had authorised this in the growing belief that the Spanish squadron would never come out. It was a thin chance, but it gave Cervera the possibility that, if he could clear the harbour entrance quickly enough, he might run through the American line.[6]

Cervera's instructions to his captains were based on the observations he had made of the movements of the blockading fleet. The arc in which the major American vessels were usually disposed ran from Daiquiri in the east. At that end of the line the *Indiana* led the *New York, Oregon, Iowa* and *Massachusetts*, with the *Brooklyn* at the western end. The smaller cruisers lay between these. Cervera planned to escape from the harbour, at once turning to the west. The *Maria Teresa*, leading his squadron, was to engage the *Brooklyn*, endeavouring if possible to ram her, while the three remaining cruisers, not pausing to support the flagship, should proceed westwards at their maximum speed. The destroyers were also to steam away at high speed, taking no part in the battle unless a good opportunity arose to attack an isolated enemy ship. Those ships that got away would head for Cienfuegos or Havana. Concas described the response of the captains to Cervera's plan:

> The words of the Admiral were received with enthusiasm, and we all clasped each other's hands fervently, as soldiers who knew how to meet death and destruction, from which no power could save us. There were harsh and well merited denunciations of many statesmen who remain as calm as if they owed nothing either to God or their country, and we swore that if any of us should survive he would defend the memory of those who perished in the encounter.[7]

Concas went ashore to concert the arrangements with Toral, while Cervera arranged to deliver to the Archbishop of Santiago a package of all the documents relating to the mission of the squadron; this, Concas was later to write, enabled those who served under Cervera, and the whole navy, to protect their honour against 'interested imputations.' Concas also had a final meeting on shore with Villaamil, the commander of the destroyers. During the night the gunboat *Alvarado* was to go down to remove six of the mines which blocked the channel to the West of Cay Smith.

Early on the morning of Sunday, July 3 Cervera sent Concas in the *Alvarado* to the harbour entrance to make a final check on the position of the blockading ships. As dawn broke, it was misty, but as the sun came up the mist dispersed; it was going to be a hot, still day. Concas noted that the *Indiana* was closer inshore than usual; more importantly, he realised that the *Massachusetts* had left the blockade (she had gone to Guantánamo to coal), while the *Brooklyn* had moved closer to the *Texas*; a small yacht was in the space which Schley's flagship had previously occupied. Concas attempted to measure the apparent distances offshore of the American ships, but the range of the stadimeter he was using was limited to 7656 yards (7000 m), and he could see that the Brooklyn's distance was some 2000 yards more than this. His observations completed, Concas returned to the *Maria Teresa* to report to Cervera.

Leaving the harbour was not entirely straightforward. The entrance was a narrow channel about 1100 yards in length, made still narrower near the outlet by the Diamond Bank, where the width was reduced to 76 yards; the narrows turned slightly, limiting the speed at which they could be taken, which meant that only one ship at a time could enter the narrows. Concas described the effect of this:

> It was necessary therefore that the ships go out a considerable distance apart, and although this circumstance in itself would not be prejudicial to our line, it had, on the other hand, the serious drawback that the ship which went out ahead, as well as each successive ship, would have to suffer alone the fire of all the enemy's vessels, resulting in a battle of only two available guns against more than 200.[8]

Cervera now gave orders to the squadron to weigh anchor; when all the ships reported that this was done, the signal for the sortie, 'Viva Espana,' was given, and led by the *Maria Teresa* wearing her battle flag the squadron moved towards the entrance. After she had passed the Diamond Bank, Cervera turned to the chief pilot of Santiago: 'Goodbye,' he said, 'Go, and be sure that you let them pay you because you have earned it well.'[9] As she emerged from the harbour entrance, it could be seen that the American ships were hurriedly getting under way, and Concas asked permission to open fire. As the notes of the bugle giving the signal for this died away, Concas turned to Cervera: 'Poor Spain,' he said. Cervera answered by an expressive motion, as though to say that he had done everything possible to avoid it, and that his conscience was clear.[10]

Aboard the *New York* Sampson had been preparing to go ashore for his conference with Shafter. He and Lieutenant Staunton, who was to accompany him, had put on brown canvas leggings and spurs in preparation for a hot cross country ride, to which neither of them was looking forward. At about 8:50 p.m. the *New York* displayed the signal: 'Disregard movements of commander-in-chief,' and accompanied by the gunboat *Ericsson* and the armed yacht *Hist* steamed slowly eastwards towards Siboney. Goode, who was watching him, noted that the admiral was not in very good health, and thought him 'well-nigh worn out with the tremendous strain of the past month.' Sampson glanced through his telescope at the blockading fleet as the *New York* steamed eastward. He was standing on the cruiser's flying bridge, dictating a memo to his clerk, when a cry rang out from the signal bridge: 'Smoke in the harbour!' This was followed by another shout: 'The fleet's coming out!' The flagship went at once to action stations, and turned hard aport.[11] Chadwick, who was also to accompany Sampson to the conference, was in his cabin getting ready. He heard a distant gun, and then the scurry of feet as the ship went to general quarters. Making his way to the bridge, he saw that the *Maria Teresa* had already cleared the harbour entrance; as he watched, a second cruiser appeared. When the *New York* had completed her turn, she was some 7 miles to the east of the harbour entrance. It was now about 9:35 a.m.[12]

After so long watching and waiting for the Spanish to come out, expectation that they would do so had faded among the men of the blockading fleet. Captain Philip, of the *Texas*, afterwards recalled: 'Cervera's sally had been so long expected that when it actually came it was unexpected. I, for one, did not dream that, after declining the issue for a month, he would come out in broad daylight.'[13] That Sunday, the usual Sunday quarters and inspection began at 9:30 a.m. throughout the fleet; being the first Sunday of the month there would be the reading of the Articles of War, followed by the muster of the crew and divine service. The process had already begun aboard the *New York*, and was beginning also in the rest of the fleet. No one could of course have foreseen that the sortie should have taken place when Sampson's departure had left Schley for the time being in actual command of the blockading fleet. Margaret Leach, among other historians, was struck by the remarkable irony that

> on that morning hour, of all the days and hours, [Sampson] should have been required to dance attendance on the bungling general; that Cervera should have chosen the westward course, carrying the battle ever farther from the American commander-in-chief, casting its honours to the insubordinate Commodore whose conduct he despised.[14]

As the flagship began to work up to full steam in pursuit of the rest of the American fleet, Sampson's thought was 'Oh, that we had wings!' Even the calm unemotional Sampson allowed himself a moment of bitter regret that it should have been while he was on his way to a conference with the uncooperative Shafter that Cervera should have chosen to put to sea.

The general muster was beginning aboard the *Brooklyn* as three bells were struck, and her captain and executive officer came on the quarterdeck in dress uniform and wearing their swords. Schley, with no sense of what was about to happen, was relaxing, as Graham recorded:

> Dressed in a pair of white duck trousers, a shabby blue coat, and officer's white summer hat, with no insignia of rank upon him, Commodore Schley braced his white shod feet against a hatch combing, tilted his chair back, plucked rather nervously at his imperial, and remarked, 'This is pretty slow.[15]

Although columns of smoke had been seen rising in Santiago harbour in the still morning air, there was no thought of what this might mean, and the church parade on board the *Brooklyn* and other ships of the fleet got under way as usual. Graham remembered noticing the gaps on the western side of the blockading line 'that must have offered tempting invitation to a foe desirous of, and eagerly looking for, a chance to escape.' At that moment the *Brooklyn*'s forward engines were uncoupled, and none of the ships had steam for more than 10 knots.

Schley went below to change into Sunday rig; 'then returning on deck to a seat under a small awning spread on the after part of the quarterdeck to protect the officers from the heat of the sun as it mounted higher and higher,' he made a survey of the harbour entrance. It was only moments later that there came a cry from the forward bridge, as Lieutenant Commander Hodgson called out through a megaphone: 'Tell the Commodore that the Spanish fleet are coming out!'[16]

Schley described the position of the American ships at the moment that Cervera's squadron was sighted:

> The *Brooklyn*'s head at this moment was in the direction of Cabanas Cove, to the westward of the entrance to Santiago, or to the westward of north. The enemy ships were seen from the starboard side of the *Brooklyn*'s quarterdeck coming out. The *Texas* was approximately a point or more abaft the *Brooklyn*'s starboard beam, heading to the eastward. The *Iowa* was slightly ahead of the *Texas* or, looking from the *Brooklyn*, to the left of the *Texas* and eastward. The *Oregon* was east again of the *Iowa*. The *Indiana* was still east of the *Oregon*, while the *Gloucester* appeared to be lying in near Aguadores, and the *Vixen* near Cabanas.[17]

The *New York*, Schley observed, 'was out of sight and signal distance, even with glasses from the forward bridge;' her position left Schley in no doubt that he was now in effective command of the American fleet. Graham was standing by him at that moment:

> Commodore Schley was on his feet in an instant, and reaching over back of me to where his binoculars lay on the steel hatchway cover, as he grabbed them up he exclaimed, 'Come on, my boy. We'll give it to them now!'... The Commodore sprang forward through the superstructure, elbowing his way among the men, who in their excitement and delight were paying little attention to rank or station. He was making for the little bridge around the conning tower.[18]

The 'little bridge' was a wooden platform which he had had built a few weeks before, raised about three feet above the deck, to enable him to be in touch with Captain Cook during a battle, and to give him a better point of observation.

'Signal close in,' Schley said to Flag Lieutenant Sears, and then: 'Signal they are going to the west.' To Captain Cook, he said: 'Open fire, Cook, and fire deliberately.' Next, he looked for the *New York*; telling the offices near him that he could not see her he asked if any of them could. Told that she was not in sight he remarked: 'Then it's our fight.'[19] It would be surprising if Schley did not at that moment feel a measure of self-satisfaction at the chance that had left him in immediate command of the fleet as the action developed.

Aboard the *Iowa*, Evans had had breakfast with his son. Although at sunset the previous evening, the columns of smoke rising in Santiago harbour had been pointed out to him, he paid little attention; the Spanish ships frequently moved about the harbour. Evans was getting ready for the captain's inspection of the crew, when the alarm went off for general quarters, and six hundred men rushed to their action stations. His biographer wrote: 'Evans' eyes were fixed upon the fast stepping *Infanta Maria Teresa,* clearing the entrance and rounding the shoals, with guns flaming and looking her noblest in fresh black paint, shining brightwork and resplendent battle flags of red and gold.'[20] The signal number 250 was hoisted: 'The enemy's ships are escaping.' The night before, when Evans had ignored the smoke in Santiago harbour, his quartermaster had been more prescient, and had laid the three relevant signal flags ready for use. The American ships all saw the *Maria Teresa* at about the same time; the first to do so, due to her position in the blockade line, was probably the *Iowa*.

The difference in fighting power between the American and Spanish vessels was enormous. When the battle began, the American fleet consisted of four battleships, an armoured cruiser, two converted yachts and a torpedo boat; Cervera had four armoured cruisers and two destroyers. The Americans had seventy six large guns, all of which were in reliable working order and fully provided with ammunition; the Spanish had forty two, a number of which were unreliable and short of ammunition. There was an approximate equivalence in the number of crew engaged; there were 2,341 American sailors compared to 2,261 Spanish.[21]

Accounts of the battle which followed vary one from another, as is only to be expected. The way in which individual incidents were described did, however, sometimes owe something to their authors' desire to put a particular spin on what occurred. This, naturally, was the subject of lengthy controversy during the Court of Inquiry, at which Schley's lawyers were able to point out instances which, as James Parker subsequently wrote, showed variations intended to reflect less well on the performance of the *Brooklyn*. They also put the *New York* as nearer to the scene of action than was actually the case.[22]

One particular record to which Parker was referring was that compiled during the course of the battle aboard the armed yacht *Vixen*. Her commander Lieutenant Sharp had, at the suggestion of his executive officer Lieutenant Harlow, ordered that this be made. A copy of this was attached to the report which Sharp sent to Sampson on July 6. Several typewritten copies of the record had been made; but the manuscript copy purportedly attached to his report differed in a number of particulars from the typed copy which was attached to the *Vixen*'s logbook. The longhand version was written by the yeoman of the *Vixen*, a man named Wainwright. Although Schley's lawyers asked for his attendance at the inquiry, the judge advocate failed to produce him. Each and every one of the variations and omissions had the effect of which Schley's lawyers complained. The inference is obvious; but it was not a matter to which the court in due course paid much attention.

Given that some of the later accounts of the battle might have been affected by a desire to put matters in a particular light, the *Vixen*'s record assumes some importance, as being a contemporary document actually written during the course of the battle, by someone with no axe to grind. Many of the incidents that occurred were of course beyond question, although where facts were unarguable, motives were frequently in issue. As for the record attached to the *Vixen*'s logbook, Parker notes that both Sharp and Harlow testified to its accuracy.

21

Santiago: The Battle

Within minutes of the *Maria Teresa* emerging from the harbour entrance the gunners on both sides were in action. Each of the American ships headed for the entrance, opening fire as they did so. Very soon the smoke from the guns began to obscure the visibility. The *Brooklyn*, on the western side of Santiago, was the closest of the American vessels. Captain Cook described the movements of his ship in relation to the enemy in his evidence to the Court of Inquiry in these terms:

> As soon as I saw this fleet, and saw that they were heading south-west, they seemed to be coming straight for the interval between the *Texas* and *Brooklyn*, we being headed for the fleet, about north-east. I went into the conning tower and directed the helmsman, told him what I wanted to do – to keep straight for the head of the fleet... The *Texas* was well on our starboard, and she was heading to the northward and eastward (how much I do not know)... The Spanish ships were well to the westward. We held to the north-east. When I saw that, I ported the helm, perhaps halfway over.[1]

As he saw that the Spanish ships had put their helms aport to pursue an escape to the west, Cook realised that he must alter course; by then the *Brooklyn*'s head had come round almost to the east and he gave the order 'hard aport to the helmsman,' and then ran to the starboard side to see the rest of the American fleet, and its position in relation to the *Brooklyn*:

> Instantly, quicker than I can tell it, the Commodore called to me: 'Cook, hard aport,' or 'is your helm hard aport?' My answer was, 'It is hard aport: she is turning as rapidly as possible.' As I saw the *Texas*, I saw her port bow. I never saw her starboard side; and changing her bearing very rapidly, *the Brooklyn* turned very rapidly along the port side of the *Texas*... We made a complete turn, and a very rapid turn with the helm hard aport, from previously 'port' until we came around, and paralleled the Spanish fleet on the other side.[2]

This account absolutely accorded with Schley's recollection. The issue that arose at the hearing concerned Schley's reaction to the warning allegedly given by Hodgson, the navigator, that the turn to starboard risked cutting down the *Texas*. To this Schley was said to have replied: 'Damn the *Texas*. She must look after herself.' Their exchange was heard by neither Cook nor Graham, both of whom were within earshot. Cook told the inquiry that there had been no danger of any collision between the *Brooklyn* and the *Texas*; he said that the navigator came across to him and said: 'Captain, do you see the *Texas*?' Cook was looking directly at her: 'just about then we were pretty well clear of her – I mean opening out her stern. I said 'oh, yes' and he told me that entirely reassured him, and he walked away.'[3] It was at this point at the hearing that Dewey interrupted to ask Cook how near the *Brooklyn* had passed to the *Texas*, and Cook replied that they had passed at about 400 yards. He went on to observe that this was the hottest part of the action, and that there was no time for indecision. Looking at the situation later, he thought that if he had turned the other way there would have been the chance of disaster. It appeared to him, and to those on the *Brooklyn*'s bridge, that the movements of the *Maria Teresa* indicated an intention to try to ram. Although at the hearing there was some dispute about the evidence, it seems that whether or not the *Texas* needed to to do so, she backed her engines to avoid any risk of a collision with the *Brooklyn* as the flagship made her turn.

When the *Brooklyn* had completed her turn, which came to be described as 'the loop,' she seemed to Schley and Cook to be momentarily alone in facing the Spanish squadron, now heading westward at maximum speed; a heavy pall of smoke obscured the position of the other American ships, and Schley observed: 'Well, Cook, we'll have to stay alone with this crowd.' Just then the *Oregon* emerged through the smoke, firing a salvo from her forward 13-inch guns, and behind her came the *Texas*. Schley, in his memoirs, describes the scene as it was at about 1030:

> For the next 15 minutes, with [the *Oregon*] on the *Brooklyn*'s quarter, the fighting was terrific. Both ships were a sheet of flame fore and aft, and what rapid gunfire meant was truly realised. Not many minutes had passed in this terrific onslaught before the leading ship of the enemy was observed to be badly hurt and wobbling like a bird wounded, and apparently lagging. Smoke was seen issuing from her ports, and, but a few minutes afterwards, from her hatches, in columns mounting straight into the air.[4]

It was clear that the *Maria Teresa*'s end was already near, and Schley remarked to Cook: 'We have got one. Keep the boys below informed of all the movements. They can't see, and they want to know.'

Soon after this it was apparent that the *Oquendo* had also been badly hit, and was on fire, and within minutes both she and the *Maria Teresa* had turned in towards the land. It seemed to Flag Lieutenant Sears that the *Maria Teresa* had surrendered, but having caught fire her crew could not haul down her flag; Schley told Cook to cease firing on her. By now both the *Oregon* and the *Iowa* were also concentrating their fire on Cervera's flagship. Behind her the *Vizcaya* and the *Colon* had emerged quite close together, and they were drawing ahead of the *Oquendo*.

By the time the *Oquendo* had come out, the situation of the *Maria Teresa* had indeed become desperate. Concas described what he called her' deathblow,' which he believed came from the *Iowa*, some 2000 yards astern of the Spanish flagship: 'She lodged in us two 12-inch shells, which, exploding on the poop, burst the steam pipe of the main pump and broke some pipes of the engines, which was the decisive cause of the loss of the ship.' Concas dismissed the claim of Captain Taylor, of the *Indiana*, that shells from his ship had hit the *Maria Teresa*, reckoning that since the *Indiana* had been firing at the two destroyers, at a range of up to 4500 yards, and these had come out half an hour after the *Maria Teresa*, the *Indiana* could not have seen the effect of shells fired towards the Spanish flagship.

Concas reckoned that but for the damage caused by the *Iowa* there might have been a chance of escape, for only the *Brooklyn* was fast enough to keep up. But the wreckage on the poop, and in the engine room, was fatal. Just at this moment another shell hit the *Maria Teresa* wounding Concas and the only two bridge officers still on their feet, and Cervera took personal command. It was immediately clear to him and the officers near to him that there was no choice but to run the ship ashore, both to prevent her being captured and to save the crew. Turning to starboard, the ship was run ashore about 5 miles from the harbour entrance.[5]

Last of the four armoured cruisers to leave the harbour, the *Oquendo* ran straight into the concentrated fire of three battleships, to which she could make no effective reply. Her captain, Juan Lazaga, was killed as she turned to the west; within minutes her port side was a mass of flame. Her forward turret was put out of action by an 8-inch shell, so she was fighting with one gun against all of the American guns. At full speed, she passed the *Maria Teresa* as the flagship turned inshore, and burning furiously, and still under heavy fire, she was beached about a mile to the west.[6]

Behind the *Oquendo*, Villaamil's two destroyers, the *Furor* and the *Pluton*, did not immediately emerge from the harbour entrance. Why this should have been so, Concas could not say; Villaamil was killed in the action, so his reasons were unknown. Cervera had ordered that the destroyers come out behind but close up to the armoured cruisers; under their protection, the intention was that they keep close inshore until they were able to get out of range by virtue of their speed. As it was, they came under fire immediately, and were destroyed within minutes, the *Furor* sinking in deep water and the *Pluton* beaching herself at Cabanas. Losses among their crews were high, each losing about one third of her men, most of whom were killed. The two destroyers were finished off by the armed yacht *Gloucester*, which had been at the eastern end of the blockade line. She was commanded by Lieutenant Commander Richard Wainwright, who had been executive officer of the *Maine* when she blew up in Havana harbour.

Meanwhile both the *Vizcaya* and the *Colon* had been making their way westward, momentarily benefiting by the American concentration on the other two armoured cruisers. The *Vizcaya* was putting up a brave fight against the *Brooklyn*, but being slower than the *Colon* she was soon passed by her, and began to receive the concentrated fire of all the American heavy ships. She struggled on for as long as she could, taking heavy punishment. In the confusion of the battle, however, the American battleships were at risk of getting in each other's way. Captain Clark of the *Oregon* was to describe to the Court of Inquiry a narrow escape from collision with the *Iowa* as the battleships turned westwards in pursuit of Cervera's squadron:

> I put my helm a-starboard, and sheared off; and then I saw the *Iowa* again. She had evidently changed her course to the westward very sharply at almost the same time; and I was fearful that she would collide with us – that she would swing too far. I therefore put my helm hard a-starboard, to clear her, and we went by her; and I saw no more of her during the entire action.[7]

It was not only the *Iowa* that Clark had to watch out for:

> I saw the *Texas* just after I passed the *Iowa*. Whether she was moving rapidly, or lying in the water without any movement, or how she was moving, I cannot recall, I was so concerned

> about striking her. I was just clearing the *Iowa* when the *Texas* was reported on the port bow, and I had no time except to give one glance at her; and then give the order 'hard aport.' Then I had to jump over to the other side to see if I was going to clear the *Iowa*. I was afraid my speed would not be sufficient to carry me by; and yet I had to get past; and I really cannot tell whether I saw the bow or stern of the *Texas*.[8]

Clark's evidence was that of an unbiased witness of truth, and so may be accepted as an accurate record of the confusion among the American battleships. The narrow escape of the *Oregon* from collision with the *Iowa* was confirmed by the latter's navigator, Lieutenant Commander Scheutze, who told the inquiry that the ships passed at about 150 to 200 feet.[9]

In another not unimportant respect Clark's evidence was helpful to Schley's claim to have been in actual command during the battle:

> I remember a signal, made by Commodore Schley from the *Brooklyn*, 'follow flag,' because I ordered it repeated. We did close up. I thought it was 'follow flag.' It may have been 'close up.' My memory is distinct in this, – that it was made immediately after we came out of the smoke and discovered the Spanish fleet ahead of us. On our first discovery of the *Brooklyn* this signal was flying, or it was reported to me immediately after that time.[10]

Meanwhile in their westward progress, the *Colon* had overtaken the *Vizcaya* and drawn clear of her, so that for the moment the latter was the target for the American pursuers, as Concas related:

> To add to her bad luck the *Vizcaya* was left behind by her companion; therefore, being nearer, she was instinctively attacked by all the ships of the enemy; the same circumstance of two of our guns pitted against all those of the enemy occurring again as before; and hardly had the hostile ships gained in distance when fire broke out on the beautiful cruiser, which all the heroic courage of her defenders could not control, and at about half past eleven she ran ashore at Aserrados, her flag consumed by the flames, like those of her two companions, so that not one flag was lowered... The *Vizcaya* carried a beautiful silk flag, the gift of the historical society of the ancient province of the same name, and knowing the ship lost Eulate had it lowered and burned, hoisting another one to the main truck, and this one was never lowered until the fire caused the whole mast to fall into the flames devouring the poop, their pointed tongues seeming to wait for the flag of our country to fall into them, that it might never serve the enemy as a trophy.[11]

As had been the case with the *Maria Teresa* and the *Oquendo*, the crew of the *Vizcaya* had to jump overboard, the wounded being carried ashore by those who could swim. In her case, however, a boat was saved, and thanks to a nearby reef most of the crew survived.

It was during the exchange of fire with the *Vizcaya* that the *Brooklyn* received most of her damage, several shells hitting her superstructure and one penetrating the gun deck. Sending to know how many men had been killed and wounded, Schley and Cook were amazed to learn that there had been only two slightly wounded. Soon after this, however, the *Brooklyn* suffered her only fatal casualty, when Chief Yeoman Ellis was killed while taking the range of the *Vizcaya*. As two men prepared to throw his body overboard, Schley saw what they were doing:

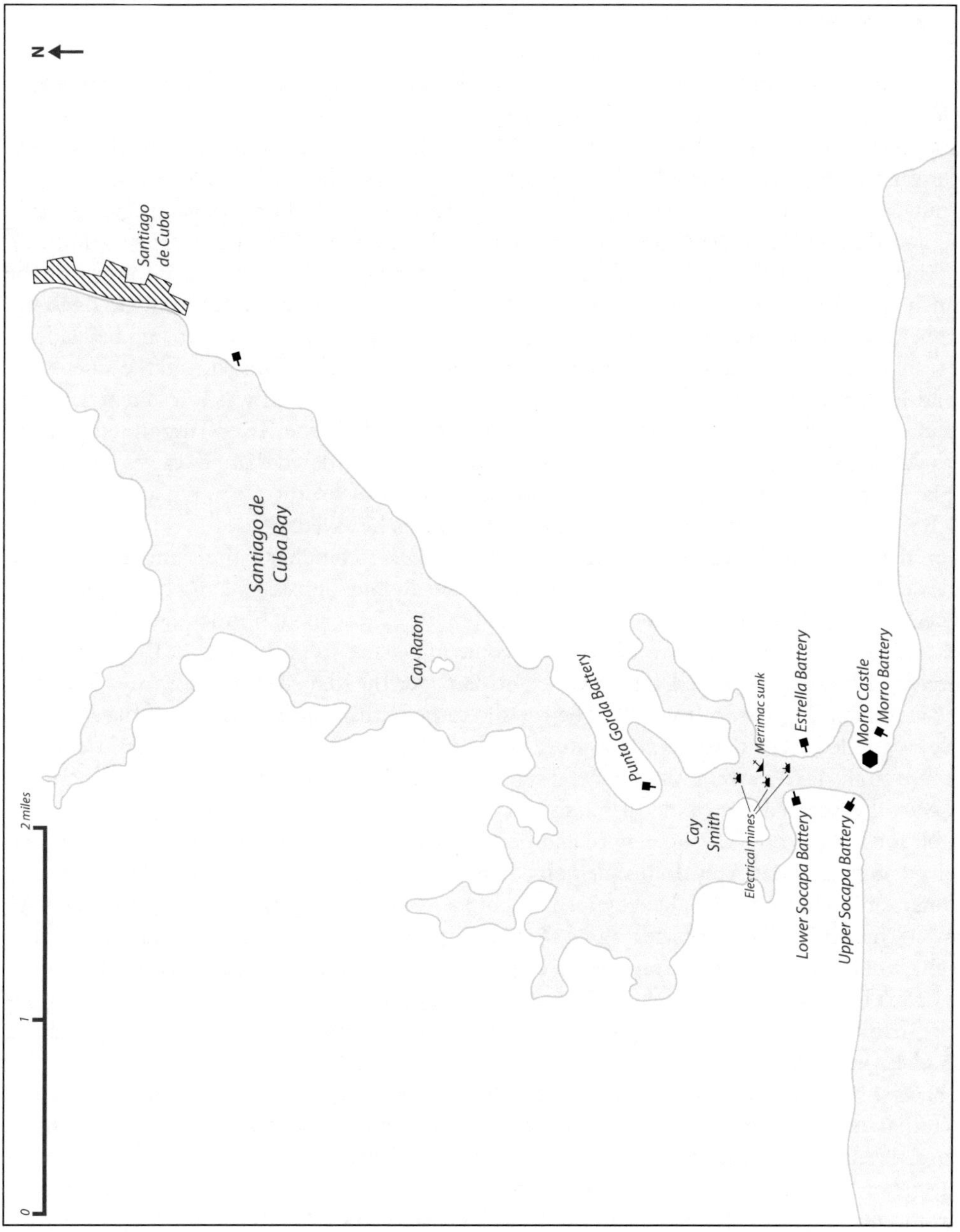

6 Santiago de Cuba.

> In the midst of all this hot action, with all this tremendous responsibility upon his shoulders, with the shells bursting over his head and the small projectiles rattling against the turret, from the heat of battle this commander found time to turn and say: 'Don't throw that body overboard. Take it below, and we'll give it Christian burial.'[12]

This account, by one of Schley's principal cheerleaders, was characteristic of the terms in which the journalists reported the events of the battle.

The destruction of the Vizcaya left the *Colon* as the only remaining prey for the leading American warships. She had only her secondary armament, so was unable to fire at long range at her pursuers. Graham noted that the chase, led by the *Brooklyn* and the *Oregon*, began at 11:25 a.m., and that by 12:15 the *Colon* was some four and a quarter miles ahead. Slowly, however, the Americans gained, and by 12:50 Schley reckoned that she was now within range of the 13-inch and 8-inch guns of the *Oregon* and *Brooklyn*; he signalled to the battleship to open fire with her main armament, as did the *Brooklyn*, and soon shell splashes close to and beyond the *Colon* showed that she could not get away. Her captain Emilio Diaz Moreu, and the squadron's second-in-command, Commodore Jose de Paredes, could see that all was lost and at 1:15 she turned towards the shore, running aground near the mouth of the River Turquinio, some 50 miles west of Santiago. As her flag was hauled down, Moreu ordered that her valves be opened. Unlike her three companions, which had run ashore on to rocks, the *Colon* ran ashore on sand which was to give an apparent opportunity for the ship to be saved.

For the moment, however, the surrender of the *Colon* completed the American victory. Schley ordered Cook to take a boat over to the cruiser to take possession, and hoisted a signal: 'The enemy has surrendered,' which was repeated by the *Texas* about 5 miles away, to the *New York*, which was hurrying westward. She had come under fire from the forts at the entrance to Santiago harbour as she passed, but sustained no damage. That day she fired only three four-inch shots at the sinking *Furor.* It was 1:45 before she came within signal distance of the *Brooklyn*. Schley signalled: 'We have gained a great victory. Details will be communicated.' The only response from the *New York* was a general signal: 'Report your casualties.' To those aboard the *Brooklyn*, this seemed a curt and dismissive reply, and Schley, thought Graham, was offended. He followed up his original signal with another: 'This is a great day for our country,' but this too received no substantive reply. In his memoirs Schley observed: 'It is to be regretted that no word of congratulation, so much valued by men and officers on such occasions, issued from the flagship.'[13] Schley busied himself with signals to the other ships that had taken a prominent part in the chase of the Spanish squadron. To the *Oregon*, he sent: 'Thanks for your splendid assistance. If it hadn't been for you, we might well not be here;' and to the *Texas* he sent: 'You did glorious work. Thank you for keeping with us.' As the American ships lay offshore, they exchanged cheer after cheer in wildly euphoric excitement.

The first signs of what was to come were noted by Graham, who amidst all the enthusiasm noted that 'from the *New York* there came never a sound of joyfulness and never a cheer.' Those aboard the flagship, Graham thought, 'were naturally disgruntled,' but there was, he considered, great disappointment at the lack of any message of congratulation. The *New York*, on arrival, ordered Cook, who was returning from the *Colon*, to report aboard the flagship, which he did, taking with him some of the Spanish officers, before himself returning to the *Brooklyn*. Thereafter Schley went over to the *New York* to report to Sampson. They had a brief discussion, and were joined by Clark from the *Oregon*. Almost at once came news that another unknown warship had been sighted, which was believed to be Spanish, and Sampson ordered that the *Brooklyn* and *Oregon* should intercept her, although shortly revoking the order in respect of the *Oregon*. As she headed east, the *Brooklyn* encountered the *Vixen*, aboard which was Lieutenant Staunton, Sampson's assistant chief of staff, who told Schley that he believed the stranger to be the battleship *Pelayo*. As the *Brooklyn* neared her, however, she made a signal, and it was realised that she was the Austrian cruiser *Kaiserin Maria Teresa*, en route to Santiago, and seeking permission to enter the harbour to pick up Austrian subjects. Schley told her captain that it would be prudent not to attempt to do so at night, and that it would be wise to remain 20 miles offshore.

Back at the River Turquinio, Chadwick had gone over to the *Colon*, where he met with Commodore Paredes and Captain Moreu; he found that the ship had taken on a lot of water, but according to his account was told that everything was tight. From this, he concluded that the *Colon* could be floated off and that her valves were secure. A prize crew from the *Oregon* went on board. It soon became clear that assurances about the valves, repeated to Sampson by Moreu, were not to be relied on, as the ship was making water fast. At 6:10 p.m. the prize crew reported six feet of water in the hold, and at 7:45 that she was still leaking badly. It was clear that unless something was done she would sink in deep water; only the bows were aground and the sea bed shelved steeply towards her stern. The *New York* closed on her, and put her bows against the *Colon*'s starboard quarter, and then pushed her around until the stern took the ground. However, it was too late to save her, and the prize crew and the Spanish engineers who had remained on board were taken off; at 10:30 the *Colon* sank, turning on her side.

Sampson and Chadwick later complained that the valves had been opened treacherously, on the basis that this was done after the *Colon*'s flag had been lowered. Concas argued that this was incorrect, 'not only because neither the distance nor the condition of the ship made any precipitation necessary, but also because the ship did not surrender until she was thought to be at a total loss.' He thought it strange that the American people should attempt to give lessons in morality 'when that which they profess is of a peculiar kind, as the whole world knows.'[14]

Graham recorded a further episode in the burgeoning issue as to who could claim credit for the victory, having witnessed a confrontation between Sharp, the *Vixen*'s captain and Lieutenant Harlow, his executive of officer, on the one hand and Lieutenant Staunton on the other, who

> were getting into a rather bitter dispute, the two former declaring that the *New York* was never a moment in the fight or even within signal distance, while the *Brooklyn* had borne the brunt of it, and Lieutenant Staunton arguing that while they hadn't fired a gun from the *New York*, they had been fairly near the fight and it was therefore Admiral Sampson's victory.[15]

This had taken place as the *Vixen*, with Goode as well as Graham on board, had headed for Siboney to send from the cable station established there Sampson's report of the battle, a trip that was temporarily aborted by the sighting of the *Kaiserin Maria Teresa*. Staunton made a further attempt to send the cable, by going aboard the torpedo boat *Dupont* to get to Siboney. He took with him the text of the message which Sampson had signed. Since Chadwick was aboard the *Colon* at the material time, it was probably Staunton who had drafted it. Goode went with him. When they got there they met Sears, Schley's flag lieutenant, who wanted to send the commodore's dispatch. Staunton would have none of it saying that all communications to the

Navy Department must go through the senior officer present. Although agreeing that the death of Chief Yeoman Ellis should be mentioned, he did not include this in the text of the report which he sent, which soon attracted a good deal of criticism. It read:

> The fleet under my command offers the nation as a Fourth of July present the whole of Cervera's fleet. It attempted to escape at 9:30 this morning. At two the last ship, the *Cristobal Colon*, had run ashore 75 miles west of Santiago and hauled down her colours. The *Infanta Maria Teresa*, *Oquendo* and *Vizcaya* were forced ashore, burned and blown up within 20 miles of Santiago. The *Furor* and *Pluton* were destroyed within 4 miles of the port.[16]

The boastful style is certainly uncharacteristic of Sampson, and suggests that he was not the author; the clumsy attempt to invoke the memory of General Sherman's famous Christmas message to Abraham Lincoln announcing the capture of Savannah struck a particularly false note.

Although the *New York Times* at once hailed 'Sampson's Fourth of July victory,' and congratulations poured in from all directions to the Admiral, it was not long before, as Richard West wrote, 'Sampson's publicity went sour:'

> During the 12 day interval before his battle report could be completed a phenomenon occurred which defies precise explanation. Reporters hinted at dissension between the two leaders. Editors noted that in his first brief announcement… Sampson had not mentioned Schley. In The *Baltimore American* Schley's close friend General Felix Agnus proclaimed on July 6 that ' Schley is the real hero,' and that Sampson had not had 'the grace even to mention Schley's name... He was in command. He began the destruction of the Spanish fleet... He did the work. Now give him the honours.[17]

On July 5 Representative Berry of Kentucky proposed a motion that Congress give Schley a vote of thanks, also arguing that Schley was the real hero. The controversy was thus well and truly launched.

It had of course been a comprehensive victory. Only Chief Yeoman Ellis had died on the American side. On the other hand, according to Concas, the Spanish squadron suffered a total of 323 killed and 151 severely wounded; there were few only slightly wounded. This amounted to 22% of all the crews; although this was an enormous number, it was nevertheless fewer than Concas and his colleagues had expected, and this was he thought due to the fact that ' fire had hastened the destruction of the cruisers.'[18]

Subsequent research showed that Cervera's armoured cruisers had sustained a total of 123 hits. The *Oquendo* suffered the most, being hit 57 times; the *Maria Teresa* and the *Vizcaya* each sustained 29 hits. According to Trask, the *Colon* was hit eight times as it left the harbour before getting beyond the range of her pursuers, suggesting that the decision of Paredes to beach her was based not on the damage she was suffering, but on what the near misses from the *Brooklyn* and *Oregon* told him was going to happen. It certainly appears that his mind was made up by the information that the coal remaining aboard was of poor quality, meaning that the ship's speed must shortly be reduced.[19] Trask reckoned that this supported Concas's view that the principal disparity between the two sides was in gunnery. Of the American ships directly engaged, the *Brooklyn* was hit directly 20 times by whole shot, of which two were six-inch, three were 4.7-inch and the rest smaller shells. Captain Cook reported that 'no injury was done to the ship... The smokestacks were hit in several places; the signal halyards, rigging and flags were cut in many places. The flag at the main was destroyed, being much cut by shot and flying pieces of shells.'[20] The *Texas* suffered extensive damage from one 6-inch shell; the *Iowa* was hit nine times, twice by 6-inch shells; the *Indiana* was hit twice by shell fragments; the *Oregon* sustained three hits causing considerable damage, and the *Gloucester* was not hit at all. This was, as Chadwick pointed out, only to be expected from the huge disparity in numbers of guns, as well as in the strength of armour.

These comparative statistics do not, however, reflect a great deal of credit on the American gunnery in absolute terms. The total number of shots fired during the battle was 9,429 – these were divided between the *Brooklyn*, 1,973; *Oregon*, 1,903; *Indiana*, 1,876; *Iowa*, 1,473; *Texas*, 835; and *Gloucester*, 1,369. The ammunition thus expended broke down as to 47 thirteen-inch, 39 twelve-inch, 319 eight-inch, 171 six-inch, 473 five-inch, 251 four-inch and 8,129 projectiles of a lesser calibre. The proportion of hits to shots fired was therefore rather less than one and a half per cent, and this was in spite of the fact that the American gunners were firing at an adversary with a very limited ability to respond.

Cervera escaped from the *Maria Teresa* and swam to the shore, where he was picked up by a boat from the *Gloucester*. After she had finished off the two destroyers, she was active in rescuing the crews of the Spanish flagship and the *Oquendo*, her men frequently risking their lives to board the cruisers and destroyers while ammunition, guns and boilers were exploding. Cervera was conducted on board the *Gloucester*, where he was received with great kindness and consideration by her officers before being transferred to the *Iowa*. Bob Evans described his reception aboard the battleship:

> As the brave old admiral came over the side scantily clad, without shirt or hat, yet an admiral every inch of him, the officers saluted, the marines presented arms, and the buglers sounded the salute for an officer of his rank... The meeting between the late commander-in-chief, who had with him his son, acting as his flag lieutenant, and the commanding officers of the torpedo boats, and Captain Eulate and his men, was touching and pathetic.[21]

Eulate had been rescued from the blazing *Vizcaya*, and was brought aboard the *Iowa*, where he offered his sword in the traditional manner to Evans, who brushed it aside before assisting him to his cabin. Before going below, Eulate turned to look at his ship: 'Adios, *Vizcaya*!' he said, and just as he spoke her forward magazine exploded.

Cervera, after meeting with both Schley and Sampson, went ashore to Guantánamo. He asked permission to send a telegram to Blanco in Havana, which was granted. In it he wrote:

> In compliance with your Excellency's orders I went out from Santiago yesterday morning with the whole squadron, and after an unequal battle against forces more than three times as large as mine my whole squadron was destroyed. *Teresa*, *Oquendo* and *Vizcaya*, all with fire on board, ran ashore. *Colon*, according to information from Americans, ran ashore and surrendered. The destroyers were sunk. Do not yet know of loss of men, but surely 600 killed and many wounded (proportion of latter not so large). The survivors are United States prisoners. Gallantry of all the crews has earned most enthusiastic congratulations of enemy. Captain of *Vizcaya* was allowed to retain his sword. I feel very grateful for the

generosity and courtesy with which they treat us. Among dead is Villaamil, and, I believe, Lazaga; Concas and Eulate wounded. We have lost everything, and I shall need funds.[22]

To this Blanco replied a week later, saying that he was deeply impressed and greatly admired the conduct of commanders, officers and crews. He went on to observe, in a remark that must have profoundly annoyed Cervera: 'Perhaps if another time had been chosen for sortie result would have been different. Sampson states in his report he sustained only three casualties. Is that possible?'[23]

Cervera, who was by now at Portsmouth, New Hampshire, where he had arrived on July 10, responded at once to the implied criticism:

> Am deeply grieved that all my actions meet with your Excellency's censure. Trust I may be able to justify them when time comes, as the facts have taken care of showing that there was no exaggeration in my opinions expressed to your Excellency, which you also censured. The sortie at night would not have obviated the loss of squadron, and surely the number of dead would have been tripled, provided the sortie could have been effected at all, which the pilots doubted. Many thanks for your offers. In my former telegram I have already asked for $70,000 gold.[24]

When he came to write his detailed report of the battle, after he had received reports from the commanding officers of all his ships, he did not revisit the issue of whether he could have conducted the sortie at night, feeling no doubt that he had made his position on this entirely clear.

Sampson, however, had a view on this, writing in the following year in the *Century* magazine:

> When we come to consider the strategy of Admiral Cervera in leaving the harbour, it must be said first of all that it would have been much better, if he could have done so, to leave by night. That he could not do so is the testimony of officers of his fleet. We know from what they said subsequently, while they were prisoners, that this plan had been considered by the admiral and his officers. Two advocated going out by night; the others were all in favour of the sortie by day. The great difficulty in a night attempt was our dazzling searchlight. A searchlight shining direct in one's eyes prevents him absolutely from seeing anything else; it is as though he was looking at the sun; and it was that effect upon them, taken in connection with the necessity of seeing their way out of the channel, that made them hesitate.[25]

Those aboard the blockading ships did not attach so much importance to the dazzling effect of the searchlights. Captain Clark thought that Cervera should have made the attempt to go out by night:

> He could have placed as guides to the channel, along the shore and on the smokestack or mast of the sunken *Merrimac*, lights screened toward the sea, so that we could not have detected them. His best chance would have been to get up his anchors and begin to move about dusk, when he would have had light enough to see the shore and the channel marks, timing his movement so that he could dash out just as darkness fell. We could not have closed upon him without great danger to ourselves.[26]

In Clark's opinion, the searchlights would have soon become ineffective in the smoke, even if the blast of the guns did not extinguish them, while the commanders of the American ships would not have been able to see what each of the others was doing, as well as the movements of the enemy: 'It was the difference between certainty and uncertainty.'

Schley did not, in his memoirs, express a view about the timing of the sortie, but he did take the opportunity of a further meeting with Cervera, when the *Brooklyn* visited Guantánamo a few days after the battle, and before the Spanish admiral was transferred to Portsmouth, New Hampshire. Cervera told him, he recorded, that his intention had been 'to concentrate the fire of his ships upon the *Brooklyn,* as well as to ram her, believing that this plan would increase the chances of escaping with the others, the *Brooklyn* being regarded as the fastest vessel of the American squadron.'[27] Schley thought that if the *Brooklyn* had been disabled, and in the absence of the *New York*, it was an open question as to what the outcome would have been. While at Guantánamo Schley received from Lieutenant Sharp of the *Vixen* his report of the battle referred to previously, and wrote his own report, which he forwarded to Sampson on July 6.

This was not however, his first attempt to deliver a report to the Commander-in-Chief. On the evening of the battle Schley composed a fairly brief report of the action which he took with him to the flagship next day before leaving in the *Brooklyn* for Guantánamo Bay. Sampson read it, and handed it back. His reason for not accepting it was that it made no mention of the *New York*, and suggested to Schley that it should mention that the *Indiana* and the *Gloucester* were nearer to the flagship. Clearly Sampson was extremely sensitive about the fact that he had played no part in the battle. This exchange with Schley was the first intimation of what would become a bitter future conflict. Although the two men would be punctiliously correct in their relations with each other, each had supporters who would show no such restraint.

22

The End of the War

Once it had become clear that Camara's squadron was bound for the Far East, Sampson's operations off Santiago were free from interference. The State Department, upon the urgent request of Secretary Long, was doing its best to hamper Camara's progress by instructing American consuls to protest strongly to authorities in neutral ports about the coaling of the Spanish squadron there or in territorial waters under their jurisdiction. The Naval War Board took a particular interest in Camara's progress, recommending on June 20 the purchase of the armoured cruiser *O'Higgins* from Chile to prevent Spain from acquiring it. The dispatch to Manila of the monitors *Monterey* and *Monadnock* would, it was hoped, be sufficient to strengthen Dewey's squadron to enable it to counter the threat from Camara.

The Naval War Board's assessment of the overall naval situation remained cautious:

> The success in both East and West depends upon control of the sea; that is, upon being constantly superior in both quarters, to any probable combination of the enemy... We have neither force enough to be constantly superior to him in all quarters, nor the power to anticipate his arrival in any one quarter, being ignorant of his destination.[1]

It is easy to discern Mahan's hand in this expression of the board's view. Looking beyond the immediate political situation, the board suggested that another reason to obtain the *O'Higgins*, even if it meant paying over the odds, was that there might be 'questions pressing for settlement at the close of this war' that would make it desirable to add her to the navy.

As Camara made his way across the Mediterranean, the Navy Department made plans to assemble an Eastern squadron which would include the *Oregon*, *Iowa* and *Brooklyn*, reducing Sampson's strength off Santiago to four armoured vessels. This prompted a protest from Sampson, which the Naval War Board accepted for the time being as a good reason to postpone detaching any of his armoured vessels. Commodore Watson was designated to command the Eastern Squadron, which Long intended should move as soon as possible, 'as a diversion favourable for Dewey' was necessary.

Uncertainty about Camara's progress, and concern as to his effective strength in relation to Dewey's squadron continued while a military buildup of US forces in the Philippines was under way. The second-highest ranking officer in the army, Maj Gen Wesley Merritt, was appointed on May 12 to command the expeditionary force there, the first instalment of which sailed from San Francisco on May 25. Further shipments of troops followed over the next two months, by which time a total of 16,689 men had been sent. The *Monterey* and *Monadnock* had sailed on June 11 and June 25 respectively. Dewey was unsure if they would be sufficient to meet the threat from Camara's squadron; in this he was probably right. He suggested, again correctly, that the best way of getting Camara to turn back was to threaten the coast of Spain.[2]

While these American forces were heading across the Pacific, the United States formally annexed the Hawaiian Islands, in the teeth of Japanese protests. It was the fear that Japan might herself decide to take action there that finally prompted McKinley to support the resolution for annexation which had been ready and waiting in the Senate for some time; it finally passed both houses of Congress on July 6. It was an important step in the expansion of United States power and influence, as indeed was the commencement of military operations in the Philippines.

Camara had endured an unhappy time of it when he reached Egypt, where the efforts of Deputy Consul General Watts, and the attitude of the British authorities, had ensured that coaling the squadron would be extremely difficult. Camara finally began his passage through the Suez Canal on July 5, and entered the Red Sea on July 7. Next day he was recalled to Spain. Chadwick calculated that the route to Mindanao, his destination in the Philippines, would have been over 7000 nautical miles, and that he could not in any case complete his voyage before August 17. He was scornful of the lack of sensible direction on the part of the Spanish government: 'Its admiral was to go somewhere and do nothing. To scatter his fleet hither and thither and land a few soldiers was to play at war. The one wise order was to direct his return home.' He noted that when he got back to the Spanish coast, Camara was to show himself as ostentatiously as possible, displaying the national flag illuminated by searchlights: 'Such was war from the point of view of the Spanish Ministry.'[3]

Meanwhile, on the morning of the sea battle of Santiago, Shafter had made an attempt to avoid further fighting around the city by sending a demand to Toral that he surrender, failing which he would shell the place; Toral refused. When Shafter received news of the naval victory, he repeated his demand, which Toral again rejected. Shafter permitted civilians to leave the city, and on July 4 long columns of refugees began to head for El Caney. From Washington came insistent demands that Shafter hasten his operations; he responded by pointing out that Escario, with the column from Manzanillo, had now arrived, and that he needed reinforcements. He also returned to the need which he saw for the navy to force the harbour entrance, to which he referred in a letter to Sampson of July 3 reporting the arrival of the Manzanillo column: 'Now if you will force your way into that harbour the town will surrender without any further sacrifice of life.'[4] He emphasised the point in telegrams to Alger on July 4 and July 5, and continued to press Sampson, who was frustrated that the general seemed unable to grasp what seemed to the admiral to be obvious: 'Of men there were plenty; of the all-important material – ships – there was but little; no number of men within reason, in the circumstances, weigh against a battleship.' And the Navy had to consider not only the capture of Santiago but also the threat posed by Camara's squadron en route to the Far East.

Sampson's position was strengthened by Long's telegram of July 6, which firmly upheld his attitude to Shafter's demands:

> You are instructed not to risk loss of any armoured vessels by submarine mines unless for the most urgent reasons, as the duration and result of this war will depend chiefly upon the superiority of our navy to that of the enemy. It has always been considered here that if you batter the Morro and the United States Army will assail and take, they could hold the bank of the entry, driving away infantry of the enemy from the vicinity of the minefields.[5]

That done, the mines could be cleared and the fleet could then enter the harbour and take the city.

Sampson was unwell. He sent Chadwick and Staunton ashore to meet with Shafter; and the chief of staff persuaded the general to write again to Toral to describe the extent of the navy's success, and to spell out the intention to bombard the city if no surrender could be agreed. Chadwick also agreed with Shafter on the steps to be taken in addition to the bombardment. Toral agreed to a truce, while he consulted his government. This seemed hopeful, and must have come as a relief to those of Shafter's army that were fast losing confidence in him. Roosevelt wrote a violent letter to Henry Cabot Lodge:

> Not since the campaign of Crassus against the Parthians has there been so criminally incompetent a general as Shafter; and not since the expedition against Walcheren has there been a grosser mismanagement than in this. The battle simply fought itself, three of the brigade commanders, most of the colonels and all of the regiments individually did well; and the heroism of some of the regiments could not be surpassed; but Shafter never came within three miles of the line, and never has come; the confusion is incredible.[6]

The response from Toral was to the effect that he should be allowed to abandon the city and march out, unmolested, to Holguin. This was referred to McKinley, who instructed that the proposal be rejected, and that only unconditional surrender would be acceptable. Meanwhile Shafter's nerve had cracked; he suggested that it should be accepted, but was emphatically told that this could not be. Informed of this, Toral ended the truce. Arrangements were now put in hand for the bombardment to commence; the *New York* had gone to Guantánamo to coal. Schley was thus in temporary command of the fleet, and orders went to him to begin firing on July 10. The bombardment began almost immediately; after it had continued on the following day a fresh truce was declared, and further negotiations began for the surrender of the city. Shafter, however, was still labouring under the delusion that he could compel the navy to force the entrance; in spite of the truce, he telegraphed Alger early on July 12: 'so far no attempt to enter the harbour by the navy. They should be required to make a determined effort at once.' Not surprisingly, this effusion annoyed Chadwick and Sampson very much indeed. However, General Miles had now arrived, and negotiations with Toral went forward. The latter, of course, had to obtain Blanco's approval to the proposed capitulation; but by the afternoon of July 14 it seemed that agreement for a surrender had been reached, and a meeting was agreed to settle the precise terms. A last-minute hitch occurred when the Spanish sought the right to retain their arms, but this was refused and the capitulation was agreed.

It was marked, however by a further unedifying dispute between army and navy. Chadwick attended the negotiations of the detailed terms on Sampson's behalf, and expected as his representative to be one of those signing the document setting these out, but Shafter, in a display of petulance that was unforgivable (and which was not forgiven) refused to allow it. Shafter later explained his reason to Sampson, which was that no 'claim for any credit for the capture of Cervera and his fleet had been made by the army.' The breakdown of interservice relations was further illustrated when a dispute arose as to the entitlement to the ships in the harbour, which included the gunboat *Alvarado*. Chadwick told Shafter that these should be turned over to the navy; Shafter referred the matter to Alger, who told him that they belonged to the army. After a rancorous correspondence, the issue was settled by the president, who ruled that such joint captures were not within prize law. At this Alger agreed that 'the floating marine and naval property captured should be turned over to the navy, as the War Department does not desire to be troubled with them.'[7]

The mutual suspicion of the army and the navy was seen again in connection with the operations to be undertaken against Puerto Rico. It had always been McKinley's intention that once Santiago was taken, and Cervera's squadron disposed of, an invasion of Puerto Rico should be undertaken as soon as possible. The island had a population of slightly under one million, and had been granted autonomy in November 1897. Although there were disputes between the political parties in Puerto Rico, the population was not as disposed to anti-Spanish activity as Cuba. However, General Manuel Macias y Casado, the Governor General, had very limited resources to resist an invasion. It has been estimated that he had about 8,000 regular troops and a roughly similar number of poorly trained and armed local volunteers; his naval forces were quite unable to offer any challenge to the American navy, consisting of two unprotected cruisers, two small gunboats, an armed merchantman and Cervera's third destroyer, the *Terror*, which he had been obliged to leave at Martinique. The entire Spanish defence force was thus of negligible fighting value.[8]

Mahan, in his later assessment of the campaign in the West Indies, pointed out that seizing Puerto Rico was, in purely military terms, a desirable first objective for the United States, since its possession would deny Spain a valuable advanced base in the region. However, the situation in Cuba that had led to the war made it necessary that operations there take priority. This had not, in fact, been the view of General Miles, who in early June was still arguing for a move on Puerto Rico before dealing with Santiago. To this, McKinley replied firmly in the negative. Miles finally sailed from Charleston on July 8, arriving in the first instance at Santiago, where Sampson was preparing the Eastern Squadron and a covering squadron for operations against Camara and the Spanish mainland. There followed a prolonged debate between Washington, Miles and Sampson about the best way in which to operate against Puerto Rico. It was finally agreed that the expeditionary force should land at Fajardo, at the eastern end of the island. What was not agreed was the size of the naval escort to protect the convoy of troop transports. Miles repeatedly complained that Sampson was not prepared to detail enough ships for the purpose. The two men had a meeting at Guantánamo on July 20 which was not very agreeable, and Miles wrote to Alger to express his discontent:

> There are battleships enough here to enable us to land within cannon shot of the city of San Juan. I request that positive orders be given to the navy to cover the landing of at least 10,000 troops on the island of Puerto Rico, without delay, as that number will be there within a week.[9]

He also sent a further request on similar lines to Sampson, complaining that the force proposed as an escort was inadequate. Sampson, in response, told Miles that he would somewhat increase the force, adding that 'the *Cincinnati, Yale, Columbia, Annapolis, Wasp, Gloucester* and *Leyden* are amply sufficient to cover the landing of 10,000 men.' He would however add three monitors.

The dispute between Army and Navy Departments was giving rise to serious anxiety in Washington, where Long was finding it difficult to defend Sampson against the complaints which the Army Department was raising. McKinley now intervened, and Long was obliged to send a telegram to Sampson on July 21:

> The president directs that you send ships of war enough to enable Miles to land at Puerto Rico, and to remain there as long as needed to render assistance, or to give him at once the *Indiana*, the *Newark* or something of each class as good. Act promptly. Why do you not telegraph about this convoy, some of them [?telegrams] are three days old. On the face of things you seem dilatory in this matter. The Department awaits your quick reply.[10]

Biting back the indignation which he and Chadwick felt at this, Sampson at once sent a patient and detailed reply, which brought forth from Long 'handsome amends' for his strictures, accepting that Sampson had done all that he could for Miles. Since Sampson had not in the least failed to comply with the orders he had received, which put Camara at the top of his agenda, he was entitled to Long's acknowledgement. As Chadwick pointed out, the whole difficulty 'was but a natural corollary of the want of a central directive force' such as only a general staff and a mutual understanding between the War and Navy Departments could provide

Miles had, in the meanwhile, got his expeditionary force together, and sailed from Guantánamo Bay on July 21 at 3 p.m. with 3,415 troops, covered by an escort which included the battleship *Massachusetts*, whose captain, Francis Higginson, was in command of the squadron. Another 3,600 troops were en route from Charleston, and 2,900 left Tampa on July 24. Miles now, however, astonishingly changed the convoy's destination from Fajardo to Guanica, on the south coast of the island. Higginson objected to the change on a number of cogent grounds, including the shallow waters that would keep his heavy ships further offshore, and the lack of available charts. Miles, however, convinced that there was more anti-Spanish feeling in the south of the island, insisted. It was a decision that Mahan sharply criticised in a letter to Long after the war:

> The Puerto Rico landing I once told you, at Guanica, and the initiation of operations there, appears to me a military stupidity so great, that I can account for [these acts] only by a kind of of obsession to vanity, to do a singular and unexpected thing.[11]

In the event this decision, although baffling to Alger and to Long, was not productive of serious ill effects, due to the weakness of the Spanish forces in Puerto Rico and the tactical errors made by Macias in spreading them too thinly. Ponce, in the south, was the largest city in the island, and was soon occupied, and the advance of the American army over the mountain ranges which ran east-west began on August 6. Preparations for a decisive assault to lead to an advance on San Juan were in hand when news arrived of the armistice that had been negotiated. Total American casualties were seven killed and 36 wounded; Spanish losses may have been 10 times as great.[12]

In the Philippines the Spanish government had been faced with an insurrection which began in 1896, and which General Ramon Blanco, at that time the Governor General, had proved unable to crush. His successor, the much more hardline General Camilo de Polavieja, proved rather more successful, limiting the activity of the insurgent forces to minor guerilla actions. In his turn, Polavieja was succeeded as Governor General by General Primo de Rivera, who negotiated an end to the uprising, which by then was led by Emilio Aguinaldo. The pact, which Aguinaldo intended should only temporarily terminate hostilities, took effect on December 14, 1897; it included a substantial payment to Aguinaldo, who departed in the first instance to Hong Kong, before leaving for Europe. En route, he came into contact with the American consul general in Singapore, who persuaded him to return to Hong Kong, and cooperate with

Dewey. The latter explained to a Congressional committee in 1902 that he had found Aguinaldo and his companions to be a considerable nuisance:

> They were bothering me. I was very busy getting my squadron ready for battle, and these little men were coming on board my ship in Hong Kong and taking a good deal of my time, and I did not attach the slightest importance to anything they could do, and they did nothing.[13]

After the battle of Manila Bay, Aguinaldo returned to the Philippines, landing at Cavite on May 19. Dewey's contempt for the insurgent leaders led him to pay little heed to their possible role in the subsequent course of events in the Philippines; in the event matters did not turn out well, and subsequent disputes as to what had or had not been agreed led to 'numerous charges and counter charges subsequently emanating from both sides.' One American historian summed up the position that arose:

> In happy ignorance of the Filipino aspirations for independence, Washington planned and acted on the false premise that the Filipinos were a docile people gratefully ready to accept the law and order provided by their white tutors.[14]

Not surprisingly, therefore, the insurgents soon became increasingly uncooperative with the American forces as they arrived. They soon surrounded the city of Manila, but occupied a position between the Spanish lines and the base established by the Americans. It was not until August 13 that the Americans finally advanced on the city, under the cover of a bombardment by Dewey's squadron of the key Spanish positions. A capitulation was soon negotiated; the battle, such as it was, had been fought without the cooperation of the insurgent groups, which the Americans tried unsuccessfully to prevent occupying any part of Manila. Casualties on both sides had been light, but even these were pointless; peace negotiations between the United States and Spain had already resulted in agreement for a cessation of hostilities.

The American adventure in the Philippines was, of course, far from over; for the present the aspect of Dewey's activities in Manila Bay following his victory that attracted most attention had been his relationship with the German squadron which had arrived, apparently on the lookout for opportunities arising from the imminent collapse of Spanish power in the region. There had been a number of arrivals of neutral warships in the Bay; the British gunboat *Linnet* on May 2, the French *Brieux* on May 5, the German cruiser *Irene* and transport *Darmstadt* on May 6 and the British cruiser *Immortalite* on May 7. The Japanese *Itsukushima*, and the German *Kormoran* followed, while Vice-Admiral Otto von Diederichs arrived with his flagship *Kaiserin Augusta* on May 12. His squadron was supplemented by two more German warships, the battleship *Kaiser* and the cruiser *Prinzessin Wilhelm* before the end of the month, at which time there were five German warships, three British and one each from France and Japan.[15]

Dewey was entirely ready to think the worst of German intentions. His naturally belligerent attitude had led him to see in Germany a fitting opponent, remarking in 1897: 'It is indecent to fight against Spain anyhow. Now, if France would come in too, we could save face, but best of all if Germany would come in. If only Germany could be persuaded to come in.'[16] Given the chance to appear ready to stand up against any threat, Dewey made the most in years to come of his strained relationships with his German counterpart, whose squadron, at its peak, was considerably stronger. Diederichs, who recently successfully completed the acquisition of Kiao-Chou, considered that the outcome of the Spanish American War could well be the partition of the Philippines; Alfred von Tirpitz, the State Secretary of the Imperial German Navy, was not in favour of any adventures overseas, which might threaten his plans for naval expansion. He thought that the war had come too soon to provide any opportunities for Germany. The commander-in-chief of the navy, Admiral Edouard von Knorr, was rather more ambitious, reminding Kaiser William that the navy required more bases worldwide.

In Manila Bay, Dewey was somewhat isolated, since he was obliged to send vessels to Hong Kong to send or receive cables. Not that he was much inclined to keep closely in touch, in any case; according to him, when McKinley later noted that there was no record at all of any friction with Diederichs in the files, Dewey told him: 'No, Mr President. As I was on the spot and familiar with the situation from day to day, it seemed best that I look after it myself, at a time when you had worries enough of your own.'[17] Among the conversations which Dewey had with Diederichs, he told him that although the United States had not decided what to do about the Philippines they had 'the right of possession through conquest.' The threat from the German squadron remained much in Dewey's mind, not least because he suspected, wrongly, that Diederichs was conspiring with the Spaniards. The German admiral refused to entertain the possibility of taking control of Manila, a proposal which the governor general also made to other neutral commanders in the Bay. In fact by late June Diederichs had recognised that there was not going to be any opportunity to gain a foothold in the Philippines. This did not prevent further misunderstanding when the cruiser *Irene* was engaged on a humanitarian mission; in one heated exchange with Diederichs' flag lieutenant, Dewey burst out: 'If Germany wants war, all right, we are ready!' Before leaving Manila Bay, after the fall of the city, Diederichs reported to Knorr in Berlin, and loftily commented on Dewey's choleric demeanour:

> I attached little value to blustering remarks made in a condition of extreme excitement and complete loss of self-control... And still less to his threats. I thought both were excusable considering the immaturity and rudeness of the American nation which has had neither the time nor material progress to teach its sons tact and good manners.[18]

Thinking it over, Diederichs correctly predicted both that the United States would annex the Philippines, and would then have to fight a war of insurrection.

The process of ending the war began with a meeting between Jules Cambon, the French ambassador in Washington, and President McKinley and Secretary of State William Day on July 26. Cambon had been directed to represent Spain in peace talks, and he found McKinley entirely ready to begin these with a view to bringing the war to a speedy conclusion that would leave no lasting animosities between the two countries. The president was not, however, prepared to limit the discussion in the first instance to Cuba, as Cambon proposed, and an overall settlement would in any case require the US Cabinet to agree on what terms would be acceptable. That Spain must give up Cuba and Puerto Rico was the Cabinet's unanimous view, but it was much less sure about the Philippines. McKinley had steadily progressed towards a policy of acquisition; although he had not yet finally reached that position, he was determined to keep it as an option. When he put the terms to Cambon on July 30, he made it clear that the surrender of Cuba and Puerto Rico was not negotiable; the future of the Philippines would be determined at a peace conference.

While the discussions continued, there was growing anxiety about the health of the American troops in Cuba; sickness, malaria and yellow fever had already begun to take a fearful toll. McKinley was outraged by the circulation of a round robin signed by Shafter's officers to the effect that the army was disabled by malarial fever and was at risk of its complete destruction from yellow fever; its contents reached the Press, and the president's bargaining position was seriously weakened. Despite this, McKinley held firm; Cambon warned the Spanish government, which was still reluctant to accept the American position on the Philippines, that if she rejected the terms Spain would 'have nothing more to expect from a conqueror resolved to procure all the profit possible from the advantage it has obtained.'

On the afternoon of 12 August the peace protocol was signed on a wet and gloomy day. It marked a considerable personal triumph for the president, whose popularity in the United States rose to a new high. Respect for McKinley also rose internationally; the London *Spectator* observed that he was 'now by far the most influential personage in the United States.' There remained the problem of preparing for the peace conference, to be held in Paris. This involved the selection of commissioners, about which McKinley took particular care. The commission was to be headed by William Day; McKinley selected as his successor as Secretary of State John Hay, the ambassador to Great Britain.

During the negotiations in Paris McKinley assumed a noncommittal air with regard to the final peace terms, but he had privately reached the conclusion that the Philippines should be annexed. For a long time the Spanish negotiators held out, but finally, subject to further discussion of details, the American terms were accepted. The United States acquired the Philippines, Puerto Rico and the island of Guam; Spain gave up Cuba, but not its debt, and received a payment of $20 million. It now remained to get Congressional approval to the peace treaty. This was not easy; in the Philippines, the military situation with the insurgents was deteriorating. In the end, however, the Senate voted to accept the treaty on 6 February 1899 by 57 to 27, one vote more than the minimum two thirds majority that was needed.

23

Controversy

The relationship between Schley and Sampson took a decisive turn for the worse a week after the battle of Santiago. On July 10 Sampson composed a report to Long, in the course of which he made comments on the performance of senior officers, and the rewards which they had earned. It was a confidential letter, the contents of which he did not discuss with those concerned. Nor, in respect of the others mentioned, was there any reason to do so. However, in relation to Schley he made a number of observations that could not fail to be damaging, but concerned matters which at no time had he raised with their subject. Sampson wrote:

> With regard to Commodore Schley, I much prefer that the Department should decide his case. I am unwilling to fully express my own opinion. His conduct when he first assumed command on the south coast of Cuba I assume to be as well known to the Department as to myself. Had the Commodore left his station off Santiago de Cuba at that time he probably would have been court-martialed, so plain was his duty. Were I alone in this opinion I would certainly doubt my judgement, but so far as I know this opinion is confirmed by that of other commanding officers here acquainted with the circumstances. This reprehensible conduct I cannot separate from his subsequent conduct, and for this reason I ask you to do him ample justice on this occasion.[1]

Before writing this extremely critical report, Sampson evidently discussed Schley's performance with some of his captains. Among these was the outspoken 'Fighting Bob' Evans who was invariably forthright in his criticism of Schley.

Outwardly, at any rate, relations between Schley and Sampson continued to be cordial. Ironically, it was the day that Sampson composed his damning letter to Long that Schley came to see him, having read the first batch of newspapers that hailed Schley as the victor of the battle. He brought with him a telegram which he wished to go to Long at the Navy Department:

> Feel some mortification that the newspaper accounts of July 6 have attributed victory on July 3 almost entirely to me. Victory was secured by the force under command Commander-in-Chief, North Atlantic station, and to him the honour is due. The end of line held by the *Brooklyn* and the *Vixen* was heavily assailed, and had the honour, with the *Oregon*, of being in the battle from the beginning to the end. And I do not doubt for a moment full and proper credit will be given to all persons and all ships in the official report of the combat.[2]

Sampson carefully read the telegram, and then said: 'Schley, this is kind and generous; I will transmit it at once.' Schley, remarking in his memoirs that he and Sampson had been friends for forty years during which there had been no break or misunderstanding, was entitled to record his dismay that it was not until February of the following year that he became aware of Sampson's disapproval.

At the time he wrote his telegram of July 10 to Long, Schley was of course aware of the boastful terms in which Sampson had first reported the victory, and he would not have forgotten Sampson's curt response to his signal to the flagship that 'a glorious victory has been achieved' and that it was 'a great day for our country.' Graham described his reaction at that time to the reply, which consisted only of a request that he report his casualties:

> 'Report your casualties,' repeated Schley, turning on his heel and walking over to the other side of the bridge, a pained expression on his face; and up to our signal masts went the flags 'one dead and two wounded.'[3]

Graham also recorded how offended Schley had been when his request that he might have the honour of accepting the surrender of the *Cristobal Colon* was ignored.

The aftermath of the battle left bruised feelings all round. Shafter's complaints about Sampson were written up in the press, and one story which was reported claimed, quite incorrectly, that Schley had wanted to dash into Santiago harbour, ignoring the mines and the Spanish batteries. Schley visited Sampson to deny the story, and to reassure him that he agreed with him with regard to an attempt to force the entrance. Sampson was apparently sufficiently disturbed to ask Long to investigate how the story originated; it appeared that it came not from one of the accredited journalists with the fleet but from one who had been on an *Associated Press* dispatch boat.[4] This sort of thing naturally tended to heat up the burgeoning controversy.

One newspaper, the *Springfield Republican*, accurately summarised one of the key elements which caused the controversy to flare up, and to continue unabated for so long:

> It arose largely from the determination of the slapdash writers to get a brilliant hero out of the Santiago battle at any cost. Sampson's careful, thorough and comprehensive leadership would not do at all. The hero must be a dashing and devil-may-care officer, 'standing on the bridge,' and fearlessly leading the line of battle against the enemy fleet. It was a great disappointment to the company of newspaper strategists that the battle took place as it did, and even the glory of it all, which they would heap on Commodore Schley, was a good deal dimmed by the fact that it was a running foe who was assailed and overcome. It was then reported that Schley would have led the fleet into the harbour before Cervera came out, could he have had his way. This confirmed his title to the heroship of the whole affair, and placed Sampson in the light of a halting, shrinking, feeble commander, whose fleet had finally achieved victory in spite of him by a stroke of luck and the gallantry of the officers under him.[5]

Much the same sort of comparison was made during the First World War in the British Press between Jellicoe and Beatty after the battle of Jutland, again unfavourable to the less obviously heroic commander-in-chief.

Predictably enough Mahan, whose dislike of Schley had not softened with the passing years, felt obliged to let everybody know his views on the question of credit for the victory, writing on

August 5 in the *New York Sun* that it did not matter that Sampson had not personally led the American battle line at Santiago:

> With the wise and stringent methods laid down by the admiral, it would not in the least have mattered, as things happened, with such ships and such captains, had the Commander-in-Chief and the second-in-command, either or both, been 70 miles away... Few things in the observation of the writer have been more painful than the attempt of a portion of the press and of the public to rob Sampson of his just and painfully won dues.[6]

Schley's injured feelings and Sampson's reservations about his colleague's performance were put aside when the fleet returned to New York for a review to celebrate the ending of the war. The fleet arrived there on August 20, and was met by a fleet of vessels of all kinds crowded with spectators. While the ships were getting into line they were greeted by an uproarious welcome, as Schley described: 'The manifestations of joy on the part of our people found expression in deafening huzzas and applause. These, added to sounding of whistles, the ringing of bells, and the tooting of horns, rang out a welcome as sincere as the heart could wish.'[7] All the way up the harbour, huge and wildly enthusiastic crowds packed both sides of the river to witness the 'pageant of a lifetime.' To someone of Schley's open and spontaneous nature it was an overwhelming statement of the public's recognition of the navy's achievement; and he almost immediately received an acknowledgement of his own achievement when news was brought to him during the course of the *Brooklyn*'s progress upriver that he had been promoted to the rank of rear admiral, for 'eminent and conspicuous conduct in battle.' The promotion advanced him six numbers; he did not immediately know that Sampson had been advanced eight numbers, which now carried him above Schley in seniority. It might seem a small thing; but it prompted a violent political reaction in Congress.

For the moment Schley was able to enjoy the enthusiasm with which he and the *Brooklyn* were received. The *New York Journal*, reporting that a brass band welcomed the ship by playing 'Maryland, my Maryland,' observed that 'there was no doubt about the heart in Winfield Scott Schley's welcome home,' going on to add that 'judging by the sound alone, the cheers for Schley were longer and greater than for anyone in the fleet.'[8] Publicly, at any rate, there was no sign of any official discontent with the part that Schley had played during the campaign. Ashore in New York, he and Sampson walked arm in arm at a reception at which they were welcomed by Long and other members of the Cabinet. It was a progress about which Sampson may have had somewhat mixed feelings.

These celebrations concluded, Schley went to spend a few days with his family, staying in Connecticut. While there he developed a case of the malarial fever that had swept through the army in Cuba, and was confined to his bed. Once he had recovered, he was ordered to Washington; the journey by rail gave him another opportunity to see how well he was regarded by the American public:

> Along the entire route people had gathered in vast crowds to greet and pay their respects. As the train passed further south these crowds augmented, only, however, because longer notice had been given them of the commander's presence on the train. At Jersey City, Clinton, Philadelphia, Wilmington, Baltimore and Washington the enthusiastically warm reception of the people was a touching tribute of affectionate regard. At the depot of the

> Pennsylvania Railroad at Washington the commander was received by an almost countless multitude of his fellow countrymen, whose enthusiastic applause constitutes a delightful memory. After he was seated in his carriage and had reached Pennsylvania Avenue, a core of bicyclists, numbering over a hundred, formed an escort on each flank of the vehicle as it was driven to the Shoreham Hotel.[9]

There another huge crowd greeted him. Arriving at the Navy Department, he was at once taken by assistant secretary Charles H Allen to the White House, where President McKinley welcomed him, and appointed him as a member of the commission which was to go to Puerto Rico to supervise the Spanish evacuation of the island. Schley, who valued highly the stateliness of ceremonial forms, was gratified by the wording of the commission appointing him: 'Know ye, that reposing special trust and confidence in the integrity and ability of Rear Admiral Winfield S Schley USN, I do appoint him a commissioner.'

Schley now returned to New York and went aboard the *Brooklyn*, which was being visited by thousands of sightseers. He had the satisfaction of hoisting his rear admiral's flag, which was saluted with 13 guns. On August 31 he embarked on the transport *Seneca*, and with his fellow commissioners sailed for San Juan. The work of the commission occupied him for the next seven weeks before, at noon on October 18, the American colours rose over the public buildings and fortifications of the city to mark its formal annexation by the United States. Schley remained in San Juan for another fortnight before the newly designated commander of the naval station arrived, and then returned to Washington to await his next appointment.

When Schley arrived back in Washington, he hoped that he might be appointed to command the prestigious European Squadron, but this had not yet been reconstituted. Instead, he returned to find that the Sampson-Schley controversy had by no means subsided. Indeed, it had continued to blaze in the columns of the Press, within the Navy Department and throughout the navy. Neither Schley nor Sampson took any part in the public debate. Sampson kept his own counsel throughout, apart from his ill-natured and unnecessary observations to Long of July 10. He had gone in the autumn as a member of the American commission to superintend the evacuation of Cuba by the Spanish, and while there fell ill due to overwork and malarial fever. Photographs taken of Sampson before and after the war testify to his worsening general health, which continued to deteriorate. However, he was able to remain in command of the North Atlantic Station during the ensuing year. His silence on the issues in dispute did not mean that his case was not put forward; among his cheerleaders there were a number of those whose voices were extremely influential.

Prominent among them was Mahan. In the early stages of the controversy, his contributions were positively in praise of Sampson rather than negatively in criticism of Schley. He collected evidence from various sources to show that Sampson's conduct of the blockade had been the prime cause of victory, in particular the constant employment of searchlights to illuminate the entrance to Santiago harbour. He wrote to Senator Lodge: 'The attacks of the press upon Sampson, either virulently or by constant sly innuendo, have kept my blood boiling. It is my belief that the closeness of the watch at night largely induced the sortie by day – unwise as that was.'[10] At first, he did not see the controversy as likely to be prolonged, observing to a fellow author that 'there will be no scandal unless indiscreet friends of Schley provoke it. Of this I have some fear, but will use my influence against it as far as I can, unless of course the abuse of Sampson becomes intolerable.'

Mahan's self restraint did not last long. As the furore over Sampson's promotion above that of Schley grew, he took up the cudgels with vigour, particularly when a Congressional vote of thanks to Sampson, Schley and Dewey was proposed. He told Long that Schley was incompetent, and should not again be entrusted with command. He told his family lawyer that Schley had 'done nothing to merit distinction' during the war. He wrote articles in *McClure's Magazine* praising Sampson to the skies, and using words such as 'delay,' uncertainty,' and 'mistakes' in describing Schley's performance.[11]

The ferocity of the continuing dispute, both in the Press and within the navy, continued to deepen and was becoming so serious as to gravely damage the morale and confidence of the navy itself. It was not a vast organisation, and its senior officers, who took sides in the controversy, were relatively few in number. It raged among them with such fury that in November 1899 Long felt obliged to issue a circular order prohibiting naval officers on active duty from discussing the case in public. Chadwick, who had allowed himself to be interviewed by a journalist on the subject, received an official reprimand. The prohibition did not stop the arguments continuing in private, however, if anything with increased fervour. A recent historian of the navy's battles during the war, evidently anxious to preserve a picture of its essential unity, has claimed that 'there was little controversy within the Navy itself,' an assertion that is surely wrong.[12] By no means all officers took Sampson's part, as became clear at the Court of Inquiry.

Considering the extent to which John Long was responsible for conducting the campaign against Schley, the hypocrisy of his observations in his memoirs on the subject of the controversy is staggering:

> History will certainly do justice to both men, giving them praise where deserved and blame where due. Would that the recent discussion of their merits, too often inflamed and unreasonably blind to anything but its own preconceptions and prejudice, could have been inspired with the calm and generous spirit with which history at a later day and with judicial balance will record its verdict![13]

Long's prohibition, of course, did not inhibit Mahan who was not on active duty, and the vindictiveness of his campaign against Schley grew in intensity. In a letter to the editor of the *Century* magazine he referred to Schley having begun his blockade of Santiago only after he had 'plucked up courage to remain nearer than 25 miles' from the entrance to the harbour. To Long in mid December 1899 he sneered that since Schley had not demanded a Court of Inquiry to clear himself of the allegations made, he was not entitled to promotion to the rank of vice admiral; on this, he argued, there was no room for differing opinions, and such a promotion would be a 'disgrace.' In his letter to Long he summed up the basis of his case against Schley:

> Personally, I consider that Schley's utter unfitness for command is conclusively demonstrated, over his own signature, by two facts. One is the well-known telegram announcing his purpose to return to Key West; the other is the statement, in his letter of May 30, that the speed of the squadron was reduced from 7.5 to 8.5 knots to 4 or 5, going from Cienfuegos to Santiago, to enable the *Eagle* to keep up. The man who, under all the circumstances, could do those two things is demonstrably unfit for command; and I have always purposed, in case my opinion were asked, to rest it on these two statements. In my judgement, as a student of military history, there is no escape from this conclusion.[14]

Schley, while in Puerto Rico, had not been aware of one of the first acts of the Navy Department which related to issues raised in the course of the controversy about Santiago. On September 2 the navigators of the ships taking part in the battle were convened by Sampson as a board to plot the positions and movements of the American fleet and Cervera's squadron during the battle. The only one of the commanding officers who appears to have been consulted by this board was Chadwick, apart possibly from Cook on the last day of the board's sessions. The board reported on October 8; it was presided over by Lieutenant Commander Richard Wainwright, the captain of the *Gloucester*. Its conclusions were somewhat tentative; the board felt 'that under the circumstances, it is as nearly correct as is possible so long after the engagement.' Schley bitterly observed that although subsequently abandoned by the Judge Advocate at the Court of Inquiry as being worthless as an accurate record, it had in the meantime become the basis of attacks upon him; and was even reproduced in Long's memoirs when they were published in 1904.[15]

McKinley, on the advice of his Navy Secretary, had promulgated on August 11 the promotion of both Sampson and Schley, the former being advanced eight numbers and the latter six. The effect was to put Sampson one number above Schley in the Navy List. By the time this reached Congress there was a considerable head of steam in the campaign to reject this as being wrong and unfair to Schley. On January 23, 1899 the Senate resolved that the Secretary of the Navy should be 'directed to furnish the Senate with the facts and military records in the possession of his department' affecting the proposed promotions. Long thereupon appointed a board of officers to assemble the required information. To ensure that this board adopted the position which he required, he chose captains Robley Evans and Henry Taylor, both of whom were confirmed critics of Schley, as well as Ensign Henry H Ward, who was of the same view. He added Lieutenant James H Sears, a devoted friend and admirer of Schley, no doubt to give the board some semblance of balance; there was not a lot, though, that he could do to overcome the bias of his superiors. The documents which this board finally sent to the Senate under the bar of secrecy did not include the orders, contained in what became known as Documents Nos 6 and 7, whereby Sampson ordered Schley to remain off Cienfuegos. They did, however, include Sampson's secret letter to Long about what he described as Schley's reprehensible' conduct. Not surprisingly, Schley's supporters in the Senate reacted badly, and resolved that the board's report, and the accompanying documents, be disclosed to Schley for comment. In this way he learned for the first time of the contents of Sampson's secret letter. In Schley's extremely detailed response, he was able to include the orders omitted from the Navy Department's submission. This was the first occasion on which he was himself able to put forward his own case. The issue before the Senate of the relative seniority of Sampson and Schley was in itself of no practical consequence, but it was seen to be an important symbol of the injustice which Schley was believed to have suffered. His production of Document No 7 caused considerable embarrassment to Long, who hastily issued a statement denying that the department had suppressed it. In the end the Senate passed a new bill regulating the promotion of senior officers, which McKinley accepted; Schley and Sampson were confirmed as rear admirals, subject to confirmation by a Scrutiny Board.

Schley's supporters in the Press continued to plead his cause; but McKinley also received advice from a more unbiased source, when Alexander K McClure, the editor of the *Philadelphia Times* wrote to him on the subject. Having had no contact with either Sampson or Schley, apart from a brief meeting with the latter when he visited Philadelphia, he could claim to be impartial. He wrote: 'It is evident to any intelligent and dispassionate observer of existing conditions, that the administration and the Navy Department have become committed to an act of great injustice to the navy and the country, by the proposed promotion of Sampson over Schley.' He went on to set out in some detail why it was that Schley deserved the credit for the victory, and pointed out the way in which Sampson had acted with regard to him. He was writing, he said, entirely privately, to save the administration 'from a blunder that will be little less than a crime.'[16] McKinley forwarded this to Long, who appears to have paid no attention to it.

In the spring of 1899 Schley became involved in a public dispute over an article in the *New York Sun*, which quoted an account by the *Brooklyn*'s navigator of an exchange with Schley over the cruiser's turn to starboard which had resulted in the 'loop' that was to be much discussed. Lieutenant Commander Alban C Hodgson said that he questioned this, and that Schley's response was that they were near enough to the enemy. Upon Hodgson saying that the turn meant that they would 'cut down the *Texas*,' Schley allegedly gave the reply previously quoted to the effect that the Texas should look out for herself. Schley now wrote to Hodgson, asking him to deny this 'oft repeated calumny.' After an exchange of correspondence, Schley pressed for a short letter denying that this 'colloquy' took place. Hodgson provided this, but wrote a further letter suggesting that some such exchange on the lines reported had in fact occurred. Schley had the denial published but not Hodgson's further letter; and refused permission for Hodgson to publish the whole of the correspondence. At this, Hodgson complained to the Navy Department, asking that it either take steps to exonerate him in the eyes of the public or give him permission to publish the correspondence.[17]

In the summer of 1899 Dewey returned to New York in the *Olympia*, and was received by a huge public turnout for the parade of 35,000 men, which on September 30 wound its way through the city and under a triumphal arch specially erected to honour him. Dewey stood for six hours beneath the arch reviewing the procession. His carriage led the parade; Schley and others followed. Schley described the bombardment of flowers from housetops and windows, from doorsteps and pavements. The air, he wrote, 'seemed to be filled with flowers,' and he reflected that 'the millions who had gathered to honour the great Dewey with their tribute of affection could find no grander prototype in the days of Imperial Rome.'[18] It was, he thought, an 'offering of love from a nation of free men to all who had wrought well for the honour of home and the glory of country,' and they would never forget it. Ever since Santiago, Schley had been deeply moved by the public response to the events of the war.

In November 1899 Schley was appointed to the command of the South Atlantic Station. It was a sensitive appointment due to the outbreak of the Boer War; South Africa fell within his area of responsibility. Schley, not altogether unreasonably, took the appointment as an official 'endorsement that the professional record of the rear admiral was approved and stood unblemished and unblameworthy.'[19] Sailing in his flagship, the *Chicago*, on November 25, 1899, Schley was soon involved in a busy round of public engagements in various of the republics of South America. He was especially moved by a presentation made to him by Americans living in Buenos Aires, finding that 'it was not easy on the moment to frame a reply that should convey to his countrymen how deeply this souvenir of their affection had touched the recipient.' Schley was met by similar receptions elsewhere during the term of his command, which was scheduled in any case to end in the autumn of 1901. In the event, he was ordered home in April that year; he hastened home to be with his son, who was seriously ill in hospital with blood poisoning, and it was several weeks before he was out of danger.

In the spring of 1900, Dewey's huge popularity led to what his biographer Ronald Spector has called 'the most bizarre episode of his career.' This was the 'Dewey for president' boom. It had begun, in a modest way, almost immediately after the victory of Manila Bay. Various prominent individuals began canvassing the possibility that Dewey might run in the presidential election of November 1900. At first he dismissed the possibility entirely, although his denials were taken as merely the routine gestures of modesty expected of a candidate. One problem was that no one knew whether Dewey was a Republican or Democrat. If the former, he would have to defeat McKinley for the nomination; if the latter, and he was prepared to oppose the annexation of the Philippines, he might appear to be an ideal candidate. However, in November 1899 he signed the preliminary report of the Philippine commission, which deprived him of an issue which would have been the central plank of the Democratic campaign. It has been pointed out that it was in the weeks after his return to the United States that he would have had his real moment of opportunity; thereafter, his real chance was gone. His new wife, Mildred Maclean Hazen (he had remarried in October 1899) was interested in the possibility of his candidature, and Dewey was beginning to think he should do something about it.

Unexpectedly, on April 3, 1900, he announced in an interview given to a young reporter of the *New York World* that he had indeed decided to become a candidate. However, in doing so he explained that he had become 'convinced that the office of the president is not such a very difficult one to fill, his duties being mainly to execute the laws of Congress.' If chosen, he said, he would execute those laws as faithfully as he had always executed the orders of his superiors. Spector remarks that his announcement was greeted with mingled incredulity and amusement: 'the appalling combination of egotism, complacency and naivete revealed in the interview was the subject of much comment in the press.'[20] Although, in spite of the absurdity of his pronouncements there was for a few weeks a real feeling that having claimed to be a Democrat, he might be a viable candidate, there was no endorsement of his candidature by any of the leaders of the party, and by May 18 Dewey abandoned it. He told reporters: 'I don't understand how I got the idea in the first place.' Dewey had been a brave and competent, if lucky, squadron commander; he was not, however, very astute politically, as this incident demonstrated, and he would probably have made a shatteringly bad president.

Throughout Schley's posting to the South Atlantic, he was detached from the controversy that continued to rage. He was reported to have expressed the wish that the whole question be allowed to rest. Sampson, meanwhile, had continued in command of the North Atlantic Station until October 1899, when his deteriorating health compelled his transfer to a less demanding post. He was appointed to the command of the Boston Navy Yard, which if not entirely a sinecure, was much less stressful. He was able to make a number of public appearances towards the end of that year, but he was not well enough to see out the full term of his appointment at Boston. He had, however, been able during his last year at sea to write a number of articles, both with regard to the events of the Spanish American War and to the lessons to be learned from it. He offered a realistic appraisal of the current situation of the U.S. Navy:

> If our easy victories over the fleets of a weak naval power fill our people with the belief that we have now a navy that is large enough for all our needs, then those victories will have done us harm instead of good... We have still much to learn about modern warships. They are as yet in the experimental stage.[21]

Like Schley, Sampson still made no personal public contribution to the continuing controversy.

He had no need to do so. Mahan continued his relentless campaign against Schley. He wrote to Lodge in February 1901 to describe a meeting which he had had with his old adversary Rear Admiral Henry Erben; he had been gratified to find that he shared Mahan's views:

> It must be remembered that history has yet to speak in this matter. There can be no question what her verdict will be, or that it will be plainly spoken. The mere fact that under such grave imputations Schley did not ask for a court... will receive, can receive, but one interpretation. He dared not.[22]

In June 1901 there was published the third volume of *A History of the United States Navy from 1775 to 1901*. The two earlier volumes, published in 1893 and 1898, were in use as textbooks at the Naval Academy. The author was Edgar Stanton Maclay, a clerk in the Brooklyn Navy Yard. The terms in which the book described Schley's conduct during the war at once caught the attention of the American Press, and Schley began to receive from all over the United States press cuttings which included quotations from Maclay's book.

The tone of the book in its comments on Schley was throughout extremely hostile. There were a number of passages in particular which Schley found especially offensive. In relation to the movement of the Flying Squadron from Cienfuegos to Santiago, Maclay wrote: 'Here we have another illustration of the lack of decision and enterprise which was so apparent in Schley's failure to promptly ascertain whether or not Cervera's squadron was in Cienfuegos.'[23] Maclay had quoted with satisfaction the comment of Robley Evans on the period spent before Cienfuegos to the effect that the Flying Squadron 'proceeded to drift leisurely... off and on, Micawber- like, waiting for something – we hoped the Spanish squadron – to turn up.'

On the subject of the squadron's need for coal, Maclay wrote:

> In his report about the coal supply of the vessels under his command Schley exhibited either a timidity amounting to absolute cowardice or of prevarication of facts that were intrinsically falsehoods.[24]

Turning to Schley's report that he was, by reason of the need for coal, obliged to return to Key West, Maclay compared it unfavourably with the famous response 'I'll try, Sir' given by Colonel Miller at the battle of Lundy's Lane when ordered to storm a battery:

> Schley, on May 28, 1898, sullied this brightest of American mottoes by penning: 'Much to be regretted, cannot obey orders,' and turned in caitiff flight from the danger spot toward which duty, honour and the whole American people were most earnestly urging him. Viewed in whatever light it may be, the foregoing dispatch can not be characterised otherwise than as being, without exception, the most humiliating, cowardly and lamentable report ever penned by an American naval officer.[25]

Dealing with the battle of Santiago, Maclay described the *Brooklyn*'s 'loop' as turning tail and running away:

> To anyone who reads consecutively Commodore Schley's official reports from the beginning of this naval campaign, May 22 – it not being necessary to bring in the undisputable

> facts advanced by his alleged enemies – his conduct at this crisis seems pre-eminently characteristic.[26]

Maclay went on to observe that 'Schley's contribution to naval strategy', as shown by his conduct throughout this campaign, was 'avoid your enemy as long as possible, and if he makes for you, run.' Schley was, he said, 'perfectly willing to avoid blanketing the fire of the other two American warships, even at the risk of a disastrous collision with the *Texas*, so long as he could escape getting too close to danger.'[27]

In the preface to his book, Maclay acknowledged the 'hearty and valuable cooperation' which he had received from Rear Admiral Crowninshield. It is not difficult to guess at what would have been tone of his contribution on the subject of Schley. Sampson's name appears among those whose 'valuable assistance' is acknowledged, together with that of Chadwick and a number of other officers known to be severely critical of Schley's performance. It is entirely possible that one or more of his contributors read the book in draft. It would be particularly shocking if Sampson did so, but for any of them it would have been thoroughly discreditable to let Maclay's insulting and abusive comments on Schley pass without the strongest protest.[28]

Quite what prompted such a vicious personal attack by Maclay is not apparent, but it is not surprising that it moved Schley to feel that he must take action. There were, essentially, two proactive options open to him. One was to demand a court of inquiry. The other was to bring civil proceedings for defamation against the author and publishers of the offending work. Schley will have been advised by his lawyers that comments about his exercise of professional judgement, even if wrong, might rely upon the defence that they were fair comment on a matter of public interest; and that in any case there would no doubt be plenty of witnesses prepared to endorse the criticisms made of him. The outspoken allegations of cowardice, however, fell into a different category. There was not a vestige of truth in them, and they were clearly defamatory, entitling Schley to sue.

However, although success in such a claim would clear his name of the charge of cowardice, it would not provide Schley with a vindication of his performance as commander of the Flying Squadron, and would not do anything to confirm his claim for all or a large part of the credit for the victory of Santiago. This meant that the alternative course, of asking for an inquiry, would have seemed more attractive to him. He may not have been aware of Mahan's jibes on the subject of whether he would dare to seek an inquiry; but any senior naval officer would be very conscious of his right to do this, and he may have been thereby goaded into this course of action. This was what he decided to do, although his letter to Long calling for an inquiry appears to suggest that he had considered the alternative of civil proceedings.

He had two other options. He could have issued a press statement dismissing Maclay's work for the rubbish which is undoubtedly was; or he could have continued to maintain a dignified silence, in the knowledge that his supporters in the American Press could be relied upon to put forward his case to the public. It is of course a matter of speculation to interpret the psychology of an individual at a remove of more than a century, based only upon his conduct or his writings. Schley's autobiography does not provide much of a clue to his thinking. He commented that the controversy 'had grown in bitterness from day-to-day, and it was promoted by irresponsible and cowardly innuendo, which the writer could not with dignity or self-respect notice any more than a Royal Dane could heed the snarls of the little cur at his heels.'[29] Now, however, he deemed it proper 'to appeal to the protection of the Secretary against the low flings of an employee under the Department.'

Schley's personality was very different from that of Sampson, who was, outwardly at any rate, a calm and thoughtful individual, disinclined to personal demonstration, and capable of taking clear-sighted and rational decisions even when grievously provoked, as for instance by Shafter or Miles. Beneath this modest, unassuming exterior, however, he was capable of strong feelings, as his needlessly harsh treatment of Schley in his letter of July 10, 1898 had demonstrated. Sampson might well have been capable of ignoring abusive and ill informed comment. Schley, on the other hand, was a much more open and impulsive personality, responsive to the manner in which others perceived him, and in his turn sensitive to their feelings. Richard West observes that 'in the best sense of the word he was sentimental.' This manifested itself in his generosity and spontaneity, as described in the sympathetic visit which he paid to Cervera after the battle:

> The bedraggled Spaniard, wearing a borrowed suit and feeling greatly depressed by the loss of his men and his ships, burst into tears when Schley spoke to him in Castilian Spanish, assuring him of the high regard in which he was held and offering to help him in any way that he could.[30]

After three years in which he and his conduct had been so much in the public eye, Schley had perhaps in a sense become a captive of his own reputation, feeling that he must now stand up for the popular belief that it was to him that much of the credit for Santiago should go. Not to demand a public inquiry could be seen as a passive endorsement of the criticisms of his detractors. It was a point which Long had made in the letter he wrote to McKinley after Senator Louis B Macomas of Maryland had told him that he was bringing a delegation from Baltimore to complain about the Secretary's persecution of Schley: 'It is inconceivable that any self-respecting naval officer would for a moment rest under criticism, much less the persecution, of a superior authority and not demand at once the hearing of a court of inquiry.'[31] In this observation, as with his other correspondence on the matter, Long was almost certainly expressing the views of Schley's detractors within the Navy Department such as Crowninshield, as well as those of Mahan and others. Indeed, it is entirely possible that his letters were drafted for him within the Department.

Schley therefore on July 22, 1901 wrote formally to Long to call for action:

> Within the past few days a series of press comments have been sent to me from various parts of the country of a book entitled 'The History of the Navy' written by one Edgar Stanton Maclay. From these reviews it appears that this edition is the third volume of the said history, extended to include the late war with Spain, which the two first volumes did not contain and were in use as textbooks at the Naval academy.
>
> 1. From excerpts quoted in some reviews, in which the page and paragraph are given, there is such perversion of facts, misconstruction of intention, such intemperate abuse and defamation of myself as subject Mr Maclay to action and civil law. While I admit the right of fair criticism of every public officer, I must protest against the low flings and abusive language of this violent partisan opponent, who has infused into the pages of his book so much of the malice of unfairness as to make it unworthy of the name of history, or of use in any reputable institution of the country.
> 2. I have refrained heretofore from all comment upon the innuendos of enemies muttered or uttered in secret and therefore in safety to themselves. I think the time has now

come to take such action as may bring this entire matter under discussion under the clearer and calmer review of my brothers in arms, and to this end I ask such action at the hands of the Department as it may deem best to accomplish this purpose.

3. But I would express the request that whatever this action may be, it occur in Washington, where most of my papers and data are stored.[32]

The Department responded with astonishing speed; only four days after the date of Schley's letter, Long signed an order convening a Court of Inquiry and setting out the precept upon which its investigation and opinion were to be based. This was drafted by the Navy's Judge Advocate General, Captain Samuel C Lemly; its terms made no reference whatever to the question of credit for the victory of Santiago, and were certainly intended to focus attention on each and every one of the criticisms that had been aired publicly of Schley's conduct. The court was to comprise Admiral George Dewey as president, and Rear Admirals Louis A Kimberley and Andrew EK Benham as members. Kimberley was too ill to serve, however and was replaced by Rear Admiral HL Howison. The hearings were to commence on September 12, 1901. Schley immediately protested that the reference in paragraph 5 of the precept to his 'disobedience' should be amended, since it was an expression of the Department's opinion. This request was refused, since Schley had acknowledged in his telegram of May 28, 1898 that he was unable to obey the Department's orders.

Schley now had six weeks to prepare his case. In the meantime, Maclay was dismissed by the Navy Department, and in due course Congress forbade the use of the book at the Naval Academy. The publishers D Appleton and Sons recalled the book, and only a limited number of copies containing the offending passages remained in circulation. This may well have been in response to a threat of a civil claim.

Meanwhile Sampson, who of course had been made aware of the pending Court of Inquiry, expressed a wish to give evidence at the hearing. His health, however, had deteriorated to the point where this was quite out of the question. Mahan, who visited him at about this time, was shocked at Sampson's appearance, noting that 'his prolonged frail health and incipient decay had wasted the vigorous frame I had once known, and set on him the mark of death's approach.' That September, Sampson suffered a stroke, and thereafter lived in seclusion at Lake Sunapee, New Hampshire. His doctor diagnosed him as being 'in the throes of a mental depression, the most constant symptom of which is a certain form of aphasia characterised by his mixing up words.'

Between the making of the order convening the Court of Inquiry and the commencement of the hearing, the American people had been stunned by the assassination of William McKinley at the Pan American Exposition held in Buffalo New York. Shot by Leon Czogolsz on September 6, he died eight days later, and Vice President Theodore Roosevelt was sworn in as his successor. The nation grieved for a president who was seen as having changed the course of American history. After lying in state, his body was transported to his home town of Canton, Ohio for a Methodist funeral.

24

The Court of Inquiry

Schley had assembled a strong team to represent him at the hearing. Judge Jeremiah M Wilson, born in Ohio in 1828, was one of Washington's most distinguished lawyers. He became a circuit court judge in Indiana before being elected to Congress in 1871, where he served for two terms, after which he remained in Washington. Isidor Rayner was born in Baltimore in 1850, and was admitted to the Maryland bar in 1871. He served first in the Maryland House of Representatives and then in the Maryland Senate from 1878 to 1886, when he was elected to Congress. Defeated in 1888, he was elected to the two following Congresses, after which he declined re-election. In 1899 he became Attorney General of Maryland, a post he still held at the time of the Schley Court of Inquiry. The third member of the team was retired US Navy Lieutenant Commander James Parker. Born in Ohio in 1832, he served in the Mexican War of 1846-1847, retiring from the navy in 1856 to take up the practice of the law in Ohio. When the Civil War broke out he returned to the navy, serving with distinction in the Fort Fisher campaign. After the war he returned to the law.

Schley's lawyers were opposed by Captain Samuel C Lemly, who had been Judge Advocate General of the United States Navy since 1892. It was he, with the assistance of other members of the Navy Department, who drafted the precept which determined the remit of the Court of Inquiry. Mindful of the long running controversy involving the supporters of Schley and Sampson, he was determined to ensure that the Court did not enquire into the actions of Sampson at any time during the hearing. He was assisted by Edwin P Hanna, described in some accounts as an attorney in the Judge Advocate General's office, but who was the Solicitor General of the Navy, an office that made him the senior civilian legal adviser to the Secretary of the Navy, and which he had held since 1899.

Determining the membership of the Court of Inquiry had, in the particular circumstances, presented quite serious difficulties for the Navy Secretary. Long himself was of course an unabashed supporter of Sampson in the controversy with Schley. He must also have had a pretty clear idea of the opinions of most if not all of the senior officers from whose number the members of the Court would be selected. It is of course impossible at this remove to know how many of these had not already formed a concluded view in favour of one side or the other.

When they came to review the composition of the Court, Schley's lawyers could be confident of at least a sympathetic hearing from Dewey, who was an old friend of Schley. However, the same could certainly not be said of Howison, who had been openly partisan in the semi-public comments he had made about the affair. It was plain that objection must be taken to his membership of the Court. Howison could, of course, have recused himself. Instead, he wrote a mealy-mouthed letter to the Assistant Navy Secretary, denying much of what he was alleged to have said, and seeking to justify the rest, leaving it to the Navy Department to decide if he should serve.[1] It was a course of action which he was soon to regret.

In support of the objection Rayner called three witnesses, whose testimony as to remarks which they had heard Howison make left little doubt of his decided opinions on the issues raised. Lemly was obliged to put Howison on the witness stand in an attempt to rebut the evidence of these witnesses. Unfortunately, Howison did not stand up well to Rayner's cross examination. By turns shifty and truculent, he was obliged to concede much of what was put to him, and by the time his evidence was concluded the other two members of the Court could have had little difficulty in deciding that he should be excused.

It was during Howison's evidence that Lemly took the opportunity to emphasise his view of the scope of the proceedings. He argued that the issues before the Court were limited to those arising from Schley's conduct, consistent with the way in which the precept had been drafted:

> The conduct of Rear Admiral Schley is in question, not only at the battle of Santiago, but in the whole Santiago campaign; but I might as well say here that the question of Admiral Sampson's conduct on these occasions is not before the Court in any way.[2]

Rayner was having none of that, retorting at once that it was intended to prove that Sampson was not at the battle of Santiago at all; and if he was not, then Schley was the commander-in chief. If Howison had already made up his mind that Sampson won the battle it would effectively throw the burden of proving his innocence on Schley, instead of the other way about. It was his submission that the question of who was in command was a very pertinent inquiry:

> That will be one of the questions involved here, not a comparison between Schley and Sampson, but as to who was practically, legally, officially, and technically the commander at the battle of Santiago – to whom credit is due, if, as the admiral has said, credit is due to the officer who was in charge.[3]

It was an issue that in one form or another would frequently arise during the course of the hearing. To exclude all consideration of Sampson would be a serious handicap to the lawyers putting Schley's case. Parker regarded it as a demonstration that Lemly intended, as far as he could, to make the proceedings take the form of a court martial, rather than a Court of Inquiry solely concerned with getting at the truth, and he cited the way in which Lemly had chosen to call witnesses:

> Instead of summoning all the witnesses who knew, or were supposed to know, anything about the matters to be inquired into, in order that all the facts might be presented to the Court, as it was his duty to do, only those witnesses, with a few exceptions, were summoned by the judge advocate who were known or believed to be unfavourable to Admiral Schley, and who could be relied upon to discolour or conceal such facts as might be favourable to him.[4]

It was left to Schley's lawyers to call the witnesses required to rebut the allegations made against him. In one instance at least it appears that Lemly discreditably attempted to suppress the evidence of a witness who might be favourable to Schley.

It was also a matter of serious complaint that although the Court of Inquiry was convened as a result of Schley's request for an investigation, neither he nor his lawyers were given any chance to contribute to the precept, as Rayner protested during the course of the hearing:

> We asked for this investigation, and instead of letting us give the precept under which we would like the inquiry to take place you framed a precept, and we are here under the specifications of your precept which you have stated in open court you framed yourself. There is not a single specification of this precept that we ever framed. Here is an applicant asking for a Court of Inquiry and he is not allowed to frame a single specification. He wants to be inquired into, but the government, by its Judge Advocate, frames the precept.[5]

Again and again questions arose which touched on Sampson, and whenever they did, Lemly objected; and Rayner, every time, argued that it was impossible to keep Sampson out of the case:

> You will find that you cannot keep Admiral Sampson out of this. I know you are trying very hard to do it, but you cannot do it. You cannot keep him constructively from the presence of this Court. You may actually but not constructively. It is impossible to do so if this case is to be properly investigated.[6]

Ironically, it was Sampson who was responsible for the question of his role in the battle being brought up during the hearing. His lawyer WH Stayton, of the firm of Stayton and Campbell, wrote seeking the right to be heard by the Court of Inquiry, and arrived on September 27 to present a letter from Sampson asking that they be permitted to appear as his counsel to represent his interests. The Court denied the request; when Stayton attempted to speak, Dewey firmly refused him leave to do so. It was not to be the last attempt which Sampson made to intervene in the disposal of Schley's case.

Parker's complaint about the way in which Lemly had dealt with the selection of witnesses was well founded. There was never any doubt that he had discussed their evidence with them before they gave it, although it cannot be known how far he went in preparing with them the evidence which they would give. There was a brief exchange on the subject when Lieutenant Commander Southerland was giving his evidence. Rayner asked him if he had discussed his evidence with anyone since the Court of Inquiry was ordered. Southerland; evidently uncomfortable, turned to Lemly, and asked: 'Do you want that question answered?' Lemly replied: 'Oh yes; of course,' and Southerland admitted that he had discussed it with Lemly.[7]

Jeremiah Wilson's participation in the hearing came to an abrupt end on September 24, when he died suddenly of heart failure in his room at the Shoreham Hotel. Announcing this, Rayner applied for an adjournment, which was duly granted. Schley was personally extremely distressed by the news of Wilson's death. Asked by journalists for a comment, he said: 'The news is so shocking that I cannot trust myself to give expression to my estimate of the man. I can only say that I have lost not only a clear headed and brilliant counsel but also a dear and much beloved friend.'

The procedural success on the part of Schley's lawyers in removing Howison from the Court of Inquiry did not go down well with Lemly, and from the start there was a good deal of personal rancour in the exchanges between counsel. Lemly and Hanna seem to have felt themselves at times to be somewhat outgunned by their opponents, particularly Rayner. The removal of Howison did not, though, achieve the aim of ensuring an impartial court. First, Howison's replacement was Rear Admiral Francis M Ramsay, who had been involved in such violent disputes with Mahan in days gone by. He may not have been as openly prejudiced as Howison, but he appears nonetheless to have been a firm supporter of Sampson in respect of the major issues of the controversy.

Secondly, however, there was another serious problem with the composition of the Court, of which Schley and his advisers were at the time unaware, as Parker later explained:

> Neither he nor either of his counsel knew that Rear Admiral Benham, as a member of the Board, had already decided the important question of who was in actual command in the battle of Santiago. If we had known that, Admiral Benham would have been objected to as a member of the court, and would probably have been excused.[8]

Parker, not unreasonably, concluded that Benham, in the circumstances, ought not to have served as a member of the Court, or at least disclosed the matter to Schley and his counsel.

With the issue of the membership of the Court out of the way, Lemly began to call the Navy Department witnesses. Much the most offensive of Maclay's allegations in his book had been the suggestion that Schley had displayed cowardice in the face of the enemy, and this was a subject that was directly or indirectly addressed by the precept, in particular in paragraphs 1, 7, 8 and 9. One of the earliest witnesses was Rear Admiral Francis Higginson, captain of the *Massachusetts* during the Santiago campaign. Schley had transferred his flag from the *Brooklyn* to the *Massachusetts* for the conduct of the bombardment of the harbour entrance and the *Cristobal Colon*, which was in plain sight. Higginson said that they had developed the batteries, drawn their fire and got an idea of what they consisted. Asked by Lemly what had been Schley's manner, he replied firmly that it was that of a commander-in-chief, an answer that Lemly must have found disappointing.

There followed a prolonged legal wrangle over a question put by the Court as to whether every effort incumbent on the commanding officer of a fleet in such circumstances was made by Schley to capture or destroy the *Colon*. Higginson replied that he did not think it was. Wilson and Schley both objected to the question as calling for an opinion, Rayner weighed in with a powerful argument:

> From the time of the trial of Admiral Keppel, which was perhaps one of the greatest naval trials that ever took place, down to the present day, the courts have consistently declined in trials before expert boards to permit witnesses to give an opinion.[9]

Rayner quoted extensively from a number of legal authorities in support of his submission on the issue; in the end, in spite of Lemly's protests, the Court withdrew the question, and the answer was said to be 'expunged from the mind of the court.'

The question which had been put to Higginson about Schley's conduct while aboard the *Massachusetts* was repeated to all the witnesses who had observed him in combat. These included Captain Francis A Cook, the commander of the *Brooklyn* and the vessel's navigator, Lieutenant Commander Albon C Hodgson (who had no reason to be sympathetic to Schley) and a large number of other officers and men of the *Brooklyn* and of the *Massachusetts*. All save one testified unequivocally to Schley's coolness, bravery and enthusiasm, and spoke of the confidence which his bearing inspired in those around him.

The exception was the navigator of the *Massachusetts*, Lieutenant Commander Templin M Potts. His reply to the question about Schley's manner was that 'his bearing was that of a man who was suffering under extreme mental excitement, of one who had a disagreeable duty to perform. And he performed it reluctantly, and he tried to get through with it as soon as he could.' Not surprisingly, Rayner gave Potts a very hard time; and when he came to make his closing submissions enjoyed himself mightily at the expense of Potts, and, indirectly, of Lemly:

> I think, if I had one witness after another testifying to the heroism of Commodore Schley, I would not stain this record with any such remark as this. Of course, Potts has gone into history, too. He has covered himself with renown. His name will echo through the ages of undying fame. When Manila will have been forgotten, and Santiago have been buried in oblivion, the name of Lieutenant Potts will live… The shadow of Potts has struck more terror to the souls of admirals and commodores and captains than could the substance of ten thousand sailors. Whenever an admiral or a commodore or a captain is engaged in the carnage of mortal conflict, beware of Potts. Beware of your looks. Be careful how you walk. Be reserved and reticent in your speech.[10]

There was more of the same, and it provoked Lemly to complain that Rayner was 'traducing the reputation of an officer who is well known to you, an officer of ability, an officer of high standing.' There followed a violent argument in which Lemly asserted that Rayner was not correctly stating the evidence of the witness. Rayner's response was withering. 'You have no right to traduce the reputation of Commodore Schley, sir. I shall traduce the reputation of any man whom I think has not established his reputation.' When Lemly repeated his claim that the witness was being misquoted, Rayner said loftily: 'I thought my brother had abandoned this. We have been getting on so well that I thought that my brother would not get in any more of these tempestuous rages.' Stung by this, Lemly became even more angry: 'I am present here not because I wished to be. I am here because it was made my duty. I was ordered to come. I think it is unjust, and it shows how utterly unreliable he is in his statements when he gets up here – '

At this point Rayner intervened: 'I do not think this interruption will justify this. You must not make a statement of that sort. I will not permit it. You are not only unreliable, but you are very offensive.' Dewey intervened to calm matters down, saying that of course the Court would read all the testimony that had been given. He seems to have had one eye on the clock, for he added significantly: 'We only have one day more here'.[11]

To be fair to Lemly, he must have known that there was never likely to be any credible evidence of cowardice on Schley's part. Since, however, the suggestion figured so heavily in Maclay's book, and had been put about so long by Schley's detractors, he was more or less obliged to include the personal conduct of Schley in the precept of the matters to be considered by the Court, and to call such evidence as he could to address the point. It was however, impossible to argue that Schley had shown cowardice when so many witnesses testified to the opposite. Typical was the evidence of Lieutenant Edward Simpson: 'His bearing was that of a brave man, self-possessed, alert to his duties, and encouraging the officers and men in their duties.'[12] Lemly at least had the grace, when he came to make his closing address, to deal with the point directly:

> I have never believed nor do I claim from the evidence, that personal misconduct – or, to call a spade a spade, cowardice – was exhibited by Commodore Schley in any part of his

> career as commander-in-chief of the Flying Squadron. But I regret to submit that … the Commodore exhibited unsteadiness in purpose and in push and in failure to obey orders. The characterisation of this conduct is, however, for the Court.[13]

Lemly had arranged for the display of large charts in the courtroom to assist witnesses to explain the position of vessels at various times, but it soon became apparent that these, as evidence, were almost entirely worthless. One witness, Lieutenant Bristol, who had made a chart purporting to show the position of the ships during the battle of Santiago, encountered Rayner at his fiercest. In the course of his cross-examination, Rayner comprehensively demolished the accuracy of the measurements on which the chart was based. He also demonstrated the unreliability of Bristol's evidence as to what he had personally seen of the Spanish batteries at the harbour entrance.

The question of the inaccuracy of the charges which were put before the Court frequently arose. It did so, for instance, during the evidence of Lieutenant Commander William H Schuetze, the navigator of the *Iowa*, who had been a member of the board of navigators assembled after the battle to produce a report of the position and movement of the ships. He told the Court that he had signed the report under protest, because he believed it was incorrect; he did so because Commander Richard Wainwright, who was chairman of the board, had said that it was the best they could do, even if they stopped until doomsday. These discussions about the accuracy of charts purporting to show the tracks of the ships engaged demonstrated just how imperfect were the recollections of the various witnesses. In the end, the Court had to make do with a large number of conflicting and subjective impressions.

Judges invariably dislike it when personal conflicts erupt between counsel, especially in lengthy or high profile cases. It is by no means infrequent, and during this hearing the court was to encounter a very considerable number of clashes, particularly between Rayner and Lemly. Disputes over procedure and the admissibility of evidence led to a large number of rancorous exchanges between them, but Parker and Hanna were also frequently involved in bitter disputes. At one point, for instance, Hanna complained that one of Rayner's objections had 'taken more time to discuss than the matter itself would have required:'

> Rayner: I am very tired of the suggestion of yours; I am, really.
> Hanna: And I am tired of making it.
> Rayner: You had better stop making it, then.
> Hanna: And I hope the occasion for making it will not occur again.
> Rayner: Every objection I make you seem to think is an interruption, when it is important to us.[14]

A similar exchange was prompted by a complaint from Lemly, during his prolonged and uninspired cross-examination of Schley, that Rayner was raising objections simply to disrupt the process. Rayner sighed heavily: 'My dear sir, I have interfered with you less than you have ever been interfered with before. I have sat here for three days with my patience gone, physically, (not intellectually) worn out by the questions.'[15] Rayner had soon discovered that Lemly and Hanna were unable to deal effectively with sarcasm or, indeed, humour of any kind, and he exploited this whenever he could. During the course of a lengthy argument about the admissibility of evidence that cast doubt on whether Schley had said 'Damn the *Texas*' during the

Brooklyn's turn, Hanna said that he wished to say a few words, 'prompted by the fact that when the objection was made counsel on the other side looked me directly in the face:' Rayner replied that Hanna was so pretty that he could not help looking at him, which produced a furious complaint from Lemly.[16]

There was another such altercation between Rayner and Hanna when the former complained about the inaccuracy of the charts that had been put in:

> Rayner: Do you object to my asking any questions about this chart?
> Hanna: I object to your saying 'Then your map is wrong,' and so on in that style. It is outrageous –
> Rayner: Oh, well, I will change the style.
> Hanna: It is an outrageous method of examining an officer, and has been resorted to more than once in this inquiry.
> Rayner: I will make my style as pleasant as I can.
> Hanna: Please make the style a little more respectable.
> Rayner: Do not criticise. I think my style is all right.
> Hanna: You have a good opinion of it, no doubt.[17]

Likewise, during a further lengthy dispute over the accuracy of the charts Rayner cheekily referred to Hanna as his 'learned and solemn friend,' a remark that seriously annoyed Lemly, who called it 'improper,' adding: 'All these left handed compliments that are thrown in here are entirely unusual in courts of inquiry.' Rayner said that he withdrew them, although saying that he did not think Hanna would object if he called him 'solemn,' whereupon Lemly said: 'I call you funny.' To this, Rayner, who was enjoying himself, replied: 'I do not call you a bit funny.'[18]

Dewey remained remarkably patient during rancorous exchanges of this kind, even when they became extremely heated. On the twenty first day of the hearing Lemly, annoyed at having been overruled by the Court, accused Rayner of not reading accurately from a paper he was holding, which caused Rayner to explode: 'I have been careful, in a practice of over thirty years, never to state anything inaccurately.' Dewey brought the argument to an end for the moment: 'That will do, gentlemen;' but it flared up again before the Court adjourned, Rayner calling attention to 'very disagreeable conduct on the part of the Judge Advocate':

> Throughout this case I have endeavoured to conduct myself with the utmost degree of courtesy and politeness; but – and this is something that has occurred not merely once but has occurred over and over again in this case – the least little objection that is made brings the Judge Advocate to the most irritable humour that is possible.[19]

So many of the specifications of the precept called simply for an opinion as to whether Schley had done all he might that there was considerable scope for the scoring of valuable points in cross examination – if, that is to say, the Court was approaching these issues with an open mind. Certainly Rayner obtained useful results in his cross examination of a number of key witnesses. On the subject of the bombardment of May 31, and the extent to which it was the batteries or the *Colon* which was the primary target, he explored in some detail with Captain Folger of the *New Orleans* the conclusions to be drawn. At the end of this, he asked: 'Then the reconnaissance, taking it as a reconnaissance was successful for the purpose of developing the number and strength of the batteries at Santiago?' To this, Folger replied 'Eminently so.' Later in the hearing Ensign Macy testified that so far as the bombardment on May 31 was concerned, Schley's principal concern was to reconnoitre the batteries, rather than to destroy the *Colon*; and that he had much in mind the importance of not risking any of his ships in a contest with the forts. This, of course, directly contradicted the evidence on the point which Lemly had called.

Rayner was particularly effective in dealing with Captain Sigsbee of the *St Paul*, who gave evidence at considerable length of his conversations with Schley when the Flying Squadron first arrived at Santiago. In the knowledge that he would be calling witnesses who would challenge Sigsbee's account, Rayner pressed him hard. He compelled him to acknowledge that when Schley's ships first arrived off the port, he had thought at first that their smoke was that of Cervera's squadron. Pouncing on this, Rayner pointed out that if Sigsbee had thought it might have been Cervera arriving, he could hardly have believed that the Spanish were already there. Sigsbee, who became decidedly shifty in the course of his evidence, was much concerned with what he had been publicly reported as having said to Schley about the presence or otherwise of the Spanish squadron, and continued to deny that he had told Schley that it was not there. Rayner called George Graham, who testified that he heard Sigsbee say in reply to Schley's question: 'No, they are not here. I have been here a week and they are not here.' Graham's evidence was confirmed by two other witnesses. An orderly, Dennis J Cronin, said that he had been standing close at hand while Schley and Sigsbee spoke, and overheard the conversation; while another witness, Ensign Marble, said much the same, recalling that Sigsbee had said that the Spanish ships could not be there without his knowing of it. Here, then, was a direct conflict of evidence; on balance, there would seem to be a greater ring of truth in Schley's account, as confirmed by Graham, Cronin and Marble, than in that of Sigsbee.[20] It was an important point, since Schley relied on what Sigsbee had told him as justifying his brief westward movement before he returned to blockade Santiago.

One witness upon whom Lemly could certainly rely for evidence hostile to Schley was 'Fighting Bob' Evans, particularly on the subject of the speed with which the Flying Squadron had moved. While several times irritably asserting that he was there to answer questions, he became testy under cross-examination, and was on occasion deliberately obstructive in his replies to Rayner. Chadwick, on the other hand, was decidedly vague in his recollection of events. He did, however, recall part of Schley's visit to Sampson at Key West on May 18:

> My only distinct recollection in regard to the conversation was Commodore Schley's statement to the Admiral that he desired to be perfectly loyal; that he was very pleased to be under his command, and that the Admiral could be sure he would be perfectly loyal in all his conduct. Chadwick also remembered the occasion of Sampson's despatch to Schley of May 29, in which he sent his congratulations; he had protested to Sampson about this, which he thought was 'improper.'[21]

A witness for Schley with whom Hanna did quite well in the course of a ponderous cross-examination was Lieutenant Wells, who served as Schley's Flag Secretary. By the end of his evidence the actual date of the receipt by Schley of orders had become extremely confused, as was the identity of the vessel bringing them. In general, though, neither Lemly nor Hanna made much headway with the witnesses called on Schley's behalf.

Naturally Rayner's chief witness was Schley himself. He was on the witness stand from the early afternoon of Thursday October 24, which was the 31st day of the hearing, until 3:00

p.m. on Wednesday October 30, which was the 34th day. He gave his evidence in chief in the form of a lengthy narrative, covering the specifications of the precept from the time the Flying Squadron was formed at Hampton Roads until the conclusion of the battle of Santiago. As he progressed through the events which occurred during the course of his command, Rayner and Parker brought out matters in greater detail by putting questions to clarify Schley's narrative. Considering the length of time that had elapsed, he showed considerable command of the relevant facts.

Lemly's cross examination began on Monday October 28, soon after the commencement of the hearing on that day. Early in the course of this there was a sharp passage of arms over the issue of whether it was necessary for a plan of battle for the captains of the ships concerned to be put in writing. As Rayner pointed out, nowhere in the regulations of 1896, in relation to the duties of a commander-in-chief, was this prescribed, and Schley was firm in his stated belief that it was not necessary.[22]

One of the aspects of Schley's evidence with which Lemly was understandably concerned was the extent to which he was acting as commander of the fleet on July 3; he put to him that Schley had not prior to the inquiry claimed to have made the signal:'Follow the flag.' To this Schley replied: 'I think I have kept my mouth pretty close about all subjects relating to that matter,' which was a fair comment. Lemly was, of course, also concerned to make much of the *Brooklyn's* 'loop.' Schley insisted that it was made not only to avoid the cross fire of other vessels of the fleet; it was also to enable him to continue the battle, and was 'the movement that decided the events of that day.'[23] He accepted entirely that although it was Cook who had given the order 'Hard aport,' which began the *Brooklyn*'s turn it was he who was entirely responsible for it, and would have given the same order in a second.

Apart from Schley himself, much the most important witness on whom Rayner relied was Captain Francis A Cook, whose evidence as captain of the *Brooklyn* traversed the whole of the period covered by the precept. He was called in the first instance by Lemly, but his account, supporting as it did the case which Schley put before the Court, was especially valuable. As to the *Brooklyn*'s turn, he confirmed that he gave the order before Schley said the same thing, to which he replied that the helm was already hard aport. Significantly, Cook brought out two key points about the turn; first, that it did not in any way hazard the *Texas* and secondly, that by turning to starboard the *Brooklyn* avoided any possibility that she could be rammed by the *Maria Theresa*. In answer to the often repeated question about Schley's conduct and bearing, Cook was emphatic, saying that he 'always regarded him as an enthusiastically brave and patriotic officer – never in any other light.'[24]

Rather unnecessarily, and perhaps as Parker wrote in his book 'in its effort to find something which might throw discredit upon Admiral Schley,' the Navy Department pursued the issue of what had passed on the bridge of the *Brooklyn* on July 3 immediately before the 'loop'. The exchanges of correspondence on the subject in 1899 had left Lieutenant Commander Hodgson extremely dissatisfied. Schley published the brief denial, in the *Washington Post* but not the longer letter of explanation; this, it was suggested, was disingenuous, and the Navy Department later that month ordered Hodgson to make a statement to Chadwick, which he did. In this statement Hodgson said that he did not intend in his published note of denial intend to convey 'the idea that no such colloquy took place.'[25] It was all rather a storm in a teacup but it was one of the specifications of the precept, and as such the Court heard evidence on it at length.

On Monday November 4 the evidence was finally completed, and there remained only an argument about the admissibility of various documents before the closing addresses began. By agreement between the parties it was Hanna who was the first of the advocates to present his closing submission to the Court. He rose to speak at 2:00 p.m. He began by saying that he aimed to be brief; but he went on to promise a careful, exhaustive review, with citations, of the evidence. As he remarked, these objectives were incompatible, and brevity was not a feature of his presentation. He spoke for the rest of that day, and continued the following morning, offering a laboured analysis of the evidence, the arguments put forward, and each of the specifications of the precept. He was still speaking at the lunch adjournment on November 5, after which he went on for a further hour. In conclusion, he thanked his opponents 'for the exceedingly, considerate manner in which our relations have been conducted,' a description that was certainly courteous but scarcely accurate.[26]

He was followed by Parker, who spoke for the rest of that afternoon and went on for another half hour on the following morning. He drew attention to the remarkable feature of the case:

> There never has before been a case, so far as my knowledge and research into naval history has shown me, wherein the man who was, without controversy, completely victorious and did his whole duty, has felt compelled to ask an inquiry as to that conduct before a tribunal of his brother officers.[27]

He spoke, of course, as a retired naval officer, and frequently drew on his seagoing experience to make his points. He closed with an appeal to the Court to say of Schley that it was 'impressed with the fact that on that day he, with the officers and men who were engaged in that struggle, fulfilled in the very noblest degree the traditions of the American Navy.'

It was not Parker's last word on the issues with which the Court was concerned. In 1910 he published an angry and rather untidy book about the campaign, illustrated by reference to the evidence before the Court, and attacking the conclusions which it had reached. He protested again, as he and Rayner had done throughout the hearing, that whereas Schley had asked that the Navy Department should 'take such action as may bring this entire matter under clearer and calmer review of [his] brothers in arms,' the Department had confined the precept to an investigation of Schley's conduct:

> One who reads that precept cannot fail to see that the object which Judge Advocate Lemly, who drew it, had in view, was an indictment of Admiral Schley, to prove and sustain which every possible effort was to be directed. And this purpose was relentlessly pursued.[28]

Mindful no doubt of Hanna's gracious remarks, and notwithstanding the rancour which had characterised so many of the exchanges during the course of the proceedings, Rayner rose to begin his final remarks with a stately, but possibly somewhat insincere compliment to Hanna for his 'highly capable argument' and both to him and to Lemly 'for having managed this case with a most judicial impartiality.' He went on to deliver a closing address that was remarkable for its lucid grasp of the detailed facts and the inferences to be drawn from them. His demolition of the government's case was scathing, frequently witty or bitingly sarcastic; and although never directly accusing witnesses of lying, effectively destroyed the credibility of their evidence. Or, at least, that would have been the effect before an impartial Court; but that, almost certainly, was not what he was facing.

Rayner ended his address with the kind of flamboyant language that was a feature of the oratory of the time:

> Such a trial as this has never to my knowledge taken place in the history of the world. It seemed to my mind that this case had hardly opened with the testimony of Captain Higginson before it commenced to totter, and from day to day its visionary fabric has dissolved from view. When Captain Cook, their last witness, was put upon the stand, the entire structure collapsed, and now after the witnesses from our own ships and the gallant captain and crew of the *Oregon* and Admiral Schley have narrated their unvarnished tale, the whole tenement, with all of its compartments, from its foundation to its turret, has disintegrated and lies like a mass of blackened ruins. It has taken three years to reveal the truth. There is not a single word that has fallen from the tongue of a single witness, friend or foe, that casts the shadow of a reflection upon the honoured name of the hero of Santiago. He has never claimed the glory of that day. Let it be known he has never claimed the glory of that day… And what is more than all, which has been revealed in this case as matchless as his courage, and as unsullied as his honour is his beautiful character and the generous spirit that animates his soul and the forgiving heart that beats within his bosom…For three long years he has suffered and now, thank God, he believes that the hour of his vindication has come. With composure, with resignation, with supreme and unfaltering fortitude, he awaits the judgment of this illustrious tribunal, and if that deliverance comes, he can from the high and exalted position that he occupies look down upon his traducers and maligners and with exultant pride exclaim: 'I care not for the venomous gossip of clubs and drawing rooms and cliques and cabals, nor for the poisoned shafts of envy and of malice. I await, under the guidance of Divine Providence, the verdict of posterity'.[29]

As he ended, the audience broke into tumultuous applause; attempting to restore order, Dewey insisted: 'This is not a theatre.'

Lemly asked for the hearing to be adjourned early, and it was not until the afternoon of November 7 that he rose to deliver his final address. As with those who had spoken before him, Lemly took the Court through the evidence of the witnesses, quoting extensively from the documentation. Like them, he too quoted from instances in naval history, including in particular British naval history. But there were no verbal pyrotechnics to compare with Rayner's performance, and he spoke for only one and three quarter hours, about a third of the time of his opponent. He ended, after acquitting Schley of the charge of cowardice, by arguing that he had 'exhibited unsteadiness in purpose and in push and failure to obey orders,' and concluded:

> I trust that I may be pardoned if I remind you, gentlemen, that the first importance of the matters before you is not as they relate to any individual, but as they concern the naval service. It is for you to lay down a standard of conduct to be followed in future similar cases – a standard such as that set by our great naval commanders like John Paul Jones, Decatur, Perry, Farragnt, the Porters, and others. A sense of propriety forbids me to mention the living.[30]

Having adjourned on what was the fortieth day of the hearing, the Court of Inquiry proceeded to consider its decision. Considering the enormous amount of oral and documentary evidence before them, its members may be said to have achieved a remarkably speedy result in being able to produce their decision by December 13. This was particularly striking since, in the end, they were unable to arrive at a unanimous conclusion. The decision took the form of a section headed 'Facts,' which actually included a number of expressions of opinion critical of Schley; and a section headed 'Opinion,' which read as follows:

> OPINION
>
> Commodore Schley, in command of the Flying Squadron, should have proceeded with utmost despatch off Cienfuegeos and should have maintained a close blockade of that port.
>
> He should have endeavoured on May 23rd, at Cienfuegos, to obtain information regarding the Spanish squadron by communicating with the insurgents at the place designated in the memorandum delivered to him at 9:35 a.m. of that date.
>
> He should have proceeded from Cienfuegos to Santiago de Cuba with all despatch, and should have disposed his vessels with a view of intercepting the enemy in any attempt to pass the Flying Squadron.
>
> He should not have delayed the squadron for the *Eagle*.
>
> He should not have made the retrograde turn westward with his squadron.
>
> He should have promptly obeyed the Navy Department's order of May 25th.
>
> He should have endeavoured to capture or destroy the Spanish vessels at anchor near the entrance of Santiago Harbor on May 29th and 30th.
>
> He did not do the utmost with the force under his command to capture or destroy the *Colon* and other vessels of the enemy which he attacked on May 31st.
>
> Bt commencing the engagement on July 3rd with the port battery and turning the *Brooklyn* around with port helm Commodore Schley caused her to lose distance and position with the Spanish vessels, especially with the *Viscaya* and *Colon*.
>
> The turn of the *Brooklyn* to the westward was made to avoid getting her into dangerous proximity to the Spanish vessels. The turn was made towards the *Texas*, and caused that vessel to stop and to back her engines to avoid possible collision.
>
> Admiral Schley did injustice to Lieutenant Commander A.C. Hodgson in publishing only a portion of the correspondence which passed between them.
>
> Commodore Schley's conduct in connection with the events of the Santiago campaign prior to June 1, 1898, was characterized by vacillation, dilatoriness, and lack of enterprise.
>
> His official reports regarding the coal supply and the coaling facilities of the Flying Squadron were inaccurate and misleading.
>
> His conduct during the Battle of July 3rd was self possessed, and he encouraged, in his own person, his subordinate officers and men to fight courageously.[31]

As president of the Court, Dewey was obliged to sign the document; but he strongly dissented from its conclusions, and wrote a minority report which read as follows:

> In the opinion of the undersigned the passage from Key West to Cienfuegos was made by the Flying Squadron with all possible despatch, Commodore Schley having in view the importance of arriving off Cienfuegos with as much coal as possible in the ships' bunkers.

> The blockade of Cienfuegos was effective. Commodore Schley in permitting the steamer *Adula* to enter the port of Cienfuegos expected to obtain information concerning the Spanish squadron from her when she came out.
>
> The passage from Cienfuegos to a point twenty-two miles south of Santiago was made with as much dispatch as was possible while keeping the squadron a unit.
>
> The blockade of Santiago was effective. Commodore Schley was the senior officer of the squadron off Santiago when the Spanish squadron attempted to escape on the morning of July 3, 1898. He was in absolute command, and is entitled to the credit due to such commanding officer for the glorious victory which resulted in the total destruction of the Spanish ships.[32]

The Court's recommendation was that in view of the length of time which had elapsed since the Santiago campaign, no further action should be taken.

Epilogue

Admiral Dewey may not have been the sharpest tack in the box when it came to matters of presidential politics, but he was perfectly aware of the real issue concerning the battle of Santiago in the court of public opinion. Whatever, therefore, Rear Admirals Benham and Ramsay may have wanted to say about Schley's performance prior to the battle, he was not going to pass up an opportunity to put the record straight, as he saw it, as to the battle itself. His minority report firmly assigned the credit for the victory to Schley, and that, for the American press and public, was that. More than one cartoonist, when the news of the court's decision was received, portrayed Dewey congratulating Schley, with his colleagues on the court disregarded. Their views were always going to cut a lot less ice than those of Dewey, who remained a great national hero; and even they had been obliged to dismiss the allegations of cowardice, albeit in awkward and grudging terms. On the other hand, Dewey's dissenting opinion was widely seen as cancelling out much of their criticism of Schley before Santiago. For Schley and his supporters, Dewey's conclusion that he was in command during the battle was a prize that was a valuable reward for undergoing the ordeal of the Court of Inquiry.

Nevertheless, Rayner and Parker prepared a detailed statement of exceptions to the majority report of the Court of Inquiry, which was submitted to Long on December 18. In view of his well-known opinions on the issues raised, there was no expectation on their part that it would have any effect. It was however, a comprehensive attack on the reasoning of the decision; it restated trenchantly their case put forward at the hearing, and pointed out the failure of the court to take account of uncontradicted evidence which supported that case. Schley was not the only one to submit such a statement of exceptions; on the following day Sampson's lawyers delivered a request to the Secretary of the Navy that he expressly disapprove Dewey's dissenting opinion. For their part, Lemly and Hanna submitted on December 20 a paper in response to the statement from Rayner and Parker, which they criticised as containing a number of misstatements and in particular made an 'inaccurate and misleading' use of the words 'the majority of the court'.[1]

Predictably, Long wasted no time in approving the findings of the Court of Inquiry, and also the conduct of the majority in making no finding on the issues raised by Dewey in his minority report. His letter to this effect was published on December 20, which scarcely indicates any very considered review of the matters put before him. Schley, in his memoirs, suggested that Long had conveniently forgotten his report to the Senate in 1899, in which he had stated that Sampson had proceeded to Siboney to meet General Shafter under his orders; and argued that Long was evidently not correctly informed of the *New York*'s actual position when the battle began, quoting in full an affidavit from James O'Shaughnessy, of the *Chicago Chronicle*, which described the situation of the flagship when gunfire was first heard.[2]

Schley and his lawyers were not prepared to leave the matter where it stood after Long's confirmation, and prepared a detailed petition to the president by way of appeal. Roosevelt took the task of reviewing the whole of the issues extremely seriously. He considered the detailed terms of Schley's appeal, and the response of the Navy Department, and all the official reports, logbooks and signal books, as well as the testimony before the Court of Inquiry, and interviewed the four surviving captains of the major vessels at Santiago. He published his findings in a memorandum of February 18, 1902. His conclusion on the points on which the members of the court were unanimous was that 'on the whole the court did substantial justice'. He thought that there was a reasonable doubt whether Schley had moved 'with sufficient expedition from port to port', but thought that his gravest error was the 'retrograde movement'. However, he dismissed all the issues arising before the battle when he wrote:

> The majority of those actions which the court censures occurred five weeks or more before the fight itself, and it certainly seems that if Admiral Schley 's actions were censurable he should not have been left as second-in-command under Admiral Sampson. His offences were in effect condoned when he was not called to account for them. Admiral Sampson, after the fight, in an official letter to the Department, alluded for the first time to Admiral Schley's 'reprehensible conduct' six weeks previously. If Admiral Schley was guilty of reprehensible conduct of a kind which called for such notice from Admiral Sampson, then Admiral Sampson ought not to have left him as senior officer of the blockading squadron on July 3 when he (Sampson) steamed away on his proper errand of communication with General Shafter.[3]

Roosevelt went on to consider the question of who was in command during the battle, which he took to be in effect an appeal from the decision of President McKinley as to promotion, and he decided that neither Schley nor Sampson had exercised command. He thought that the *Brooklyn* could have turned westward rather than eastward when making her loop; if it was the more dangerous course, it also offered more danger to the Spanish. McKinley's promotion recommendations were, he concluded, appropriate. He ended his findings with a firm statement of his hope that they would bring the matter to an end: 'there is no excuse whatever for either side for any further agitation of this unhappy controversy. To keep it alive would merely do danger to the Navy and the country'.[4]

Of the two protagonists in the dispute, Schley had perhaps more reason to be content with Roosevelt's conclusions, even if they did not exonerate him from charges of errors of judgement. His supporters were legion and were in no way shaken in their admiration of him. Dewey had received shoals of letters commending his minority position opinion, and there were many public and private expressions of support for Schley. Lieutenant-General Nelson A Miles had incurred a reprimand from the Secretary of War by publicly announcing his agreement with Dewey. The outcome of the Court of Inquiry provoked a new round of honours and presentations to Schley all around the country; there had previously been many such demonstrations of public gratitude to him following the Battle of Santiago.

Schley, who had retired from the Navy on October 9, 1901, was profoundly touched by the public response. When he published his memoirs in 1904, he recorded his appreciation of the 'many manifestations of high regard and affection of friends from one end of our country to the other who presented him with many souvenirs of priceless value in testimony of their affection'.

He was especially grateful for the public statements from state legislatures and governors, which 'formed the highest tribute of distinction that could be paid to a fellow citizen'. These things, he wrote, had brought him 'satisfaction that, in all the trying experiences of a long professional career his conduct had stood approval by the people of his country'.[5]

Sampson, meanwhile, was gradually sinking. His health made it impossible for him to respond personally to all that was being said, even had he wished to do so. On May 6, 1902 he died in Washington. His funeral was attended by President Roosevelt, the Cabinet, the Supreme Court, members of Congress and senior naval and military figures; and an impressive funeral cortege, including a large body of sailors from the North Atlantic Squadron, escorted his body to Arlington Cemetery.

He was deeply mourned by his many friends and colleagues in the Navy. Foremost among these was French Ensor Chadwick, who had done much to inflame the controversy with Schley by both public and private statements. He wrote of Sampson that he was 'one of the greatest characters in our Navy and one of the finest in the country'. Among the various steps which he took to bring Schley into disrepute, the most decisive was, in the end, the information which he gave to Maclay. With the contribution from other Sampson supporters, this prompted Maclay to publish the violent invective which led Schley to seek a court of inquiry. Chadwick's statements to the press, which earned him a serious reprimand, damaged his own reputation within the Navy, where he was regarded as breaching trust by exposing internal conflict within the service.[6] He retired from the Navy in February 1906, and turned to a new profession in which he displayed outstanding ability, becoming an extremely successful historian. Among his key works was his three volume history of the Spanish-American War. He died on January 27, 1919, soon after the ending of the Great War, at the outset of which he had been among the few prominent American defenders of Germany.

Roosevelt's hope that discussion of the Schley-Sampson controversy would now cease was not fulfilled. Among those who contributed to its continuance was John D Long. Before the presidential election of 1900 he had been touted as a possible candidate for the vice presidency; after McKinley's re-election he continued as Navy Secretary until he resigned in May 1902, partly because his relationship with Roosevelt was not good. Other factors were the fact that he had not escaped public criticism about his role in the war of 1898, due to what emerged during the Court of Inquiry; and also to the death of one of his daughters in October 1901 which left him profoundly depressed. In 1903 he published his memoirs under the title *The New American Navy*; in this book he was, predictably enough, heavily critical of Schley. Retiring thereafter from public life he died on August 28, 1915.

Mahan, perhaps the most malignant of Schley's critics, was dismayed by Dewey's magisterial upholding of Schley's claimed credit for the Battle of Santiago. In December 1901, when *The Independent* took a strongly pro-Schley position, Mahan angrily terminated his relationship with the magazine. In 1903, still pursuing his hatred of Schley, he told Roosevelt that he was outraged that men of intelligence and position continued to have a relationship with Schley, whom he regarded as a liar.[7] He had come some considerable way since August 1898 when he had described Schley as a 'gallant man and a good officer'. He kept up his persecution of Schley when he wrote a short history of the Naval War Board for the Navy Department in 1906; in this he wrote that Schley's 'uncertain course [and] … vacillating action, as shown by his telegrams had destroyed the confidence of the Department and of the Board in him, as a commander-in-chief'.[8] Mahan had also assisted Long in the preparation of the latter's memoirs, and maintained a close relationship with the former Navy Secretary. Mahan himself had published his *Lessons of the War with Spain* in 1900, which comprised a number of magazine articles, but in these he did not directly address the controversy. He died on December 1, 1914.

Among the principal participants in the Court of Inquiry, Rear Admiral Andrew Benham was the first to go, dying on August 11, 1905. Rear Admiral Francis Ramsay who like Benham had retired from the Navy well before the Court of Inquiry, died on July 19, 1914. Edwin P Hanna died on July 3, 1909, while still in office as Solicitor General of the Navy. Samuel C Lemly continued as Judge Advocate General of the Navy, stepping down in June 1904 after serving 12 years in the post.

Isidor Rayner continued his political career. At one point during the inquiry, Lemly had jeered at his aspiration to become governor of Maryland; it was, however, as Democrat Senator for that state that he achieved his political ambition, when he was elected in 1905. He served in the Senate with distinction until he died on November 25, 1912. In the course of a memorial address to the Senate, Senator Talbott said:

> He was called upon to represent the hero of Santiago, Admiral Schley, in his defence before the Court of Inquiry. Mr Rayner's splendid effort in this notable case will long be remembered as a masterly defence of a brave and heroic man by a great and accomplished lawyer.

Dewey's influence on the Navy continued to be enormous. In 1900, when Long established the General Board of the Navy, he appointed Dewey as its president. Dewey did not, however, enjoy a particularly good relationship with the Navy Secretary and this was unlikely to have been improved by his minority decision at the Court of Inquiry. When Long stood down, however, he was succeeded by William H Moody; Roosevelt's choice was determined by the fact that Moody was an outspoken advocate of a strong Navy who was also very receptive to Dewey's advice, and the admiral's influence grew during his term of office. Dewey would not have been sorry to see the back of Rear Admiral Arent S Crowninshield, who left the Bureau of Navigation and was replaced by Rear Admiral Henry Taylor, the former commander of the *Indiana*. Crowninshield retired abruptly from the Navy in May 1903 when, as commander of the European Station, he was to his fury deprived of the battleship *Illinois* as his flagship, and was given instead the cruiser *Chicago*. Dewey continued until his death on January 11, 1917 to be at the forefront of those calling for a strong Navy; one historian summed up his post war career in these terms: 'Dewey remained firmly in control of what could be described as a moderate course of change using traditional avenues to accomplish modernisation and improvements in the Navy'.[9]

David L Trask, the outstanding modern American naval historian of the period, commenting on the effect of the Court of Inquiry upon the U.S. Navy, has written:

> Although the dispute between Sampson and Schley did not lead to a general overhaul of the Navy Department, it helped publicise the need for new and improved vessels, adequate communications by means of bases and naval stations, and improved operational performance, especially in gunnery.[10]

The creation of the General Board in 1900 was also a response to the experiences of 1898 although it was not until 1915 with the appointment of a Chief of Naval Operations that anything approaching a general staff was established.

After publishing his memoirs Schley continued to lead an active life, accepting many invitations throughout the country. In 1909, however, his health began to fail, and on October 2 1911, while in New York after a vacation with his wife, he collapsed and died suddenly while crossing a street. As had been the case with Sampson before him, Schley was given an impressive funeral in Washington. The mourners were, in the absence of President Taft in Nebraska, led by Navy Secretary George von Lengerke Meyer and Admiral Dewey, accompanied by the members of the Supreme Court, the diplomatic corps and members of both houses of Congress. Taft requested that all veterans of the Spanish American war be given leave to attend the funeral. Six retired rear admirals, a retired Supreme Court Justice and General Nelson A Miles acted as pall bearers. The funeral procession to Arlington cemetery included one hundred midshipmen from the Naval Academy and five companies of sailors and six of marines.

During his captivity in the United States, Cervera had become an increasingly popular celebrity, widely respected for his chivalry, particularly in his treatment of Lieutenant Hobson and the crew of the *Merrimac.* He refused an offer of parole which would have enabled him to return to Spain; but he was soon released in any case. When he got back to Spain he was, regrettably, not very well received. The Press and public were looking for a scapegoat, and the Spanish government was content to let Cervera bear the responsibility for the naval disaster. He and his officers even had to face a lawsuit, which was ultimately dismissed. The publication of his collection of documents meant, however, that the true causes of the defeat became apparent. In February 1901 justice was done when he was promoted to the rank of vice admiral, and in 1903 King Alfonso XIII appointed him a life Senator. His last appointment was as commander of the naval district of Ferrol in 1906-1907, after which, his health beginning to fail, he retired. He died at his home in Southern Spain on April 3 1909.

As commanders, the thoughtful and analytical Sampson was abler than the warmhearted, impulsive Schley. It is undeniable that some of Schley's operational decisions, while in command of the Flying Squadron, were tentative, and his judgment was not always sound. However, Sampson's description of his conduct during this period as 'reprehensible' was spiteful and discredited its author. Roosevelt was justified in brushing aside the criticisms made by the Court of Inquiry of those aspects of Schley's contract while in command of the Flying Squadron which had not prompted either Long or Sampson to do anything about them. Operationally, Schley had been an adequate commander; his blockade of Cienfuegos and later of Santiago was sufficient for the purpose. Differing opinions might reasonably be held about the 'loop', but his conduct during the battle of Santiago was otherwise beyond reproach.

Sampson's judgment was also at times at fault; his original scheme to launch an attack on Havana immediately on the outbreak of war was probably unwise; and his futile bombardment of San Juan was certainly a mistake. On the other hand, he conducted an efficient blockade of Santiago particularly in his use of searchlights. Whether the sinking of the *Merrimac* was the correct decision is debatable; Schley, for one, was more anxious to see that Cervera emerged from the harbour rather than for him to be blocked in.

Sampson's behaviour towards Schley does seem very much out of character. Perhaps it is the case that, once the tumult of war had died away, it was his bitter disappointment at having missed the battle of Santiago which accounted for this. Soon after his death, Mahan wrote an essay on Sampson for *McClure's Magazine* in which he noted that there were 'certain moral faculties which are not acquired by practice, though they may by it be improved and enlarged' which were prominent among the aptitudes of the competent commander. He found these in Sampson:

> Upon him responsibility sat easily … anxiety did not overrun the due bounds of reasonable, though watchful, precaution … he could rest with quiet mind in the certainty that all had been done which reason could prescribe, untroubled by fears of improbable, though not impossible, eventualities.[11]

Given the emotions of the time, it was to be expected that Mahan should express himself in such terms; perhaps, in his comparison with other great naval leaders, he somewhat overstated the case.

It was Sampson's misfortune that chance had led him away from his fleet at the critical moment, and in a sense it was Schley's misfortune as well. Certainly, had Sampson been able to preside over the inevitably easy victory at Santiago, Schley would not have been so viciously persecuted by those around Sampson who felt that he should not be seen as entitled to the credit for it.

The naval war of 1898 was one which the United States Navy could not fail to win. The hunger of the assertive American Press and the loyal American public for authentic heroic achievement conferred on the naval leaders a reputation which was, perhaps, rather more than their abilities deserved. As the man at the centre of the controversy that so long and so damagingly divided the U.S. Navy, Schley's abilities, and all his actions, were subjected to unprecedentedly minute scrutiny, both in the columns of the Press and the lengthy proceedings of the Court of Inquiry. Perhaps the fairest and most dispassionate assessment was made by the British historian HW Wilson, who defended the controversial 'loop' and thought it strange that Schley should have been condemned for it. He went on:

> Yet we do not think that posterity, when it reviews his career, would disagree with the general tendency of the majority verdict. Schley showed too much hesitation and indecision at critical moments to claim the proud fame of a great admiral … There is no foundation whatever for the imputation of cowardice, and it is a thousand pities that it was ever made.[12]

As to the suggestion that Sampson deserved the credit for the victory of Santiago because he planned the dispositions of the fleet, Wilson added: 'but rarely will the Anglo-Saxon mind believe that the brain which plans is as much entitled to renown as the hand which executes'. Perhaps the last word can be left with Schley, who ended his memoirs with the words he wrote immediately after the battle: 'I'm glad that I had an opportunity to contribute in the least to a victory that seems big enough for all of us!'

Notes

Prologue

1 *Mariposa Gazette*, August 24 1901.
2 James Parker, *Rear Admirals Schley, Sampson and Cervera* (New York 1910) p.317.

Chapter 1

1 Harold and Margaret Sprout, *The Rise of American Naval Power 1776-1918* (Princeton 1946) pp.165-166.
2 Ibid, p.170.
3 Ibid, p.224.
4 Stephen Howarth, *To Shining Sea* (London 1991) p.219.
5 Ibid, p.224.
6 Rear Admiral George R Clark and others, *A Short History of the United States Navy* (Philadelphia 1939) p.408.
7 Walter R Herrick, *The American Naval Revolution* (Baton Rouge 1966) p.27.
8 Captain Edward L Beach, *The United States Navy: A 200 year History* (Boston 1986) p.323.
9 Kenneth J Hagan, *This People's Navy* (New York 1991) p.187.
10 Herrick, p.18.
11 Allan Nevins, *Grover Cleveland: A Study in Courage* (New York 1941) pp.218-219.
12 Herrick, pp.31-32.
13 Quoted Howarth, p.236.
14 Richard S West, *Admirals of American Empire* (Indianapolis 1948) pp.43-44.
15 West, pp.92-93.
16 Herrick p.34.
17 Herrick, p.35; Joseph G Dawson II, 'William T Sampson: Progressive Technologist as Naval Commander' in *Admirals of the New Steel Navy*, ed James C Bradford (Annapolis 1990) p.154.
18 Herrick, pp.35-36.
19 Ibid, p.38.
20 Sprout, p.207.
21 Quoted Herrick, p.44.
22 Ibid, p.45.
23 Herrick, p.61.
24 John C Reilly Jr and Robert L Scheina, *American Battleships 1886-1923* (London 1980) p.52.
25 Sprout, p.213.
26 Reilly and Scheina, pp.54-68.
27 Sprout, p.214.
28 Ibid.
29 West, p.147.
30 Alfred T Mahan. *The Interest of America in Sea Power, Present and Future* (London 1897) p.8.
31 Ibid, p.7.
32 Quoted West, pp.149-150.
33 Robert Seager II, *Alfred Thayer Mahan* (Annapolis 1977) p.215.
34 Quoted Seager, p.215.
35 Quoted Captain W D Puleston, *Mahan* (London 1939) p.116.
36 Quoted Robert Seager II, 'Alfred Thayer Mahan' in *Admirals of the New Steel Navy*, p.41.

Chapter 2

1 Quoted Herrick, p.107.
2 Quoted Warren Zimmermann, *First Great Triumph* (New York 2002) p.121.
3 Mahan, *The Interest of America in Sea Power*, p.12.
4 Robley D Evans, *A Sailor's Log: Recollections of Forty years of Naval Life* (New York 1910) pp.259-260.
5 Puleston, p.121.

6 Quoted Seager, *Mahan*, pp.237-238.
7 Quoted West, p.149.
8 Quoted, Herrick, p.126.
9 Herrick, p.127.
10 Quoted Herrick, p.130.
11 Ibid, p.141.
12 Reilly and Scheina, pp.72-81.
13 Quoted, Herrick, p.157.
14 Ibid, p.160.
15 Sprout, p.219.
16 Clark, pp.442-443.
17 Reilly and Scheina, pp.83-95.
18 Ibid, pp.97-113.
19 Herrick, p.179.
20 Quoted Puleston, p.147.
21 Ibid, p.145.
22 Quoted Seager, *Mahan* p.282.
23 Quoted Puleston, pp.164-165.
24 Seager, *Mahan*, p.307.

Chapter 3

1 Rear Admiral Winfield S Schley, *Forty Five years Under the Flag* (New York 1904) p.4.
2 West, p.23.
3 Seager, *Mahan*, p.27.
4 Schley, pp.6 and 8.
5 Ibid, p.38.
6 Ibid, pp.45-46.
7 Ibid, p.57.
8 West. p.116.
9 Quoted West, p.100.
10 Harold D Langley, ' Winfield Scott Schley' in *Admirals of the New Steel Navy*, p.189.
11 Schley, p.135.
12 Quoted Langley, p.192.
13 West, p.113.
14 Schley, p.189.
15 Ibid, p.183.
16 Ibid, pp.184-185.
17 Quoted Seager, *Mahan*, p.184.
18 Ibid, pp.184-185.
19 Schley, p.236.
20 Ibid, p.240.

Chapter 4

1 Captain Alfred T Mahan, *Retrospect and Prospect* (Boston 1903) p.291.
2 Captain Alfred T Mahan, *From Sail to Steam* (New York 1907) p.186.
3 West, pp.58-59.
4 Quoted West, p.59.
5 Mahan, *Retrospect and Prospect*, p.302.
6 Admiral of the Navy George Dewey, *Autobiography* (New York 1913) pp.139-140.
7 West, p.116.
8 Ibid.
9 Quoted West, p.117-118.
10 West, p.126.
11 Quoted Dawson, p.155.
12 Quoted West, 336.
13 Dawson, p.157.
14 West, pp.182-183.15
15 West, p.185-186.
16 Reilly and Scheina, pp.83-133.
17 Quoted West, p.190.
18 West, p.190.

Chapter 5

1 Dewey, pp.21-22.
2 Ibid, pp.46-47.
3 Ronald Spector, *Admiral of the New Empire* (Baton Rouge 1974) p.12.
4 Quoted Spector, p.12.
5 Dewey, p.52.
6 Ibid, p.55.
7 Idib, p.69.
8 Ibid, pp.110-112.
9 Vernon L Williams, 'George Dewey: Admiral of the Navy' in *Admirals of the New Steel Navy*, p.228.
10 Ibid.
11 West, p.38.
12 Ibid, p.68.
13 Ibid, p.69.
14 Dewey, p.142.
15 West, p.73.
16 Spector, p.28.
17 Dewey, p.149.
18 Spector, p.24.
19 Dewey, p.151.
20 Spector, p.29.
21 Dewey, p.151-162.
22 Spector, pp.27-28.
23 Quoted West, p.135.
24 Dewey, p.164.
25 Quoted West, p.137.
26 Dewey, p.165.

Chapter 6

1 Lewis L Gould, *The Spanish American War and President McKinley* (Lawrence 1980) p.1.
2 Edmund Morris, *The Rise of Theodore Roosevelt* (London 1979) p.560.
3 John D Long, *The New American Navy* (New York 1903) ii p.173.
4 Quoted Morris, p.567.
5 Ibid, p.513.
6 Long, ii p.174.
7 Morris, p.569.
8 Quoted Morris, p.569.
9 Ibid, p.571.
10 Morris, p.573.
11 Spector, p.85.
12 Ibid.
13 Quoted Spector, p.37.
14 Morris, p.579.
15 Quoted Morris, p.581.
16 Ibid, p.590.

Chapter 7

1 Philip S Foner, *The Spanish-Cuban-American War and the Birth of American Imperialism*, (New York 1972) I p.xvi.
2 Joseph Smith, *The Spanish American War* (New York 1994) pp.2-3.
3 Quoted Allan Keller, *The Spanish American War* New York 1969) p.2.
4 Rear Admiral French Ensor Chadwick, *The Relations of the United States and Spain: Diplomacy* (New York 1909) p.10.
5 Foner, I p.xviii.
6 Chadwick, *Diplomacy*, p.287.
7 Ibid, pp.289-290.
8 Ibid, p.306.
9 Ibid, pp.338-339.
10 Quoted Sprout, p.175.
11 Foner, I p.xxii.
12 Ibid, I p.xxxii.
13 Ibid, I p.10.
14 David F Trask, *The War with Spain in 1898* (New York 1981) p.7.
15 Trask, p.9; Smith p.19.

Chapter 8

1 Raymond Carr, *Spain 1808-1939* (Oxford 1966) p.342.
2 Ibid, p.348.
3 Quoted Smith, p.9.
4 Chadwick, *Diplomacy* p.432.
5 Ibid, p.440.
6 Ibid, 457.
7 Trask, p.12.
8 Carr, 386.
9 Quoted GJA O'Toole, *The Spanish War* (New York 1984) p.56.
10 Chadwick, *Diplomacy*, p.482.
11 Ibid, p.491.
12 Gould, p.9.
13 Gould, p.25.
14 Quoted Trask, p.13.

Chapter 9

1 Trask, p.17.
2 Quoted O'Toole, p.88.
3 Quoted Gould, p.29.
4 Diane E Cooper, 'Diplomat and Naval Intelligence Officer' in *Crucible of Empire*, ed James C Bradford (Annapolis1993) p.5.
5 Chadwick, *Diplomacy*, p.510.
6 Ibid, p.522.
7 Gould, p.31.
8 Quoted Gould, p.31.
9 Chadwick *Diplomacy*, p.531.
10 Ibid, p.536.
11 Ibid, p.539.
12 *Annual Report of the Secretary of the Navy*, 1898.
13 Quoted Chadwick, *Diplomacy*, p.543.
14 Quoted Malcolm Muir Jr, 'French Ensor Chadwick: Reformer, Historian and Outcast' in *Admirals of the New Steel Navy*, pp.101-102.
15 Trask, p.35.
16 H W Wilson, *The Downfall of Spain* (London 1900) p.37.
17 Michael Blow, *A Ship to Remember* (New York 1992) pp.431-434.
18 Chadwick, *Diplomacy*, p.554.
19 Ibid, p.558.
20 Trask, pp.33-34.
21 Quoted Morris, p.610.
22 Trask, p.44.
23 E T S Dugdale, ed, *German Diplomatic Documents 1871-1914* (London 19929) III pp.500-501.
24 Ibid, III p.506.
25 Chadwick, *Diplomacy*, p.572.

26 Ibid, p.581.

Chapter 10

1 Rear Admiral Pascual Cervera, *A Collection of Documents Relating to the Squadron Operations in the West Indies* (Washington 1899) p.20.
2 Rear Admiral Pascual Cervera, *Views of Admiral Cervera regarding the Spanish Navy in the Late War* (Washington 1898) p.8.
3 Wilson, pp.61-62.
4 Ibid, p.59.
5 Ibid, p.65.
6 Cervera, *Documents*, pp.12-13.
7 Ibid, p.22.
8 Ibid, p.24.
9 Ibid, p.25.
10 Wilson, pp.76-77.
11 Cervera, *Documents*, p.28.
12 Ibid, 31.
13 Ibid, pp.31-33.
14 Ibid, p.38.
15 Ibid, p.42.
16 Rear Admiral French Ensor Chadwick, *The Relations of the United States and Spain: The Spanish American War*, (New York 1911) I p.108.
17 Captain Victor M Concas y Palau, *The Squadron of Admiral Cervera* (Washington 1900) p.23.
18 Cervera, *Documents*, pp.45-46; Concas, p.27.
19 Concas, p.27.
20 Ibid, p.30.
21 Wilson, pp.98-99.

Chapter 11

1 Trask, pp.75-76.
2 Ibid, pp.76-78.
3 Quoted Trask, p.79.
4 Quoted Morris, p.594.
5 Quoted Zimmermann, p.243.
6 Trask, p.81.
7 Chadwick, *Spanish American War*, I pp.29-32.
8 Trask, p.86.
9 West, p.212.
10 Seager, p.363.
11 Schley, pp.257-258.
12 Langley, *Admirals*, p.194; *Crucible*, p.71.
13 Long, I pp.212-213.
14 Ibid, I p.211.
15 Chadwick, *Spanish American War*, I pp.20-21.
16 Wilson, p.113.
17 Ibid, pp.108-109.
18 Edwin A Falk, *Fighting Bob Evans* (Freeport, 1939) p.253.
19 Schley, pp.259-260.
20 Chadwick, *Spanish American War*, I p.75.
21 Quoted Smith, p.59.
22 Wilson, p.104.
23 Chadwick, *Spanish American War* I p.87.
24 Ibid, I p.130.
25 Quoted Wilson, p.117.
26 Smith, p.61.
27 Quoted Smith, p.63.
28 Chadwick, *Spanish American War*, I pp.53-54.

Chapter 12

1 Spector, p.39.
2 Dewey,, pp.167-169.
3 Ibid, p.170.
4 Ibid, p.179.
5 Quoted Morris, p.603.
6 Dewey, p.181.
7 Quoted Jim Leeke, *Manila and Santiago* (Annapolis 2009) p.41.
8 Dewey, p.195.
9 Ibid, p.205.
10 Quoted Spector, p.49.
11 Spector, pp.49-50.
12 Ibid, p.52.
13 Chadwick, *Spanish American War*, I p.161.
14 Ibid, I pp.167-168.
15 Wilson, p.131.
16 Ibid, p.132.
17 Chadwick, *Spanish American War*, I p.170.
18 Dewey, p.205.
19 Spector, p.57.
20 Ibid.
21 Leeke, p.64.
22 West, p.202.
23 Chadwick, *Spanish American War*, I p.179.
24 O'Toole, p.186.
25 Dewey, p.218.
26 West, pp.205-206.
27 Dewey, pp.219-220.
28 Chadwick, *Spanish American War*, I p.190.
29 Dewey, pp.224-225.
30 Chadwick, *Spanish American War*, I p.212.
31 Quoted West, p.210.

32 Nathan Sargent, *Admiral Dewey and the Manila Campaign* (Washington 1947) p.48.
33 Beach, p. 349.
34 Sprout, p.441.
35 Chadwick, *Spanish American War*, I p.203.
36 William R Braisted, *The United States Navy in the Pacific 1897-1909* (New York 1964) p.26.
37 Chadwick, *Spanish American War*, I pp.203-204.
38 Wilson, p.149.
39 Ibid, p.152.

Chapter 13

1 Wilson, p.179.
2 Ibid, pp.186-188.
3 Chadwick, *Spanish American War*, I p.150.
4 Quoted West, p.215.
5 Ibid.
6 Seager, p.370.
7 Quoted Seager, p.361.
8 West, p.216.
9 Ibid, p.217.
10 Ibid, p.216.
11 Ibid, p.219.
12 Ibid, p.220.
13 Smith, p.72.
14 Chadwick, *Spanish American War*, I p.214.
15 Ibid, I p.216.
16 Ibid, I p.219.
17 Ibid, I p.220.
18 Ibid, I p.225.
19 Wilson, p.193.
20 Quoted Wilson, pp.194-195.
21 William Goode, *With Sampson Through the War*, (London 1899) p.71.
22 Chadwick, *Spanish American War*, I p.234; Wilson, p.196.
23 Chadwick, *Spanish American War*, I p.234.
24 Ibid, I pp.234-235.
25 Wilson, p.197.
26 Ibid, 198.
27 Chadwick, *Spanish American War*, I p.142.

Chapter 14

1 Concas, p.43.
2 Ibid, p.43.
3 Ibid.
4 Alfred T Mahan, *Lessons of the War with Spain* (London 1900) p.122.
5 Cervera, *Documents*, p.73.
6 Ibid, p.76.
7 Wilson, p.211.
8 Concas, p.50.
9 Cervera, *Documents*, p.80.
10 Ibid, p.82.
11 Ibid, p.83.
12 Concas, p.52.
13 Ibid, p.13.
14 Chadwick, *Spanish American War*, I pp.243-244.
15 Ibid, I p. 244.
16 Ibid, I p.246.
17 Ibid, I p.262.

Chapter 15

1 *Record of Proceedings of a Court of Inquiry in the Case of Rear Admiral Winfield S Schley, US Navy* (n.d) II p.142.
2 Chadwick, *Spanish American War.*, I p.266.
3 Wilson, pp.217-218.
4 Chadwick, *Spanish American War*, I p.272.
5 Schley, p.270.
6 Ibid, p.271.
7 Parker, pp.103-105.
8 Wilson, p.220.
9 Goode, p.114.
10 Ibid, p.108.
11 Parker, p.108.
12 *Proceedings*, I p.854; quoted Parker, p.108.
13 Goode, pp.114.
14 George E Graham, *Schley and Santiago* (Chicago 1902) pp.126-129.
15 Chadwick, *Spanish American War*, I p.293.
16 *Proceedings*, I p.887.
17 Chadwick, *Spanish American War*, I p.300.
18 Ibid.
19 Ibid, I p.291.
20 Ibid, pp.294-295.

Chapter 16

1 Schley, p.276.
2 Graham, p.160.
3 *Proceedings*, II pp.1471-1472.
4 Schley, p.278.
5 Quoted Trask, p.124.

6 Chadwick, *Spanish American War*, I pp.306-307.
7 Long, I p.276.
8 Ibid, pp.276-277.
9 Chadwick, *Spanish American War*, I p.324.
10 Ibid, pp.327-328.
11 Concas, p.53.
12 Cervera, *Documents*, p.88.
13 Ibid, 91.
14 Ibid, pp.91-92.
15 Concas, p.57.
16 Cervera, *Documents*, pp.96-97.
17 Concas, p.57.
18 Wilson, p.245.
19 *Proceedings*, I p.427.
20 Graham, p.177.
21 Wilson, p.233; Schley, p.283.
22 Concas, pp.58-59.
23 Chadwick, *Spanish American War*, I p.326.
24 Wilson, p.234.
25 Cervera, *Documents*, pp.98-99.
26 Concas, pp.57-58.

Chapter 17

1 Richmond Pearson Hobson, *The Sinking of the Merrimac* (New York) p.6
2 Ibid, p.15.
3 Graham, p.204.
4 Goode, p.144 and 146; Long, I pp.268-269.
5 Quoted Trask, p.531n.
6 Chadwick, *Spanish American War*, I p.285.
7 Hobson, pp.29-30.
8 Ibid p.41.
9 Chadwick, *Spanish American War*, I p.340.
10 Hobson, pp.47-48.
11 Ibid, pp.69-79.
12 Ibid, p.95.
13 Chadwick, *Spanish American War,* I p.343.

Chapter 18

1 Chadwick, *Spanish American War*, I p.348.
2 Quoted Trask, p.176.
3 Schley, p.288.
4 Quoted Wilson, pp.253-254.
5 Chadwick, *Spanish American War*, I p.352.
6 Goode, p.159;Graham, 238.
7 Quoted Goode, pp.162-163.
8 Cervera, *Documents*, p.101.
9 Ibid.
10 Ibid, pp.102-103.
11 Schley, p.289.
12 Quoted Wilson, pp.258-259.
13 Chadwick, *Spanish American War*; I pp.355-356.
14 Trask, p.137; Chadwick, *Spanish American War*, I p.357.
15 Chadwick, *Spanish American War*, I pp.363-364.
16 Cervera, *Documents*, p.105.
17 Goode, pp.173-174.
18 Schley, p.291.
19 Ibid.
20 Cervera, *Documents*, p.105.
21 Mahan, *Lessons*, p.181.

Chapter 19

1 Trask, p.146.
2 Quoted Trask, p.178.
3 Chadwick, *Spanish American War*, I p.370.
4 Trask, p.188.
5 Quoted Smith, p.117.
6 Mahan, *Lessons*, pp.191-192.
7 Anon, *Squadron Bulletins of the North Atlantic Squadron* (New York 1898) p.11.
8 Chadwick, *Spanish American War*, I p.386.
9 Ibid.
10 David F Trask, 'American Intelligence during the Spanish American War,' in Bradford, *Crucible*, pp.37-38.
11 Trask, p.204.
12 Trask, p.205; Chadwick, *Spanish American War*, II pp.23-24.
13 Quoted Trask, p.205.
14 Major General Joseph Wheeler, *The Santiago Campaign 1898* (Boston 1898) p.13.
15 Chadwick, *Spanish American War*, II pp.33-34.
16 Concas, p.60.
17 Cervera, Documents, p.108.
18 Ibid, p.111.
19 Ibid, p.112.
20 Ibid, p.114.
21 Ibid, p.115.
22 Chadwick, *Spanish American War*, II p.58.
23 Trask, p.223.
24 Quoted, Trask, p.241.
25 Smith, p.141.
26 Quoted Trask, p.248.

27 Chadwick, *Spanish American War*, II pp.106-107.
28 Ibid, p.107.
29 Trask, pp.251-252.
30 Quoted Jack C Dierks, *A Leap to Arms* (New York 1970) p.148.

Chapter 20

1 Chadwick, *Spanish American War,* II p.121.
2 Ibid, II p.122.
3 Cervera, *Documents*, p.118.
4 Ibid, p.119.
5 Concas, p.68.
6 Wilson, p.281.
7 Concus, p.69.
8 Ibid, p.70.
9 Quoted Ivan Musicant, *Empire by Default* (New York 1998) p.442.
10 Concas, p.74.
11 Goode, p.194.
12 Chadwick, *Spanish American War*, II pp.131-132.
13 Quoted Trask, p.262.
14 Margaret Leech, *In the Days of McKinley* (New York 1959) p.257.
15 Graham, p.208.
16 Schley, p.300.
17 Ibid.
18 Graham, p.306.
19 Graham p.372.
20 Falk, p.323.
21 Trask, p.262.
22 Parker, p.227.

Chapter 21

1 *Proceedings*, I p.895.
2 Ibid.
3 Ibid, II pp.1769-1770.
4 Schley, p.303.
5 Concas, p.76.
6 Ibid, p.77.
7 *Proceedings*, II p.1338.
8 Ibid, II p.1339.
9 Ibid, I p.779.
10 Ibid, II p.1340.
11 Concas, pp.77-78.
12 Graham, p.330.
13 Schley, p.310.
14 Concas, p.80.
15 Graham, pp.358-359.
16 West, p.266.
17 Ibid, p.287.
18 Concas, p.83.
19 Trask, p.265.
20 Quoted Chadwick, *Spanish American War*, II p.183.
21 Quoted Falk, p.338.
22 Cervera, *Documents*, p.121.
23 Ibid, p.123.
24 Ibid, p.135.
25 Quoted, Chadwick, Spanish American War, II p.185.
26 Chadwick, *Spanish American War*, III p.187.
27 Schley, p.322.

Chapter 22

1 Quoted Trask, p.274.
2 Chadwick, *Spanish American War*, II p.378.
3 Ibid II pp.389-390.
4 Ibid.
5 Ibid, II pp.202-203.
6 Trask, p.290.
7 Chadwick, *Spanish American War*, II pp.247-252.
8 Trask, p.338.
9 Chadwick, *Spanish American War*, II p.276.
10 Ibid, II p.279.
11 Quoted, Trask, p.335.
12 Smith, p.175.
13 Trask, p.400..
14 Brailted, p.43.
15 Trask, p.378.
16 Quoted Terrell D Gottshall, *By Order of the Kaiser* (Annapolis, 2003) p.186.
17 Dewey, p.252.
18 Quoted Gottshall, p.208.

Chapter 23

1 West, pp.288-289.
2 Schley, p.335.
3 Graham, p.352.
4 West, p.290.
5 Quoted West, pp.291-292.
6 Ibid, pp.290-291.
7 Schley, p.341.
8 Quoted West, pp.296-297.
9 Schley, pp.343-344.
10 Quoted Seager, p.401.

11 Seager, p.402.
12 Leeke, p.154.
13 Long, II p.49.
14 Quoted Seager, p.403.
15 Schley, p.365.
16 Quoted Langley, *Crucible*, pp.89-90.
17 Langley, *Crucible*, pp.90-92.
18 Schley, p.298.
19 Ibid.
20 Spector, pp.110-114.
21 Quoted West, p.294.
22 Seager, p.403.
23 Edgar Stanton Maclay, *A History of the United States Navy* (New York 1901) III p.293.
24 Ibid, pp.296.
25 Ibid, p.298.
26 Ibid, p.364.
27 Ibid, p.365.
28 Ibid, pp.vi-vii.
29 Schley, p.409.
30 West, p.296.
31 Quoted Langley, *Admirals of the New Steel Navy,* p220n.
32 Schley, pp.409-410.

Chapter 24

1 *Proceedings*, II pp.18-19.
2 Ibid, I p.23.
3 Ibid.
4 Parker, p.321.
5 *Proceedings*, I p.257.
6 Ibid, I pp.154-155.
7 Ibid, I p.324.
8 Parker, p.319.
9 *Proceedings*, I pp.52-54.
10 Ibid, II p.1774.
11 Ibid, II p.1775.
12 Ibid, II p.1836.
13 Ibid, II p.1823.
14 Ibid, I p.320.
15 Ibid, II p.1524.
16 Ibid, p.631.
17 Ibid, p.691.
18 Ibid, I p.702.
19 Ibid, I p.874.
20 Ibid I pp.420, 1224 and 1236.
21 Ibid, I p.841.
22 Ibid, II p.1418.
23 Ibid, II p.1511.
24 Ibid, II p.894.
25 Parker, p.311.
26 *Proceedings*, II pp.1674-1719.
27 Ibid, II p.1719.
28 Parker, p.325.
29 *Proceedings*, II pp.1786-1787.
30 Ibid, p.1823.
31 Ibid, I p.1824.
32 Ibid, II pp.1824-1830.

Epilogue

1 *Proceedings*, pp.1831-1843.
2 Schley, pp.426-428.
3 *Proceedings*, pp.1927-1928.
4 Ibid, p.1936.
5 Schley, pp.430-431.
6 Muir, pp.109-110.
7 Seager, p.405.
8 Dawson, p.170.
9 Seager, p.405.
10 Williams, p.244.
11 Trask, p.485.
12 Mahan, *Retrospect and Prospect*, pp.298-300.
13 Quoted Langley, *Admirals of the New Steel Navy*, pp.220-221.

Bibliography

Anon., *Squadron Bulletins of the North Atlantic Squadron* (New York 1898)

Beach, Captain Edward L, *The United States Navy: A 200 Year History* (Boston 1986)

Blow, Michael, *A Ship to Remember* (New York 1992)

Bradford, James C, Ed., *Crucible of Empire* (Annapolis 1993)

Bradford,, James C, Ed., *Admirals of the New Steel Navy* (Annapolis 1990)

Braisted, William R, *The United States Navy in the Pacific 1897-1909* (New York 1969)

Carr, Raymond, *Spain 1808-1939* (Oxford 1966)

Cervera, Rear Admiral Pascual, *A Collection of Documents Relating to the Squadron Operations in the West Indies* (Washington 1899)

Cervera, Rear Admiral Pascual, *Views of Admiral Cervera Regarding the Spanish Navy in the Late War* (Washington 1898)

Chadwick, Rear Admiral French E, *The Relations of the United States and Spain: Diplomacy* (New York 1909)

Chadwick, Rear Admiral French E, *The Relations of the United States and Spain: The Spanish-American War* (New York 1911)

Clark, Rear Admiral George R, and others, *A Short History of the United States Navy* (Philadelphia 1939)

Concas y Palau, Captain Victor M, *The Squadron of Admiral Cervera* (Washington1900)

Dewey, Admiral of the Navy George, *Autobiography* (New York 1913)

Dierks, Jack C, *A Leap to Arms* (New York 1970)

Dugdale, E T S, Ed., *German Diplomatic Documents 1871-1914* (London 1929)

Evans, Robley D, *A Sailor's Log: Recollections of Forty Years of Naval Life* (New York 1910)

Falk, Edwin A, *Fighting Bob Evans* (Freeport 1939)

Foner, Philip S, *The Spanish-Cuban-American War and the Birth of American Imperialism* (New York 1972)

Freidel, Frank, *The Splendid Little War* (Boston 1958)

Goode, William, *With Sampson Through the War* (London 1899)

Gottshall, Terrell D, *By Order of the Kaiser* (Annapolis 2003)

Gould, Lewis L, *The Spanish American War and President McKinley* (Lawrence 1980)

Graham, George E, *Schley and Santiago* (Chicago 1902)

Hagan, Kenneth J, *This People's Navy* (New York 1991)

Herrick, Walter R, *The American Naval Revolution* (Baton Rouge 1966)

Hobson, Richmond P, *The Sinking of the Merrimac* (New York 1899)

Howarth, Stephen, *To Shining Sea* (London 1991)

Keller, Allan, *The Spanish American War* (New York 1969)
Leech, Margaret, *In the Days of McKinley* (New York 1959)
Leeke, Jim, *Manila and Santiago* (Annapolis 2009)
Long, John D, *The New American Navy* (New York 1903)
Maclay, Edgar Stanton, *A History of the United States Navy*: Vol 3 (New York 1901)
Mahan, Alfred T, *From Sail to Steam* (NewYork 1907)
Mahan, Alfred T, *Lessons of the War with Spain* (London 1900)
Mahan, Alfred T, *Retrospect and Prospect* (Boston 1903)
Mahan, Alfred T, *The Interest of America in Sea Power, Present and Future* (London 1897)
Millis, Walter, *The Martial Spirit* (Cambridge 1931)
Morris, Edmund, *The Rise of Theodore Roosevelt* (London 1979)
Musicant, Ivan, *Empire by Default* (New York (1998)
Nevins, Allan, *Grover Cleveland: A Study in Courage* (New York 1941)
O'Toole, G J A *The Spanish War* (New York 1984)
Parker, Commander James, *Rear Admirals Schley, Sampson and Cervera* (New York1910)
Puleston, Captain W D, *Mahan* (London 1939)
Record of Proceedings of a Court of Inquiry in the Case of Rear Admiral Winfield S Schley US Navy (n.d)
Riley, John C and Scheina, Robert L, *American Battleships 1886-1923* (London 1980)
Sargent, Commander V, *Admiral Dewey and the Manila Campaign* (Washington 1947)
Schley, Rear Admiral Winfield S, *Forty Five Years Under the Flag* (New York 1904)
Seager, Robert, *Alfred Thayer Mahan* (Annapolis 1977)
Smith, Joseph, *The Spanish American War* (New York 1994)
Spector, Ronald, *Admiral of the New Empire* (Baton Rouge 1974)
Sprout, Harold and Margaret, *The Rise of American Naval Power 1776-1968* (Princeton1946)
Trask, David F, T*he War with Spain in 1898* (New York 1981)
West, Richard S, *Admirals of American Empire* (Indianapolis 1948)
Wheeler, Major General Joseph, *The Santiago Campaign* (Boston 1898)
Wilson, H W, *The Downfall of Spain* (London 1900)
Zimmerman, Warren, *First Great Triumph* (New York 2002)

Index

INDEX OF PEOPLE

INDEX OF PLACES

INDEX OF SHIPS

INDEX OF GENERAL & MISCELLANOUS TERMS